FIELDS OF HONOR

Union forces at Cumberland Landing, Virginia, 1862.

FIELDS OF HONOR

EDWIN C. BEARSS

NATIONAL GEOGRAPHIC
WASHINGTON, D.C.

Published by National Geographic Partners, LLC.
1145 17th Street NW Washington, DC 20036-4688 USA

ISBN 978-1-4262-0093-9 (paperback)

First printing in paperback 2007

The Library of Congress has cataloged the hardcover edition as follows:
Bearss, Edwin C.
Fields of honor: pivotal battles of the Civil War/ Edwin Cole Bearss.
p.cm.
Includes index
ISBN: 0-7922-7568-3
I. United States—History—Civil War, 1861-1865—Campaigns. I. Title.

E470.B43 2006
973.7'3—dc22 2005058372

Since 1888, the National Geographic Society has funded more than 13,000 research, exploration, and preservation projects around the world. National Geographic Partners distributes a portion of the funds it receives from your purchase to National Geographic Society to support programs including the conservation of animals and their habitats.

Get closer to National Geographic explorers and photographers, and connect with our global community. Join us today at nationalgeographic.com/join

Interior design by Peggy Archambault.

Printed in the United States of America

22/VP-PCML/7

TABLE OF CONTENTS

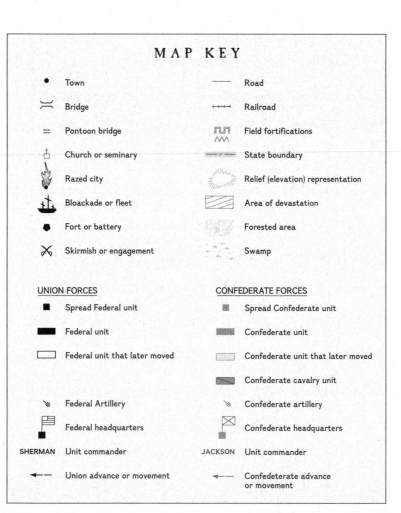

MAP KEY

Town

Bridge

Pontoon bridge

Church or seminary

Razed city

Bloackade or fleet

Fort or battery

Skirmish or engagement

Road

Railroad

Field fortifications

State boundary

Relief (elevation) representation

Area of devastation

Forested area

Swamp

UNION FORCES

Spread Federal unit

Federal unit

Federal unit that later moved

Federal Artillery

Federal headquarters

SHERMAN Unit commander

Union advance or movement

CONFEDERATE FORCES

Spread Confederate unit

Confederate unit

Confederate unit that later moved

Confederate cavalry unit

Confederate artillery

Confederate headquarters

JACKSON Unit commander

Confedeterate advance or movement

Federal troops occupy a line of breastworks on the north bank of the North Anna River, 1864.

PREFACE

Edwin C. Bearss

I served in the United States Marine Corps during World War II and know how a battlefield feels, sounds, and smells. Frankly there is nothing like it. Anyone who has ever been there will never forget it.

I have been leading battlefield tours since the 1950s, and in each instance I find that the sites continue to teach me. In that time I've met hundreds of thousands of people from all walks of life—two Presidents of the United States, foreign leaders, executives of international corporations, senior officers of the United States and foreign militaries as well and the "rank and file soldiers," jurists, members of Congress, and countless "history buffs"—each coming for reasons that are as unique as they are. Most of the people I have the opportunity to lead and teach are serious about trying to learn what these battlefields mean. I have taken people to sites from the French and Indian Wars, the American Revolution, the War of 1812, the various Indian and Plains wars, the Civil War, and World War II. While each has its students, the American Civil War stands out above all of them.

I believe the enduring interest in America's Civil War comes from the direct connection many people feel with the people who fought in it. It is a conflict that attracts both professional and amateur historians in large numbers. By walking the fields they extract nuggets that might otherwise be overlooked. I am frequently asked to read manuscripts for books on various aspects of the Civil War. No other conflict even comes close in terms of interest and active scholarship.

I try to accommodate as many programs as I can. My schedule regularly exceeds 250 days per year on the road giving lectures or leading tours. Some are regular programs that I reserve each year: The Civil War Round Table of Chicago was the first such group in the United States, and only one man has been on more of their annual tours than I have. Charlie Falkenberg still accompanies me on many fields. For years I did two programs a year in support of Jerry Russell's Civil War Roundtable Associates and the Confederate Historical Institute. Ted Alexander does an annual program for the Chambersburg Chamber of Commerce, and of the many Civil War Round Tables, the relatively new Low Country Civil War Round Table represents the continuing interest in the war—friends Jack and Joyce Keller are gracious hosts for my annual March lecture—when over 400 people attend. There are other groups too numerous to mention but all are wonderful hosts.

This book is the story of the Civil War as I have presented it on the battlefield tours I give. It is a special piece of work and to accomplish it I turned to my friend Len Riedel, Executive Director of the Blue and Gray Education Society (BGES). Since 1994 Len's father Bill, aka "Dad," and Steve Halcomb have been recording my tours and lectures. They have built an archive that is approaching 400 taped hours. In cooperation with my friends Rob Zaworski and Sam Craghead, who have been assembling tapes and my publications from various tours and archive sources, the Blue and Gray Education Society helped me place and establish my personal archives at Marine Corps Base Quantico in the Marine Corps University Library Archives.

Len worked closely with the National Geographic Society and members of his nonprofit educational organization to produce more than 2,500 pages of transcripts from my special series for the BGES entitled *Ed Bearss's Essential Civil War.* They were turned over to historian Brooks Simpson and editor Harris Andrews, who drafted a concise narrative that relies on my actual presentations on the field.

I am a man of the battlefields. The narrative you are about to read is the story of these fields as I have learned it. I am as enthusiastic today about the various programs that I lead as I was when I first took a group out. All in all—it is a good life and I am thankful to all for helping to keep me young.

INTRODUCTION

James M. McPherson

When Edwin C. Bearss was growing up on a Montana ranch before World War II, he named cattle after Civil War battles and gave names of Civil War generals to the milk cows and their calves that roamed the ranch. His favorite milk cow was Antietam; one of her calves was Sharpsburg. Ed first encountered the Civil War when he was in sixth grade. He had earlier fallen in love with ancient history. And he seemed genetically programmed for a fascination with military history. A third cousin had received the Medal of Honor as a marine fighting against the Philippine insurrectionists. Ed's father, Omar Bearss, had been a Marine Corps officer in World War I. When Ed's parents rented a house in Billings so Ed could attend sixth grade there instead of in the one-room schoolhouse near the ranch, Ed found books about the Civil War in the house. He was forever hooked.

That was in 1934 and 1935. During the next several years, events in Europe and Asia built toward the conflicts that would erupt into World War II. Ed followed these events avidly. He acquired maps of Spain, China, and central Europe and moved flags across the maps to follow the advances and retreats of various armies. His knowledge of world geography and current events was extraordinary. In his junior year in high school he scored highest on a current events test in the entire state; the following year he did the same in U.S. history. His total recall of historical facts was even more impressive. Ed denies that he has a photographic memory. "I can't scan a poem and quote it back to you." But he undoubtedly could do so if he was interested in poetry, for he admits that "anything I am interested in I never forget." Above all, he has never forgotten anything he has read about history or any feature of terrain he has seen on a map or walked over on the ground itself. It is these qualities of encyclopedic memory that make him a legendary tour guide of historical sites, especially battlefields.

I have been on many historical tours with Ed—not only of Civil War battlefields but also of Waterloo, the Somme, and World War II sites from the Normandy beaches to the Huertgen Forest and Remagen. I remember one occasion that illustrates his mastery of the detail of several wars. Ed and I were members of the Civil War Sites Advisory Commission created by Congress in 1991 to survey the threats to Civil War battlefields and the opportunities to forestall these threats by land acquisitions, easements, and other means. The commission traveled to many Civil War battlefields, where Ed gave his patented tours, and we held hearings in nearby cities. We made our final site visit in 1993. Ed not only brought alive the battle that took place there in January 1865 but also described the hurricane that washed away part of the fort in the 1920s and the building of an airstrip during World War II that destroyed part of the remainder in such vivid detail that we were sure he had been there on all three occasions. The following day, as our bus rolled out of Wilmington for a tour of the Bentonville battlefield, we passed the battleship U.S.S. *North Carolina* tied up in the Cape Fear River. For the next 20 minutes Ed described all the actions in which the ship had participated in World War II, the battle stars she had won, and what she had done after the war before arriving in Wilmington to become a ship museum. As he finished this dramatic account, we passed the Moore's Creek National Battlefield. Without missing a beat, Ed shifted from 1944 to 1776 and told us the story of that patriot victory over the Loyalists.

Ed has experienced war firsthand. Six months after he graduated from high school the Japanese attacked Pearl Harbor. Ed enlisted in the Marine Corps and in July 1942 shipped out for the South Pacific. On January 2, 1944, his unit attacked Japanese pillboxes on New Britain Island, where Ed was hit by several machine-gun bullets. At the risk of their own lives a couple of buddies pulled him out of range and got him to an aid station. Eventually evacuated to the United States, Ed spent the next 26 months recuperating in military hospitals—and reading about the Civil War.

Discharged in 1946, he went to Georgetown University on the GI Bill and graduated in 1949. For several years he worked as a geographer in the Naval Hydrographic Office in Washington and spent his spare time visiting Civil War battlefields. That avocation soon became his vocation. He went to Indiana University, where he earned an M.A. in history with a thesis on Confederate Gen. Patrick Cleburne. Ed had already learned that one cannot understand a Civil War battle without walking the ground. "I realized that at Gettysburg, when I visited the battlefield in the early 1950s," he told me. "The ground over which Pickett's Charge took place was not at all how I visualized it from my reading." So before he wrote his thesis Ed decided to visit the battlefields where Cleburne fought. At Shiloh he had an epiphany of sorts. The park historian walked him over the field for six hours. "That six-hour ramble through the woods and fields of bloody Shiloh," Ed recalled, "changed my understanding of events of that late afternoon 92 years before." But even more significant were "the interpretive skills and electrifying personality" of the park historian, Charles Shedd. Then and there Ed decided that he wanted to pursue a similar career. He applied to the Park Service and in 1955 was hired as the historian at Vicksburg National Military Park.

From there Ed never looked back. He was promoted in 1958 to regional research historian for the National Park Service's Southeast region, still working out of Vicksburg but visiting virtually every battlefield in the western theater of the Civil War, writing up reports for other park historians, giving tours himself, and developing his unique style, which blended on-the-spot descriptions of tactics and terrain, colorful anecdotes about Civil War personalities both great and obscure, and an appreciation of the larger strategic and political contexts of specific battles. During these years Ed met Margie Riddle, a schoolteacher with an interest in and knowledge of the Civil War that matched Ed's own. They married in 1958. For the next eight years they lived in Vicksburg, where Margie began editing and proofreading Ed's books and research reports. She also helped him with one of the great coups of his career—the raising of the ironclad gunboat U.S.S. *Cairo* from its watery grave in the Yazoo River north of Vicksburg, where it had been sunk by Confederate "torpedoes" (mines) in December 1862. As Ed and colleagues reconstructed the gunboat for exhibit at the park—the pièce de résistance of Civil War artifacts—Margie spent some 3,000 hours cleaning, identifying, and researching 10,000 items that came up with the boat, ranging from silverware to frying pans to boat hardware—many of them on exhibit at the park's U.S.S. *Cairo* museum.

By the time of the Civil War Centennial in the 1960s, Ed had earned fame as the most knowledgeable Civil War historian in the National Park Service. In 1966 he moved to Washington as part of a new research team of Park Service historians. Here, too, his workaholic energy and encyclopedic knowledge produced superb reports and recommendations for improvement at national parks from Guam to the Klondike, from Fort Moultrie to Fort Donelson. In 1981 Ed became chief historian of the National Park Service, a position he held until a year before his retirement in 1995.

But for Ed, retirement meant more time than ever for his favorite activity—tours of every kind of historical site for organizations of all kinds—the Smithsonian Institution, the Civil War Preservation Trust, History America Tours, the Blue and Gray Education Society, Civil War roundtables, the U.S. Army and Marine Corps—and on and on. Ed's tours have reached tens of thousands of people, many of whom return again and again as self-described Bearss groupies. Although other tour guides have tried, none can match Ed's unique style, which personalizes the generals and politicians and sergeants and privates who populate his battlefield tours. His stentorian voice carries easily not only to those in his tours but also to the dozens of others who attach themselves to Ed as he walks the ground at Gettysburg and other fields.

The following transcripts of Ed's tours of the principal Civil War battlefields make it possible for those who have never been privileged to take an actual tour with him to take a virtual tour. And for those who have walked these fields with Ed, the transcripts bring back the details of terrain and tactics, personalities and command decisions that first opened their eyes to the reality of those battles—and of that war. To read the following pages is the next best thing to being there.

A Word About Organization in the Armies of the North and South

In 1861, the United States Army had an authorized strength of 25,000 officers and men, but actual musters numbered about 16,000. The senior commanders had an average age past seventy, and Winfield Scott, the general-in-chief since 1841, was seventy-five, obese, and could not leave his chair without assistance. Of the 1,100 Regular Army officers active when Fort Sumter was fired upon, nearly 400 resigned their commissions and joined forces with the Confederate States of America. With one-third of the officer corps of the Army and one-fourth of the Navy's joining the Confederacy, it's little wonder that the two armies were somewhat similar in organization; all the officers had, in fact, trained with the same manuals, most particularly the one known as *Hardee's Tactics.* Its author, William Joseph Hardee, after publishing the manual in 1856, served as commandant of cadets at the U.S. Military Academy until January 1861, when he resigned and subsequently was made a brigadier general in the Confederate Army.

At First Manassas, the initial full-scale conflict to pit members and former members of the U.S. Army officer corps against each other, eight of the thirteen senior Union commanders had never seen combat, whereas twelve of the fifteen Confederate generals were experienced battle commanders, most of them West Pointers. Still, as President Lincoln pointed out to General Irvin McDowell (a longtime staff officer elevated to his first command), who hesitated to do battle until his troops were more "experienced," both sides in the coming conflict were equally "green." Confederate General Joe Johnston commented on the outcome of the battle by saying that "whichever army had stood a while longer on that day, the other would have given way."

The two armies facing each other, the Union Army of the Potomac and what later would be called the Army of Northern Virginia, reflected the general tendency for Confederate armies to be named for the "territory" in which they were organized and for Union armies to be named for principal rivers in their area of operation, among those the James, the Ohio, and the Tennessee. There were at least sixteen Union and twenty-three Confederate bodies known as an "army," those on both sides often bearing the name of their "Department," or territorial organization, such as Department of East Tennessee. Among the armies, the next largest designation was a "Corps," and for the Federals the corps were numbered, whereas for the Confederacy most were known by the names of their commanders, as in "Longstreet's Corps." Each corps was divided into at least two numbered divisions (also known by the names of their commanders), which were further broken down into "brigades," and then into "regiments," which numbered about 1,000 men each on muster in and were the basic fighting units in most battles. They were made up of "companies" (since for the most part "battalions" were not then designated), which were further divided into "platoons," and then "squads." In the Union army, brigades were most often identified by a number whereas in the Confederacy they continued to bear the names of their initial commanders, most notable with the Stonewall Brigade, which retained its name even after General "Stonewall" Jackson moved on to higher commands and was subsequently killed. Exceptions to custom in the Union army were brigades known as "Irish," "Iron," and "Vermont," among others. Regiments, in both armies, were usually drawn from a single area (or ethnic background or occupation, such as firemen in the "11th New York Fire Zouaves") and bore that name as well as a number, as in 20th Maine or Eighth Georgia. Toward the end of the war, most regiments, through disease, desertion, and battle casualties, were well below their starting strength, since there was little provision at the time for replacements, except by forming new units.

In addition to infantry, there were artillery and cavalry organizations, besides the usual headquarters, quartermaster, engineer, and signal units. Each army corps included an artillery brigade (or battalion in the Confederate Army), which was divided into "batteries," which were the basic operational units, initially limbering six cannon in the Union Army (four guns by the Spring of 1864) and usually four in the Confederacy. Most often batteries were assigned where needed in battle, combined together into a larger force, or kept in reserve.

The cavalry, which operated more or less independently as the "eyes" of field commanders, was most often formed early in the war at regimental strength, divided into battalions and then into ten or twelve "troops" designated by letters, which were further divided into "squadrons" consisting of two companies, the smallest operational unit in horseback combat. Within a year the horse soldiers were being organized into brigades, then divisions, and finally corps, and being employed as mounted infantry. Then (and forever after), many cavalry forces were popularly identified by the romantic figures that led them, most notably J.E.B. Stuart, Phil Sheridan, John Hunt Morgan, John Buford, Nathan Bedford Forrest, and Wade Hampton, as in "Hampton's Legion."

1859

Seen from the vantage point of the U.S. armory as it was located in 1859, the much traveled Armory Firehouse—the place that radical abolitionist John Brown's men were to have stormed and taken—was where Brown and his "army of liberation" would make their final stand on October 18, 1859. Having miscalculated the eagerness of Harpers Ferry slaves to join the insurrection, Brown found himself holed up in the firehouse with a small band of men. After losing most of their group, including two of Brown's own sons, Brown finally surrendered to United States Marines under the command of Lt. Col. Robert E. Lee.

PRELUDE TO WAR

JOHN BROWN'S RAID

OCTOBER 1859

During the "four score years" that followed the founding of the American Republic, the persistent question of whether slavery should be tolerated in a society that promised equality and professed democratic ideals had become more and more divisive politically. Confrontations between the free states of the North and the slaveholding, agrarian South increasingly gave way to violence and force of arms. By mid-century three decades of constitutional argument and legislative debate had led to the Compromise of 1850, a series of stopgap measures that temporarily balanced the interests of slave and free factions. In 1854, when Congress passed the Kansas-Nebraska Act, opening up two new western territories for settlement, it left to "popular sovereignty" the decision whether slavery would be allowed to expand into these new lands. In other words, the white male inhabitants of the territories would decide for themselves. Northerners and Southerners alike soon rushed westward, determined to control the political processes of the new territories. Both sides were armed, and before long a vicious guerrilla war broke out between pro-slavery "Border Ruffians" and free-soil "Jayhawkers." In describing the anarchy, eastern press headlines screamed "Bleeding Kansas."

One of the leading figures in this bloodshed was militia captain John Brown, who had established a free-soil settlement on the Osawatomie. An ardent abolitionist who grasped his inspiration from the stern and vengeful God of the Old Testament, Brown took it upon himself to strike back at members of the pro-slavery faction after some of their number had attacked the antislavery stronghold of Lawrence, Kansas, on May 21, 1856. Three days later, on the night of May 24, Brown and several of his numerous sons attacked a pro-slavery community called Dutch Henry's Crossing along Pottawatomie Creek and seized and murdered five men in cold blood. Pro-slavery forces later struck back, attacking the settlement of Osawatomie on August 30, killing one of Brown's sons and burning his home.

Although authorities claimed to want Brown apprehended, he remained free and somewhat elusive, but eventually was forced out of Kansas. As the decade neared its end, he was addressing groups in the East, rallying them to the abolitionist cause with passionate rhetoric. At the same time, however, Brown began to talk privately about the possibility of instigating a slave insurrection. He believed that the Federal arsenal and armory at Harpers Ferry, Virginia, offered a promising initial target; if he could secure enough arms and begin to rally escaped slaves to seek out a secure stronghold, a freedman's "republic" in the Appalachian Mountains, he might well create a rebellion that would spread and liberate slaves throughout Virginia and the South.

At Harpers Ferry the Potomac receives the waters of the Shenandoah River. To the west of town is Bolivar Heights, part of the Blue Ridge Mountains. South of the Shenandoah (an Indian term meaning "Daughter of the Stars") and south of the Potomac is Loudoun Heights, part of the Blue Ridge Mountains. North of the river, in Maryland, are Maryland Heights and South Mountain. At Harpers Ferry the river valleys of the Potomac and Shenandoah form natural routes of travel. Anthropologists believe that long before the coming of whites, Indians moving north and south were in the habit of crossing the Potomac River in and around the Harpers Ferry area.

Harpers Ferry is named for Robert Harper, who in 1747 began operating a ferry across the Potomac and Shenandoah rivers. He established himself there at a good time for an entrepreneur. He saw the beginning of a heavy migration from the northeast to the southwest, opening up the area down the Shenandoah Valley toward western North Carolina. That same year,

The Shenandoah River runs into the Potomac at Harpers Ferry, West Virginia. Strategically important for travelers heading West, the town was home to the Federal armory and arsenal.

Dr. Thomas Walker, an English chap, traversed an ancient Indian trail through a defile in the Appalachians and named it Cumberland Gap, by way of which hundreds of settlers were able to reach Kentucky, including Daniel Boone. The crossing at Harpers Ferry soon became just as important a travel route for the white man as it had been for the Indians.

Young George Washington becomes familiar with the lands to the west of the Blue Ridge as a surveyor. The French were beginning to move aggressively southward from Canada, in what would become the French and Indian War, and establish Fort LeBoeuf on the portage between waters draining into Lake Erie and the stream forming the headwaters of the Allegheny. Washington passes through this area in 1753 as a 22-year-old with a message from Virginia Lt. Governor Robert Dinwiddie telling the French commandant at Fort LeBoeuf that he is trespassing on territory chartered to England in 1609 and must withdraw. The French are unimpressed with this message. The next year, Washington leaves Williamsburg with a small detachment, passes through Harpers Ferry, and proceeds westward. About 20 miles east of the confluence of the rivers forming the Ohio, Washington builds a fort at Great Meadows, which he calls Fort Necessity, having learned that the French have already arrived at the confluence of the Monongahela and Allegheny Rivers. Washington is lucky. His men ambush a force of Indians and Frenchmen commanded by Ens. Joseph Jumonville. Washington's Indian allies ritually murder Jumonville by smashing his skull and removing his brains. Jumonville's brother responds by leading an attack against Fort Necessity, forcing Washington to surrender. Fortunately for what will become the United States, the Frenchman controls his Indians, and they do not murder our future President. Washington will come back through this area with Maj. Gen. Edward Braddock in an attempt to oust the French from Fort Duquesne, near modern Pittsburgh, but the British are badly beaten and withdraw in July 1755.

Washington buys land in the country surrounding Harpers Ferry. By 1791, as President of the United States, he's in a position to do something for the region. It's been decided by Congress that the future capital of the United States will be sited just below the falls of the Potomac River, in what will be called the new District of Columbia. As a military man, George Washington looks to establish an armory nearby. The only other one in the United States is at Springfield, Massachusetts.

Now, it's important to distinguish between an armory and an arsenal. You manufacture arms at an armory; you store arms and repair them at an arsenal. The new armory must be near a source of water power, and relatively close to the capital. Washington decides to site the second U.S. armory at Harpers Ferry, 61 miles northwest of the capital.

Washington also has an interest in economic development and will be a force behind the Potomack Canal, which precedes the Chesapeake & Ohio Canal. The Potomack Canal is planned to provide water routes around the obstacles of Great Falls and Little Falls. Through its militia system, the United States had established arsenals as well: The one in Virginia is located here, so Harpers Ferry will have both an arsenal and an armory. By 1859 Harpers Ferry is also the intersection of two major railroads, the Baltimore & Ohio and the Winchester & Potomac. Because it's at the hub of strategic transportation corridors, with an armory and an arsenal situated near the Mason-Dixon Line, the accepted divider between slave and free states, Harpers Ferry becomes a key objective as John Brown matures his plans. It is a gateway to and from the slaveholding South.

John Brown was born in 1800 in Torrington, Connecticut, but grew up in Ohio, where his abolitionist father maintained a stop on the Underground Railway. Up until his antislavery activities in Kansas, John Brown was far from successful in life except at fathering children. By two women he fathered twenty children, seven by his first wife and the rest by his second. Largely thanks to his notoriety in Bleeding Kansas, Brown becomes something of a hero among abolitionists in Massachusetts and the other New England states. He is closely associated for a while with the former slave Frederick Douglass. However, when the self-educated Douglass learns of Brown's plans to organize an Army of Liberation to support a slave insurrection, he urges caution. "An attack on the federal government," Douglass argues, "would array the whole country against us."

Brown arrives in Harpers Ferry on the second day of July 1859 and will identify himself variously as Isaac Smith, Nelson Hawkins, and Shabel Morgan. He talks to some local people and says he wants to rent an isolated farmhouse. They tell him about the Kennedy place, which is located in a secluded valley on the west side of Elk Ridge, five miles northwest of Harpers Ferry. He rents it and begins to assemble his Army of Liberation. Brown arrives in Harpers Ferry with his sons Owen and Oliver. He is soon joined by Oliver's wife Martha, his son Watson, and 16-year-old daughter Annie. The other Army of Liberation volunteers drift in. Another veteran of Kansas, the well-educated John Henry Kagi will be secretary of state for Brown's provisional government. Initially, they have an English soldier of fortune, Hugh Forbes, who had fought with Garibaldi in Italy, prepare a plan for guerrilla warfare that will free slaves. Forbes presents Brown with his plan, called "the drill manual," but never actually visits the Kennedy Farm. While on a speaking tour in Connecticut, Brown contracts to have one thousand pikes—long, spear-like instruments—made. With Kagi's help, Brown had drafted a "Provisional Constitution and Ordinances for the People of the United States" in 1858. After about a month and a half Forbes decides this is a crackbrained idea and that Brown is a madman. He quits in August.

Brown is now confronted by a mutiny in his army. The soldiers are discontented with the long periods of confinement and inactivity on the farm. Frederick Douglass urges that they call the raid off, but Brown is a charismatic speaker. He addresses the army. The army agrees to stay. There are five blacks in the army. They can only come out at night—Virginia and Maryland are slave states. What are the neighbors going to say if they see unfamiliar whites and blacks running around together during daylight hours? The blacks have to stay up in the Kennedy farmhouse garret. A number of the whites are Quakers. Quakers eschew violence, but some have come to the conclusion that violence in liberating the slaves can be justified by their church. Others had followed Captain Brown in Kansas. Brown is going to sleep 23 people in the Kennedy house, 25 counting Annie and Martha.

Brown sends out John E. Cook to pose as a book salesman, aiming to ingratiate himself with Lewis Washington, great-grandnephew of George. He visits Washington in his home, Bellair, and scouts out his house. During their actual raid Captain Brown will send Aaron Stevens with five people to seize Lewis Washington as a hostage, and Cook goes with them.

Six leading members of the abolitionist movement, five of them from Massachusetts, fund Brown's uprising. We know them now as the Secret Six. There is Samuel Gridley Howe, a world-renowned physician and the husband of Julia Ward Howe. There is clergyman and writer Thomas Wentworth

Higginson, a leader in the intellectual community in Massachusetts who will command a black regiment during the Civil War. Manufacturer George Stearns is another—he will be in charge of recruiting blacks when the Lincoln Administration starts organizing black units in 1863. Franklin Sanborn is a Boston editor and educator. Theodore Parker is a prominent Boston Congregationalist minister. They are joined by former antislavery Congressman Gerrit Smith of New York. These are the Secret Six.

By mid-October Brown feels that the time has come to strike. Concerned about arousing the suspicions of neighbors around the Kennedy farm, Brown feels compelled to act despite the fact that several members of his "army" have not yet arrived. On the evening of October 16, 1859, he turns out his army.

Brown tells his men to get "on your arms." Owen Brown, Francis Merriam, and Barclay Coppoc remain at the Kennedy farm with most of the army's pikes and guns, as well as a number of incriminating letters that later will show that the raid is being funded by the Secret Six. The rest of his Army of Liberation, 19 strong including Brown, sets out for town. Brown knows it will be quiet in Harpers Ferry that night. There has been a revival meeting with singing, praying, and shouting, so the townspeople will retire early. Imagine Brown driving his wagon loaded with pikes and Sharps carbines down the hill leading to the Potomac. He sees the lights flickering off in Harpers Ferry as the last of the "night owls" go to bed. Brown knows it was a Methodist revival. It would have been better if it had been a Baptist revival, because the Baptists are generally a lot more fervent than Methodists. He sends John Cook and Charles Tidd to cut the telegraph line that leads to Washington and Baltimore.

About 11:30 Brown reaches the long covered bridge crossing the Potomac. Bill Williams, the bridge watchman, waiting to be relieved at midnight, is sitting in a guard shack on the Harpers Ferry side of the river. He hears men coming toward him, and he accosts them. They are

Ardent abolitionist John Brown, pictured here in a circa 1846 portrait, led a violent antislavery attack in Kansas in 1856 before planning to instigate a slave rebellion in Harpers Ferry.

wearing heavy shawls and slouch hats. Brown confronts Williams as two of his men put pistols in his face and overpower him. Williams asks "What have I done?" Brown replies "You've done nothing to me but enough to the poor blacks. I mean to capture Harpers Ferry, and if resisted I must burn the town and have blood." So, trussing Williams up, they go to the armory gate. There Danny Whelan, the 17-year-old gatekeeper, a good Catholic boy, is confronted and captured as he whispers a prayer. The lock and chain are broken and Brown seizes the armory. Brown then sends five men out with his wagon, guided by John Cook and led by Aaron Stevens, to seize hostages. An important hostage will be Lewis Washington, descendant of the first President. In the early morning hours of the 17th, they break into his house and into his bedroom. Washington recognizes Cook. They tell him to get ready to come with them, but they want two things that he owns. They want the sword given George Washington by Frederick the Great that bears the inscription "From the World's Oldest General to the World's Greatest," and a pistol that had belonged to Lafayette. Stevens, a veteran of Bleeding Kansas, points to Osborne Anderson and tells Washington, "Give him the sword." Anderson is one of the five blacks who march with Brown. They take Lewis Washington, who dresses immaculately but refuses to ride in the wagon. They also seize his slaves.

Brown hopes that as soon as the slaves have heard that he has possession of Harpers Ferry, they will rise up and spark a servile insurrection. But this is not the Deep South, where slavery exists in a far harsher form, and the blacks might well have swarmed to him. If slavery is ever less demeaning and arduous, it's in this part of the nation. This is not a Louisiana sugar plantation or Mississippi cotton country. These are household slaves. Brown has not picked a good place to begin an insurrection.

The Lewis Washington slaves get into the wagon. The raiders stop at the Allstadt House, where they seize John Allstadt and his son and take their six slaves. By the time they return to Harpers Ferry there has been bloodshed. The eastbound express comes in at 1:30 a.m. Dr. John Starry hears the chuffing of an engine idling and hears a shot. Like a good physician he grabs his medical bag and heads down toward the railroad depot, located adjacent to the Wager House Hotel. He finds a badly wounded man, Hayward Shepherd, a free black who works as a baggage man. He has been shot in the groin by one of the raiders; it's obvious to Dr. Starry that he's not going to live long. So the first man killed by the Army of Liberation is one of the very people they've come to liberate.

Now it is 5 a.m. and Brown and his raiders have stopped a Baltimore & Ohio train. When conductor Andy Phelps asks, "Can I proceed?" Brown, concerned about innocent travelers, says yes, but the conductor is worried. Perhaps the raiders have sabotaged the bridge, so Brown gets a lantern and leads the train across the bridge. Phelps stops the train at the Monocacy Junction station, where the telegraph line is operational, and sends a message warning, "Insurrectionists are in possession of Harpers Ferry."

It was not an auspicious beginning. By stopping the train, then letting it proceed, Brown ensured that people would too quickly learn of his raid. Still, Brown had succeeded in securing control of the bridge leading into town; before long both the arsenal and armory were under his control, along with the nearby Hall's U.S. Rifle Works. He took control of a small group of prisoners, including several armory workers who showed up early on the morning of October 17. But his success was short-lived. Dr. Starry quickly spread the word as to what had happened; militia companies from Virginia and Maryland began to converge on Harpers Ferry. Some townspeople also picked up weapons and joined in the fray. Before midday they had reclaimed control of the bridge and begun advancing on key points. Brown attempted to negotiate a truce, but those efforts failed, and by afternoon several members of his army were killed, captured, or wounded as local townsfolk and militia tightened their circle around the survivors of Brown's beleaguered band.

Brown and a number of his remaining men take refuge in the armory engine house. The armory has a brick wall around it. The engine house is located near two arsenal buildings situated close to the foot of Shenandoah Street, on the south side of the armory. Here the authorities keep their fire engines, but the building would gain fame as John Brown's Fort.

Before long, there is more bloodshed in the town. Dr. Starry, after treating Shepherd, goes up to the Lutheran Church and tolls the bell and sends messengers to nearby Charles Town and Shepherdstown. The word spreads—insurrectionists are in possession of Harpers Ferry. The militia turns out, but it's not particularly well organized or disciplined. Shortly after 9 a.m. Thomas Boerly, a local grocer, is shot by a raider as he walks down High Street; there he lies with his blood flowing into the gutter. Ex-West Pointer and candidate for sheriff of Jefferson County George W. Turner is gunned down as he rides along High Street. Also shot is the friendly, popular, 72-year-old Mayor Fontaine Beckham, who is the guardian of a black family and a black man who will be freed upon his death. They will be the only blacks liberated by the raid, winning their freedom when Beckham's will is probated. A number of the raiders have also been killed—Dangerfield Newby, a black man whose wife and family are held in bondage in Virginia and the oldest of the raiders next to Brown; William Leeman; John Kagi; Lewis Leary (black); and William Thompson. Aaron Stevens has been wounded and John Copeland (black) captured.

As darkness closes in, Brown is barricaded in the engine house. The raiders in John Brown's Fort with the "old man" are Dauphin Thompson and Jeremiah Anderson; Oliver and Watson Brown, both mortally wounded; Stewart Taylor, who will be killed sometime during the long night; Shields "Emperor" Green (black); Edwin Coppoc; and 11 hostages, including Lewis Washington and the Allstadts, father and son. A number of the "liberated" slaves have been reluctantly armed with pikes.

During the long night Watson Brown dies; when John Brown hears his other son, Oliver, moaning, he snaps, "Shut up and die like a man." Before long Oliver dies.

News that something bad has happened at Harpers Ferry arrives at the War Department in Washington City on the morning of October 17. Upon hearing the news President James Buchanan goes to the War Department. In the office that day is James Ewell Brown Stuart, a lieutenant in the First U.S. Cavalry on leave from Fort Riley in Kansas Territory. He's in Washington seeking to patent an invention to hitch a saber to a belt. There is only one senior line (combat) officer of the U.S. Army in Washington. Every other one is a staff officer. The only line troops in Washington are at the Marine barracks. Already the Navy Department has been alerted, and Lt. Israel Green with some 90 marines boards a special train en route for Harpers Ferry. Stuart is sent to find Lt. Col. Robert E. Lee, who is known to be at Arlington, his wife's family home, on a long leave of absence to settle his father-in-law's estate. Stuart finds Lee in civilian clothes at Ledbetter's Pharmacy in Alexandria. Reporting to Secretary of War John B. Floyd and the President, Lee receives orders to proceed to Harpers Ferry and take charge of the marines. The marines had been ordered to halt and detrain at Sandy Hook, a mile and a half downstream on the Potomac. Lee will not arrive at Sandy Hook until after dark on the 17th.

By the morning of October 18, Colonel Lee, having crossed the river, deploys Green and his marines in front of Brown's Fort, and orders the saloons closed. He asks the commander of the Virginia militia, "Will you storm the engine house?" The reply is no: The militia will leave that job to the professional military. Lee then approaches Col. Edward Shriver and asks if the Maryland militia would like to seize the engine house. Shriver gives the same reply. It's going to be up to Colonel Lee, Lieutenants Green and Stuart, and the marines to get the insurrectionists out.

No one knows that it's *the* John Brown who's in the engine house; everyone still assumes it's a man named Isaac Smith. Lee directs Stuart to approach the engine house, white handkerchief in hand, and parlay with the leader of the insurrection. Lee adds that if they surrender and do not harm the hostages, he will guarantee their safety as prisoners. Meanwhile, Lieutenant Green has formed up a detail of marines with sledgehammers, in case they have to storm the engine house. As Jeb Stuart nears the engine house, the door opens a crack and Stuart is surprised by who he sees. Having been stationed at Forts Leavenworth and Riley, in Kansas Territory, Stuart recognizes "Old Osawatomie" Brown, as he was known there. He tells Brown of Lee's terms. Brown says, "Let me march out with my army. Let me cross the bridge, and I'll keep the hostages until we get across the bridge, and then I will release them unharmed." Stuart's orders are not to negotiate. He steps back from the door and waves his hat—the signal to

On October 17, Lt. Col. Robert E. Lee (pictured here in a circa 1855 photo that was later retouched) received orders to take charge of the marines at Harpers Ferry and stop the insurrection.

storm the engine house. A team of brawny marines comes forward with sledgehammers and attacks the engine house doors, but there is too much give in the doors, and the planks do not shatter. Green then sends forward a team of marines with a fire ladder. Using the fire ladder as a battering ram, they batter away part of the lower corner of one of the doors.

Israel Green has brought with him a light dress sword rather than a heavier combat saber. He crawls through the door on his hands and knees, followed by other marines. As he crawls through the door he sees Brown, crouching, with his Sharps carbine. Lewis Washington points Brown out. Green rushes at Brown and puts a deep cut on his neck with his sword. Green then tries to run Brown through, only to have the blade strike a button or some other hard item and bend double. He then rushes at Brown and uses the blunt end of the broken sword to beat Brown into submission. He leaves

Brown badly bleeding, slumped on the floor. One marine who was following behind him is mortally wounded, possibly by a shot fired by Brown, and a second is wounded in the brief melee. A marine lunges at Dauphin Thompson, pinning him to the wall with his bayonet. Thompson, with this bayonet through him, turns with his center of gravity and ends up pinned to the wall head downward. Jeremiah Anderson is shot and killed. Brown is captured alive, along with Coppoc and "Emperor" Green. On the floor are Stewart Taylor and Oliver and Watson Brown, who all died during the night from their wounds. None of the hostages is harmed.

Arriving here shortly after the capture are Senator James M. Mason and Governor Henry Wise, both of Virginia, and a busybody from Ohio, U.S. Representative Clement Vallandigham. They question Brown. Wise soon makes the worst decision, in my opinion, that any governor of any state has ever made. He claims Brown for the Commonwealth of Virginia, instead of having the federal government prosecute Brown for murder. Wise will have him charged as having committed treason against Virginia, and having conspired with slaves to foment servile insurrection. Wise is impressed when he questions Brown. Brown is outspoken and straightforward about himself and his objectives. Colonel Lee will remain in Harpers Ferry until they have transferred Brown and the other prisoners to Charles Town on October 19, where they will be jailed and held for trial.

Brown's trial for insurrection and treason lasts from October 27 to October 31. Brown represents himself. The jury's verdict is handed down, and on the second of November the judge announces the verdict—death by hanging—and sets December 2 as the date for this to be carried out.

There is a lot of noise among abolitionists that they will rescue Brown. It is rumored that abolitionist forces are assembling in Bellaire, Ohio. Brown sends word that "I don't want to be rescued." He knows he is going to be more valuable to the cause as a martyr than rescued. During the trial, Brown puts the institution of slavery on trial. On the day of his execution, Brown will write in a note handed to his jailer that he is "now quite certain that the crimes of this guilty land will never be purged away but with blood."

On the day Brown is to be executed, Colonel Lee is back at Harpers Ferry with a large force of federal soldiers to keep order. Mary Ann Brown is also in Harpers Ferry. She visits her husband on December 1, but she does not go to the hanging. The VMI Corps of Cadets also attends, its artillery contingent led by a Maj. Thomas J. Jackson. Also present is one who will be at center stage on April 14, 1865. Actor John Wilkes Booth was performing in Richmond and temporarily joins the Richmond Grays, a militia unit dispatched to Charles Town.

As Brown comes out of the jail, in a scene to be recorded in paintings and lithographs, legend has it that black women hold up their children to be blessed by Brown. He rides a half-mile from the jail to the hanging site. He mounts the 13 steps. The hangman ties his seven knots. Brown says, "Make it quick." And he's gone. Booth is impressed. He loathes everything that Brown stands for, but he's impressed with the way Brown goes to his death. Would he remember this day in April 1865?

Repercussions sweep the country throughout the remainder of 1859 and into 1860. The publication of the trial transcript inflames people; so does the indictment in Virginia of the Secret Six. When authorities sent by Lee arrive and search the Kennedy farmhouse, they find the correspondence tying Brown to the Secret Six. To their horror, Southerners discover that what at first looked to be the action of a "madman" has been backed by responsible people in the North—leaders of the abolitionist movement and leading intellectuals. The Virginia court indicts them. The only one that flees the country is Theodore Parker. The others stay because they know that when the legal people deliver extradition papers, they will not be honored.

Many Southerners see Brown as an agent of abolitionists seeking to incite a servile insurrection in the South, such as had happened with severe consequences more than 50 years earlier in Haiti. Southerners also see that Brown is being aided and abetted by people that enjoy great public support in the North. Brown is looked on as a saint by millions of Americans, and by equal numbers as a madman, and yes, a terrorist. Southern legislatures vote large sums of money to buy arms and equipment; the pro-secession "fire eaters" strengthen their position in the southern states. If I'm a good Southerner at the time, I can see why I might decide to join the militia. To many, Brown has made his gallows as sacred as the cross and the crown of thorns worn by the Savior on Calvary. To most Southerners he is the devil incarnate.

Brown's body is turned over to Mary Ann; she transports it northward with considerable show. Up in Philadelphia they ring the Liberty Bell. He is buried in North Elba, New York, on a farm purchased for him years before by Gerrit Smith.

The fate of the respective members of the Army of Liberation, as Brown called his followers, is as follows: Brown, 59, hanged. Annie Brown, 16, sent home. Martha, daughter-in-law, 17, sent home. John Kagi, killed in the Shenandoah River as he flees. Aaron Stevens, hanged. Oliver and Watson Brown, killed. Jeremiah Anderson, killed. John E. Cook, hanged. Charles Plumber Tidd, escaped. William Thompson, killed—shot, dumped in the river, and for days passersby could see his ghostly face looking up at them. Dauphin Thompson is bayoneted in John Brown's Fort. Albert Hazlett, hanged. Edwin Coppoc, hanged. Barclay Coppoc, Francis Merriam, and Owen Brown, left as rear guard at the Kennedy farm, escaped. John Copeland, hanged. William Leeman, killed. Stewart Taylor, killed. Osborne P. Anderson, escaped. Dangerfield Newby, killed. Lewis Leary, killed in the Shenandoah River. Shields "Emperor" Green, hanged.

It is my belief that the Brown raid and its linkage with the Secret Six is the vital catalyst that leads to secession, the Civil War, and the liberation of more than four million black Americans.

1861

Twentieth-century fortifications—modern and enlarged from the shelled and destroyed original brick structure of Fort Sumter—look toward Charleston, South Carolina. On April 12, 1861, "shot and shell went screaming over Sumter as if an army of devils were swooping around it," recalled a member of the Union Garrison. The fort, under the leadership of Major Robert Anderson, held out for 36 hours against the heavy bombardment of Confederate General Pierre Gustave Toutant Beauregard—Anderson's assistant at West Point. Remarkably, none of the 68 defenders were killed. On April14th a battered Stars and Stripes was lowered and replaced by the Stars and Bars of the Confederacy, with seven stars representing the Southern states that had seceded from the Union. Within two months of Sumter's fall, four other states would secede.

I

FORT SUMTER

APRIL 1861

The victory of Republican Party candidate Abraham Lincoln over a fragmented Democratic Party in the election of 1860 spread fear and anger throughout the South. Southern "fire eaters" denounced Lincoln and the "Black Republicans" and argued that the South could not tolerate an administration that would not support states' rights and property rights (i.e., slavery) in the new territories. A Mississippian wrote to his local newspaper, the Natchez Free Trader, *"the minds of the people are aroused to a pitch of excitement probably unparalleled in the history of our country."*

The Democrats had gone into the election with their political base divided between proslavery Vice President John C. Breckinridge of Kentucky and Senator Stephen A. Douglas, whose appeal was primarily to northern Democrats. A third party, Tennesseean John Bell's Constitutional Union, further divided Democrats and their supporters. In the end, Abraham Lincoln and the Republicans won with only 40 percent of the popular vote but with a firm 180 electoral votes against Breckinridge's 72. Furthermore, Lincoln's victory was overwhelming in the northern states, totaling more than 60 percent of the electorate. As Lincoln's Inauguration loomed, fear, despondency, and alarm spread throughout the Deep South. Rumors of new John Browns and of slave insurrections flared throughout the southern states. For many Southerners Lincoln's victory could mean only one thing—secession.

It began in South Carolina. On December 20, 1860, a convention held in Charleston voted 169 to 0 to adopt an Ordinance of Secession severing all ties between the sovereign state of South Carolina and the Federal Union. Mississippi followed suit on January 9, and, in quick succession, so did Florida, Alabama, Georgia, Louisiana, and Texas. On February 4, 1861, representatives of six of the seven seceding states, meeting in Montgomery, Alabama, formed the Confederate States of America. The delegates created a provisional constitution, and on February 18 swore into office the provisional Confederate president, Jefferson Davis of Mississippi—the former U.S. secretary of war.

In the North, both outgoing President James Buchanan and President-elect Abraham Lincoln spoke of reconciliation with the South but firmly opposed secession. In his Inaugural Address in March, Lincoln stated firmly that he would use "all the powers" at his disposal to "hold, occupy, and possess Federal property," but made no mention of specific actions he might order against the seceding states. By the spring of 1861, the tensions of a nation were focused on Fort Sumter, a tiny island fortress at the mouth of Charleston Harbor in South Carolina.

South Carolina secedes from the Union in December 1860. On the night of December 26, 1860, Maj. Robert Anderson, commander of Fort Moultrie, abandons the Sullivan's Island fortification and orders his troops to row through the darkness to Fort Sumter, which is more easily defended.

The next morning, Gov. Francis W. Pickens sends a delegation headed by his aide-de-camp, Col. J. Johnston Pettigrew, to meet with Anderson. Pettigrew informs Anderson that the governor is surprised he has reinforced Sumter. Anderson answers that he has simply removed his command from Fort Moultrie, which was within his rights as commander of all the forts in the harbor. He tells Pettigrew that he can get no information or positive orders from Washington and that he hopes by relocating his men to Fort Sumter the matter can be settled peacefully. "In this controversy between the North and the South," Anderson adds, "my sympathies are entirely with the South." Nevertheless, Anderson is a man who will do his duty.

Today Fort Sumter still stands near the entrance to Charleston Harbor. It is built on a stone and rock riprap island that was deposited between 1830 and 1845. Fort Sumter is about one-half as high now as it would have been at the beginning of the Civil War. In 1861 the fort had two lower casemate tiers, the second tier still under construction, and one top tier en barbette, with guns in the open behind the parapet. The outer walls were about 50 feet tall and 5 feet thick. During the siege of 1863–65, to recover the fort, Federal batteries battered away most of the upper two tiers. In the 1870s the rubble was removed and Fort Sumter rebuilt as a two-tier fortification. In 1898–99, the fort was modernized with the construction of Battery Huger, mounting two 12-inch guns in a reinforced concrete emplacement inside the fort's brick walls.

Brevet Maj. Pierre Gustave Toutant Beauregard is an important figure in the U.S. Army in 1860. An engineer officer, he had just been assigned as superintendent of West Point when his native Louisiana seceded from the Union on January 26, 1861. He immediately resigns from the Army and holds the dubious distinction of having served the shortest tenure of any superintendent of a U.S. military academy.

Beauregard is sent by the Confederacy to Charleston as its first field commander, a brigadier general, then the highest rank in the Confederate States military, and he will be in charge of operations that eventually result in the surrender of Fort Sumter. The South Carolinians have already begun construction of fortifications at other points around the harbor when Beauregard arrives, and he continues to fortify Charleston. Fort Moultrie, abandoned by Anderson and now occupied by South Carolina forces, sits on

OPPOSITE: *On December 26 Maj. Robert Anderson, commander of the Federal forces at Charleston, moved his garrison from Fort Moultrie to the more defensible Fort Sumter, commanding the entrance to Charleston Harbor. On April 11, 1861, General Beauregard, commanding provisional Confederate forces, demanded the surrender of the fort. Anderson refused, and at 4:30 a.m. on April 12, Confederate batteries at Fort Johnson on James Island opened fire, quickly joined by other Rebel guns sited on Sullivan's Island. For a day and a half Anderson returned fire bravely but ineffectively. On April 13, with the fort badly damaged, Anderson surrendered, evacuating his garrison on the following day.*

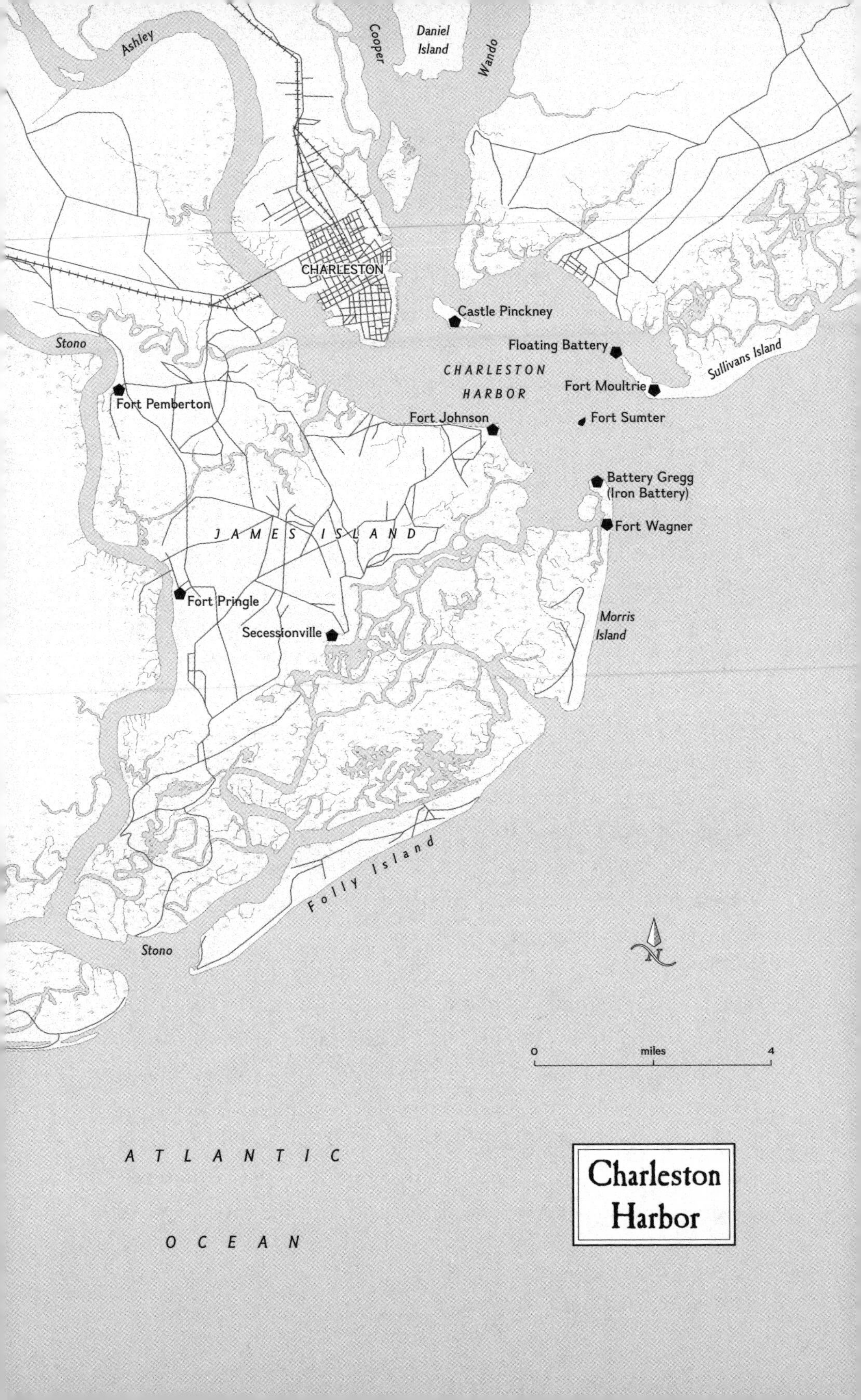
Ashley
Cooper
Daniel Island
Wando
CHARLESTON
Castle Pinckney
Floating Battery
Sullivans Island
CHARLESTON HARBOR
Fort Moultrie
Stono
Fort Pemberton
Fort Johnson
Fort Sumter
Battery Gregg (Iron Battery)
Fort Wagner
JAMES ISLAND
Fort Pringle
Secessionville
Morris Island
Folly Island
Stono
N
0 miles 4
ATLANTIC OCEAN

Charleston Harbor

Sullivan's Island, one mile across the water northeast of Fort Sumter. The Confederates have erected two sand batteries there and anchored a floating wooden battery to the north of Sumter, all spaced along the curving western end of Sullivan's Island, which is across the Cooper River from Charleston. A mile and a half to the west of Anderson's refuge, on the opposite side of the harbor, the South Carolinians have constructed two earth-and-sand mortar batteries at Fort Johnson, on James Island, and have placed several guns and an ironclad battery at Cummings Point on Morris Island, three-quarters of a mile due south of Fort Sumter. Along the harbor's edge in Mount Pleasant, approximately one mile northwest of the fort, the Confederates have placed a mortar battery. Soon Anderson's troops at Fort Sumter will be surrounded by a ring of fire.

Anderson sets his men to work improving the defenses of the fort. The soldiers add earth and wood traverses at vulnerable places along the parapet, to keep enemy shot from enfilading the barbette tier guns, and construct bombproof shelters. Passages are cut to connect the officers' quarters, and a stone-and-brick wall is constructed to protect the main gate (sally port). Anderson also orders that five Columbiad cannon barrels, four 8-inch and one 10-inch, be placed on the parade ground to serve as makeshift mortars. Despite all of his preparations for battle, Anderson maintains communication with the Confederate authorities to prevent misunderstandings.

On the morning of January 9, 1861, a supply ship, the *Star of the West,* loaded with troops and provisions, steams across the Charleston Harbor bar on its way to Fort Sumter. Belowdecks is Lt. Charles R. Woods and a company of about 200 reinforcements. Maj. Peter F. Stevens, commanding the Morris Island defenses, orders Cadet George E. Haynesworth of the Citadel military college to open fire from the "sand hill battery." The *Star of the West* then runs along the coastline taking more fire, being hit twice with no damage by the Citadel cadets.

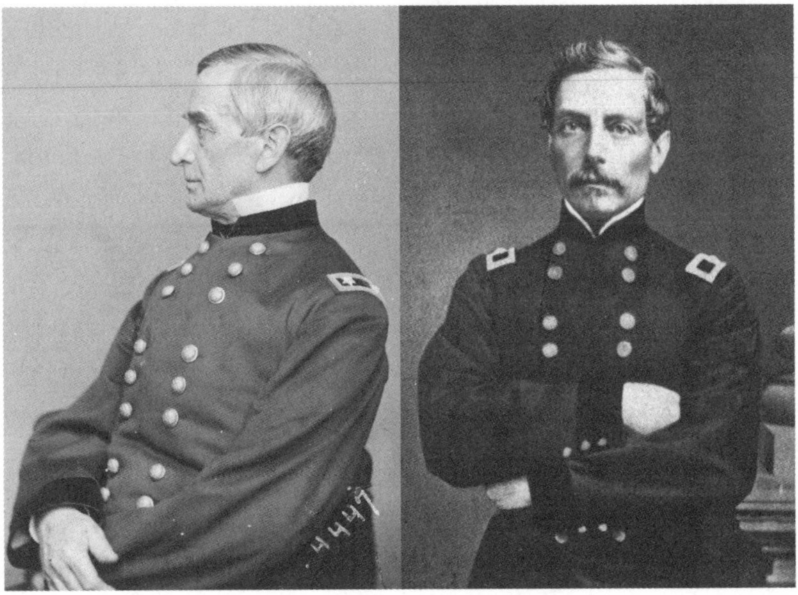

Confederate Gen. Pierre Gustave Toutant Beauregard (right) directed the bombardment of Fort Sumter and Maj. Robert Anderson's (left) Federal troops that opened the war.

It maneuvers toward the channel and seeks to pass between Sumter and Moultrie, taking fire from Moultrie, and then aborts its mission. These will be the first cannon shots of the Civil War, but Major Anderson does not want to provoke an attack. He does not answer the South Carolinians' fire. With lessened hope of new supplies, he is forced to rely on the provisions transferred from Fort Moultrie to Fort Sumter on December 26, 1860. On March 5 President Lincoln learns that Anderson's supplies will run out by mid-April. On March 19, he sends former naval officer Gustavus V. Fox, who has proposed a naval expedition to relieve Fort Sumter, to Charleston to assess the situation. Fox meets with Governor Pickens and General Beauregard, and is permitted to go to Fort Sumter. Meeting with Anderson, he hints at a plan to reinforce the fort. On his return to Washington, Fox argues the feasibility of his plan, setting April 15 as the deadline for resupplying the fort.

After much agonizing over triggering a crisis, Lincoln orders another attempt to resupply Fort Sumter. On the afternoon of April 4 he calls Fox to the White House and tells him that he has "decided to let the expedition go." Lincoln has already heard from Anderson that he has rations to last for "about a week." The President sends a message to Anderson by the postal service that a relief expedition "will go forward," and he urges Anderson to hold out until "the 11th or 12th."

To guard and transport his expedition the Navy provided Fox with the warships *Powhatan, Pocahontas,* and *Pawnee* and the revenue cutter *Harriet Lane* as escort, and the large commercial steamer *Baltic* was engaged to transport men and supplies. With considerable difficulty Fox secured the services of three civilian tugs, the *Yankee, Uncle Ben,* and *Thomas Freeborn.*

On April 6, the frigate *Powhatan* prepares to sail from New York, and the other vessels, including the cutter *Harriet Lane* and tugs *Uncle Ben* and *Yankee,* are readied to head south. The sloop of war *Pawnee* sails from Norfolk, Virginia, on April 9, and the *Baltic,* with Fox on board, puts out to sea the same morning from New York Harbor. Shortly after the *Baltic* sails, a heavy gale scatters the expedition's vessels.

Beauregard demands that Anderson surrender Fort Sumter on April 11. Though short of food and supplies, Anderson refuses, but admits that unless he receives reinforcements he will be starved out by the 15th. This answer is unsatisfactory to Beauregard. He is under orders from the Confederate government in Montgomery to fire on Fort Sumter to prevent reinforcement if absolutely necessary. He is faced with a dilemma.

The fatal gun—a 10-inch seacoast mortar—goes off at 4:30 in the morning on the 12th day of April. The shot is fired as a signal from the east mortar battery in Fort Johnson. It was ordered by Capt. George James and fired by a Lt. Henry Farley. Tradition has it that Edmund Ruffin of Virginia fired the first shot that hit Fort Sumter. Unfortunately for tradition, the next firing after the signal shot comes from Fort Moultrie. The Ironclad Battery on Cummings Point next opens fire; its battery is manned, of course, by the Palmetto Guard. The Palmetto Guard had a prominent volunteer coming down to join them, Edmund Ruffin, Virginia's answer to South Carolina's archsecessionist Robert Barnwell Rhett. Ruffin is an agricultural reformer, prominent in advocating the use of blue marl and other fertilizers to restore depleted soil, but he becomes better known as an ardent advocate of secession. So as his home state vacillates over what to do about secession, he rushes to Charleston to fish in troubled waters during this crisis. He pulls a lanyard on one of the three massive 8-inch Columbiad cannon placed in the Ironclad Battery as the firing on Fort Sumter spreads around what soon becomes the ring of fire from the Confederate batteries.

This morning, Mrs. Mary Chesnut, destined to gain fame as a premier Civil War diarist, finds herself in a Charleston hotel room fronting the Battery, listening to the opening gunfire that heralded the bombardment of Fort Sumter. Her husband James, one of Beauregard's emissaries that has been negotiating with Anderson, is somewhere out in the harbor. She writes in her diary that upon hearing the guns "I sprang out of bed and on my knees—prostrate—I prayed as I have never prayed before."

From within the fort the defenders could see Federal warships lurking just beyond the bar. It was Gustavus Fox's relief expedition. A few hours earlier on April 12, the Baltic *had arrived off Charleston Harbor, but only the* Harriet Lane *had then made the rendezvous. By 6 a.m., the* Pawnee *joined the force, but orders required her captain to await* Powhatan*'s arrival. To further plague Fox's mission, the tug* Thomas Freeborn *never sailed from New York, and the* Uncle Ben *was seized after being forced to seek shelter from gales at Wilmington, North Carolina. Only the tug* Yankee *reached Charleston Harbor, after being delayed by the rough weather.*

There was another disaster: Poor communications in Washington diverted the Powhatan *to an expedition to relieve Fort Pickens in Florida, one of two other military installations still under Federal control in the Confederacy. Unfortunately for Fox the* Powhatan *carried the armed launches and crews necessary to land troops and supplies from the* Baltic. *In the end, Fox and the men of his expedition could only watch helplessly as shot and shell rained down on Fort Sumter.*

The bombardment is one-sided for several hours. It will be about 7:00 or 7:30 a.m., however, before the Union guns return fire. Anderson is not only short on food but also on ammunition. Capt. Abner Doubleday, who later claims to have invented baseball, will fire the first return shot for the Federals from a right gorge angle casemate, sighting on the Confederates' Cummings Point Ironclad Battery on Morris Island.

Mortar shells fired from the batteries on Sullivan's Island and Fort Johnson soon made the parade ground and the open parapet of Fort Sumter dangerous places, and Anderson ordered that the barbette tier guns should not be manned. Despite Anderson's orders, a few men ventured onto the barbette to fire guns facing the Confederate batteries. Fired in haste, the shot did little damage but served to boost the morale of Sumter's defenders.

Three times during the day the barracks were set on fire by exploding shells, but each time the flames were quickly extinguished. Throughout the rest of the day and into the night Confederate projectiles battered Sumter's walls and interior without yet causing serious damage. After nightfall, Rebel batteries fired shells only every ten or fifteen minutes. Short on cartridge bags, Major Anderson ordered teams of men to stitch them from cloth obtained by cutting up extra clothing and hospital sheets.

At daylight on the 13th the Confederates increased their rate of fire, and the bombardment began to take effect. A lucky shot from Cummings Point sprayed shell fragments into a casemate, wounding a sergeant and three men. Later a civilian worker was severely wounded by debris from a mortar shell explosion. By now the Confederates began to fire hot shot, solid shot heated to cherry-red temperatures in a special furnace, from Fort Moultrie. These missiles set fire to the officers' quarters, forcing the Federals to seal off their magazines to prevent an explosion.

The fort's garrison watched helplessly as the fire spread to the enlisted barracks. Ready ammunition stored in the stair towers and nearby rooms exploded. The flagstaff was struck down by shot seven times during the day, only to be raised again. When finally the flagstaff was destroyed, the flag was secured by Lt. Norman Hall and Sgt. Peter Hart to a temporary staff, rigged on the parapet.

About one o'clock Louis T. Wigfall, a former U.S. senator from Texas and South Carolina native who was serving as a volunteer aide on Beauregard's staff, rowed to the fort through the bombardment to demand its surrender. After a brief discussion with Anderson, the two men agreed that the fort would be surrendered.

A comic opera scene follows when Beauregard's official emissaries return to the fort soon after Wigfall's departure and an embarrassing interregnum ensues. Tempers flare as the emissaries learn that Wigfall has exceeded his authority and Anderson threatens to "run up my flag and open fire again." It will be 7 p.m. before passions cool and reason prevails, and Beauregard and Anderson agree to accept the terms of surrender previously agreed to by Wigfall and Anderson. The victorious Confederates agree to allow Anderson and his command to march out of the fort with their colors and arms, after firing a salute to the flag they had so gallantly defended. Major Anderson and 81 defenders had held Fort Sumter for 34 hours and endured the rain of more than 3,300 lethal projectiles before conceding defeat.

Sadly, during a planned hundred-gun salute to the flag, a cannon discharges prematurely on the 47th round, killing Pvt. Daniel Hough instantly and setting fire to a nearby pile of cartridges, which explode, seriously wounding five men, one of whom, Pvt. Edward Galloway, soon dies. Shortly afterward, with banners flying and with fifes and drums beating out "Yankee Doodle," the men of the Fort Sumter garrison march onboard the transport that is to carry them to the steamship *Baltic.*

Imagine the cheers that go up from the Charlestonians when word comes that the fort has surrendered. Thousands stand about on the

Confederate soldiers stand by guns mounted on Fort Sumter's parade ground. The Confederate "Stars and Bars"—seven stars representing seven seceded states—flies from a makeshift flagpole.

waterfront shouting, stamping their feet, and singing. Governor Pickens proudly proclaims, "The day has come; the war is open, and we will conquer or perish. We have defeated their 20 million, and we have humbled the proud flag of the Stars and Stripes that never before was lowered to any nation on Earth." But the residents of Charleston do not realize what this historic event will mean for their city over the painful course of the next four years.

And then again, imagine how it would look out here on April 14, 1865, when Robert Anderson, now a brevet major general, returns with the same huge garrison flag that he had lowered four years earlier and raises it once again in formal ceremonies over a battered Fort Sumter. The fort, however, does not resemble the fort he had surrendered in 1861, since, because of the terrific pounding it had received over the course of four long years of war, it is now a single-tier fort and all but unrecognizable.

If you were here in April 1865, you would see a war-devastated city, fire-blackened ruins, rubble-filled streets, and shuttered and tumbled down brick buildings, especially fronting the Ashley River. You would see numerous earthworks thrown up to protect the heavy guns of the emplacements near the waterfront. These guns would be of a caliber, size, and power undreamed of in April 1861.

By late May of 1861 Virginia, Arkansas, Tennessee, and North Carolina joined South Carolina, Mississippi, Florida, Alabama, Georgia, Louisiana, and Texas in seceding from the Union, and the Confederacy transfers its capital from Montgomery, Alabama, to Richmond, Virginia, to position itself to take on Washington, D.C.

The Confederate victory at Fort Sumter may have caused rejoicing in the South, but the firing on the Stars and Stripes galvanized the North, and preparations for war soon began in earnest. Federal troops gathered in Washington, D.C., and prepared to cross into Virginia to meet the Rebel armies assembling south of the Potomac. "On to Richmond!" was the cry, but the first meeting would occur northwest of that city, along a creek called Bull Run.

2

FIRST MANASSAS

JULY 18–21, 1861

No sooner had news arrived in Washington of the firing upon Fort Sumter than President Abraham Lincoln issued a call for 75,000 militia to help put down what he called an insurrection. They were to serve in the Army for 90 days, and it would not be the last call for volunteers that year. During the following several weeks, Virginia, North Carolina, Tennessee, and Arkansas would cast their lot with the Confederacy, while Maryland, Kentucky, and Missouri teetered in the balance.

Virginia's Ordinance of Secession, although it required ratification by the voters, placed the nearby national capital at risk, and the uncertainty of continued allegiance in eastern Maryland and Baltimore made the protection of Washington even more imperative. Troops from the northern states were rushed to the defense of the city. On April 19, a regiment from Massachusetts shot their way through mobs of southern sympathizers in Baltimore. By the end of the day four soldiers were dead, twenty more were injured, and a score of civilians lay dying or wounded.

Virginia's secession, ratified by a popular vote on May 23, had already led to the seizure of Norfolk's Gosport Navy Yard and the Harpers Ferry Armory and Arsenal, and to the Confederate government's decision to transfer its capital to Richmond, Virginia, some hundred miles south of Washington, transforming the area between the two capitals into prime battlegrounds. On the morning of May 24, Federal troops crossed the Potomac and seized the old port town of Alexandria, with its rail links to Richmond and the Shenandoah Valley, and Arlington Heights.

With a solid foothold in northern Virginia, Federal General in Chief Winfield Scott, now 75 years old, obese, and unable to mount a horse without considerable help, began collecting his forces. By early July, the Union had organized two sizable commands south of the Potomac. Some 35,000 men under the command of Brig. Gen. Irvin McDowell, a tall and rotund West Pointer from Ohio, prepared to advance south toward the Confederate capital. Another 18,000 men, commanded by 69-year-old Maj. Gen. Robert Patterson, would move down from Pennsylvania into the Shenandoah Valley. Patterson's assignment was to pin in place a Confederate force, some 11,000 strong, commanded by Brig. Gen. Joseph E. Johnston. Patterson was to prevent Johnston from reinforcing the main Confederate Army, approximately 23,000 men, gathering around Manassas Junction, about 25 miles southwest of Washington, under the leadership of the hero of Fort Sumter, Brig. Gen. Pierre G. T. Beauregard. This key rail junction was located a few miles southwest of a winding creek known as Bull Run, which lay across the main routes from Washington south; one of the junction's rail lines, the Manassas Gap Railroad, ran westward to Strasburg and Mount Jackson in the Shenandoah Valley, some 50 miles away, offering Johnston, if he could evade Patterson, a quick way to unite forces with Beauregard.

McDowell was under political pressure to do something dramatic. The U.S. Congress was on call to convene in special session in Washington on July 4, and the enlistments of the Union Army's 90-day volunteers were about to run out. When he complained to the President that his men were ill prepared to assume the offensive at this point, Lincoln replied, "You are green, it is true, but they are green also; you are all green alike."

Hardly reassured, McDowell set his army in motion on July 16, heading first to Fairfax Court House, then to Centreville, from where he would pivot southwest to confront Beauregard's force deployed beyond Bull Run. In Washington, socialite Rose O'Neal Greenhow, apprised of McDowell's advance, sent coded word to Beauregard that the campaign was under way. In fact, Beauregard was probably already well aware of McDowell's advance. Ill-disciplined Federal columns took a full day to advance six miles to the villages of Annandale and Vienna. Orders went out from Richmond directing Johnston to move his men via rail and to link up with Beauregard. Fortunately for Johnston, on the day McDowell advanced, Patterson withdrew to the vicinity of Harpers Ferry, leaving the Confederates free to board their trains.

Twenty-three years after his graduation from West Point, Brig. Gen. Irvin McDowell (fifth from right) commanded Federal forces against Confederate Gen. P. G. T. Beauregard at Manassas.

As he waited for Johnston's four brigades to arrive, Beauregard readied his defenses. The Confederate commander had chosen Bull Run, with its steep banks, as his defense line. A single stone bridge, carrying the Centreville-Warrenton Turnpike crossed the creek here, while the Orange & Alexandria Railroad crossed downstream at Union Mills. Beauregard posted more than half of his forces between Mitchell's Ford, where the road between Centreville and Manassas crossed, and Union Mills Ford. He dispatched one brigade of South Carolina and Louisiana troops to guard Stone Bridge and left Sudley Ford, on upper Bull Run, undefended. On July 18 McDowell's men finally arrived at Centreville in Beauregard's front.

The Confederates had established their line covering the crossings of Bull Run along a seven-mile front from Stone Bridge, where the Warrenton Turnpike crosses Bull Run northwest of Ball's Ford, extending down to Blackburn's and Union Mills Fords. The Federals enter Centreville at mid-morning of July 18 with Brig. Gen. Daniel Tyler's division in the lead.

They find the road toward Manassas strewn with thrown-away gear, indicating a rapid Rebel retreat from Centreville.

Tyler's division consists of four brigades. The lead brigade is commanded by Col. Israel B. Richardson, a West Point graduate and Mexican War veteran who had left the Army and was living in Michigan at the outbreak of the Civil War. Known to some as "Fighting Dick," his swarthy complexion leads other to call him, behind his back, "Greasy Dick." I'm sure he preferred "Fighting Dick."

Marching southwest, the Yankees approach the enemy position at Mitchell's Ford. Tyler is under orders to make a reconnaissance and not to bring on an engagement. However, as he gets on the high ground overlooking Bull Run, it appears to him that the Confederates are in rapid retreat, and he gets carried away. Israel Richardson deploys most of his brigade in support of his artillery batteries. On the commanding ground overlooking Mitchell's Ford, he positions two light 12-pounder howitzers of Capt. Romeyn B. Ayres's Company E, Third U.S. Artillery, and sends the 12th New York, preceded by three companies of the First Massachusetts, to reconnoiter and force their way across Blackburn's Ford, downstream a bit. Not a very smart idea, as they will find out.

About a mile below Blackburn's Ford is McLean's Ford, where you have the brigade commanded by Confederate Brig. Gen. David R. Jones. Brig. Gen. James Longstreet's brigade, supported by four guns of the Washington Artillery, is assigned to guard Blackburn's Ford, where the 12th New York is nosing around. Although "Old Pete" Longstreet has skirmishers on the north side of Bull Run, his main force is on the south side. In reserve is a brigade commanded by Col. Jubal A. Early. Upstream about a half mile as the crow flies, but a mile as Bull Run meanders, is Mitchell's Ford, defended by Brig. Gen. Milledge Bonham's brigade. There are a number of fords scattered upstream, such as Ball's Ford and Lewis Ford, guarded by Col. Philip St. George Cocke's brigade; Col. Nathan "Shanks" Evans's brigade is at Stone Bridge.

Jubal Early is ordered to reinforce Longstreet when the Confederates open fire on the 12th New York, whose men are not hardened combat veterans. The New Yorkers are finding out that in war people get killed; that people get very badly wounded. It is not quite as much fun as they had expected when marching out of New York to come down south. And then the Confederates counterattack—Rebels cross the stream. Soon the 12th New York is frightened and fleeing. Captain Ayres has to get his guns out of here. The Yankees see 22 of their own, now dead, carried to the rear. They see badly wounded men—and worse is the sight of panic-stricken soldiers. Confederate morale soars. Just like the Southern politicians said: One Rebel can lick ten Yankees. The Yankees are cowards.

McDowell spends the next two days out with Capt. John G. Barnard reconnoitering the fords and determining how best to cross Bull Run and assail the Confederates.

Realizing that Patterson could not interfere in time, Johnston marched from Winchester, crossed the Blue Ridge to Piedmont, and there began loading his men onto trains on the morning of July 19, to quickly shift most of his force to Manassas Junction. A veteran of the War of 1812, Patterson had gone so far as to say that the War Department could arrange for his execution should he fail in his duty of holding Johnston in the valley. His resignation after the First Manassas campaign served the same purpose. If Johnston can successfully bring his force to join Beauregard, the two opposing armies will be fairly evenly matched; the Federals have lost their numbers bulge.

Johnston began loading the first of his four brigades on trains for the journey to Manassas on the morning of July 19. These included a brigade of Virginians commanded by a strange fellow who had taught artillery tactics at the Virginia Military Institute—a West Pointer some of his former students still called "Tom Fool" Jackson or "Old Blue Light."

By July 21, a Sunday, both armies are ready to attack one another. Each commander hopes to strike his opponent's left flank: Beauregard plans to push northward across the fords at Union Mills, McLean's, and Blackburn's, while at Sudley Ford McDowell intends to swing northward around the Rebel left, cross Bull Run, and then slam southward into the enemy's left flank. Part of his force advances west, across Cub Run, toward a small Confederate force deployed behind Stone Bridge.

Stone Bridge is on the Warrenton Turnpike where it spans Bull Run. The Union plan is to turn the Confederate left with the Union right, employing two of their five divisions. The Confederate plan is to turn the Union left with their right, committing 7 of 12 of their brigades. McDowell has spent two days reconnoitering and formulating his plan; he commences it earlier than the Confederates. If the Confederates had triggered their advance a couple of hours earlier, it's possible that the outcome of this battle would have gone the other way, because both armies are new to the art of warfare. Their leaders have never commanded such large numbers.

The Union plan is that Daniel Tyler is going to lead the march out of the Centreville encampment, move down the Warrenton Turnpike, and demonstrate against the bridge to keep the Confederates thinking that this is where the attack will come. Then the turning column, the division commanded by Col. David Hunter in the lead, with Col. Samuel P. Heintzelman's division following, will march along circuitous roads passing to the north, and cross Bull Run at Sudley Ford beyond Sudley Church, positioning them to carry out their mission and turn the Confederate left. To be successful they must move rather rapidly, while Tyler's demonstration must keep the Confederate defenses pinned down along Bull Run.

The Confederates have four brigades in their right flank at Blackburn's, Mitchell's, McLean's, and Union Mills Fords, with more in reserve, including the brigades of Brig. Gens. Barnard Bee and Thomas Jonathan

Jackson, and Cols. Jubal Early and Francis Bartow. All are to be committed to the Confederate attack on the Union left. Action starts at Stone Bridge about 6:30 a.m. Who does the Union have to watch their left flank and rear? Here is one of the "great names of military history!": Col. Dixon S. Miles, who will face a court of inquiry for drunkenness during this battle. With three brigades he is charged with covering the Union left and making a demonstration to hold the attention of the seven Confederate brigades. There are five brigades in McDowell's turning column, with three of Tyler's to bluff the Stone Bridge Rebels.

Beauregard has appointed Capt. E. Porter Alexander as his chief signal officer. After Alexander arrives in June he picks a dozen intelligent privates for the signal service. Now, all privates are intelligent, so that means there are 12 intelligent privates that he teaches the "wigwag" signal system he learned from then-surgeon Albert Myer, the Union Army's first signal officer. The Confederates also erected four signal stations. One station is on Van Pelt Ridge, just north of the Warrenton Turnpike and west of Bull Run; another is on Wilcoxen's Hill, south of Manassas Junction.

It's Sunday morning. McDowell is a large man and he has also been a staff officer most of his military life. He got his job principally because Secretary of the Treasury Salmon Portland Chase knows he is from Ohio, and Chase and Chase's daughter are both convinced that Salmon P. Chase and not Abraham Lincoln should be sitting in the White House. Chase wants his own man in command; he went to bat and McDowell got the job.

The Confederates in the Stone Bridge area are commanded by South Carolinian Nathan "Shanks" Evans. He got the name "Shanks" at West Point. At West Point you get your nickname not because of your beauty. In the eyes of his fellow cadets he was not good looking. Shanks's problem—he had rather spindly legs. What does he have to defend this bridge with? He has the Fourth South Carolina Infantry. He has a colorful unit out of Louisiana, the First Louisiana Special Battalion, soon to gain fame as the "Louisiana Tigers," commanded by Maj. Roberdeau

Unfamiliar with the terrain at Manassas, Gen. Joseph Johnston, the highest ranking Regular Army officer to join the Confederacy, shared command with Gen. P. G. T. Beauregard.

L. Wheat. If you had a football team you'd want to recruit Wheat as a linebacker. He's the son of an Episcopal rector, stands some six feet three, and weighs about 250 pounds. He served with William Walker—"the gray-eyed man of destiny"—in Nicaragua and Giuseppe Garibaldi in Sicily. Many of his men are Irish and had worked as stevedores in New Orleans. They wear distinctive Zouave uniforms. Evans has two cannon attached to him and two companies of cavalry. It's a small force, under a thousand men.

The Yankees come down off the ridge separating Cub Run and Bull Run. The lead gun, a 30-pounder Parrott rifle weighing three tons, is commanded by Lt. Peter Hains of Company E, Second U.S. Artillery, fresh out of West Point. He throws that big 30-pounder into position and trains it toward the Van Pelt house, along the ridge north of the Warrenton Pike and West of Bull Run. Three shots crash in the vicinity of the house, one of which goes through the signalman's tent. Tyler's men keep Evans's Confederates pinned here while David Hunter's men—leading the turning column—move around their flank. The first to arrive at Stone Bridge is Brig. Gen. Robert "Fighting Bob" Schenck. He ought to be able to bluff, because he wrote the book on playing stud poker, but he doesn't do a very good job today. He throws forward the Second New York on either side of the Warrenton Pike. Then he tells Col. Alexander D. McCook's Ohio boys to move down a side road to Lewis Ford and keep the Rebs busy there. Evans isn't taken in by any of this. He doesn't think the Yankees are aggressive enough to mean trouble. Meanwhile, Col. William T. "Uncle Billy" Sherman, commanding a brigade of troops from New York and Wisconsin, reconnoiters the east bank of Bull Run above Stone Bridge. About 8:30 he spots a large man—Major Wheat—riding down and across at a farmer's ford. Sherman puts that information in his back pocket until he finally crosses Bull Run at 11 a.m. at Farm Ford.

Nathan Evans is getting increasingly suspicious. The Federals are not pushing very hard against his front for this to be anything but a feint. His position is protected by a formidable abatis of felled timber—the wooden equivalent of barbed wire—extending from the bridge north and southwest of the turnpike about a quarter mile. As

OPPOSITE: *On the morning of July 21, McDowell sent several brigades across Bull Run at Sudley Ford to attack Beauregard's left flank. By late morning Federal forces had pushed aside the Confederates holding Matthews Hill and advanced on Henry Hill south of the Warrenton Turnpike. There the Federals launched a series of assaults to drive Rebel forces off the hill. By late afternoon, Beauregard dispatched reinforcements to Chinn Ridge, and two Confederate brigades struck the left flank of the Federals, and the Yankees began to withdraw from the battlefield in a retreat that soon turned into a rout.*

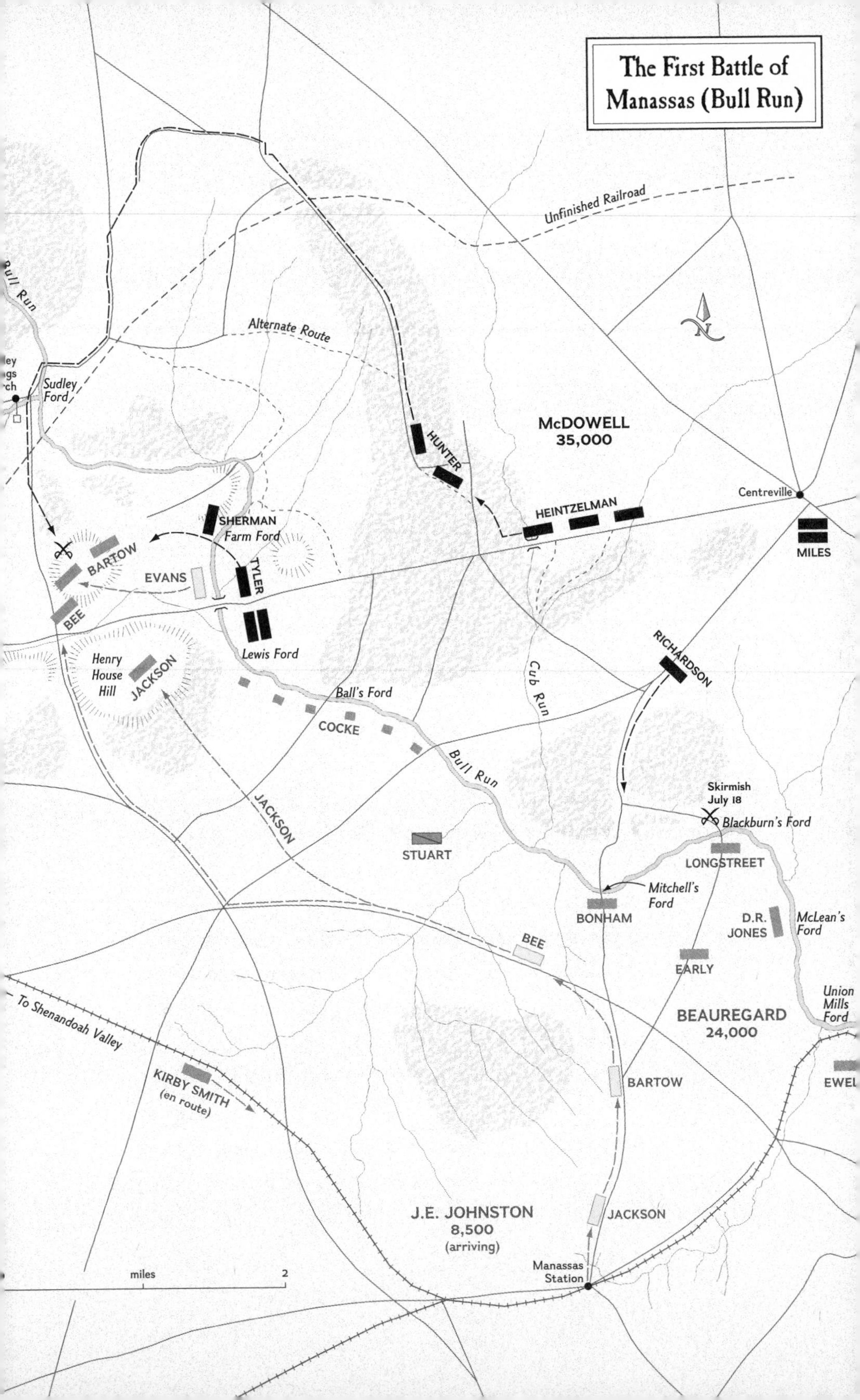

The First Battle of Manassas (Bull Run)
Unfinished Railroad
Bull Run
Alternate Route
Sudley Ford
McDOWELL
35,000
HUNTER
HEINTZELMAN
Centreville
MILES
SHERMAN
Farm Ford
TYLER
EVANS
BARTOW
BEE
Henry
House
Hill
JACKSON
Lewis Ford
Ball's Ford
COCKE
Cub Run
RICHARDSON
Bull Run
JACKSON
Skirmish
July 18
Blackburn's Ford
STUART
LONGSTREET
Mitchell's
Ford
BONHAM
D.R.
JONES
McLean's
Ford
BEE
EARLY
Union
Mills
Ford
BEAUREGARD
24,000
To Shenandoah Valley
KIRBY SMITH
(en route)
BARTOW
EWEL
J.E. JOHNSTON
8,500
(arriving)
JACKSON
Manassas
Station
miles
2

Captain Alexander gazes out from his signal station on Wilcoxen's Hill in an easterly direction, he sees Brig. Gen. Richard S. Ewell's Confederates at Union Mills. He sees D. R. Jones's men preparing to cross at McLean's Ford, and Longstreet at Blackburn's. As he is looking toward the north, he sees columns of infantry coming out of the woods, sunlight flashing off brass cannon and bayonets. It's Hunter's Yankees closing on Sudley Ford. Alexander signals to Evans at the bridge: "Look to your left. You are turned."

Evans immediately takes six companies of the Fourth South Carolina, Wheat's battalion, and two cannon, and heads toward Pittsylvania (the Carter House); he then redeploys his men astride Sudley Road. Later in the day Evans pulls two more companies, leaving only two companies at Stone Bridge. It is going to be well into the afternoon before Fighting Bob Schenck crosses this bridge and moves west.

Throughout the morning the Union forces continue to march northwest in their effort to turn the Confederate left. It is midmorning before they finally cross Bull Run at Sudley Ford. As the long blue columns turn south on the Sudley Road, only Evans's people stand in their way. Beauregard, realizing that his flank is in danger, reconsiders his own offensive thrust against the Union left and begins shifting brigades to meet the attacking Yankees.

At Sudley Ford five Union brigades made their way across Bull Run. David Hunter's division has the lead. An ex-staff officer—a paymaster—Hunter owes his position to being in the right place at the right time. If I wanted to get ahead in the Civil War, I would be sure to be in Springfield, Illinois, on February 11, 1861, aboard the train that left that day, carrying President-elect Abraham Lincoln to Washington. For the next 11 days I'd have a chance to make an impression on the new boss. Look who was on that train—John Pope, then a captain; Edwin Sumner, already a colonel; and David Hunter—three future generals.

Hunter leads his men southward. Ahead of them on Matthews Hill is Nathan Evans, with his less than a thousand Confederates supported by two cannon, one gun on Buck Hill and the other north of the turnpike in front of "Gentleman" James Robinson's house. (Gentleman Jim was the widow Judith Carter Henry's half-brother.) Hunter plans to run over the Confederates and secure Matthews Hill. He doesn't even take the time to put out cavalry to see what's in front of him. The Rebs open fire; Hunter goes down; it takes time for his replacement, Col. Andrew Porter, to take over. Col. Ambrose E. Burnside's brigade, part of Hunter's division, is already confused. Things are becoming a mess.

Accompanying Burnside's First Rhode Island Regiment is the governor of Rhode Island himself, William Sprague. Among the other unofficial observers on the battlefield are two men destined for major roles in the Civil War. Congressman John A. Logan will end up a corps commander. In the future, Sherman's worst mistake will be when he gives Oliver O. Howard command of the Army of the Tennessee, passing over Logan. Logan believed he had been passed over because he was not a West Pointer. If Logan had been elected President in the postwar years, West Point would have been in deep trouble.

Another civilian here is Joseph Hooker, a West Pointer who had served in the Mexican War. He has a lot of nerve. He has made enemies. After leaving the Army, he had gone broke in California; he played too much poker in Sonoma Square. So he borrowed money from banker William T. Sherman and stiffed him. If somebody stiffs you for your money, you never forget it. He had also stiffed Henry Halleck, the future general in chief, for money, and he was on the outs with General in Chief Winfield Scott. So he can't get a commission. The day after the battle he meets with President Lincoln and tells him, I don't know how good a general I would be, but I will tell you one thing—I am a helluva lot better then any of those you had out there yesterday. So Lincoln writes a memorandum to Secretary of War Simon Cameron, and Hooker becomes an instant brigadier general.

While Evans's men to the north of the Warrenton Turnpike face the Federal onslaught on Matthews Hill, two more Confederate brigades, under the command of Barnard Bee and Francis Bartow, hurry north from the Blackburn's Ford sector to join them. Unbeknownst to them, two of Tyler's Union brigades, under William T. Sherman and Erasmus Keyes, are about to cross Bull Run at Farm Ford and advance westward into the right and rear of the Confederates' Matthews Hill line. South of the Warrenton Turnpike, on Henry House Hill, Thomas J. Jackson will arrive about noon, following the route north pioneered by Bee and Bartow, and prepare his Virginians for combat.

When Burnside finally gets his act together, he deploys his brigade. In an open field on Matthews Hill, facing Buck Hill, he positions the six guns—James rifled cannon—of Capt. William H. Reynolds's battery of Rhode Island artillery, which is attached to the Second Rhode Island Volunteers. The James rifle is a ripoff. You take a good smoothbore gun, you rifle it and convert it into a substandard rifled gun. The bronze being relatively soft, you have to use resin for your rotating band to give the projectile a spin, but resin isn't satisfactory. One third of McDowell's 57 guns at First Manassas are James rifles, but two years later, there are few if any James rifles at Gettysburg. They would be replaced by better rifled guns—ten-pounder Parrotts and three-inch ordnance rifles.

Burnside forms his men for the assault on Matthews Hill. He outnumbers the Rebels three to one. He's got them outgunned, eight cannon to two counting the 71st New York's two boat howitzers. Johnston and Beauregard realize that the Union has seized the initiative. They scrub their attack on the Yankees' left and rush men to support Evans's people in the fight for Matthews Hill. The first reinforcements to arrive are Barnard Bee's. A West Pointer, Bee has two regiments and two companies of a third. He now must make a crucial decision. Evans asks for help. Bee doesn't hesitate, he leaves Henry Hill and crosses Young's Branch to support Evans. He is heavily outnumbered. Later Bartow will arrive on

Sudley Ford, shown here in 1862, was a key crossing point for Federal troops attempting to turn the Confederate left during the Battle of First Manassas, or Bull Run.

Henry House Hill, and he will advance one of his two regiments, the Eighth Georgia, to be soon reinforced by the Seventh Georgia. You don't want to belong to the Eighth Georgia because you're going to get blown away in the Matthews Hill fight. The Eighth is going to lose almost half its men—killed, wounded, or missing—in 20 minutes. The Rebels carry the fight to the enemy. That is going to keep the enemy off-balance and buys time for Jackson and his five Virginia regiments to reach Henry Hill. He isn't Stonewall yet, and his command isn't yet the Stonewall Brigade. By the time Jackson arrives about noon things are coming rapidly unglued for the Rebels. But for the better part of an hour Bee's, Bartow's, and Evans's brigades had carried the fight to the enemy.

Who are the Yankees involved in this fight? There is Ambrose Burnside's brigade, they have Andrew Porter's brigade, and it's getting worse for the Rebels, because Col. Samuel P. Heintzelman's division is arriving, with Brig. Gen. William B. Franklin's First Brigade leading the way. That is bad news for the Eighth Georgia over on the extreme right of the Confederate line, because they are assailed by the First Minnesota, and those boys are going to shoot the daylights out of the Eighth Georgia. Bartow, who is nearsighted, doesn't recognize whether they are Yankees or Rebels out there in the woods. To the right and rear of the Confederates fighting for Matthews Hill, Sherman leads his men across Farm Ford, upstream from the Stone Bridge. He heads eastward following the sound of the guns. Also coming up are the cannoneers, using whips and spears on the teams, Capt. Charles Griffin's and Capt. James Ricketts's batteries. They unlimber their 12 guns on Dogan Ridge, on either side and fronting east of the John Dogan house. The cannon are supported by William B. Franklin's two Massachusetts regiments. Col. Orlando Wilcox's New Yorkers and Michiganders now come up to further increase the odds against the Confederates.

The Rebels see Yankees to their front and Yankees in heavy numbers to their right rear. They pull back. The Confederate regiments are disorganized and fall back in confusion. But what have they done? They have gained two hours. Two hours in the fight for Matthews Hill. Some will say that in the confusion Bee looked back and saw Jackson standing on Henry House Hill, and muttered something about him standing as still as a stone wall. At least that's a South Carolinian's version. Col. Wade Hampton's "Legion," barely 600 strong, arrives on the field and makes a brief stand along the Warrenton Turnpike.

Col. Erasmus D. Keyes, who had crossed Farm Ford behind Sherman, advances his brigade toward Henry House Hill. Three of his four regiments had the best weapons on the battlefield. The First, Second, and Third Connecticut are partially armed with Sharps breech-loading rifles—the same weapon with which Col. Hiram Berdan will arm his elite First U.S. Sharpshooters. He also has the Second Maine. A force of 2,500 men moves against Wade Hampton's 600 South Carolinians. Hampton's men break. About this time Keyes arrives at the foot of Henry House Hill, near the Robinson House. In the woods behind Jackson's Virginians, milling around and regrouping are Hampton's, Bartow's, Bee's, and Evans's people. What an opportunity for Keyes—there's Jackson's right flank inviting attack. But opportunity knocks only once, and Keyes fumbles his opportunity.

Coming on the field, Irvin McDowell senses impending victory for the North. Rather than pressing on to seize Henry House Hill, however, he pauses to reorganize his command under the hot July sun. McDowell waits for more than one hour before resuming his advance. By this time he has more than 18,000 men under his control. The beleaguered Confederates have been given a chance to realign their forces, disturbed only by an unsupported attack near the Robinson House by two of Erasmus Keyes's regiments, the Third Connecticut and Second Maine.

Awaiting the Federals on Henry House Hill is the Virginia Brigade of Thomas J. Jackson. Beauregard and Johnston use the lull to shift more brigades north to meet the Union threat.

The Confederates by accident have come up with a good system of command when Johnston arrives at Manassas Junction. Superior in rank to Beauregard, Johnston is to be overall commander. But he is new to the area, so Beauregard calls the shots on the field. With Beauregard commanding on the battlefield, Johnston will manage the flow of manpower and reinforcements to points of danger and opportunity. Beauregard is a student of Napoleon and probably knew more about the French commander's tactics than anyone else on the field. And seeing himself as an "in gray" Napoleon, he anticipates a battle of annihilation. If you read Bonaparte closely, he doesn't fight many battles of annihilation. Johnston is a cautious man; a military engineer like many officers in the Civil War,

Fierce fighting raged around the Stone House, which became a makeshift refuge for wounded soldiers. It is one of the few remaining Civil War-era structures standing at Manassas today.

he has moved from a staff position to being a decision-maker in command of an army. At a critical moment on Sunday, July 21, Johnston makes a key decision that changes the flow of the battle as he exclaims, "I ride to the sound of the guns." Beauregard accompanies Johnston, who takes the lead. Beauregard overtakes him before they arrive with their staffs on Henry House Hill, overlooking the Stone House. Brig. Gen. Thomas J. Jackson has already formed his men in the edge of the timber. Upon reaching here, the two senior officers again divide their responsibilities. Johnston backtracks to what became his field headquarters at Portici, also known as the Lewis House for its owner, Francis Ware Lewis. There he's better positioned to send arriving reinforcements to either Henry House Hill or Chinn Ridge, as warranted. Beauregard remains on Henry House Hill. Here he not only sends the newcomers where they are most needed, but also on occasion leads them into battle. Beauregard is arguably the most important man on Henry House Hill. His is an inspiring presence. But unfortunately for Beauregard, Jackson overshadows what he does. In contrast, Union commander Irvin McDowell is out of touch with much of his army; he is too far forward to exercise effective command of his force. It's left to his subordinates to do the best they can on their own.

After a hiatus of more than an hour the Federals are ready to resume the fight. They find that the Confederates have not abandoned the area. Jackson has come up this wood road from near Blackburn's Ford, passing Portici en route. When he gets to the edge of the woods, he forms his five regiments into a line that extends from the ravine southeast of the Robinson House, overlooking Warrenton Turnpike southwest nearly to Sudley Road. They furl their colors; then lie or kneel down. Here they rest. Thirteen guns take position to their front. They include the Rockbridge Artillery, commanded by William Nelson Pendleton. These guns are still at VMI. Too bad they did not then note their serial numbers or the weights so we would know which is Matthew, Mark, Luke, or John. That is what Pendleton named his four guns. He was the rector in Lexington, Virginia.

McDowell directs Chief of Artillery Maj. William F. Barry to advance two batteries up onto Henry House Hill. They are commanded by Charles Griffin and James B. Ricketts, both crusty Regular Army veterans. Ricketts's Company I, First U.S. Artillery, is armed with ten-pounder Parrott rifles. Now, it's a bad idea to advance rifled cannon to within 350 yards of smoothbore Confederate guns. You're taking a weapon that has accuracy and range, but you're putting it within canister shot of smoothbore guns. Ricketts and Griffin protest the decision to advance their guns, and they ask, "Will we have infantry support?" Yes, they are told. They unlimber their guns within dangerous proximity to Rebel infantry they cannot see and 13 smoothbore enemy cannon. Worse, the Federals are going to lose one gun crossing Young's

Branch. Griffin comes up with only five guns of his Company D, Fifth U.S. Artillery—two Howitzer smoothbores and three Parrott rifled guns.

Earlier in the day, the widow Judith Carter Henry, who lives in the house on the hill that bore the family name, had been taken to the springhouse by one son and her only daughter. Mrs. Henry's husband had been a surgeon on the U.S.S. *Constellation* in the quasi war with France in 1799 and 1800. But she soon asks to be taken back to her house. An artillery duel is on in the vicinity; the Federal cannoneers are unhappy and wonder, "Where is our infantry? Why haven't we had any infantry sent up to support us?" The Confederates have sharpshooters deployed in and around Mrs. Henry's house. And they are going to make a bad mistake. They fire on Ricketts's gunners. Ricketts orders two of his guns to wheel to the left and fire on the Henry House. They set it afire; a shell goes off and all but severs one of Mrs. Henry's feet. So Mrs. Henry becomes a fatal war casualty. Not by malicious intent, simply because the Confederates are using those buildings to shelter their sharpshooters.

The bombardment continues. Chief of Artillery Barry tells Captain Griffin to take two 12-pounder howitzers beyond Ricketts's Parrotts and put them into position where he can enfilade the left of Jackson's line. He again reassures Griffin that he will be supported by infantry.

Ricketts's rifled guns are ineffective against infantry at this range, and most of the shells sail over their heads into the trees, providing showers of wood but causing no real damage to Jackson's people.

While the artillery duels, senior Confederate officers in the woods behind Jackson's Virginians rally and offer their units. Bartow, Bee, Evans, and Hampton bring some order out of chaos. Reinforcements continue to arrive. Bee rides over to one regiment and says, "What unit is this?" They say, "Sir, don't you recognize your own men? The Fourth

Alabama!" He says, "Follow me to where the fighting is." "We will follow you, sir, but where is that?" This is when he says the famous line "Yonder stands Jackson like a stone wall. Let us go to his assistance." After the war "rally around the Virginians," is added and a legend is born. In the ensuing action Bee, as well as Bartow, is mortally wounded at the head of his men, as he leads them forward.

As fighting rages along the Henry House Hill front, Griffin and Ricketts finally receive their first infantry support from the 11th New York Fire Zouaves, decked out in their newer blue uniforms. Due to the heat they are not wearing their blue jackets, making their bright red fireman's jackets visible.

The 11th New York is an elite regiment. It had been led by Col. Elmer Ellsworth. He was the mid-19th-century equivalent of the leader of a popular rock band. That was what drill teams like his were thought of then. He had been a law clerk and is known to Lincoln, having been on the February 11 train from Springfield that carried the President-elect to Washington for his Inauguration. The New Yorkers are hell-raisers. Having put out a fire in Washington's Willard's Hotel, they will be designated by none other than Lincoln to spearhead the units sent to occupy Alexandria on May 24. There Ellsworth is killed. Having pulled down a Confederate flag from atop the Marshall House tavern, he becomes a martyr to the cause, complete with a White House funeral. The Fire Zouaves are now led by Lt. Col. Noah L. Farnham. As they advance near Sudley Road, to take position on the western slope of Henry House Hill in support of Ricketts's guns, they are charged by what the Yankees dub the "Black Horse Troop" or the Fourth Virginia Cavalry, Company H. The Zouaves are mistaken, their antagonists are two companies of Jeb Stuart's First Virginia cavalry. Many of the Zouaves break and flee. Griffin and Ricketts fire away at the Confederate line, impatiently waiting for more of their promised infantry support.

"Yell like furies," VMI instructor Thomas Jonathan Jackson commanded his men as they charged at First Manassas, thus sounding the first "Rebel yell."

Up on Henry House Hill, taking position in the woods is Jackson's left flank regiment, the 33rd Virginia, led by Col. Arthur C. Cummings. They wear blue uniforms. They form in the woods and start coming across a rail fence to the right front of Griffin's two howitzers that had unlimbered to enfilade the left flank of Pendleton's gun line. Behind the Federal guns Maj. John G. Reynolds is bringing up his U.S. Marine battalion to support the artillery. But they have not yet arrived. Neither has the 14th Brooklyn nor the 1st Minnesota. So Griffin's two guns are terribly alone, backed up by a handful of shaken Zouaves and marines. Suddenly the Confederates cross the fence en masse and form into line of battle. Griffin looks to the right toward Cummings's people.

Up rides Chief of Artillery Barry. He confers with Griffin. Through the smoke they see hundreds of blue-uniformed people come over the fence. Are they friend or foe? Barry thinks they are friends; Griffin argues they're enemy. Rank is going to have its privilege until the Confederates are about 25 yards off. It's too late when Barry realizes he is wrong and Griffin is right; the Virginians fire a volley, shooting down most of the artillery horses, and charge and capture the guns. Then all hell breaks loose, and that sets off an advance along the entire Rebel line. The rest of Jackson's brigade surges forward. Men of Bartow's, Bee's, and Hampton's commands, who have re-formed, join in the charge. They capture Ricketts's six rifled Parrotts and Griffin's other three Parrott guns but are driven off by Federal infantry that comes up too late to blunt Jackson's initial surge. Fighting for the Federal guns rages as the First Michigan, of Wilcox's brigade, and two Massachusetts regiments of Franklin's brigade join in the fray but are driven back in turn.

Once again the Yankees recover their lost guns, led by some of Sherman's men, including the 2nd Wisconsin and the 13th, 69th, and 79th New York. Had Sherman committed his entire brigade at the same time, he might have carried the day, but he commits it piecemeal, one regiment at a time. The Sixth North Carolina, the fourth regiment in Bee's brigade, arrives in time to spark a second attack that gives the guns back to the Confederates. Then the Yankees retake them. And then the Rebels' return is spearheaded by a battalion of the 49th Virginia led by Col. William "Extra Billy" Smith. The cannon change hands again five times in two hours. If they change hands five times you know who ends up with them—the Confederates. The fight for Henry House Hill ends with the Confederates victorious.

As both sides wrestled for control of Henry House Hill, additional Confederate reinforcements arrived on the field. Two regiments of infantry under Philip St. George Cocke moved up on Jackson's threatened left, followed by two of Brig. Gen. Milledge Bonham's South Carolina regiments. Finally Jubal Early's brigade joined the weight of Confederate infantry massing on the Federal right and moving onto

Chinn Ridge, a low ridge extending to the southwest of the intersection of the Warrenton Turnpike and Sudley Road.

The last of Johnston's Shenandoah brigades to reach the battlefield was that of Brig. Gen. Edmund Kirby Smith. Kirby Smith's men detrained at Manassas Junction about noon and marched through the blazing July heat toward Henry House Hill. As they passed Johnston's Portici headquarters, the general shouted, "Go where the fire is hottest." By 4 p.m. Kirby Smith had moved his men to Bald Hill, to the southwest of Henry House Hill, across and west of Sudley Road.

Confederate reinforcements are rushed to Chinn Ridge to counter the arrival of Howard's sweat-lathered New Englanders. Howard's three Maine and one Vermont regiments had huffed and puffed more than eight miles by way of the roundabout route pioneered hours earlier by McDowell's flanking column. They cross Sudley Ford to reach Chinn Ridge.

I am not a great admirer of Oliver O. Howard. I am going to tell this story on him. Howard writes his mother almost every day while he is at West Point. Nothing wrong with writing to your mother. But you don't really want your mother to save all of the letters. He graduates in 1854. Who is superintendent of the military academy in 1854? Robert E. Lee. Howard writes momma saying, "I would be number one in the class if not for nepotism." He complains he would be number one in his class except for the presence of Superintendent Lee's son Custis. If this is true, Howard should graduate number two, shouldn't he? But he graduates number four.

The Confederates extend their flank westward, seeking to get in the rear of the Henry House Hill Yankees. Howard's regiments rush to Chinn Ridge to keep that flank from being enveloped. But the Confederates bring more men to bear. They call up Jubal Early with three regiments. Edmund Kirby Smith, delayed by a derailment on the Manassas Gap Railroad, arrives, detrains, and pushes his men from Manassas Junction up the Sudley Road, which runs between Chinn Ridge and Henry House

Hill. As they come up, Kirby Smith is wounded, and Col. Arnold Elzey assumes command. Also arriving is Col. Joseph Kershaw with the Second and Col. E. B. C. Cash with the Eighth South Carolina, and Capt. Delaware Kemper's Alexandria Artillery from Mitchell's Ford, and he puts them in position to the left of Philip St. George Cocke astride Sudley Road. The Confederates build up a formidable force west of Henry House Hill. To reach Chinn Ridge, Howard had pushed his men hard. Some have dropped out, a few die of sunstroke; no time to refill canteens. They deploy along Chinn Ridge facing across the valley of Chinn Branch.

If you push troops, even veteran troops, you are going to lose a lot from straggling. The Confederates have had to go some distance too, but the farthest any of them had to hurry is six miles. Howard, after a pause, moves against Elzey. But with Early's brigade on the field, supported by four cannon of the Culpeper Artillery, there are too many Confederates for Howard to master. The Rebels overlap Howard's right flank. Howard seeks to advance again, and the Confederates counterattack. Howard gives way and retreats into the valley of Young's Branch. Maj. George Sykes's Regulars cover Howard's retreat.

What at midday had seemed like an overwhelming Union victory had turned into a disaster. Outflanked on Chinn Ridge, their center at Henry House Hill driven back, by 4:30 p.m., the Union's dispirited soldiers began leaving the field in sullen groups and retreating in disorderly fashion along the Sudley Road and across Matthews Hill. Soon the retreat was general as mobs of beaten men trudged back to Sudley Ford or across the Stone Bridge and Farm Ford to Centreville.

When the Yankees retreat later that afternoon, almost everybody goes back the way they came in. Fighting Bob Schenck retires across Stone Bridge. Sherman and Keyes go back across Farm Ford. Those brigades who've come the long way round by way of Sudley Ford go back via that route. When the Federals approach the Cub Run suspension bridge, the

Ruins of the Stone Bridge, one of several Bull Run crossings employed by retreating Federal troops.

Confederates have their cannon positioned, on the ridge separating the Cub Run and Bull Run watersheds, and are firing on them. A wagon tips over and blocks the span, and what had been a disorderly retreat becomes a rout.

Here you see three powerful United States senators who had come out to witness a Union victory heading for the rear. They are exhausted. Jim Lane of Kansas, hated by Missourians; he'll commit suicide in 1866. Then you see Ben Wade of Ohio, future head of the Committee on Conduct of the War. Had the Republicans convicted the impeached Andrew Johnson in 1868, they may have gotten Wade as President of the United States. He hates the South. And there was Henry Wilson of

Massachusetts, rumored to be the person who told Confederate spy Rose O'Neal Greenhow about the Union orders to march.

As visitors who had flocked to the Virginia countryside to see the battle hurriedly boarded their carriages and mounted their horses in haste to get away, Confederate President Jefferson Davis arrived on the field and conferred with his generals as to what to do next. However, the victorious Confederates were almost as exhausted as the defeated Yankees, and there was no serious attempt at a pursuit. As it was, the Rebels had inflicted almost 3,000 casualties (killed, wounded, and missing), while losing just under 2,000 of their own men.

Beginning early on July 22 dispirited Federal troops began to straggle back into their old camps around Washington and Alexandria. Within five days Winfield Scott had replaced McDowell with a young and vigorous engineer officer—Maj. Gen. George B. McClellan. The new commander's mandate was to reorganize, train, and refit the battered Federal forces and organize the tens of thousands of recruits answering "Father Abraham's" call for more volunteers. In just the 18 days following the battle, 91,000 had responded, and by November the Union Army exceeded its original strength by more than 500,000. In the wake of the battle, Union resolve stiffened, as it became evident that this war would take longer than expected.

In the South, jubilation knew no bounds. Johnston and Beauregard were promoted to full general by order of President Davis, and the Confederacy's press hailed Beauregard as the new Napoleon. Once the weeks of rejoicing ended, however, the realization sank in that the size and ferocity of the Battle of First Manassas—or Bull Run, as it was known in the North—portended more and greater battles to come.

1862

September 17, 1862, would see more than 23,000 casualties during the Battle of Antietam. Forever after the day would be known as the bloodiest day in American history. The ground of "Bloody Lane," above, was strewn with the fallen from both sides. Though the battle was indeed a Union victory and the Confederate Army fell into a limping retreat, an overly cautious General George McClellan let them retreat unpursued. Abraham Lincoln himself traveled to Antietam to spur Union movement, but McClellan argued against pressing on. Lincoln ordered him to advance; 19 days later he "had a man across the river," recalled an unsatisfied Lincoln. On November 5th, Lincoln ordered McClellan relieved of command.

3

SHILOH

APRIL 6–7, 1862

By the fall of 1861, Gen. Albert Sidney Johnston, the officer responsible for the defense of much of the Confederacy's western regions—an area extending from the Cumberland Mountains to beyond the Mississippi River—faced a crisis of manpower. With fewer than 20,000 poorly armed and trained soldiers under his control, Johnston believed that he faced overwhelming Union pressure. He was acutely aware that the western Confederacy was divided by a series of great navigable rivers that provided ready-made lines of advance for his adversaries. The greatest was the Mississippi, already the target of Federal General in Chief Winfield Scott's "Anaconda Plan," a series of combined land and naval operations intended to encoil the South and strangle the seceding states. Other strategic rivers included the Cumberland, which flowed through north-central Tennessee before joining the Ohio, and the Tennessee, with its 200 miles of navigable waters reaching all the way down to northern Alabama. The Tennessee also emptied into the Ohio, not far from the mouth of the Cumberland.

To defend his western border, Johnston had 11,000 men under Maj. Gen. Leonidas Polk blocking the Mississippi with fortifications on the river bluffs at Columbus, Kentucky. Johnston also dispatched Brig. Gen. Simon Bolivar Buckner's forces to Bowling Green, Kentucky, to guard the approaches by rail to Nashville and threaten the key Union position of Louisville. By the winter of 1861–62, Buckner had been superseded by Maj. Gen. William Hardee, and the Confederate force there increased to 22,000 men. Other forces were sent to cover access to Cumberland Gap, while earthwork fortifications, Forts Henry and Donelson, were constructed near the Kentucky line, where the Tennessee and Cumberland Rivers were but 12 miles apart, to control the traffic on the water routes south.

By late winter two Federal Armies, totaling perhaps 37,000 men, faced Johnston—the Department of the Missouri, headed by Maj. Gen. Henry W. Halleck with his headquarters at St. Louis, and the Department of the Ohio, commanded by Brig. Gen. Don Carlos Buell. In mid-January the defeat of Confederate politician-general Felix Zollicoffer's and West Pointer and Brig. Gen. George Crittenden's combined forces at Mill Springs, Kentucky, resulted in the collapse of the right flank of Johnston's 300-mile line. Belatedly Johnston sent orders to strengthen Forts Henry and Donelson, but he was far too late. The Federal Army commander at Cairo, Illinois, a quiet and scruffy-looking brigadier general named Ulysses S. Grant, had been made aware of the forts' weaknesses and quickly made plans to capture them in preparation for a thrust deep into Tennessee. Grant's forces were supported by a fleet of U.S. gunboats under the command of Flag Officer Andrew H. Foote. In early February 1862, Grant ordered his men to board river steamboats, and the armada steamed up the Ohio toward the Confederate forts.

The river navy attacked first, with Foote's gunboats pounding Fort Henry on February 6. The fort's commander, Brig. Gen. Lloyd Tilghman, with many of his batteries flooded by high water, evacuated most of his garrison and remained behind with 90 men to face the Federal gunboats, four of them ironclads. After a sharp exchange of gunfire, Tilghman capitulated. Heavy rain delayed Grant's investment of Fort Donelson until February 12. Hoping to buy time to evacuate troops from western Kentucky, Johnston reinforced Donelson, sending 12,000 men under Brigardier Generals John B. Floyd, Gideon J. Pillow, and Buckner to strengthen the fort, bringing the number of defenders to 17,000.

Despite the fact that he was now outnumbered, the ever aggressive Grant closed in on Fort Donelson's outer defenses with two divisions under Brig. Gens. Charles F. Smith and John A. McClernand. On February 14 the Federal naval flotilla attacked the fort, only to be turned back by Rebel cannon emplaced in the fort's water batteries. Despite their success in repelling the gunboats, Floyd, as senior officer and in command of the troops in Fort Donelson, launched a breakout attempt on the following morning. Although the Confederates broke through the Federal lines and secured a route of escape, determined counterattacks led by Federal Brig. Gen. Lew Wallace and Brig. Gen. C. F. Smith caused the Rebels to withdraw back into the fort's perimeter. General Floyd and his second in command, General Pillow, escaped from the fort with most of the former's men, leaving General Buckner to request terms of surrender from Grant. There would be no terms offered, replied Grant, only "unconditional surrender." Nearly 13,000 Confederate soldiers were taken prisoner. Wags in the Union press and Army soon essayed that the general's initials must now stand for "Unconditional Surrender."

During the next fortnight Grant fended off an effort by a jealous Henry Halleck to replace him. Nearly four weeks later another force, under Union Maj. Gen. John Pope, captured New Madrid, Missouri, and then on April 8 Confederate Island No. 10, opening the Mississippi south to Fort Pillow, Tennessee. The back of Albert Sidney Johnston's defensive line was broken, and the Confederate heartland opened to invasion. Abandoning Kentucky and much of middle and west Tennessee, Johnston withdrew his forces, abandoning Nashville as well. He reached Decatur, Alabama, by March 15. Polk had already withdrawn from Columbus, Kentucky, leaving the Mississippi north of Fort Pillow under Federal control.

The Confederates began to regroup at Corinth, Mississippi, just south of the Mississippi/Tennessee line. Gen. P. G. T. Beauregard had arrived in the western theater in early February, and Johnston had immediately assigned him the task of marshaling reinforcements from the Confederate forces in the lower South. Brig. Gen. Daniel Ruggles arrives from New Orleans with 5,000 men while Maj. Gen. Braxton Bragg comes north with more than 11,000 troops from Mobile, Alabama, and Pensacola, Florida. By March 24, Johnston and Beauregard have 44,000 men concentrated at and around Corinth.

Henry Halleck, the Federal commander, directs the armies of Grant and Buell to rendezvous at a rural steamboat fueling point along the west bank of the Tennessee River known as Pittsburg Landing, which is less than two dozen miles northeast of Corinth. By April 1, Grant had concentrated nearly 40,000 men around Pittsburg Landing, and on March 16, Buell began his slow, 120-mile overland march from Nashville. Once these forces were united, Halleck planned to take personal charge for an advance on Corinth. For the moment Grant was ordered to avoid a general engagement. Rather, he is to drill his new recruits and his Fort Donelson veterans, preparing for a forward movement.

Union steamboats at Pittsburg Landing in 1862. Gen. Ulysses S. Grant arrived at the scene of the fighting at Shiloh aboard the Tigress, *shown second from the right.*

As the Union troops disembark at Pittsburg Landing they go into camp. William T. Sherman and John A. McClernand arrive. McClernand, now a major general, outranks Sherman, but Grant is a West Pointer. Sherman is also a West Pointer, and he is camped closer to the enemy, so Sherman is in command at Pittsburg Landing. There are five divisions at Pittsburg Landing—the First, under John A. McClernand; the Second, under Maj. Gen. C. F. Smith, who will be fatally injured by skinning his shin and developing a blood infection, and who will turn his command over to Brig. Gen. W. H. L. Wallace; the Third, under Maj. Gen. Lew Wallace; the Fourth, under Brig. Gen. Stephen A. Hurlbut; and the Fifth, under Brig. Gen. William T. Sherman. Lew Wallace's Third Division is posted to the north, at Crump's Landing on the west bank of the Tennessee. Grant locates his own headquarters on the east bank of the river at Savannah,

Tennessee, eight miles downstream from Pittsburg Landing. He's waiting there for Don Carlos Buell.

Last to arrive at Pittsburg Landing is the newly constituted Sixth Division. It is organized on the first day of April, and it will be commanded by a man Grant dislikes: Brig. Gen. Benjamin Prentiss. Prentiss and Grant had previously feuded over rank. Rank is always important to soldiers, but particularly to general officers. Prentiss's raw division includes a regiment that has seen combat, led by Col. Everett Peabody. Peabody, now a brigade commander, had been captured by the Rebels in the siege of Lexington, Missouri, the previous September. Prentiss's people camp in a vulnerable position: They are between three of Sherman's four brigades encamped around Shiloh Church, a tiny backcountry Methodist meetinghouse. Col. David Stuart's brigade is posted way out on the Union left, on bluffs overlooking Lick Creek and the Tennessee River, to guard the road to Hamburg Landing.

The officers drill the men; the weather improves; the trees bloom. The Johnny-jump-ups come up and the peaches blossom. The soldiers get bored—a lot of these guys are homesick. They drill, but they do not entrench. Why don't they? The prevailing tactical doctrine was crafted in the days of smoothbore muskets, which were notoriously inaccurate and with an effective range of 75 yards. Why entrench if the firepower is so weak? Shock and melee, the bayonet—those were the keys to infantry combat. More important, the Yankees establish Pittsburg Landing

OPPOSITE: *With the fall of Forts Henry and Donelson, Confederate General Johnston withdrew his forces into west Tennessee, northern Mississippi, and Alabama. In early March, Grant received orders to advance his Army of West Tennessee up the Tennessee River into the Confederate heartland. Grant moved to Pittsburg Landing to await the arrival of General Buell's Army of the Ohio from Nashville. Once combined, both Federal Armies would advance and break the Memphis & Charleston Railroad at Corinth, Mississippi, to sever the Confederacy's main rail communications between the Mississippi Valley and the East. Confederate Generals Beauregard and Johnston concentrated their forces at Corinth, hoping to strike at Grant at Pittsburg Landing before Buell could arrive.*

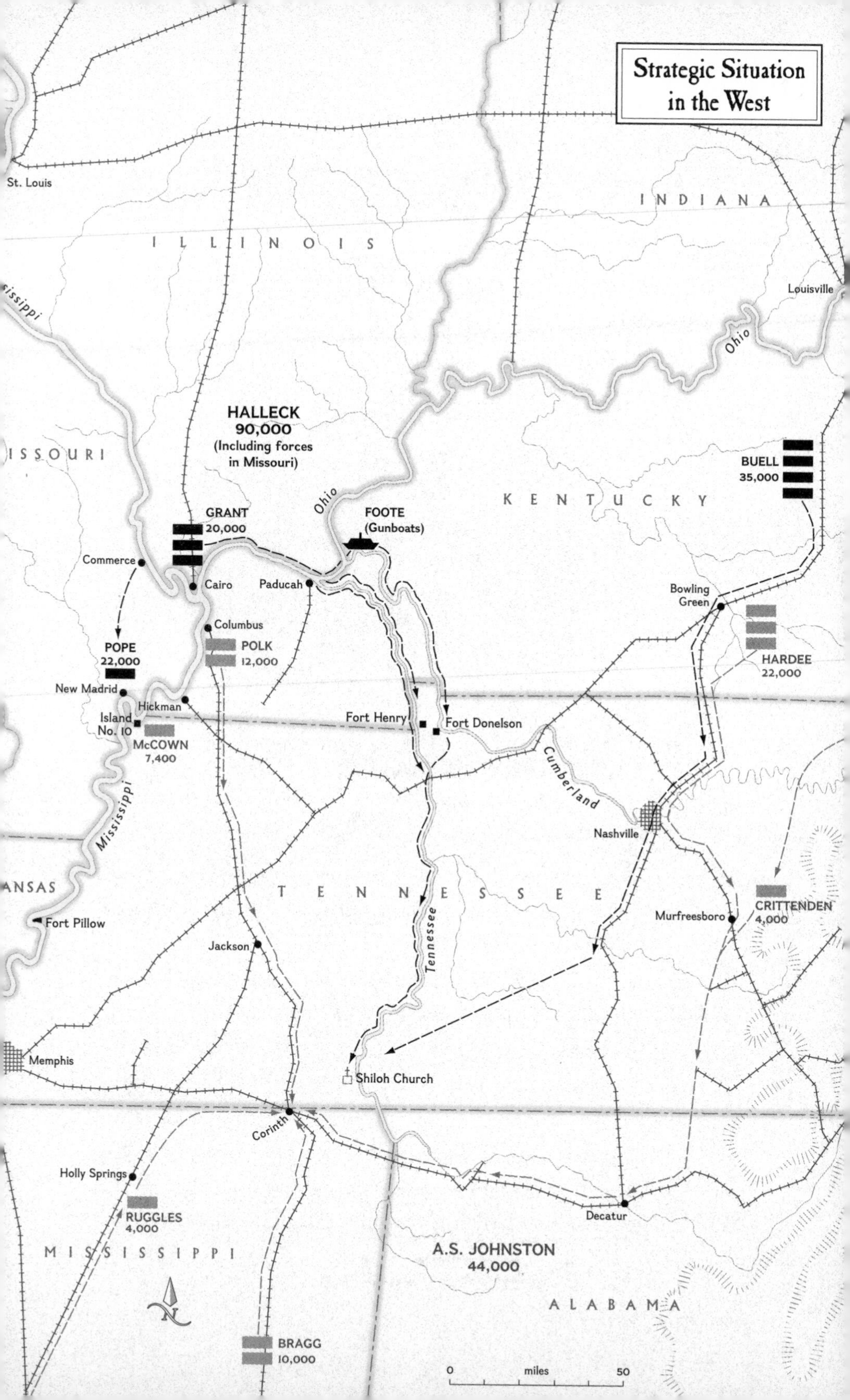
Strategic Situation in the West
St. Louis
ILLINOIS
INDIANA
Mississippi
Louisville
Ohio
HALLECK
90,000
(Including forces in Missouri)
MISSOURI
BUELL
35,000
KENTUCKY
GRANT
20,000
Ohio
FOOTE
(Gunboats)
Commerce
Cairo
Paducah
Bowling Green
Columbus
POLK
12,000
HARDEE
22,000
POPE
22,000
New Madrid
Hickman
Island No. 10
McCOWN
7,400
Fort Henry
Fort Donelson
Cumberland
Mississippi
Nashville
ARKANSAS
TENNESSEE
Tennessee
CRITTENDEN
4,000
Murfreesboro
Fort Pillow
Jackson
Memphis
Shiloh Church
Corinth
Holly Springs
RUGGLES
4,000
Decatur
MISSISSIPPI
A.S. JOHNSTON
44,000
ALABAMA
N
BRAGG
10,000
0 miles 50

A West Point error turned Hiram Ulysses into Ulysses Simpson Grant. Following his victories in the West at Forts Henry and Donelson, Grant earned the nickname "Unconditional Surrender."

as their offensive base and think that if anyone's going to be attacking, it will be them. They're just passing time at Pittsburg Landing before they get the word to move out.

Meanwhile, at Corinth, the Confederates create an army from disparate units. The Army of Central Kentucky is brought down by Generals Johnston and Hardee after it evacuates Bowling Green via Nashville. They're also going to have a good part of Brig. Gen. John C. Breckinridge's force that had been beaten badly at Mill Springs, Kentucky, where they were led by Generals Crittenden and Zollicoffer. They're joined by a large force led by Braxton Bragg, who arrives by rail from the Gulf Coast. Bragg's soldiers may not love him, but they're the Confederacy's best drilled and organized troops. Stripping New Orleans of its garrison, Daniel Ruggles's men come up from the Crescent City. Pierre G. T. Beauregard will bring down Bishop Leonidas Polk's army, which had evacuated Columbus, Kentucky, following the loss of Fort Donelson. They create an army of 44,000 men in and about Corinth, and on April 3, on learning of the rapid approach of Buell's army, the Confederates take the field. They plan to attack and best Grant's army on Friday, April 4th, a most unrealistic schedule!

Sherman is in the habit of sending patrols down the Corinth Road. Out goes the 54th Ohio on April 3, and they see some people on the other side of a field, and then they go back. On the fourth the 72nd Ohio, another of Sherman's regiments, and Maj. Elbridge Ricker's battalion of the 5th Ohio Cavalry again go out the Corinth Road and clash with the vanguard of Hardee's corps near Mickey's. Sherman is beside himself: He had explicitly told his subordinates not to bring on an engagement. Also, Sherman is going to have a visitor that evening. Ulysses S. Grant is in the habit of undocking his headquarters boat, going eight miles upriver, and visiting the camps. They talk over the situation, and Sherman convinces Grant that the enemy is still at Corinth. Grant has bad luck. It's raining—muddy. En route back to the landing, his horse falls, and it falls hard. It doesn't break Grant's ankle—it's bruised badly and swells up. The next day Grant doesn't come up—his leg is hurting him. In fact he is going to fight the Battle of Shiloh on crutches. He stays at Savannah on April 5 when Buell's vanguard, the Fourth Division, under Brig. Gen. William "Bull" Nelson, arrives late in the day and goes into camp.

The Confederates, having closed to within several miles of Shiloh Church, have all day April 5 to finalize their attack plan. They won't be interrupted by any more Union patrols. The Fifth Ohio Cavalry has been covering the army's right, the Fourth Illinois Cavalry the army's left, and they pick that day to reorganize and change their missions. Consequently, no mounted patrols go out on Saturday, and the one infantry regiment that goes out feels its way in the wrong direction—to the northwest—to encounter any Rebels.

The Federal camps, clustered to the south and southwest of Pittsburg Landing, are bounded on the east by the Tennessee River, to their west by Owl Creek, with a tributary, Shiloh Branch, to the southwest. Several smaller creeks, draining eastward into Lick Creek, form a series of deep ravines to the south. Three of Sherman's four brigades are camped on a plateau fronting Shiloh Branch. But one of his regiments is camped in Rhea's Field and separated from the others by a ravine. This unit is the 53rd Ohio, commanded by Jesse Appler, and several hundred yards separate these men from the camps of their comrades, the other two regiments of Jesse Hildebrand's brigade. Soldiers of the 53rd Ohio see Rebels out there, but no one at headquarters believes them. Sherman, frustrated by Appler's reports of Confederate activity, tells him to "take your damn regiment and go back to Ohio!"

What is Sherman's mind-set with all of these activities going on? He knew the Confederates were out there. He knew there were cavalry and infantry units, but he believed that those Confederates out in the woods were merely scouts trying to detect when the Federal advance on Corinth would occur. He was thinking that he'd do the attacking. He also knew that he commanded inexperienced personnel. He kept telling everybody that these were volunteer officers, from civil life, and that they didn't really have the experience and background that he had as a West Pointer and Regular Army officer. These men had as much idea of fighting a war as children, he said, and he used that terminology to demonstrate that the way of doing things in the Regular Army was that you discipline your men. You don't go off half-cocked if you see Confederates lurking in the woods. You don't think that you will be attacked—you're not going to be an alarmist.

Grant shared Sherman's perspective and trusted his reports. Aware that many of his men were raw recruits, he preferred to see them drilled to having them throw up field fortifications. He also believed that it would be up to the Union forces to bring on a battle by advancing against Corinth. Johnston and Beauregard had different ideas.

Beauregard draws up the attack plan. He knows that if the Confederates are going to win the battle, and the war, it must be a battle of annihilation. His goal is to crush the Yankees with succeeding waves of infantry, seize Pittsburg Landing, and drive the enemy into the river. In theory, if you are going to do that, you would mass your strength on your right, instead of forming your men in tandem. As at Manassas, Beauregard's thinking is Napoleonic. He plans to deploy the Confederates across a broad front, like the French emperor had done at Austerlitz and Waterloo. Now, we all know who won at Waterloo, and it wasn't the French. Advancing on a broad front might be good tactics in the open fields and sweeping vistas of Waterloo or Austerlitz, but the ground around Pittsburg Landing is broken up by woods and small farm fields, so the men cannot move together at the same speed. Indeed, the day had dawned bright and sunny and some of the Rebel staffers confidently called out "it's another sun of Austerlitz." But there the terrain and ground cover differed. When men advancing elbow to elbow come to an open field, they're going to speed up, while soldiers to the right and left of them are working their way through the woods. When you attack on a broad front, as Napoleon observed, "a general who is strong everywhere, is weak everywhere." Beauregard should have remembered this.

The Confederates form by corps in successive battle lines. William Hardee's men are in front; he has four brigades, three of his and one of Braxton Bragg's. He's followed by Bragg, with five brigades; Polk, with four brigades; then Breckinridge, with three brigades. But it's not clear who's in charge. In April 1862 Beauregard was still revered as the hero of Sumter and Manassas. Although he'd had difficulties with President Davis, Beauregard was looked at as one of the premier generals of the Confederacy.

Albert Sidney Johnston, on the other hand, had taken a lot of criticism for the loss of Forts Henry and Donelson, the Kentucky frontier, and much of middle Tennessee. Although he was the ranking officer, he decided to give Beauregard too much authority in terms of running the show. After all, Beauregard had been in the area for weeks, and he was a hero.

But on April 5, the eve of battle, because of the skirmishes that had occurred, Beauregard has second thoughts. "The Union camps have to be alerted," he worries. "It took us three days to execute a march that should have taken us one; we're not going to be able to surprise these Yankees and beat them." Nervously he advises Johnston, "the Yankees are going to be entrenched to their eyes; we're not going to surprise them. I think we better march back to Corinth without doing battle." Johnston is shocked. Here's a man he's been relying on all these days to enact a bold strategy, to do something to win back the Mississippi Valley, and, on the very eve of attacking the enemy, Beauregard is losing his will. What kind of general is this?

As the two senior generals confer, the others listen. Again Beauregard expresses a reluctance to fight the battle. It is my opinion that at this time, Johnston decides he isn't going to put a lot of reliance in Beauregard. In Johnston's eyes he had displayed a surprising lack of will. Disappointed, Johnston leaves Beauregard as second in command, but places him in the rear echelon, with the task of pushing troops forward. That's not a responsible role for the man you've been relying on to plan the operation. So Beauregard at the very last minute is given a minor role, as a result of his reluctance to go ahead with the attack plan he'd been responsible for developing.

The Confederate advance beginning on April 3 proved to be poorly planned and coordinated, filled with traffic jams. What should have been a day-and-a-half march turns into a three-day march, complicated by capricious spring weather—it can be 66 degrees one day, and 40 the next. It turns cold and rainy and dark. What happens when soldiers get cold? They eat more food. They consume all their rations. To make matters worse, nothing the field commanders can do can make the troops move quietly. They cheer and sound bugles, shoot at deer and rabbits, and one regiment even advances with its band playing. The generals debate whether to continue. Finally Johnston speaks. He's willing to place his trust, as he says, on "the iron dice of battle." And he says, "I would fight them if they were a million."

It is an army of hungry, wet, irritable, and sometimes confused Confederates that finally arrives at the fringes of Grant's encampment late on April 5 and early on April 6. As they deploy for their attack Union pickets continue to sense something is wrong.

Out on patrol is Capt. Gilbert Johnson of the 12th Michigan. He is cognizant of Rebels out there in the woods, and he reports that fact to his commanding officer, William Graves. Graves goes up the chain of command to brigade commander Col. Everett Peabody, 245 pounds, more than six feet tall, who had left Massachusetts to work as chief engineer on the Mississippi & Ohio Railroad. He was living in St. Joseph, Missouri, at the outbreak of the Civil War. Peabody decides to send out a combat patrol. Maj. James Powell, who has Regular Army experience, takes three companies of his regiment, the 25th Missouri, picks up another two companies of the 12th Missouri, and begins to probe into the woods. At 4:55 a.m., as they enter Fraley Field, they come under fire. A Yankee officer gets the privilege of being the first casualty. They exchange shots with the Confederates for about an hour—that means it's now six o'clock. The firing ends, and there are casualties. Powell has lost about 30 men.

Peabody, on his own initiative, sends more men forward to find out what's going on. By the time they arrive, the Confederates are coming. Yet the Rebel generals still waver. Johnston stands firm. The order goes out to advance, and Johnston swings into the saddle of his bay gelding, Fire-Eater, remarking, "Tonight we will water our horses in the Tennessee River."

General Hardee sends the brigade of Col. Robert G. Shaver forward to deal with Peabody. The Confederates are coming in line, elbow to elbow behind Maj. Aaron B. Hardcastle's Mississippians who formed the skirmish line for Hardee's corps. Close behind Hardcastle's boys are Shaver's Arkansans and to Shaver's right you have Brig. Gen. Adley Gladden's people; Brig. Gen. S. A. M. Wood's men and then Brig. Gen. Patrick Cleburne's brigade is on Shaver's left. Powell's bluecoats fall back. Shiloh's earliest hero is Everett Peabody. Peabody mounts up and rides off to his death. His brigade will be virtually destroyed trying to hold up the Rebel advance.

Sherman's people are still getting up, the cooks brewing coffee, the men getting ready for Sunday inspection. The firing in front of Prentiss has been going on for more than an hour. Peabody's brigade battles Shaver's men and initially stops them in their tracks. On Shaver's right is Gladden's brigade. Born in South Carolina, Adley Gladden is a veteran of the Mexican War, and a Louisianan by choice. His brigade strikes Madison Miller's brigade of Prentiss's division, and that fighting continues until about 8:30 a.m. By then, Gladden has been mortally wounded, and command passes to Daniel Adams. Peabody has been struck four times. This big man sits on his horse, bleeding, as he rallies his men for one last stand. He is hit again. The bullet strikes him below the nose and above the upper lip and drives into his brain. He's dead when he hits the ground.

The 15th Michigan had just arrived at the landing; it has not even been issued ammunition. As they march out somebody says, "Was that shooting ahead?" Other soldiers reply, "I presume they're shooting at squirrels." And then as they get closer to the front they see many Sunshine Soldiers. Sunshine Soldiers are those four or five healthy men that seem to be needed to help a wounded man to the rear. It's not pleasant to see men badly wounded. And the Michiganders remark, "those squirrels bite." After briefly being engaged, the 15th Michigan is marched back to the landing, issued ammunition, and they'll participate in the afternoon's fighting.

Now the Confederates begin to forge ahead. They drive relentlessly forward as Bragg's corps comes up, as do Brig. Gen. James R. Chalmers's five Mississippi regiments and one Tennessee regiment, and Brig. Gen. John K. Jackson's brigade. They attack northeastward on either side of the Eastern Corinth Road. They drive Prentiss's men from their camp a little before nine o'clock. Many of the Yanks will not stop running until they get back to the landing. Others halt and re-form.

General Johnston arrives amid Prentiss's abandoned camps at this point. He has ordered his men to "Move forward and fire low." They always admonish you to "fire low" because of the optics of the eye. Also, if you fire low, that means you're going to hit the foe in the lower extremities, where if you wound a man it's more of a problem. He also orders, "Do not halt! Do not plunder the camps. If men break and flee to the rear, they're to be shot. You're to keep up the momentum!" The Rebels are hungry. Most have eaten their three days' rations. They arrive in the Yankee camps just as the Federal cooks are preparing breakfast, so they begin to plunder. Johnston picks up a small tin cup, and announces, "This is what I am taking; it will be my share of the spoils." He will use this cup and not his sword throughout the day to direct his men. He also does something that may well cost him his life. He calls for his chief surgeon, Dr. David W. Yandell, and tells him, "You take care of these wounded, whether they're Union or Confederate." Dr. Yandell will not be with Johnston at a crucial time between 2 and 2:30 that afternoon.

Capt. Samuel H. Lockett is a senior engineer from Alabama, second in his West Point class of 1859. While out reconnoitering he sees a Union force near the river, which he estimates to be a division. Actually, it's David Stuart's brigade, detached from Sherman's division. Looking to protect his flank, Johnston orders two brigades to attack Stuart.

Near Noah Cantrell's house, one of the few frame buildings in the area, are David Stuart's camps. Stuart is two miles as the crow flies from Sherman's Shiloh Church headquarters. By 9 a.m., as we've seen, Prentiss's division has been routed and driven out of its camps. Stuart can hear the firing. Stuart is very nervous. He's isolated out here. The nearest friendly

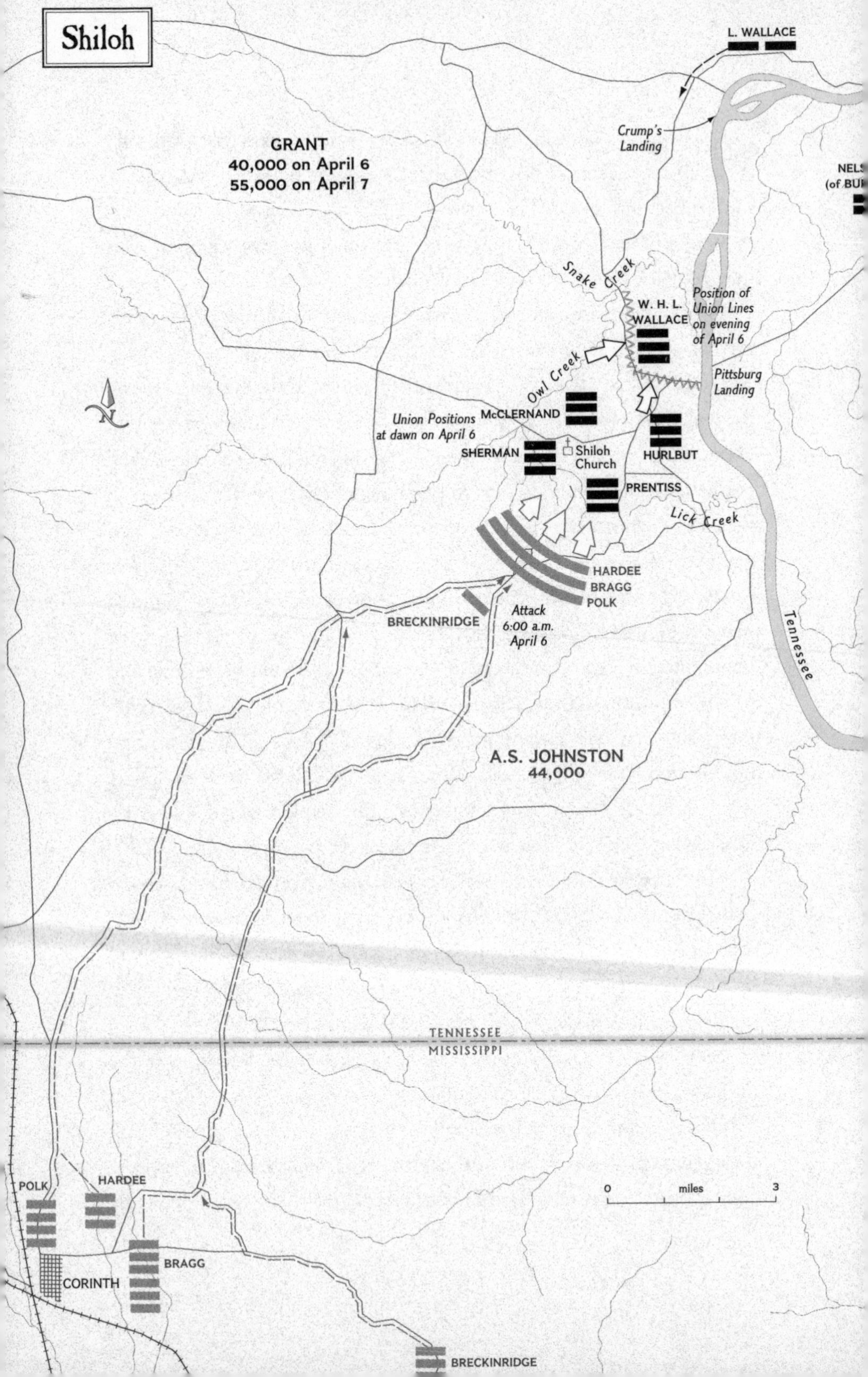
Shiloh
L. WALLACE
Crump's Landing
GRANT
40,000 on April 6
55,000 on April 7
Snake Creek
Position of Union Lines on evening of April 6
W. H. L. WALLACE
Owl Creek
Pittsburg Landing
Union Positions at dawn on April 6
McCLERNAND
SHERMAN
Shiloh Church
HURLBUT
PRENTISS
Lick Creek
HARDEE
BRAGG
POLK
BRECKINRIDGE
Attack 6:00 a.m. April 6
Tennessee
A.S. JOHNSTON
44,000
TENNESSEE
MISSISSIPPI
POLK
HARDEE
BRAGG
CORINTH
BRECKINRIDGE
0
miles
3

troops are Stephen A. Hurlbut's division, back in Cloud's Field, a mile and a quarter north. Stuart forms his three regiments in their camps on their respective color lines. Not knowing when or where the Rebels will appear, he moves from place to place. Stuart shifts his regiments about willy-nilly. Wonderful that he does this. He's going to get a bonus. Captain Lockett, seeing these movements, makes a bad decision, and when he goes back to Johnston he reports that Stuart has a division of troops rather than a brigade. That's when Johnston makes a fatal move. He sends two brigades, James Chalmers's and John K. Jackson's, to cope with Stuart. Much time will be lost, and by the time Chalmers and Jackson engage Stuart, it's noon. Think of all the time the Confederates would have gained if they'd used these two brigades to follow Prentiss's men as they retreated and re-formed in the thickets that bordered the "Sunken Road" that connects the Corinth-Pittsburg Landing and Hamburg-Savannah roads.

Sherman has camped three brigades around Shiloh Church; from left to right the brigades are commanded by Col. Jesse Hildebrand, Col. Ralph Buckland, and Col. John McDowell. Isolated in Rhea's Field in their front is Col. Jesse Appler's 53rd Ohio. He is in position to get in lots of trouble. In Sherman's camps his people hear the sounds of the opening engagement. Back at Sherman's headquarters, no one is alarmed. They figure it's a continuation of the shooting and skirmishing they heard the previous day. Finally, about 7 a.m., Appler gets very nervous. He alerts

OPPOSITE: *At dawn on April 6, Johnston's army deployed just to the south of two of Grant's camps. Despite resistance by some Federal units, the Confederates achieved almost total surprise. By mid-morning the Confederates had smashed one Federal division but faced fierce resistance on the Federal right near Shiloh Church. The Confederate attack on the right, near the Tennessee River, stalled in the dense thickets of the Hornets' Nest before finally driving back Grant's left in the late afternoon. Grant's final line at Pittsburg Landing turned back the last Confederate charge at dusk. After nightfall Buell's army moved into line on the Union left. On the following morning Grant launched a massive attack that drove back the exhausted Rebels, and Beauregard ordered a retreat.*

Sherman that the Rebels are coming. Sherman patronizingly remarks, "It's just one of Jesse's scares."

Suddenly the Rebels emerge from the woods, led by Patrick Cleburne; they struggle to get through a morass formed by low ground along Shiloh Branch. As they do, Sherman rides up. Out there in the distance, at the far end of Rhea's Field, he sees Confederates. They belong to S. A. M. Wood's brigade. Sherman puts his telescope to his eye and looks off in that direction. Yankees now come out of the woods in his front shouting, "The Rebels out here are as thick as fleas on a dog's back."

Sherman then hears a shot, and Pvt. Thomas D. Holliday, his orderly, falls. Sherman throws up his right hand and drops his telescope; he gets a buckshot in his hand.

He rides back to alert his brigade commanders that the enemy is advancing.

The Confederates have a tough time. Col. J. J. Thornton is wounded and his Sixth Mississippi suffered many casualties, more than 70 percent (the fourth highest of any Southern regiment in a single battle), as it sought to fight its way across Rhea's Field. The 23rd Tennessee, another of Cleburne's regiments, breaks. Cleburne is thrown from his horse as he seeks to cross the "almost impassible morass." Before being deserted by Colonel Appler and a number of their fainthearted comrades, the 53rd Ohio puts up a good fight—not as feeble as many writers report. But eventually they'll be dislodged. Before they finally gain the upper hand on Sherman, the Confederates have to call for reinforcements to bolster Cleburne's brigade. The Yankees shoot the daylights out of the 2nd Tennessee in its stand-up fight against the 72nd Ohio of Buckland's brigade. Brig. Gen. Patton Anderson's brigade of Bragg's corps and Brig. Gen. Bushrod Johnson's brigade of Polk's corps join the action. Still Sherman's men hold fast. Sherman may have been naive, but he is magnificent now. Inspired by Sherman, his men hold the Shiloh Church Ridge till 9 a.m. Finally, the Confederates commit another brigade, and at last Sherman's men melt away.

Shortly after the Shiloh campaign the controversial Braxton Bragg was promoted to full general, eventually relieving P. G. T. Beauregard, who suffered from ill health.

Hearing the noise of battle, Grant, at 7:30, leaves his headquarters at Savannah's Cherry Mansion, boards his headquarters boat, *Tigress,* and heads south toward Pittsburg Landing. He also sends orders to the head of Buell's column to hurry up. But there are no steamboats on hand to move Buell's troops; Brig. Gen. William "Bull" Nelson will eventually make his way by foot to a point across the Tennessee from Pittsburg Landing. Passing Crump's Landing, Grant tells Gen. Lew Wallace to "have your men ready to march at a moment's notice, in any direction to which it might be ordered." It will take some time for him to bring his three brigades together.

Grant arrives at Pittsburg Landing at 9 a.m. He rides out to Sherman's headquarters. Then he'll ride from headquarters to headquarters before returning to the landing.

Union Maj. Gen. John McClernand has three brigades. They are camped in the area north and east of the intersection of the Corinth and Purdy-Hamburg Landing roads. The brigades are commanded by Col. Julius Raith on the left, Col. C. Carroll Marsh in the center, and Col. Abraham C. Hare on the right. On McClernand's right are Sherman's people—badly intermixed—as they fall back to re-form along the Purdy Road.

The Confederates smell blood. They bring up their artillery. Sherman feels fairly confident about his command as they pull back. A Confederate shell, however, is on target as cannoneers of the Sixth Indiana Artillery unlimber their six guns. Capt. Frederick Behr is gunned down, his battery panics, and there is chaos as teams and vehicles bolt through Sherman's infantry, disrupting it. The Confederates bring the full weight of their attack on McClernand, and his division pulls back. Beauregard then makes an important command decision. He decides to coordinate operations from Sherman's former headquarters at Shiloh Church. Johnston will remain at the front and inspire the men.

Stephen Hurlbut has three brigades in his Fourth Division, commanded by Col. Nelson G. Williams, Col. Jacob G. Lauman, and Col. James C. Veatch. When called to the front, the first two take position facing south, anchoring their left along the southern edge of a cotton field, with their right strung out along the "Sunken Road." In truth the road is not truly sunken. They are soon joined by three brigades from W. H. L. Wallace's division—two, one-armed Tom Sweeny's and James Tuttle's, take position on Hurlbut's right, and the third, led by Brig. Gen. John McArthur, takes position on Hurlbut's left, south of the Savannah-Hamburg Road. Holding the position between Wallace's men on the right and Hurlbut's people on the left are about a thousand men, all that remains of Prentiss's division. You end up with about 11,000 Yankees along this one-mile front, soon to become known as the "Hornets' Nest," supported by 34 cannon. They are first tested when one of Polk's Confederate brigades under Col. William H. Stephens appears.

It numbers approximately 1,200 men. The Yankees soon lose six of their cannon when the 13th Ohio Battery, Capt. John B. Myers commanding, panics after a limber explodes, and the battery heads for Pittsburg Landing, leaving their six cannon abandoned out in Sarah Bell's cotton field.

General Bragg hurls Stephens's brigade across Duncan Field several times, against troops in a good defensive position with lots of artillery. Next on the scene for the Confederates is Col. Randall Lee Gibson's Louisiana Brigade. Like Stephens's they have no artillery support. Bragg sends Gibson's brigade through the woods and underbrush, not once, not twice, not three times, but four times—to death and destruction. Bragg gets upset about the failure to break the Federal position, and he refers to Gibson as an "errant coward." The brigade's final charge is led by Col. Henry Watkins Allen, of the Fourth Louisiana, who has been shot through both cheeks. The bullet went in one cheek and out the other. Fortunately he had his mouth open when shot, but he's bleeding badly. Bragg snaps, "I want no faltering now, Colonel Allen." Allen's men go forward to another repulse. By 3 p.m. there have been six Confederate attacks against the Hornets' Nest, each ending in a bloody repulse.

By now the Confederate efforts to envelop the Union left anchored on either side of the Savannah-Hamburg Landing Road give promise of success. David Stuart's bluecoats, assailed by Chalmers and John K. Jackson, abandon their positions at Noah Cantrell's house and retreat northward across a west-east ravine and into the rugged ground beyond. General Breckinridge comes up with the brigades of Brig. Gen. John S. Bowen and Col. Winfield S. Statham, constituting two-thirds of the Confederate reserve. General Johnston and key members of his staff are there to provide inspiration and leadership. The Confederates' goal is to overwhelm the three Union brigades (McArthur's, Williams's now led by Col. Isaac Pugh, and Lauman's) holding the left of the Sunken Road line and hopefully to seize Pittsburg Landing.

The governor of Tennessee, Isham Harris, who is serving as a volunteer aide-de-camp, accompanies Sidney Johnston. General Breckinridge doesn't

Gen. Albert Sidney Johnston was the senior ranking general holding a field command in the Confederate forces. Fatally wounded on April 6, he became the highest ranking casualty of the war.

recognize Harris, and he says, "General, I have a Tennessee regiment that won't fight." He's embarrassed when he sees the Tennessee governor, and apologizes for his derogatory remark. He identifies the Tennessee regiment that wasn't fighting, and Harris, who considers himself a good stump speaker, says, "I'll go and tend to that," and off he goes to address the 45th Tennessee.

Johnston is directing troop movements with the tin cup he picked up earlier that day. Also remember at that time he had sent off Dr. Yandell to see to the wounded, both Rebs and Yanks. Coming upon an Arkansas regiment, Johnston shouts, "We're going to charge the enemy! Remember, the enemy does not like cold steel. Do you hear me?" "Yes, we hear you!" they respond. The Confederates are fired up. Four brigades are ready to go. Johnston, mounted on Fire-Eater, rides along behind his advancing soldiers from

Mississippi, Tennessee, Missouri, Arkansas, Alabama, and Texas. The Union line collapses from left to right. John McArthur's three Illinois regiments, beginning with the 50th Illinois, crumble; a battery is nearly surrounded before it makes good its escape minus a gun. Next, the Union line in the Peach Orchard west of the Savannah-Hamburg Landing Road is folded back.

This is a great day for Johnston: It looks like he's finally scored the breakthrough that will send the Confederates thundering north to Pittsburg Landing. He's been hit four times, but only one projectile, a caliber .577 minié ball, probably fired by a Confederate, counts. Johnston sits there, and he sends off his aide, Capt. Theodore O'Hara. The only person with him at this time is Capt. W. L. Wickham. As Governor Harris rides back, he notices that Johnston looks very pale. Evidently Wickham has not noticed or not said anything about it. Harris inquires, "Are you wounded?" And Johnston says, "Yes, and I fear seriously."

They lead Johnston's horse down into the ravine and help him dismount. Harris gets down in a crouch and cradles Johnston's head in his lap. They try to get some brandy down his throat. They think that he's probably been hit in the chest because there's not that much blood, a small trickle is coming out of his right boot; the boot, unknown to them, is full of blood. They unbutton his shirt, looking for a wound in his chest. By this time, O'Hara is back, accompanied by Col. William Preston, Johnston's former brother-in-law. Harris is getting stiff, cradling Johnston, so Preston takes over. They try to get some whiskey down his throat; they get only a gurgle. Then they feel his chest, and his heartbeat has stopped.

Albert Sidney Johnston has breathed his last. Steps are taken to notify Beauregard. Harris tries to get on Fire-Eater, but the horse is wounded. He rides a short distance and gets another horse. Johnston is dead, and the word spreads like wildfire among the senior commanders of the Rebel army.

With Johnston dead, the Confederate commanders seek to sort out the situation. Who's going to command? Beauregard is in the rear; Johnston had been directing the assaults. Beauregard determines to

On April 6, 1862, these 24-pounder siege guns formed part of the Union's "Last Line" at Pittsburg Landing, during the Battle of Shiloh.

remain at Shiloh Church and, as Army commander, coordinate battle actions. Bishop Polk will command the army's left wing and Bragg the right. They're to resume attacking. They will continue to throw other brigades into the Hornets' Nest fight: first A. P. Stewart's, then in succession Shaver's, Patton's and Anderson's, and finally S. A. M. Wood's. But they're not going to secure a breakthrough until they call on Brig. Gen. Daniel Ruggles. This will be the only day in the war that Ruggles is more than a journeyman general. He gathers artillery from all over the field. He'll assemble 11 batteries, a total of 53 cannon, and at 4:30 these guns open fire on the Hornets' Nest "with the force of a hurricane."

At the same time, the defending Union forces are wearing down, contracting their front, and struggling to hold their ground. Tom Sweeny's brigade finally collapses; General W. H. L. Wallace is shot down. He remains on the field throughout the night, with rain pouring down, shot through the head. The next day Union soldiers will find the mortally wounded general and evacuate him to the Cherry Mansion, where, comforted by his wife, he dies on April 10. Prentiss's men are surrounded, and by 5:45 p.m., 2,250 Union soldiers have surrendered.

The stand at the Hornets' Nest buys precious time for Grant. As the Federals fend off attack after attack—ten in all—Grant orders his chief of staff, Col. Joseph D. Webster, to establish a last line of defense extending west from Pittsburg Landing. The line bristles with cannon; what remains of Sherman's and McClernand's divisions gathers on the right flank, fronting west.

The Union will have more than 50 cannon, including five big 24-pounder siege guns, on what becomes Grant's "Final Line." Fronting the Union left, facing south and anchored on the commanding bluff overlooking Pittsburg Landing, is the Dill Branch Ravine, 200 yards wide and adjacent to the river, with a vertical fall of 75 feet. High water from the Tennessee is backed up into Dill Branch for several hundred yards. The Union right flank is posted behind Tilghman Branch on a plateau overlooking the Owl Creek bottom, forward of the Savannah-Hamburg Road, the route over which the tardy Lew Wallace is approaching from Crump's Landing. The distance between the heads of Dill and Tilghman branches is about half a mile. By 5:45, making use of the terrain that favors the defense, Grant had cobbled together a formidable line covering Pittsburg Landing, where a linkup with Wallace could take place.

As evening approaches, with the Hornets' Nest now under Confederate control, Beauregard is faced with the choice of whether to attack Grant's Final Line. Unbeknownst to him, William "Bull" Nelson's division has finally arrived; one of his brigade commanders, Col. Jacob Ammen, hurries three regiments across the Tennessee on steamboats to form into line and fire a few shots as the Confederates tentatively advance. Then the word comes from Beauregard: enough for now—we'll finish the job tomorrow. It may have been just as well: Dill Branch, with its steep banks and undergrowth, presents more of an obstacle than one might at first expect.

Brig. Gen. William "Bull" Nelson, an acquaintance of Lincoln's, survived the bloody fighting at Shiloh only to be murdered six months later following an argument with a fellow officer.

Bull Nelson—300 pounds, six feet four—is mean as hell. He can bend a poker around his forearm. He had been a naval officer and is a close friend of President Lincoln's. On the 29th of March, back at Columbia, Tennessee, frustrated at waiting for the completion of a bridge across Duck River, he marched his men through the river. He is eager to get here. Grant, when he leaves Savannah to come upriver, doesn't leave specific instructions as to how Nelson's command is to get to Pittsburg Landing. It's going to be 12:30 before Nelson leaves Savannah. He will not bring any artillery with him because he knows the bottoms are inundated; the Tennessee River, although falling, is still high. It's going to be a hellacious sight when Nelson arrives about 5:30, on the riverbank opposite Pittsburg Landing. Nelson estimates that between 7,000 and 10,000 Army of the Tennessee soldiers, "frantic with fright and utterly demoralized, were cowering under the river bank." Grant subsequently questions the numbers cited by Nelson.

I applaud what Nelson does now. As he and his staff and escort see these panic-stricken men trying to get on their boat, he roars "Draw your sabers! Run over the bastards!"

As Colonel Ammen brings his men ashore they fight off the panic-stricken soldiers. They see Union cavalry come down and seek to drive the men away from the landing and up onto the bluffs. Whether it's 6,000, 7,000, 8,000, or 11,000—the various figures given—there are a lot of panic-stricken Yankees. Among them will be Capt. John B. Myers and Col. Jesse Appler. Jake Ammen is from Georgetown, Ohio. Who else is from Georgetown, Ohio? Ulysses S. Grant.

In the evening it gets cold, and rain sets in. Grant is outside. Grant is not disturbed by the dead, but he does not like to be around hospitals and the wounded, particularly when the doctors are doing amputations. He goes into a log cabin near the landing, and when he sees it's a hospital he can't take it, so he walks out and stands under a tree with his hat pulled down over his eyes and with his coat pulled up.

At one point during the night, Grant's chief engineer, Col. James B. McPherson, rides up and reports that much of the army is "*hors de combat*." When asked what he would do under these circumstances—retreat? Grant answered "No! I propose to attack at daylight and whip them."

During the night Union reinforcements continue to arrive, strengthening Grant's line, making a counterattack possible. All of Nelson's men are shuttled across the river by steamboats. Other divisions of Buell's Army of the Ohio arrive during the night. They come by boat, upriver from Savannah. First will be two brigades of Brig. Gen. Thomas

Crittenden's division, then three brigades of Brig. Gen. Alexander McCook's, and finally Col. George D. Wagner's brigade of Brig. Gen. Thomas Wood's division.

It is 7:30 and getting dark when Lew Wallace's three-brigade division crosses Owl Creek Bridge and files into position on Sherman's right. For both Wallace and Grant it has been a long, frustrating day, one the former will rue and seek to explain till his dying day in February 1905. When General Buell reports back to Grant, he learns that they will attack on Monday morning, April 7. Buell will be in charge on the left, Grant on the right.

Meanwhile the Confederates rest. Beauregard sends a telegram to Richmond that the army has won a "complete victory," and he will finish it in the morning. Others are not so sure. Col. Nathan Bedford Forrest hears the noise of steamboats. He puts several men into Yankee overcoats and sends them to take a closer look: They report back that they see steamboats at the landing and soldiers debarking and marching. Forrest goes looking for somebody. It's hard to find anybody in authority. In many places the Confederates pull back during the night. It rains. To make things worse, the "timberclad" gunboats *Tyler* and *Lexington,* anchored off the mouth of Dill Branch, keep up a harassing fire in the direction of the captured Union camps with their big eight-inch guns at 15-minute intervals.

Lew Wallace moves out in the morning, and what is he going to encounter? Preston Pond's brigade and four cannon. Supporting Wallace are 11 Union cannon. Wallace's men cross Tilghman Branch, drive the Rebels from Jones's Field, but slow down as they pause to wait for Sherman and McClernand to come up on their left. So we've got Grant's attack started. Cooperation between Grant and Buell's wings will be slim to none, and as they say, Slim just left town.

At the same time that Buell sets matters into motion on the left flank, Nelson's division on the Confederate right leads the way.

Under cover of darkness, the Confederates had pulled back southward to seek shelter from the rain and loot the captured Federal camps. That means the Federals are going to have a free ride early on as they advance. Nelson guides on the Savannah-Hamburg Road. On the left is Jake Ammen's brigade, in the center is the brigade of Col. Sanders Bruce, and on the right in the woods is Col. William B. Hazen's.

Before long Nelson's brigades close on the landmarks of yesterday's savage fight—the Hornets' Nest—Bloody Pond, the Peach Orchard, and the Sunken Road. Here they encounter Confederates. The Rebels have something Nelson lacks: artillery. Nelson calls up two regular batteries—Capt. John Mendenhall's Fourth U.S. Companies H and M, and Capt. William R. Terrell's Company H, Fifth U.S. Artillery. General Hardee orders his men to attack, and they hammer the Yanks near Bloody Pond. To the Confederate left, a second attack drives Hazen back to the Sunken Road with heavy losses.

Remember, as the two armies meet here on April 7, there are dead and wounded scattered about from the previous afternoon's fighting, particularly around Bloody Pond. Dead animals and dead men lie sprawled with their faces and heads in the water. Now besides the problems of empty canteens and poor water discipline, the situation is compounded because wounded men develop thirst.

The Confederates advance again, but Hardee's warning that there are friendly troops fronting his lines proves a disaster when the Yankees open fire. Hazen's brigade, supported by some of Crittenden's bluecoats, charge and capture three cannon manned by the Washington Louisiana Artillery. With Buell's arrival, the Yankees have about 28,000 men on the line, of whom 17,000 belong to the Army of the Ohio. The Confederates have perhaps 20,000 engaged. This shows a loss of command and control by the Confederates. The Confederates counterattack and drive Hazen's men back again. The fighting in this sector then stabilizes until noon, when Union troops break the impasse and force back Hardee's right.

The Confederates fare little better against the Yankees in the center, near Duncan Field, west of the intersection of the Sunken Road and the Corinth Road. Duncan Field is important primarily on April 6, when the Confederates still have the offensive. Duncan Field gets glossed over once the Union seizes the initiative. Again fighting rages in this area as soldiers of Buell's Army of the Ohio battle Breckinridge's butternuts. One of the advantages the Confederates have on day two is that the blue-coats don't make good use of their artillery, principally because the Army of the Ohio commits only three batteries. Nelson, on the left, has no batteries with him; they have to give him the guns that come up with Crittenden. The Confederates at the same time make effective use of their cannon as they fight for time. Another problem is on the Union right. Lew Wallace, after securing Jones's Field, has to wait till after 10 a.m. for Sherman and McClernand to cross Tilghman Branch on his left, and then engage the foe. Patrick Cleburne with 800 men counterattacks the Yankees, but he's driven back.

By midday on April 7 Grant and Buell's men succeed in driving Beauregard's men southwestward. The Confederates make a series of stands, but in each case they are forced to give ground. Numbers tell: Buell and Lew Wallace have brought fresh troops to the battlefield, while only a handful of men reinforce the Confederates.

Beauregard realizes that his position is weakening: He pulls back to the Purdy-Hamburg Road. A key feature in the struggle here is Water Oaks Pond. Again, the Rebels make good use of their artillery, while the Federals do not. The Confederates are fighting like hell; they've got to because if the Union forces break through the Confederate left and reach Shiloh Church, their direct line of retreat to Corinth will be endangered. Advancing against them, guiding on the Corinth Road, is Brig. Gen. Alexander McCook's division, consisting of Brig. Gen. Lovell Rousseau's and Col. Edward Kirk's brigades. Off to his left is Thomas Crittenden's division. To the right are McClernand, Sherman, and Lew Wallace, threatening to turn Bragg's left and reach Shiloh Church.

The Confederate situation is desperate. McCook's Federals are reinforced by a third brigade, headed by Col. William Gibson. The Confederates continue to give ground, falling back from Duncan Field to beyond Water Oaks Pond. Beauregard's headquarters is next to the Shiloh Church. The Corinth Road, running by the church, is the best and shortest route to Corinth, so they must hold this area as long as possible. Beauregard calls for two successive counterattacks. S. A. M. Wood's brigade spearheads the first. The men wade Water Oaks Pond and slam into McCook's division. Kirk's reinforced brigade is running low on ammunition. It pulls back; the Rebel counterattack has bought more time. However, when Gibson arrives, he stops Wood and drives him back.

The situation is increasingly desperate. To the rescue comes Preston Pond's Louisiana boys, who have been ordered all over the field without seeing much action since early morning. This buys some time, but time is running out. One of Beauregard's staff officers turns to the Confederate commander and remarks that the army resembles a lump of sugar, soaking wet, holding together for the moment, but ready to dissolve. Beauregard understands. He orders a withdrawal. Buying time yet again, Col. Robert F. Looney's 38th Tennessee heads a final charge; before long the Confederates retreat in earnest. The time is 3:30 p.m.

Neither Grant nor Buell orders a pursuit. Grant has had enough: His men are exhausted, and he hesitates to issue orders to Buell. In truth, both sides are fought out. More than 23,700 men are killed, wounded, or captured at Shiloh, more than in all of the previous wars of the United States put together. The Confederates suffer 10,694 casualties to the Union's 13,047. Grant came under heavy criticism but retained his command; for years to come Confederates would ponder the what-ifs of the battle that represented their best chance to stop and reverse the Union advance through west Tennessee and into north Mississippi.

4

ANTIETAM

SEPTEMBER 17, 1862

Beginning September 4, 1862, long infantry columns of the Confederate Army of Northern Virginia splashed across the Potomac River at White's Ford to enter the state of Maryland. On the far shore a band played inspiring music, including the popular secession air, "Maryland, My Maryland." The Rebel soldiers were sunburned and weathered, and their threadbare gray and butternut uniforms were in tatters—many marched barefoot or in worn-out shoes—but the confidence and morale of Robert E. Lee's veterans was superb. Lt. Col. E. Porter Alexander, an artillery officer in Longstreet's wing, recalled that Lee's army "had acquired that magnificent morale which made them equal to twice their numbers, and his confidence in them, & theirs in him, were so equal that no man can yet say which was greatest."

Since late June 1862, Robert E. Lee's veterans had fought an extraordinary series of campaigns and battles that had carried them from victory to victory—from the gates of Richmond to the doorstep of the northern states. In early summer Confederate forces had faced a major Federal offensive against Richmond led by Maj. Gen. George B. McClellan, whose march up the peninsula between the York and James Rivers had pressed to within seven miles of the Confederate capital. Gen. Robert E. Lee had assumed command after the wounding of Gen. Joseph E. Johnston at the inconclusive Battle of Seven Pines (Fair Oaks), just east of Richmond, on June 1, 1862. Quickly gathering control of the army, Lee struck at McClellan on June 26, fighting a seven-day series of successful but often poorly coordinated battles at Oak Grove, Mechanicsville, Gaines's Mill, Garnett's Farm, Savage's Station, White Oak Swamp,

Glendale, and Malvern Hill. By the beginning of July, despite problems of communication and coordination, the Confederates had blocked McClellan's advance and bottled up his army at Harrison's Landing on the James River.

With McClellan inactive, Lee now faced a second threat. Maj. Gen. John Pope's 50,000-man Army of Virginia that had threatened the Shenandoah Valley was now maneuvering east of the Blue Ridge mountains to support McClellan. Lee detached one of his trusted lieutenants, Thomas J. "Stonewall" Jackson, with 24,000 men, to maneuver toward Gordonsville, Virginia, to delay Pope's advance. After an engagement between Jackson and a force under Federal Maj. Gen. Nathaniel Banks at Cedar Mountain on August 9, Lee, learning that McClellan had been ordered to redeploy most of his forces to join Pope in Northern Virginia, marched north with Longstreet's wing to link up with Jackson.

Splitting his army on the line of the Rappahannock River, Lee sent Jackson north on a turning movement against Pope's right flank, and the armies met on August 28–30 at the Second Battle of Manassas. After severe action between Pope and Jackson on August 29, Longstreet's wing enveloped the Federal left on August 30, sending Pope's forces in retreat across Bull Run to Centreville.

Maintaining the offensive, Lee again moved against his enemy's flank, striking toward Fairfax Court House. After a fierce battle at Chantilly, Virginia, Pope withdrew into the defenses of Washington. After three months in command of the Army of Northern Virginia, Robert E. Lee had conducted a remarkable series of battles and campaigns that resulted in the defeat of the two Federal Armies that threatened Richmond and driven most of the North's forces back into the defenses of Washington. Despite heavy losses in men and materiel—the Army of Northern Virginia had suffered more than 29,000 casualties since June 1—Lee was determined to keep the initiative.

Rather than hurl his army against Washington's formidable ring of forts, Lee decided to take the war into the North. In a letter to Confederate President Jefferson Davis, Lee argued that he could not afford to remain idle. By entering Maryland and perhaps Pennsylvania, he could shift the armies from war-ravaged Virginia and gather supplies in the fruitful farm country of central Maryland and Pennsylvania's Great Valley and perhaps rally Marylanders to the Confederate cause. Further, a Confederate victory on Northern soil might force the Lincoln government to open negotiations with the South.

As the Rebel forces, more than 50,000 strong, crossed into Maryland and advanced on Frederick, Abraham Lincoln acted quickly to counter the threat, sacking Pope (whom he had named head of the Army of Virginia just months earlier) and restoring the charismatic McClellan to the command. Moving with uncharacteristic speed, McClellan by September 7 had established his headquarters north of Washington at Rockville, Maryland, and began sending his army—a force of some 80,000 men—marching toward Frederick on a broad front in pursuit of Lee.

After occupying Frederick on September 7, Lee, on the ninth, devised a bold plan spelled out in Special Order No. 191. Lee planned to send three columns under Stonewall Jackson to capture the strategic communications center of Harpers Ferry, to guard his rear and to open communications with the Shenandoah Valley. Jackson was then to link up with the rest of the army 12 miles north of Harpers Ferry at the small town of Boonsboro, Maryland. From there, if all went well, Lee could maneuver into Pennsylvania to meet McClellan on ground of his own choice. Lee's army resumed its march on September 10 with Longstreet and Maj. Gen. Daniel Harvey Hill headed west through the gaps in South Mountain toward Boonsboro and Hagerstown, while two of Jackson's columns under Maj. Gen. Lafayette McLaws and Brig. Gen. John G. Walker headed westward to threaten Harpers Ferry from north and south of the Potomac. Jackson with three divisions headed west to recross the Potomac at Williamsport and approach Harpers Ferry from the west.

On September 12, McClellan's vanguard reached Frederick, and on the following day the Federal commander was overjoyed at the discovery of a lost copy of Lee's Special Order No. 191, found wrapped around three cigars in an abandoned Confederate campsite. With detailed knowledge of Lee's timetable and movements, McClellan now believed that he could defeat the Rebel forces piecemeal before they could reunite. Accordingly, McClellan sent his forces marching toward Boonsboro in pursuit of Lee and Longstreet.

While a jubilant McClellan marched out of Frederick, Jackson's columns closed on Harpers Ferry. By September 13, McLaws seized Maryland Heights and Loudoun Heights, high ground commanding the town and the Shenandoah River. By the following day, Jackson had closed the trap from the west, and his artillery opened fire on the Federal garrison.

While Jackson invested Harpers Ferry, Lee left forces under D. H. Hill to hold several of the South Mountain passes and accompanied Longstreet to Hagerstown. On the night of September 13, however, he became aware that McClellan was closing in on South Mountain in his rear and ordered Longstreet to countermarch and rejoin Hill. On the 14th, McClellan struck the Confederates, forcing his way through Crampton's Gap and battering the defenses of Turner's and Fox's Gaps. After a day of fierce fighting, compelled to abandon the South Mountain gaps, Lee with Longstreet's and D. H. Hill's people withdrew southward to the small village of Sharpsburg, close to the Potomac along Antietam Creek.

On the morning of September 15, the 12,000-man garrison at Harpers Ferry surrendered. Acting decisively, Lee ordered Jackson to join Longstreet and concentrate the army at Sharpsburg. Leaving Maj. Gen. A. P. Hill's division to parole the large number of Federal prisoners at Harpers Ferry, Jackson crossed the Potomac near Shepherdstown on September 16 with three divisions, and his exhausted men marched toward Sharpsburg.

Throughout the day on the 16th both armies gathered at Sharpsburg, exchanging artillery fire across the valley of Antietam Creek. As Jackson's troops straggled in from Harpers Ferry, Lee posted his divisions along a north-south ridge behind Antietam Creek with both his flanks anchored on commanding ground near the Potomac River. In his front, three bridges crossed Antietam Creek, an upper bridge, about two and a half miles northeast of Sharpsburg, the middle bridge carrying the Boonsboro Turnpike, and a lower bridge just southeast of Sharpsburg. Lee chooses to defend only the lower bridge.

Instead of taking advantage with his superior strength—at midday on the 15th McClellan unknowingly had faced only 19,000 Confederates—McClellan spent the entire day of the 16th organizing his troops, allowing Lee valuable time to concentrate. Finally, at sunup on September 17, 1862, the Army of the Potomac launched its massive assault against Lee's outnumbered forces.

North of the David R. Miller cornfield is the western fringe of the North Woods, bounding the Hagerstown Pike on the west, and extending down toward the southwest into a pocket with limestone outcroppings. West of these woods lies Nicodemus Heights. One-half to three-quarters of a mile behind Nicodemus Heights is a meander bend in the Potomac River. Lee positions most of Jeb Stuart's cavalry there, along

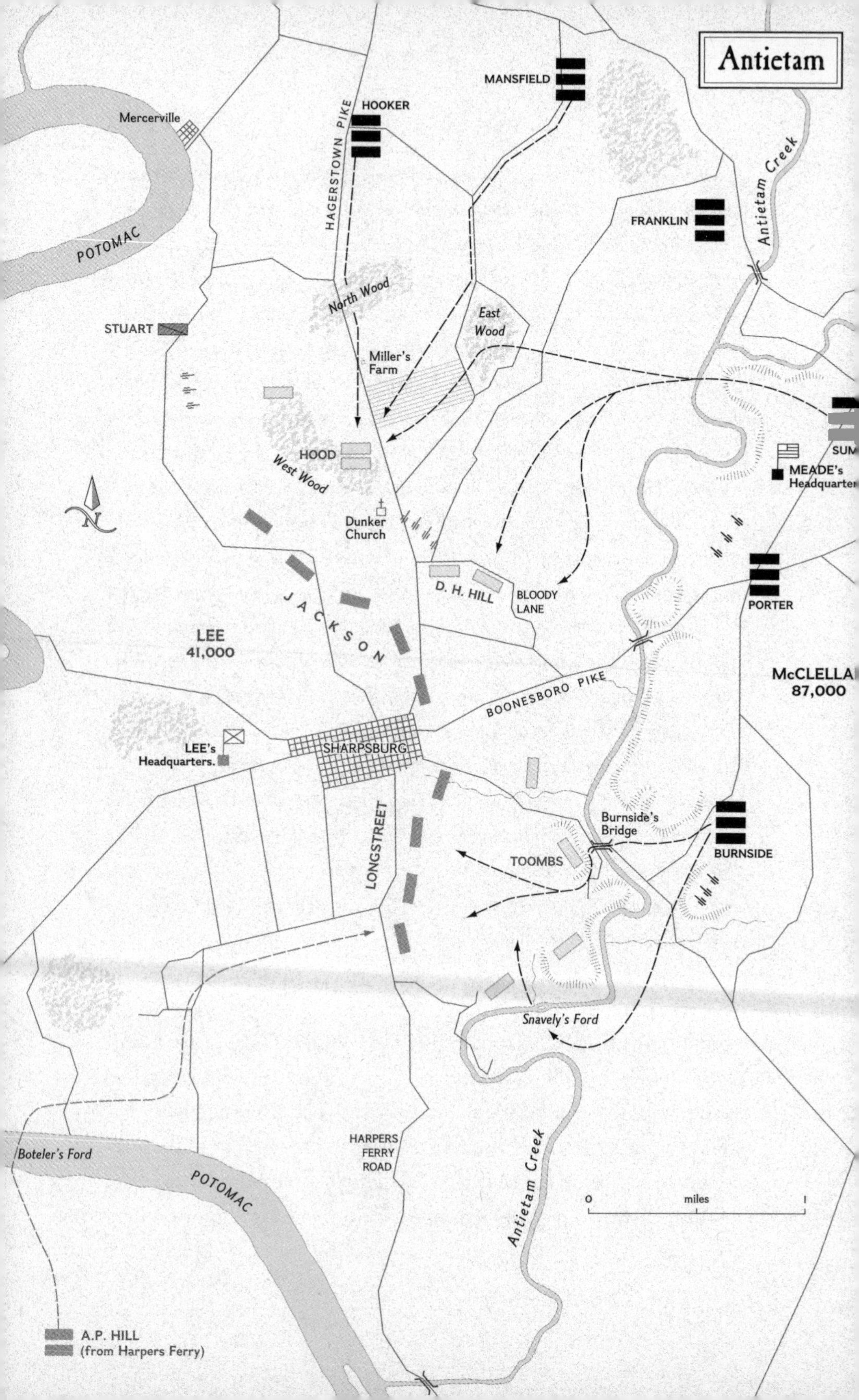

Antietam
MANSFIELD
HOOKER
Mercerville
HAGERSTOWN PIKE
FRANKLIN
Antietam Creek
POTOMAC
North Wood
East Wood
STUART
Miller's Farm
HOOD
West Wood
MEADE's Headquarters
Dunker Church
D. H. HILL
BLOODY LANE
PORTER
JACKSON
LEE 41,000
BOONESBORO PIKE
McCLELLA
87,000
LEE's Headquarters.
SHARPSBURG
Burnside's Bridge
TOOMBS
BURNSIDE
LONGSTREET
Snavely's Ford
HARPERS FERRY ROAD
Boteler's Ford
POTOMAC
Antietam Creek
0 miles 1
A.P. HILL
(from Harpers Ferry)

with the horse artillery, supported by Jubal Early's brigade. The Rebels have lots of manpower and artillery on Nicodemus Heights.

Jackson's wing holds the army's left. South of Miller's Cornfield, extending out about one-quarter of a mile northwest from West Woods, are the "Stonewall" and Capt. J. E. Penn's brigades, supported by two brigades, Col. James Jackson's and William E. Starke's. Together they constitute a division commanded by Brig. Gen. John R. Jones, one of six failed soldiers that Stonewall seems to push ahead in spite of their failings. On the east side of Hagerstown Pike from left to right are Cols. Marcellus Douglas's Georgia Brigade and James A. Walker's brigade—men of Georgia, Alabama, and North Carolina.

On the Union right is Maj. Gen. Joseph Hooker, directing the operations of the I Corps. His men are deployed north of Miller's Cornfield—soon to become "the Cornfield." His I Corps is the old III Corps, Army of Virginia, commanded by Irvin McDowell in the Second Manassas Campaign. McDowell had been relieved in the first week of September, and Hooker, new to corps command, leads the I Corps. The initial punch is going to be by the Yankee right, a haymaker powered by two corps pushing south and southwest and converging on a small white brick structure, the Dunker Church.

At 4 p.m. on September 16, the 13th Pennsylvania Reserves comes down the Smoketown Road and into the East Woods and skirmishes with John B. Hood's men. If Lee had any delusion about where General McClellan's opening blow will come, Hooker has tipped his hand. Maj.

OPPOSITE: *Lee posted his forces behind Antietam Creek west of Sharpsburg. McClellan attacked Lee's left at 6:15 a.m. with two corps, resulting in desperate fighting in the Cornfield and East Woods. By 9 a.m., assaults by a third Federal corps forced the Rebels back into the West Woods and around the Dunker Church. Later Federal assaults nearly broke through Lee's center in the Sunken Lane and fronting the Hagerstown Pike. By late afternoon Federal forces crossed the Lower Bridge and drove back Lee's right, only to be turned back by Confederate reinforcements arriving from Harpers Ferry.*

Gen. Joseph K. F. Mansfield forms up on the Smoketown Road, on the George Line Farm, a mile and a half to the left and rear of Hooker's position. It rains on the night of the 16th; it quits toward morning, and a ground fog blankets the area.

Hooker positions Brig. Gen. John Gibbon's brigade, which would receive its nom de guerre, the "Iron Brigade," in action at South Mountain, astride the Hagerstown Pike. Gibbon's Black Hats, as they are also known, are supported by Company B, Fourth U.S. Artillery. (Note that artillery units do not officially become "batteries" until after the Civil War.) Guiding on the Hagerstown Pike, they advance southward.

What Hooker should have done is send a strong force against Nicodemus Heights to drive Stuart and the horse artillery from there, but he does not. Advancing along the axis of the Smoketown Road, which converges with the Hagerstown Pike at the Dunker Church, is Brig. Gen. James B. Ricketts's division, spearheaded by Brig. Gen. Truman Seymour's brigade of Brig. Gen. George Gordon Meade's Second Division. Seymour, a member of the West Point class of 1846, will prove to be a better artist than a general. Meade's other two brigades are in reserve. Hooker's artillery opens fire. His command post is initially near Joseph Poffenberger's barn; aware of the value of public relations, he has several newspaper correspondents with him.

The attack opens shortly after 6 a.m. Seymour's brigade is supported by Ricketts's three brigades—Brig. Gen. Abram Duryee's, Col. William Henry Christian's, and Brig. Gen. George Lucas Hartsuff's. They advance through the East Woods, guiding on the Smoketown Road. If all goes well, they will crush Walker's Confederates and reach the Dunker Church. Brig. Gen. Abner Doubleday's I Corps, a division led by Gibbon's brigade, must smash the right of the Stonewall Division and the left of Douglas's Georgians, if they are to reach the Dunker Church. If the Yankees do so they will hold key ground that could give McClellan a great victory.

They've got the cornrows in front of them as they move forward through the fog, making them hard to see. Seymour's Federals pound

Walker's brigade. Two Confederate brigades rush to reinforce Walker. The Yankees punch their way forward, rolling back Walker. Gibbon's brigade, backed by Brig. Gen. Marsena R. Patrick and Col. Walter Phelps, assails the Stonewall Division. J. R. Jones, slightly wounded, heads for the rear and the Stonewall Division gives way. The bluecoats close to within 200 yards of Dunker Church. But then they're engulfed by Rebs when Brig. Gen. John Bell Hood counterattacks. Hood's people had not eaten a hot meal in more than 48 hours. They are called to battle from their cornpone and coffee and are as mad as hornets. Hood's division fans out as it storms ahead. The famed Texas Brigade led by Col. William Wofford surges into the western part of the Cornfield, while Hood's right wing—Col. Evander Law's brigade (Alabamians, Mississippians, and Tarheels)—sweeps the Yanks from the east side of the Cornfield and enters the East Woods. Among the Union casualties is General Hooker, shot in the foot.

Hooker's biggest mistake was not coordinating with Joseph Mansfield. Mansfield's men are eating breakfast when Hooker launches his attack. This is fatal for the Federals. If Mansfield had been closed on Hooker, Hood's savage surge into and through the Cornfield may have come to naught, because of the difference in manpower. Now, too late, Mansfield comes up. He is 58 years old, but looks as old as Moses with his white hair and beard. Up to two days before, he'd never held a major line command; he's been a senior staffer since 1853. Now he leads a corps.

The XII Corps includes a number of regiments that have never seen the "elephant." Brig. Gens. George H. Gordon's and Lt. Col. Hector Tyndale's brigades are exceptions, having experienced lots of fighting. They've given Stonewall Jackson hell in the Shenandoah Valley and at Cedar Mountain. Mansfield brings them forward by regimental column by company, a formation that has a narrow front and great depth. A soldier in the Tenth Maine likened the corps to a huge barn as it lurches ahead. They come under fire from soldiers on the high ground to their front. Mansfield, uncertain as to whether these people are friends or foes, rides forward to reconnoiter and is shot in the chest. He is taken to the Line Farm, but dies within 24 hours. Brig. Gen. Alpheus "Old Pop" S. Williams takes command of the XII Corps and sends Brig. Gen. George Sears Greene, 61 years old, down the Smoketown Road with two brigades. Taking over Williams's division is Brig. Gen. Samuel Wylie Crawford. A doctor at Fort Sumter, he had switched to the infantry, as he knows that if he stays a doctor his opportunities for promotion will be limited. Crawford, with his two brigades and Col. William B. Goodrich's of Greene's division, enters the East Woods and sweeps westward. There is savage fighting as the battle ebbs and flows through the East Woods and the Cornfield.

Gordon's brigade includes the Second Massachusetts, the Republican Harvard Regiment. In it is Capt. Robert Gould Shaw, who will eventually lead the 54th Massachusetts and die in the storied attack on Fort Wagner. Out in the Cornfield, Shaw is wounded. In another regiment, the 27th Indiana, is the tallest man in the Union Army. He's Capt. Richard Van Buskirk, 6 feet 11 inches, 225 pounds. When mustered in, Van Buskirk's Company F lists 35 of its 100 men as at least six feet tall and soon will be known as the "Giants in the Cornfield." (Coach Bobby Knight a century later may have found a few recruits for his "Fighting Hoosiers" in this regiment.) The struggle between Gordon's people and Hood's is particularly bitter, as photographs of the aftermath taken by Alexander Gardner on September 19 show.

By 9 a.m. Crawford's men are fought out. They cling to the Cornfield but they have taken frightful casualties. George Greene pushes ahead to within a short distance of the Dunker Church before he is pinned down.

Recognizing the grave Yankee threat to his left, Lee shuttles brigade after brigade into the battle, thinning out other parts of his line. It is a tactic he will practice all day. For now it works. With Hooker and Mansfield down, the Union attack on Jackson's wing responsible for holding the Rebel left stalls. About 9 a.m., after a brief lull in the fighting, the Federal II Corps crosses Antietam Creek planning to crush the Confederate left flank before wheeling south toward Sharpsburg.

The Union II Corps is commanded by Maj. Gen. Edwin Vose Sumner, who entered the Army as a lieutenant in 1819; he did not attend West Point. Sumner has the courage of a lion, but as a leader he commits his corps piecemeal and gets into even more trouble than McClellan does when the going gets tough. His men cross Antietam Creek at Pry's Ford.

The first Yankee division across is led by Connecticut bachelor "Uncle John" Sedgwick, a major general who plays solitaire and is popular with his soldiers. Unfortunately for the Union, Sumner accompanies Sedgwick. He does not stay behind to coordinate the movements of the remainder of his corps, the divisions of Brig. Gen. William "Old Blinkey" French and Maj. Gen. Israel B. Richardson. On the left of Sedgwick's division, marching by column as it approaches the East Woods, is Brig. Gen. Willis Gorman's brigade; on Gorman's right is a man who had to be a general, with a name like Napoleon Jackson Tecumseh Dana; and on the right is the Philadelphia Brigade led by the "Havelock" of the army, Brig. Gen. Oliver O. Howard. Sedgwick's people halt on entering the East Woods, form into line of battle, and face southwest toward the West Woods.

As they move out it is very quiet. Birds fly about willy-nilly—perhaps shell-shocked. Dead and wounded men, the human wreckage of several divisions, are scattered about the Cornfield. We'll rejoin Sedgwick's men when they enter the West Woods. General French is trailing Sedgwick by 20 to 30 minutes. French comes out of the woods, and he can't see where Sedgwick has gone. The north-south ridge—today's location of the visitor center and New York State Monument, constitutes a critical viewshed that separates French from Sedgwick as he crosses the Hagerstown Pike and enters the West Woods north of Dunker Church to meet death and destruction. Their formation invites disaster. They advance by successive brigades, the men in double ranks, elbow touching elbow, the files closers several steps behind the rear rank of each brigade.

Sedgwick's division marches across Hagerstown Pike into the West Woods, north of the Dunker Church.

We can see what the Federals are trying to accomplish by sending Sedgwick's division up the middle into the West Woods—on the far side of the woods is lower ground that extends south as far as Sharpsburg. Sedgwick's people are hemmed in by the woods. Trees in front of them, trees behind them, and trees to their left. Soon there will be Rebels in front of them, Rebels to their left, and Rebels swinging around to get into their rear. They're going to be a very uncomfortable bunch, and they will lose 2,200 men in 20 minutes, out of the 5,700-strong division.

Willis Gorman's men halt. In front of them, some 60 yards away, they see Confederates. Jubal Early's brigade has been rushed here and is posted in a wood road. Nearby is Brig. Gen. Harry T. Hays's Louisiana Tigers, already bloodied by their fight against the Union XII Corps. Gorman's men open fire. Fifty yards in back of them is Dana. Dana's bluecoats can't fire. If they do, they'll shoot into the backs of Gorman's people. Fifty yards behind Dana is Howard. Howard can't fire. Thousands of Yanks halted with only Gorman's brigade engaging the Confederates to their front.

Coming up from the south is Lafayette McLaws's division, with Brig. Gen. Joseph Kershaw's South Carolinians, Brig. Gen. Paul Jones Semmes's Georgians, and Brig. Gen. William Barksdale's Mississippians. McLaws's division had crossed the Potomac on the night of the 16th and was being held in reserve until rushed by General Lee to the point of danger. He is followed by Brig. Gen. John G. Walker's two-brigade division— sent from Lee's extreme right, near Snavely's Ford, where as yet Burnside's command is not a threat—and G.T. "Tige" Anderson's brigade. Sedgwick's men can't maneuver to cope with these Rebel reinforcements. The only Yankees who can fire at these newcomers are those on the left flank. How much more valuable it would have been if

Confederate dead lie scattered on the ground around the Dunker Church, a symbol of the bloody reality of the fighting at Antietam.

Sedgwick had a regiment moving in column on that flank. If so, that regiment could have halted and faced the newcomers.

Men in Howard's brigade panic and fire into Dana's to their front. Early in the fight, Sedgwick is wounded badly and has to leave the field. You can argue that the Yankees would have been better off if General Sumner had also been taken off the field instead of suffering a hand wound and remaining with his corps. Also wounded is Capt. Oliver Wendell Holmes, Jr., the future Supreme Court justice. What's left of Sedgwick's division flees into the West Woods, and as they do, the Confederates pursue. Unfortunately for the Confederates, the ever aggressive division led by George Greene and the artillery batteries of the I and XII Corps blast the advancing Rebels and turn back Kershaw's onrushing South Carolinians.

The next Yankee troops that appear just south of the West Woods at the Dunker Church are George Sears Greene's. Prior to Sedgwick's arrival there was a half-mile gap between Greene and the southwest corner of the Cornfield where Crawford's advance had stalled. Col. Stephen D. Lee's Rebel artillery battalion is initially positioned on a spur between today's visitor center and the Dunker Church. Greene and some of his men reach Dunker Church after Sedgwick has run into disaster. Greene is not reinforced and has to fall back in the face of a Rebel counterattack.

During the battle you see a major difference between Robert Lee's and McClellan's leadership style. Lee rides about the field. By 10 a.m., he is up near the Dunker Church, when a begrimed young private comes up and speaks to him. Lee does not recognize him until he exclaims, "Father, don't you know me? This is your son Rob!"

For much of the morning McClellan remains in and around his Philip Pry House headquarters. At times he goes up into the attic, stands on a barrel, and from that elevated height looks out the trapdoor to the roof. Other times he goes over to a fence where key staffers study distant battle actions on the far side of Antietam Creek through telescopes and binoculars. He crosses to the west side of the Antietam only once. There he meets and confers with his close friend and VI Corps commander, William B. Franklin. General Franklin, number one in the 1843 class of West Point, arrives from Pleasant Valley in time for W. S. Hancock's brigade to support Union guns that discourage the Confederates as they attempt to follow up the defeat of Sedgwick's division. Franklin goes to McClellan, which is strange because Franklin is also cautious. He urges McClellan to commit his VI Corps. Unfortunately for the Federals and fortunately for the Confederates, Sumner, known as the "Bull of the Woods," has not been wounded badly enough to be sent to the rear. He has been shocked and sickened by what has happened to Sedgwick's division. Sumner is pessimistic about the chances of Franklin's scoring any successes. In view of Sumner's attitude, McClellan decides it would be unwise to commit Franklin. Franklin's would be a good corps to be in because at veterans' reunions you could boast that you were at Antietam but were unlikely to be a casualty. Indeed only one of Franklin's six brigades, Col. William H. Irwin's,

After his success in forcing McClellan away from Richmond during the Seven Days campaign, Gen. Robert E. Lee took command of the forces he named the Army of Northern Virginia.

is seriously engaged, when late in the day the Seventh Maine is sent on a "mission impossible" to attack across the Sunken Road onto the Piper Farm, which is easily repulsed.

With Greene and Sedgwick thrown back, the combat on the Confederate left draws to a close. The next Union advance will be against the Confederate center. There the Confederate infantry are deployed facing north along a sunken farm road to the north and east of the Piper Farm.

When Maj. Gen. Daniel H. Hill's division arrives on the field, it is assigned to defend the Confederate center. Hill has five brigades. Initially, three of these advance northward and join in the fight for the East Woods. Col. Duncan McRae's and Brig. Gen. Roswell Ripley's people are hit hard, and they will be pulled out of the line; Col. Alfred Colquitt falls back to the Sunken Road. His brigade is on the left, Brig. Gen. Robert Rodes's Alabamians in the center, and Brig. Gen. George B. Anderson's North Carolinians on the right. Before the Union onslaught begins, Maj. Gen. Richard H. Anderson arrives with his division. Dick Anderson won't be here long: He's wounded. The Confederate artillery is on high ground in a cornfield behind and to the northwest of the Piper House overlooking the Sunken Road.

Sumner has lost control of his corps. He should have stayed at Pry's Ford and let Sedgwick run his show. When Sumner's Third Division under General French crosses Pry's Ford, there is no one there to tell him where to go. He veers south. In his southward march he crosses a ridge, and his right flank passes on either side of the fire-gutted Samuel Mumma House. He advances in the same formation as Sedgwick, by successive brigades, one behind the other. The Confederates in the Sunken Road (soon to become known as "Bloody Lane") throw down rail fences creating breastworks.

When French passes the Mumma House ridge he advances through a hollow and up a second rise. If you are with the Fifth Alabama in the Sunken Road, you will see the Yankees when they emerge from the hollow less than a hundred yards to your front. If your unit is the Sixth Alabama, you're on lower ground. The Yankees are going to be within 60 yards before you see them. The Sunken Road is a natural trench for the Confederates, but if the Yanks can gain and hold the high ground overlooking the right flank of the lane here—to Rodes's right and G. B. Anderson's left—the Rebs are going to be in deep trouble. The Sunken Road bends here and angles to the southeast; any Yankees on that rise can fire straight down a section of the lane. Bloody Lane is now packed with Reb infantry since four of Dick Anderson's brigades—

Known for some time as the "Young Napoleon," Maj. Gen. George McClellan is pictured fifth from the left with his staff officers.

Roger Pryor's, Carnot Posey's, Alfred Cummings's, and A. R. Wright's—have come forward through Piper's Cornfield and crowd into the Sunken Road. French's first two brigades, Brig. Gen. Max Weber's leading, trailed by Col. Dwight Morris's, don't fare well, but Nathan Kimball's combat veterans do. They seize the high ground and cling to it in spite of heavy casualties until midafternoon.

Sumner might as well have been on the moon for the command and control he is exercising over French and Richardson, his First Division commander. French attacks about 9:30 a.m., and by 11 a.m. he is stymied. Richardson's division crosses the Antietam an hour after French; he advances on French's left. But French has already been checked.

Richardson, an "old Army Man," was a farmer out in Michigan when the war began. The first of his brigades to reach the Roulette Farm is one that today enjoys much esteem: the Irish Brigade, led by Brig. Gen. Thomas Francis Meagher. An Irish revolutionist, he was sentenced to death by the Queen's Government in 1849, but world opinion resulted in his exile to Tasmania. He escaped and made his way to New York City. The Irish community has a strong militia organization in New York City, and Meagher fit in well. As the Civil War approached, the Irish looked forward to it as a way to get military experience. There were two New York Irish brigades, and many of their leaders, after the war, expected to invade and seize Canada as the first step toward the independence of Ireland. Michael Corcoran commanded one and Meagher the other. At Antietam, Meagher's Irish Brigade consists of the 63rd, 69th, and 88th New York. Also present is the 29th Massachusetts, a regiment of Protestants.

Another interesting person in the brigade is Father William Corby. He's the chaplain of the 88th New York. He will not hear confessions from anyone in the Bay State regiment. The Irish Brigade will be committed first. Richardson will do as Sumner does; he commits his brigades piecemeal.

Among the Confederates defending the Sunken Road is Col. John Brown Gordon of Georgia. He lives a long time, more than 30 years after the war. He has a faculty that everybody wishes they had but few do: He can remember conversations word for word. Gordon recalls that early that day, General Lee comes along; he speaks to Gordon and tells him that he must hold this position. Gordon replies, "We will be here 'til the sun goes down or victory is won." The Confederates have already repulsed French. Some of Kimball's men cling to the high ground. Meagher's brigade advances. Does Meagher lead his men? Whether he is drunk and falls off his horse or whether he is wounded in the fighting, no one will know. The right flank comes over the hill overlooking the Sunken Road. Meagher's men are armed with muzzle-loading smoothbore muskets with a range of about 75 yards. And for the next 30 minutes, the Irish Brigade battles the Sunken Road Confederates at point-blank range before pulling back.

The next brigade that comes up is Brig. Gen. John C. Caldwell's. It includes the Fifth New Hampshire, led by ex-sailor Col. Edward Cross. He's tough and always binds a red silk bandana around his bald head to shield it from the sun. Another of Caldwell's colonels is Francis Barlow, leading the 61st and the 64th New York. Barlow, a wealthy lawyer, looks like he buys his clothes from Goodwill Industries. He carries a very heavy sword for laying across the backside of slackers. Future general Nelson A. Miles, who was a 22-year-old clerk back in the Bay State when he joined the 22nd Massachusetts, is here as a lieutenant colonel. They gain the high ground overlooking an angle in the road adjacent to Roulette's Lane. From that ground they fire down into the Sunken Road. For the Confederates this section of the road becomes a death trap. From this time on the sunken farm road will be recalled as the Bloody Lane.

Gordon has a chance to make good on what he had earlier told General Lee. He's been wounded four times in his extremities. You always see the same side of Gordon's face in photographs today. Why? He takes a fifth bullet through the face and he falls. He is fortunate that he already has a bullet hole in his kepi too or he would have drowned in the welter of his blood.

With Gordon down, command passes to Lt. Col. James Lightfoot. It is a bad time for both Lightfoot and his fellow Confederates. Rodes now calls for Lightfoot to pull back his regiment's right two companies, so they can fire directly into Barlow's people ensconced on the high ground overlooking the Sunken Road. Lightfoot misunderstands him and shouts, About Face! Forward March! He and his Alabamians head back over the ridge toward the Piper House and barn. Col. Edwin Hobson of the Fifth Alabama looks to his right and sees the Sixth Alabama next to him, fleeing. Retreating in good order, I might add, because soldiers in their memories never flee. The Yankees punch a hole in the Rebel line into which rushes Col. John R. Brooke's brigade of Israel Richardson's division. The Federals pour

Confederate dead lie in the Bloody Lane in this photograph taken two days after the battle.

through and exploit the gap in the Rebel line. They reach Longstreet's headquarters at the Piper House. They are in the Piper barnyard and Piper Orchard.

Once again bold leadership turns the tide. There stands Longstreet. He has a badly blistered foot and is wearing a house slipper. He holds the horses of his staffers to enable them to help man cannon. D. H. Hill has picked up a rifle and has rallied several hundred infantrymen. Because of the heavy fire of the Confederate artillery, this small force of Confederate infantry slows the Yankees. Dick Richardson hastens to the rear to bring up artillery, and while directing the fire of one of his few supporting batteries, he is mortally wounded by a ball of spherical case shot, fired by a Rebel battery.

The Union surge is checked and turned back by the resolute stand of a handful of Confederates. Too much time passes before

Union Brig. Gen. Winfield Scott Hancock arrives to take command. Opportunity has knocked once again for the Confederates, and they have met the challenge.

As Union attacks on the Confederate left and center sputter to a halt, to the south of the Boonsboro Turnpike, southeast of Sharpsburg, Ambrose Burnside prepares for an assault against the Confederate right. To do so, however, his men will have to cross Antietam Creek under enemy fire from a brigade of Georgians stationed atop a wooded bluff just past the west bank of the creek. A single narrow stone bridge there offers a crossing point, but the cost will be fearful. Portions of Burnside's command probe southward, looking for another place to ford the creek; as they do so, Lee, with left and center mauled, wonders whether reinforcements will come from Harpers Ferry in time to shore up the line.

The Confederates have a brigade of Georgians watching the lower bridge. It is commanded by Brig. Gen. Robert Toombs, a bombastic drinker. A politician and former U.S. senator, his ambition is to be president of the Confederacy, but the best he gets in February 1861 is secretary of state. That's not a good position from which to be elected the second president of the Confederacy. He left the secretary of state position knowing that the American public frequently elects military heroes to their highest political office. He has little use for Robert E. Lee and other West Pointers. He has just been released from arrest for challenging a superior officer, and he wants success in a big battle, and then he will leave the army. He has three Georgia regiments and a handful of South Carolinians, 502 men, and two batteries of artillery, Capt. John L. Eubanks's Virginia Battery and a company of the Washington Artillery. They are on high ground west of the bridge. Initially guarding Snavely's Ford and the Rebel right is John G. Walker's division. About 9 a.m., with nothing happening at Snavely's Ford, Walker is sent north to West

Woods, and his arrival there helps spell disaster for "Uncle John" Sedgwick's division.

Burnside is charged with crossing Antietam Creek with the IX Corps. With Burnside commanding the Army of the Potomac's right wing, the IX Corps is commanded this day by Brig. Gen. Jacob Dolson Cox, a graduate of Oberlin. A Republican politician, a good soldier, he proves to be one of the North's best political generals. Four Union batteries, six guns in each, have neutralized the eight Confederate guns supporting Toombs. Confederate cannon on high ground southeast of Sharpsburg, however, can deliver an oblique fire down the valley of the Antietam.

Union Brig. Gen. Isaac Peace Rodman is a Quaker. He will take his division plus one brigade from the Kanawha Division led by Col. Hugh Ewing and seek to cross at a cattle ford downstream from the lower bridge. Hugh Ewing is a double relative of Maj. Gen. William Tecumseh Sherman. He is Sherman's foster brother and also his brother-in-law. He spent two years at West Point before he dropped out. Rodman is guided by a local farmer. But a ford where a farmer can cross cattle and one where Rodman can cross more than 5,000 men and artillery are quite different from one another. It will be noon before Rodman abandons his efforts to cross at the cattle ford and succeeds in crossing the Antietam at Snavely's Ford.

Meanwhile Burnside's first attack begins about 9:30 a.m. It is spearheaded by the 11th Connecticut, commanded by Col. Henry Kingsbury, a West Point graduate of the class of 1861. He had been an artillerist, but seeing that you only have limited advancement in the artillery, he switched to infantry and today leads the 11th Connecticut. His men advance and engage in a firefight with the Confederates. A few seek to wade the creek but are gunned down. Kingsbury is not as lucky as John Gordon: He'll be shot five times, and the fifth wound is fatal.

Toombs's Georgians are ensconced on the far side of the Antietam and in the woods extending 500 yards south. He also has men up above in a rock quarry. The banks are steep. Remember, if you wade the river think how slippery that steep bank becomes.

Col. George Crook commands the other brigade in the Kanawha Division. Crook is a West Pointer, a good friend of Brig. Gen. Philip H. Sheridan. Reaching the Antietam upstream, he fumbles around for about two hours before finally finding a crossing where he gets his men across by dribs and drabs.

Now it's eleven o'clock. McClellan is getting upset, and a staffer gallops up with another message for Burnside to hurry and get across. Burnside and Cox call for the next try, and this time nobody is going to miss the bridge. A column of two regiments, eight men abreast, will come up that road. These regiments are the Second Maryland and Sixth New Hampshire. Up the Rohersville Road advance the two regiments. On the other side of the Antietam, at a range of 50 to 60 yards, Toombs's Georgians open fire. To them it's like a shooting gallery, except the Georgians are playing for blood. Shot to pieces, the two regiments fall back. It's now twelve o'clock, and still Burnside's men have not crossed the Antietam. The Yankees advance two 10-pounder Parrott guns manned by Kentuckians to point-blank range of the Confederates. At a range of less than a hundred yards, Union red-legs fire double charges of canister into the brush on the hillside across the creek. Brig. Gen. Samuel G. Sturgis's division has been committed. Sturgis is another graduate of the West Point class of 1846. He is also colonel of the Seventh U.S. Cavalry Regiment when Lt. Col. George A. Custer leads it to destruction at the Little Bighorn, some 14 years in the future.

Sturgis goes to the commander of his second brigade, Col. Edward Ferrero, and asks for two regiments. Ferrero's father had been the dancing master at West Point, teaching social graces to the cadets. Ferrero had followed in his father's footsteps, but he had left that employment to become a power in New York City's Tammany Hall. He entered the Union

Shown from the Confederate perspective, "Burnside's Bridge" over Antietam Creek is where Ambrose Burnside sent regiment after regiment across the creek in an attack on Lee's right flank.

Army as colonel of the 51st New York. Ferrero has recently suspended the sutler's license to vend alcoholic beverages to the men in his brigade. He picks the two regiments ordered to secure the bridge at the point of the bayonet. They are the 51st Pennsylvania commanded by Col. John F. Hartranft and the 51st New York led by Col. Robert Potter. A 51st Pennsylvania corporal, miffed at Ferrero's support of prohibition, calls, "Will you give us our whiskey, Colonel, if we take it? Colonel, do we get our whiskey?" Ferrero, being a good politician, used to promising everything, responds, "Yes, by God!"

It has been a mistake to send men up the Rohersville Road that parallels the creek's bank leading to the bridge. So when the two regiments attack, they're going to form on the reverse side of a ridge that will shield them from Toombs's riflemen until the last minute. The color companies are aligned to strike the head of the bridge.

At a little after the noon hour the signal goes out to advance. Coming down that slope, eight abreast, the two regiments close on the bridge. Soldiers of the 51st New York veer off to the right to reinforce the 11th Connecticut behind the upstream stone wall. The 51st Pennsylvania along with the New Yorkers' color guard are the first across the bridge. Worse, if possible, Toombs's Rebels have learned that Rodman's men are crossing downstream at Snavely's Ford and will soon be taking them in the flank and rear. The Yankees are now over the Antietam, but there are more problems. Ferrero and Brig. Gen. James Nagle's brigades are short of ammunition. There's another pause of an hour while they recall Sturgis's men to the east side of the Antietam to refill cartridge boxes. Burnside then pushes Brig. Gen. Orlando Willcox's First Division across. Willcox deploys his men and, when ready to advance, he forms the right of Burnside's IX Corps.

After a lengthy delay, about 3 p.m., Burnside's forces attack the Confederates holding the ridge to the west of what forever after will be known as Burnside's Bridge. They advance toward Sharpsburg, pushing Rebs back into the outskirts of town—Federal soldiers see the church spires ahead. Just before they reach the road to Harpers Ferry, however, General Lee sights Ambrose Powell Hill, adorned in his red battle shirt, leading his Confederates forward to save the day for the Army of Northern Virginia. He had left Harpers Ferry about 6:30 that morning, and his men had been marching hard all day. Hill immediately hurls his 3,000 men at the advancing Federals. James J. Archer's and Laurance O'Branch's brigades slam into and maul the Ninth New York, a Zouave regiment. General Rodman is mortally wounded. When Confederate troops under Brig. Gen. Maxcy Gregg smash into the Federal left, the inexperienced brigade of Col. William Harland breaks. Under increasing Rebel pressure, Cox orders a withdrawal of the IX Corps back to Antietam Creek.

After Burnside is repulsed, his troops fall back into the hollows on the west side of the Antietam. Pulling back into a hollow above the bridge

Union soldiers stand watch over the grave of Federal soldier John Marshall on a hill near the West Woods. More than 23,000 soldiers were killed, wounded, or captured at Antietam.

is the 23rd Ohio. Its commander, Rutherford B. Hayes, had been wounded at South Mountain three days previously, so he is not here. William McKinley is. So after the repulse, McKinley, commissary sergeant of the 23rd Ohio, serves the Buckeyes coffee. It's quite a regiment, with two future Presidents. William Starke Rosecrans had been the original colonel. In it had served a future judge of the Supreme Court, Stanley Matthews.

The final denouement comes later, when Edward Ferrero is promoted to brigadier general. The next time his command is in formation Cpl. Lewis Patterson cries out, "Where's our whiskey? How about that whiskey?" Remembering his promise, Ferrero rescinds his suspension of the sale of alcoholic beverages.

The day's final Union surge is checked and turned back by a resolute stand by a handful of Confederates and Hill's timely arrival. By sundown more than 23,000 Union and Confederate soldiers are casualties in what had become the bloodiest day in American history.

McClellan declined to renew his offensive on the 18th, and Lee remained in position on the blood-soaked battlefield. After a truce to bury the dead and collect the wounded, Lee ordered a withdrawal back across the Potomac, downstream from Shepherdstown. McClellan did not press a pursuit.

While Antietam had not been a complete Federal victory, Lee's incursion into the North had been decisively turned back. Five days after Antietam, taking advantage of the Union victory, Abraham Lincoln issued his preliminary Emancipation Proclamation. Unless Confederates returned to the Union in the next hundred days, Lincoln announced, he would declare all slaves who resided in areas controlled by the Confederacy free as of January 1, 1863. The war to save the Union was now also the war to free the slaves.

1863

In search of a decisive victory for the South, General Robert E. Lee focused on the town of Gettysburg, Pennsylvania, in late June of 1863. Devil's Den, a known picnicking and trysting spot, saw vicious fighting over the course of the battle as sharpshooters and snipers fired from the nooks and crannies around large stones, upon which they bestowed nicknames such as Table, Breadloaf, and Bathtub. In what would be the bloodiest battle of the war, Lee lost 40 percent of his army, 28,000 men; Meade lost 25 percent, 23,000. Though a disheartening defeat, the Confederates achieved a deep advance into Union territory in an hour-long attack during which Gen. George Pickett's, Gen. Johnston Pettigrew's, and Gen. Isaac Trimble's divisions lost two-thirds of their men.

5

CHANCELLORSVILLE

APRIL 30. 1863–MAY 6, 1863

After many costly and futile attempts to drive the Confederates from their positions behind the Rappahannock River at the Battle of Fredericksburg in mid-December 1862, Maj. Gen. Ambrose Burnside struggled for a month to renew the offensive. In late January 1863, Burnside attempted to flank General Lee from his positions around Fredericksburg with a march along the Rappahannock upstream of the city, only to have his hopes literally sink into the mud when his marching columns were thwarted by heavy rains. With subordinates openly questioning his competence, Burnside called for widespread removals; Lincoln did indeed respond by authorizing several changes, but the most important was the replacement of Burnside as commander of the Army of the Potomac by Maj. Gen. Joseph Hooker. Brash and egotistical, but well known for his fighting spirit, Hooker nevertheless was determined to restore luster to the Army of the Potomac. He reorganized the army's supply system, providing rations of fresh bread and meat, and through a combination of furloughs, reorganizations, and drills brought the once disheartened army back into prime fighting condition. As spring came, he prepared to take the offensive against Lee and a somewhat weakened Army of Northern Virginia. He outnumbered his opponent by two to one.

As an army commander, Joseph Hooker plans brilliantly. His plan is to force Lee to either retreat or come out of his Fredericksburg defenses and engage him on ground of Hooker's choice. To achieve this objective, he sends Maj. Gen. George W. Stoneman's cavalry corps out on a raid on April 27. Hooker then will swing westward around Lee's position with three corps as a force of maneuver. These are the V Corps commanded by Maj. Gen. George Gordon Meade, the XI Corps led by Maj. Gen. Oliver O. Howard, and the XII Corps commanded by Maj. Gen. Henry Slocum. The three corps, a third of Hooker's force, leave their camps behind Stafford Heights, north of Fredericksburg, on the morning of April 27. They march up the Rappahannock River and cross it at Kelly's Ford, about 20 miles upriver from their camps. General Hooker, with part of his headquarters, accompanies the column of maneuver. Remaining behind at Falmouth is his chief of staff, Maj. Gen. Daniel Butterfield. Hooker leaves four infantry corps behind, opposite Fredericksburg. Two of these infantry corps, the I and the VI, cross the Rappahannock on the 29th at and below Franklin's Crossing, the site below town where Burnside's left wing crossed the Rappahannock during the Fredericksburg campaign. This force demonstrates in front of the Confederates to divert Lee's attention away from the corps executing the turning movement.

The II and III Corps remain in position behind Falmouth, ready to march when the three corps that cross the river at Kelly's Ford reach the Confederate rear. Once Hooker crosses the Rappahannock at Kelly's Ford, he will march two corps to Germanna Ford and one to Ely's Ford, both on the Rapidan River, a major tributary of the Rappahannock. The three corps will then advance through the Wilderness, toward the key road junction at Chancellorsville. When they accomplish the march to Chancellorsville, they will uncover U.S. Ford, on the Rappahannock, three miles downstream from Ely's Ford. This will reduce the distance that the II and III Corps will have to march to join them. Thus, while Stoneman and most of his cavalry are on a deep penetration raid, aimed at destroying vital railroads in Lee's rear, three corps will turn the Confederate left, two corps are hidden and ready to cross at U.S. Ford when Hooker has seized Chancellorsville, and the remaining two corps are to keep Lee's attention focused on his Fredericksburg front.

As soon as the infantry crosses the Rapidan River, Hooker arrives from Falmouth. He will travel with Meade. Everything is moving smoothly, and the plan is working. By April 30 Slocum and Howard are south of the Rapidan River at Germanna Ford with Slocum out in front, five miles upstream from Ely's Ford. They march down the Germanna Plank Road toward its intersection with the Orange Turnpike at the Wilderness Tavern. By early afternoon the three corps converge on Chancellorsville. Meanwhile Maj. Gen. John Sedgwick's VI Corps and Maj. Gen. John F. Reynolds's I Corps are positioned along the Richmond Stage Road.

What is Lee's situation? The Confederate army that fought at Fredericksburg in December 1862 is larger than the army Lee will take to Gettysburg. But since the Battle of Fredericksburg, he has detached three divisions. Near Fredericksburg, Lt. Gen. Thomas "Stonewall" Jackson commands four divisions. He still has Maj. Gen. A. P. Hill's Light Division. A second division commander, Brig. Gen. Raleigh Colston, a Jackson favorite, may be a good French teacher at VMI, but as a replacement for the transferred Brig. Gen. William B. Taliaferro he does not measure up. Maj. Gen. Jubal Anderson Early and Brig. Gen. Robert Rodes, both capable veterans, lead Jackson's two other divisions.

At the Battle of Fredericksburg, Lt. Gen. James Longstreet led the largest corps of the Army of Northern Virginia, composed of five divisions. Lee now has only two of Longstreet's divisions, Maj. Gen. Richard Anderson's and Maj. Gen. Lafayette McLaws's. Longstreet has been sent off with his other divisions to southern Virginia and North Carolina to gather "hog and hominy" and to watch the Yankees who occupied Suffolk, a town to the west of Norfolk. Hooker is aware of their absence, and he knows that they can't return in time to participate in the next battle. Lee's army numbers about 60,000 soldiers, about half the troop strength available to Hooker.

In anticipation of the conflict to come at Chancellorsville, Virginia, soldiers of the 1st New York Light Artillery prepare for inspection of their bronze 12-pounder Napoleon cannon.

By the evening of April 30, the Federals have three corps in and around the Chancellorsville crossroads. Most of the army's cavalry, under Stoneman, are beyond contact far to the southwest, in Louisa County. It will be the night of May 1–2 before General Reynolds's I Corps will recross to the north side of the river, leaving only Sedgwick's people south of the Rappahannock. On the afternoon of the 30th, Maj. Gen. Darius N. Couch, the ranking corps commander, having marched from Stafford Heights with two of his three II Corps divisions, crosses the Rappahannock at U.S. Ford and closes on Chancellorsville. Close behind is Maj. Gen. Daniel E. Sickles's III Corps. This leaves for the time being at Falmouth only Brig. Gen. John Gibbon's II Corps division.

Hooker has stolen a march on Lee, placing the Confederate commander where his foe wanted him. It looked so when three Federal infantry corps, with two close behind, moved into position at Chancellorsville, named after the Chancellor Tavern located there.

The Chancellor Tavern grew in stages. The center section is late 18th century; two wings were added in 1815, with an addition to the rear built in 1840. Chancellorsville is the home of a widow, Mrs. Sanford Chancellor, and her seven children. Six of them are unmarried daughters. The house serves as a home and a tavern, since it is one day's ride in a heavily loaded wagon out of Fredericksburg. It's a nice place for a good time and a headquarters.

Why is this a key point? Chancellor Tavern is near the eastern edge of the Wilderness, a 12-square-mile region of cutover scrub timber and impenetrable thickets, with scattered farms. The Ely's Ford Road comes in from upper Culpeper County across the Rapidan. Coming from the southeast is the Orange Plank Road, from the east is the Orange Turnpike, a macadamized road. And then there's the River Road. It goes out in a northeasterly direction, parallels the Rappahannock River, and enters Fredericksburg, less than ten miles away.

When Hooker gets here on the afternoon of April 30, there is lots of daylight left. But Hooker decides to wait until morning. He is going to telegraph and also send by messenger an order directing General Butterfield, who is back at Falmouth, to expedite the march of Couch's and Sickles's corps to Chancellorsville. Hooker is on a high. Addressing his staff and other officers back in March, he had said that General Lee has but two options: either to evacuate his position at Fredericksburg and flee ingloriously toward Richmond or come out of his earthworks and attack him. "My plans are perfect, and when I start to carry them out, may God have mercy on General Lee, for I will have none."

The Federals on the morning of May 1 advance along three roads. Meade, with two divisions, takes the River Road. The River Road's disadvantage is that it follows along the river. It is a dirt track and has a lot

Maj. Gen. Joseph Hooker (seated second from right), commander of the Army of the Potomac, poses with his staff in this 1863 portrait.

more ups and downs in it than the other two roads. The divisions accompanying Meade are led by "Old Goggle Eye," Brig. Gen. Andrew A. Humphreys. People always ask, "Who has the most expletive-deleted vocabulary in the Army of the Potomac, Winfield Scott Hancock or Humphreys?" Hancock undoubtedly wins because he has a louder voice. Perhaps Humphreys is more original in his profanity, because he can spit out a long string of oaths and never use them again in the same combination. Brig. Gen. Charles Griffin is also a contender.

Moving out in the center of the turnpike is only one division. It seems strange that Meade sends only one division along the Orange Turnpike. This division is commanded by Maj. Gen. George Sykes and is composed of the army's two Regular brigades and a brigade of volunteers. Headed out the Orange Plank Road to the southeast is General Slocum with his two XII Corps divisions, led by Brig. Gen. Alpheus "Old Pop" Williams and Brig. Gen. John W. Geary. Stationed in this area in reserve is General Howard's XI Corps, strung out along the Orange Turnpike from Chancellorsville to a point just west of the Wilderness Church.

Arriving here at mid-morning will be Couch with two divisions, that of hard-drinking Maj. Gen. William H. "Old Blinkey" French and that of Maj. Gen. Winfield Scott Hancock "the Superb." Soon thereafter Sickles's III Corps comes up. By the time they arrive here the situation has changed. Having boldly seized the initiative and stolen a march on Lee, Hooker will soon lose his nerve and go over to the defensive.

By the evening of April 29, Lee is alerted to Hooker's river crossings and flanking maneuvers, and he prepares to shift his forces in response. Lee orders the two divisions under his control—Anderson's and McLaws's—each less a brigade, to advance along the Orange Turnpike to determine the Yankees' intentions. Lee directs Jackson to begin a march toward Zoan Church, a little more than five miles west on the Orange Turnpike. On May 1, Jackson moves out at 2 a.m. from his camps around Hamilton's Crossing southeast of Fredericksburg. When Jackson marches, Jubal Early, along with Brig. Gen. William Barksdale's Mississippi Brigade of McLaws's division, remains behind with five brigades—about 10,000 men—to hold the stone wall fronting Marye's Heights and the earthworks on commanding ground southeast of Fredericksburg, These earthworks are far more impressive than they were in mid-December 1862 when Burnside repeatedly assaulted them to no avail, because the Confederates have had all winter to work on them.

It is late morning when Jackson arrives at the Zoan Church, and in accordance with Lee's discretionary orders, he seizes the initiative. He sends Brig. Gen. Ambrose Ransom Wright's brigade of Georgians, part of Anderson's division, along the unfinished railroad grade that is south and parallel to the Orange Plank Road. On Wright's right, Brig. Gen. Carnot Posey's Mississippians engage Slocum's vanguard as it approaches via the Plank Road. The divisions of Jackson's corps, led by Rodes, press westward along the Plank Road in support of Posey. Jackson then advances the remaining three brigades of Anderson's division, along with the brigades of McLaws's division, via the turnpike.

As Meade feels his way along the River Road, he hears firing off to his right and rear, causing concern. Slocum continues to advance, with "Rans" Wright's Georgians on his flank about a half mile to the south and moving toward his rear. The Confederates seize the initiative and press back Sykes's division on the turnpike east of Chancellorsville. So what does Sykes do? He sends a message back to Hooker, cautioning that he has encountered the foe, and asking for instructions. Arriving at Hooker's headquarters about now is General Sickles and the III Corps. He is told to position his people on Hazel Grove, key open high ground southwest of Chancellorsville.

Hooker now sends orders for Sykes to suspend his advance and pull back into the Wilderness. Sykes is not happy with the order since he feels that he is in a good position to face the Rebels, and as he pulls back, he runs into Hancock, who has reached Chancellorsville and is hastening east on the turnpike to his assistance. Being aggressive, Hancock favors moving forward. A message goes back to headquarters questioning the decision to withdraw. The reply comes from Hooker reiterating the order for both Hancock and Sykes to pull back. As they begin to withdraw, there's a change of mind at Hooker's headquarters, but by the time Hancock and Sykes get these orders to countermarch, they have given up the high ground on either side of the turnpike at the edge of the Wilderness.

Hardly do Hooker's men reach Chancellorsville than you hear the thud of axes; Hooker has pulled back into a strong position and is entrenching and throwing up breastworks, inviting Lee to attack him. Meade digs in behind Mineral Spring Run with his left anchored on the Rappahannock. Couch's two II Corps divisions cover Chancellorsville; on their right is Slocum's XII Corps, with Sickles's III Corps and Howard's XI Corps extending the line westward past the Wilderness Church as far as the Talley Farm.

The XI Corps has severe communication problems between Howard and at least two of his three division commanders and four of the six

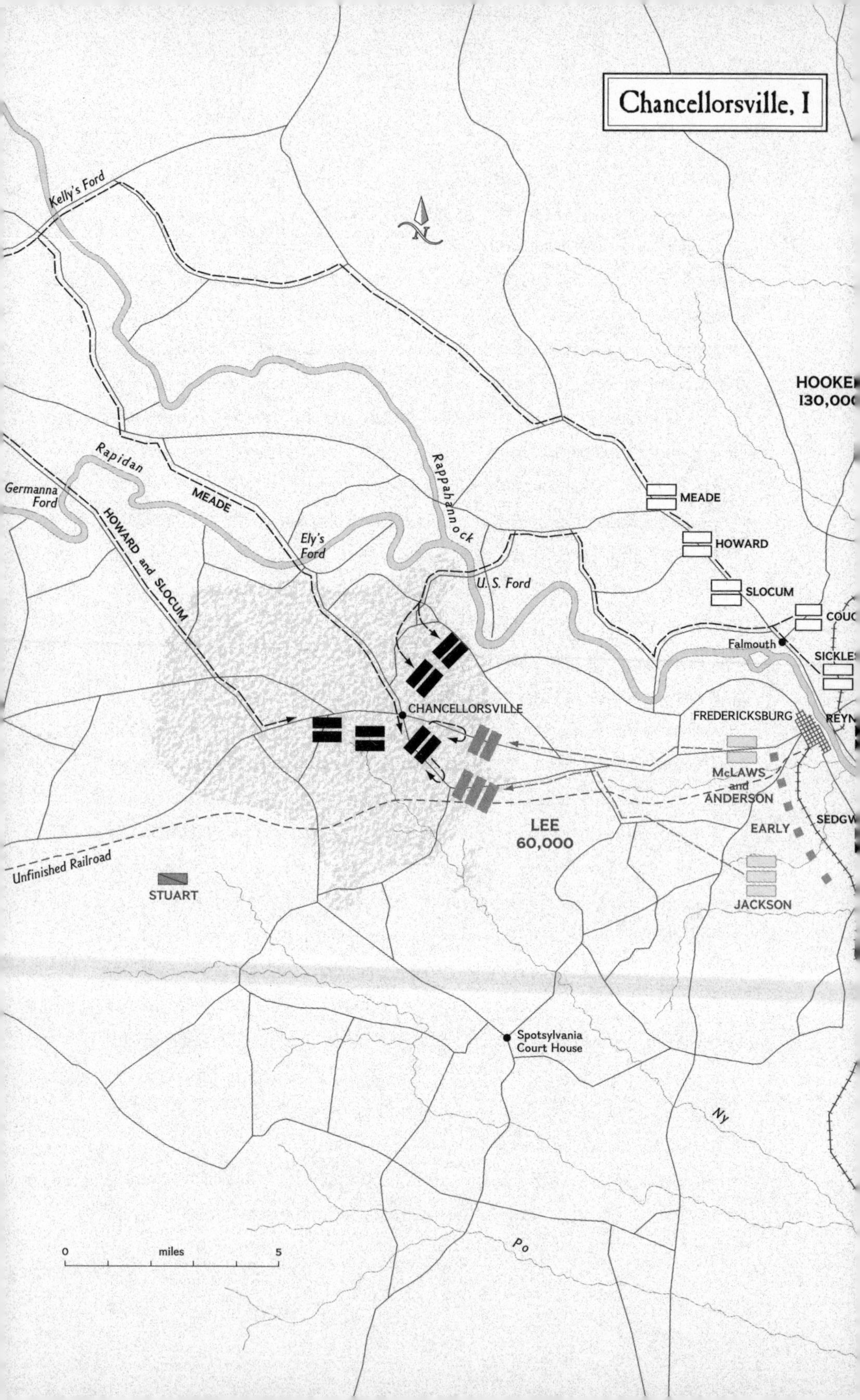
Chancellorsville, I
Kelly's Ford
Germanna Ford
Rapidan
MEADE
HOWARD and SLOCUM
Ely's Ford
Rappahannock
U. S. Ford
MEADE
HOWARD
SLOCUM
COUC
SICKLES
Falmouth
HOOKE
130,000
CHANCELLORSVILLE
FREDERICKSBURG
REYN
McLAWS and ANDERSON
SEDGW
EARLY
LEE
60,000
JACKSON
Unfinished Railroad
STUART
Spotsylvania Court House
Ny
Po
0
miles
5

brigade commanders. Many of the corps' soldiers are of German descent—most of whose first language is German. Prior to Howard's replacement of Maj. Gen. Franz Sigel as corps commander, they had boasted and sung lustily, "I'm going to fight mit Sigel."

Hooker has taken up a strong defensive position except for his right flank, which is neither refused nor posted behind a natural obstacle. By now Maj. Gen. James Ewell Brown Stuart's cavalry is roaming unopposed through the Wilderness.

Lee, an experienced engineer, reconnoiters the Union defenses, searching for a means to turn the enemy's left. There is no way to do so. Not only is the Union Army entrenched on that flank behind Mineral Spring Run, but it is an imposing physical barrier anchored on the Rappahannock River. Lee then reconnoiters Hooker's center, and, having heard the thud of axes, realizes that an attack here would be a mistake. Soon Jeb Stuart arrives in camp. He has been reconnoitering the Union right and discovers that the XI Corps' flank "is in the air." The Reverend B. Tucker Lacy, whose brother owns Ellwood Plantation, is familiar with the area, including the Brock Road near the Union right flank. He does not, however, know all the roadways in the area between Lee's campsite and the Union flank. The Confederates must find someone familiar with the road network in the Catherine Furnace area. Catherine Furnace is operated by Charles C. Welford, whose son, Charlie B., is 17 years old.

OPPOSITE: *Leaving a force facing Fredericksburg, Hooker sent three army corps to cross the upper fords of the Rappahannock and Rapidan Rivers to force Lee out of Fredericksburg. On April 29, realizing that his flank had been turned, Lee divided his army, leaving troops at Fredericksburg, and raced west to meet Hooker's advance. After an engagement near the Zoan Church on May 1, Hooker withdrew to Chancellorsville. On May 2, Lee divided his army once again, sending Jackson across the front of the Federal position to attack the exposed Union right flank. Attacking in the evening, Jackson's men routed the Federals along the Orange Turnpike, but darkness stopped the Confederate advance.*

Robert E. Lee holds a military conference at the intersection of the Orange Plank and Catherine Furnace Roads. Fitz Lee, Tucker Lacy, and Charlie Welford are present. General Lee asks, "How can we get to those people?" Lee usually referred to the enemy as "those people." Reverend Lacy outlines the road network that he knows. Charlie Welford says that there are wood roads in the vicinity of Catherine Furnace. Is a strike at the Union right practicable? Lee asks. The answer is yes.

Lee asks Jackson, "What do you propose to do?" Jackson answers, "Go around here," and he traces on a map with his finger the route he proposes to keep on. Lee then inquires about how many men Jackson will take with him on his march around the Union Army. Lee's blood must have run cold when Jackson replied, "My whole corps"—some 29,000 men in the divisions of Robert Rodes, Raleigh Colston, and A. P. Hill. What does that leave Lee? It leaves him two understrength divisions, some 14,000 men, and 24 cannon. As you remember, Barksdale's brigade of McLaws's division has been left with General Early back at Fredericksburg, and Brig. Gen. Cadmus M. Wilcox's brigade of Anderson's division is watching Banks's Ford. Still, Lee agrees with Jackson's plan.

Earlier, as they sat around the campfire, Jackson was in some discomfort. Jackson had a bad cold, incipient pneumonia. So he lay down on the ground to get some sleep, and staffer Capt. Sandie Pendleton came along and covered him with his coat. Jackson had laid his sword and scabbard up against a tree; during the night the sword and scabbard fell with a clatter. At the time, Jackson's staff thought nothing of it, but later on, as A. L. Long, Lee's aide, recalled this incident, he felt that it had a sinister meaning: the symbolic falling of the sword prefiguring the fall of their illustrious leader.

As the night passes, the Union forces continue to entrench; the Confederates also throw up earthworks. McLaws's and Anderson's divisions have a desperate mission: To rivet Hooker's attention on them while Jackson makes his famous, and last, flank march.

In the morning hours of May 2 the Confederates break camp. Jackson does not begin his march at daybreak. He moves out around 7:20 a.m. Jackson has Col. Tom Munford's Second Virginia Cavalry out in front, another VMI man. Then the divisions of Rodes, Colston, and, last but not least, A. P. Hill come in succession. The road is narrow, and Jackson is going to be moving in the neighborhood of 29,000 men. He will march 50 minutes followed by 10 minutes rest. Add a column of 108 cannon, each gun with its limber and six horses or mules and the accompanying limber and caisson with its horses. It will take four to five hours for the column to pass a given point, with stops and starts giving the column the action of an accordion: Men at the front of the column will, as old soldiers well know, march at a certain pace, and the men at the rear of the column will be double-timing to keep up.

As Jackson's men commence their march, Union forces posted near Hazel Grove, one of the few clearings in the vicinity, peer through an opening in the woods and spot their departure.

The Confederates come marching down the Catherine Furnace Road with Munford's cavalry out front. Up on Hazel Grove is General Sickles's headquarters along with his chief of artillery, Capt. George Randolph. As they look out in this direction, lo and behold, what do they see? They sight a Confederate column, seemingly endless, moving along the Catherine Furnace Road. Sickles notifies General Hooker about what he has seen, and a battery of rifled artillery (ten-pounder Parrotts) is put in position to shell the Confederate column. When he is notified, Hooker is not worried because the Catherine Furnace Road heads south and west. Hooker has said that Lee has but two alternatives: either come out of his defenses and attack, or ingloriously flee. So it looks to him like his plan is working and Lee is retreating.

The Confederates are not too concerned as they come under artillery fire, because a single shot could only strike one man and would do little other damage. The Confederate infantry double-time across this opening in the woods. But what about the 108 cannon, 216 limbers, 108 caissons, and the ambulances? What do they do? Having young Charlie Welford with them is a godsend, because he is familiar with the location of all the local wood roads. There is a parallel road east of the Catherine Furnace Road. The horse-drawn vehicles and wagons use that road, which is hidden deep in the timber.

Sickles, with permission from Hooker, sends two divisions in pursuit of the Confederates. His remaining division, Hooker's old III Corps division now under Maj. Gen. Hiram Berry, is held in reserve. One of Howard's six brigades, Brig. Gen. Francis C. Barlow's, reinforces Sickles in the "pursuit" toward and beyond Catherine Furnace. Accompanying Barlow's brigade is XI Corps commander Howard. By the time Sickles's vanguard reaches Catherine Furnace, the last of Jackson's column has moved through the area. In an attempt to discourage and distract this Union force, Lee sends Posey's brigade to threaten and harass Sickles's left flank near Catherine Furnace.

As Jackson marches, the Yankees are in hot pursuit. They drive the 23rd Georgia back to the unfinished railroad grade; it puts up stiff resistance, but is overwhelmed. In response, Jackson detaches two brigades from A. P. Hill's division to slow down the Yankees. One can imagine the reports that Hooker is receiving at his headquarters. Howard and Sickles are excited about pursuing the retreating Confederates as they press on toward the southwest and the Brock Road, their vanguard skirmishing with the Rebs' rear guard. All appears to be going well for the Union as the Confederates seemingly seek to escape the area. Throughout the morning and into the early afternoon, Jackson's column snakes through the woods, headed for the Union right.

The total march is 12 miles. It was not a particularly fast march. As the head of the column reaches the intersection of the Brock and Orange Plank roads, more than three miles southwest of Chancellorsville, at 1:45 p.m., Fitz Lee rides up and says he wants Jackson to come with him to see something interesting. Up to this time, Jackson's plan is to turn his column into the Plank Road, deploy his men, and attack up the axis of the Orange Plank Road. He orders Rodes to halt his men; this will allow the other troops to close up.

Then Jackson and Fitz Lee ride down the Orange Plank Road about a mile and a quarter until they reach the Burton Farm. North of the Burton House is high ground from where you can see the Talley Farm fields and the Orange Turnpike where Howard's XI Corps has halted and camped. Cooks and butchers have strung up beef and are busy preparing meals for the men. Troops are strolling around the camps, their arms stacked, playing cards and doing whatever troops do when they are off duty. Jackson sees that if he deploys his men to attack up the Plank Road he will strike the enemy head-on. He recognizes that if he is to launch a devastating flank attack it cannot be along the axis of the Plank Road. Fitz Lee says that Jackson becomes concerned about what he has seen at this point, and he turns his horse and rides excitedly off the high ground. He is in such a hurry that onlookers fear he will pitch forward out of the saddle and over Little Sorrel's head.

He returns to the Brock–Orange Plank Road intersection and writes his last message to General Lee. He states that "the enemy has made a stand at [Melzi] Chancellor's which is about [two] miles from Chancellorsville," and that his column is well closed up. He concludes by saying that with the help of "an ever kind Providence," he hopes to achieve a great victory. He dates the dispatch as near 3 p.m., and the courier gallops off.

Jackson then turns his attention to Rodes and orders him to continue up the Brock Road. He orders Colston to detach the Stonewall Brigade from his division. He sends it down the Plank Road along with the Second Virginia Cavalry to guard against the Yankees, who may advance a column down the road toward the Brock Road intersection.

It is not until late afternoon that Jackson reaches his new destination astride the Orange Turnpike just west of the XI Corps position. Oliver Otis Howard's men are posted parallel to and north and south of the turnpike. They are not entrenched, other than with a few crude piles of cut timber and fence rails. Even if Jackson's attack had come from the southwest along the Orange Plank Road as planned, the Confederates would not have encountered any breastworks. But to strike Howard's flank, Jackson determined that the additional two-and-a-half-mile march was warranted, even though he will need several more hours to get his men positioned, ready to attack.

Now, let's look at the Union side. Col. Leopold von Gilsa's brigade has two regiments facing west astride the Orange Turnpike. On the right is the 54th New York and on the left is the 153rd Pennsylvania, good German lads. Von Gilsa's two other regiments—the 41st and 45th New York—are posted parallel to the turnpike facing south. Two cannon at the angle are sighted west. The regiments looking west number less than 700 men.

On the left of von Gilsa is Col. Nathaniel McLean's brigade. When the fighting begins, two of his five regiments—the 25th and 75th Ohio—redeploy at right angles from their original alignment along the turnpike and face west. Along the turnpike to the left of McLean are the brigades of Col. W. Krzyzanowski and Brig. Gen. Alexander Schimmelfennig. The men of these brigades have stacked arms and are milling about enjoying themselves. To the left and east of these two brigades is Col. Adolphus Buschbeck's brigade. This brigade will end up the savior of XI Corps, because it will have time to deploy perpendicular to the turnpike before the Confederates are upon them.

Col. John C. Lee of the 55th Ohio had received reports beginning about noon from his scouts and pickets that there is Rebel activity out to the west; Col. Robert Reiley of the 75th Ohio receives similar reports. Thus several Union colonels go to their division commander, Brig. Gen. Charles Devens, with their concerns. Devens, in a patronizing manner, dismisses them and doesn't alert Howard. Even if he did believe these stories, Howard was absent from his command post, having accompanied Sickles and Barlow. Artillerist Capt. Hubert "Leather Britches" Dilger, of Company I, First Ohio Light Artillery, a veteran of the Prussian Army, also sees the enemy. When he reports what he has seen to Hooker's staff, they tell him to take his yarn to Howard's headquarters. Hooker's and

Howard's headquarters both receive advance warnings of what is about to take place, but they do not believe them.

Meanwhile, the Confederates are forming up into battle lines. Rodes's division is in the lead; Rodes deploys two brigades north and two south of the turnpike. His line extends for just over a mile from flank to flank. Five hundred yards behind Rodes's division are three of Raleigh Colston's brigades and one of Rodes's. Out in front, Maj. Eugene Blackford deploys the Fifth Alabama battalion as skirmishers. After Blackford reports to Jackson that the Fifth Alabama is ready, Stonewall turns to Rodes and tells him, "You can go forward then." The time by Rodes's watch is 5:15 p.m.

If you are one of those German boys out here, you see all sorts of wildlife—squirrels, foxes, and deer—come bounding from the woods toward you. Soon thereafter, you hear that terrible Rebel yell, as thousands of Confederates emerge from the woods as far as the eye can see and bear down on your front and flanks. You might get off a volley or two, but then it is "root hog" or die. The two guns astride the road get off a couple of rounds before they are overrun, and the 153rd Pennsylvania and the 54th New York facing west are overwhelmed by weight of numbers. In rapid succession, the XI Corps is rolled up from west to east like a wet blanket.

Buschbeck forms his brigade on the ridge east of Wilderness Church. He seeks to buy time for the corps to recover from Jackson's devastating attack. Howard returns and tries to rally his men, sitting his horse athwart the turnpike with a flag under the stump of his amputated upper right arm and a pistol in his left hand.

Back at Hooker's Chancellor House headquarters, Hooker and his staff hear firing to the west. They are not alarmed until it comes closer, and several of Hooker's staffers go out onto the turnpike fronting the house. Looking west, they see them coming! An uncontrollable mob is rapidly approaching them.

Sensational as the Confederate attack is, before long soldiers in the lead division find themselves exhausted; elsewhere, a few brigades fail to join the attack. Jackson is everywhere, pressing his men forward.

The Confederates have scored a strategic surprise, sending thousands of XI Corps troops "skedaddling" pell-mell down the turnpike. As the Confederates advance they soon encounter pockets of resistance. Several Union regiments posted south of the turnpike, including the 75th and 25th Ohio, turn 90 degrees and face west toward the oncoming Confederates. This gives Buschbeck's brigade, along with Dilger's battery, time to take position near Dowdell's Tavern on the turnpike facing west. It takes the Confederates considerable time to overwhelm the stubborn knot of resistance put up by Buschbeck's people, who have been reinforced by hard-core units that had been rallied by division commander Maj. Gen. Carl Schurz. By the time they overrun Buschbeck's brigade, Rodes's three left brigades are exhausted and their ranks becoming disorganized. South of the turnpike are three Confederate brigades led by Brig. Gens. Alfred Colquitt, Stephen D. Ramseur, and Elisha F. "Bull" Paxton that have not kept pace, because of hesitation on Colquitt's part. They do not move forward until the Confederates to their left have uncovered the intersection of the Plank Road and the Orange Turnpike. Time bought by Buschbeck and Dilger at Dowdell's Tavern helps the XI Corps slow the Confederate advance and prevents a total rout of the XI Corps.

Colston comes forward, relieves Rodes, and pushes onward. His advance is on a three-brigade front. He gains another three-quarters of a mile and halts near where the Bullock Road diverges from the turnpike. It is beginning to get dark. Soon Jackson makes what proves to be a fatal decision: He rides ahead to conduct a personal reconnaissance on a moonlit evening.

The Confederates are advancing on a broad front, with some units encountering resistance and others fighting brambles and undergrowth in the Wilderness terrain. The onslaught is beginning to lose its momentum. As night comes you begin to appreciate the effect of the delays in the march of Jackson's column, the late morning start, the impact of Jackson's midafternoon reconnaissance to the Burton Farm, and the decision to use the axis of the turnpike rather than that of the Plank Road to smite Howard's corps.

Soon, Colston's division is pulled back to re-form; the Confederates call up Hill's division. They initially bring forward Brig. Gen. James "Little Jim" Lane's brigade and the brigade of Virginians led by Brig. Gen. Henry Heth. Behind them is Brig. Gen. William Dorsey Pender's brigade. At this time, Brig. Gen. Samuel McGowan's brigade is not on the field, nor are Brig. Gens. Edward L. Thomas's and James J. Archer's. The latter two are farther behind; they have dropped back to discourage Sickles's pursuit. The Confederates will attempt to restart their attack with just two brigades.

What units does Hooker have available? He has Hiram Berry's III Corps division, as well as a II Corps brigade under Brig. Gen. William Hays. Berry's people had not joined Sickles's corps in the "wild goose chase" after Jackson's column. Instead, they remained behind and are in position along with artillery. The XII Corps is south of the turnpike, and they are rapidly constructing breastworks fronting west. Cavalry commander Alfred Pleasonton sends the Eighth Pennsylvania Cavalry in a charge down a wood road leading north from Hazel Grove in an effort to blunt the Confederate onslaught. It gets the daylights shot out of it. But the charge unnerves some of the Confederates.

Jackson has chosen an inauspicious time to go out in front of his lines to undertake his reconnaissance, but he is desperate to get his stalled attack going again. Riding with him are members of his staff and three headquarters couriers, a total of nine people. Jackson is riding Little Sorrel. Their guide, David Kyle, leads them out the "Mountain Road." Jackson wants to continue the advance toward U.S. Ford. South of the road is Williams's XII Corps division. By this time of day, many Union Army units have recovered from the initial blow delivered by Jackson's flank attack.

Having seen Hooker's re-formed defensive positions and having come under artillery and small-arms fire, Jackson seeks to return to his lines. He and his party turn their horses around and ride west. The men in Jim Lane's brigade hear them approach. They have just arrived on the front line, and they see riders approaching their position out of the darkness. They have been under artillery fire from the enemy, and there are reports of Union cavalry in the area. Soldiers in the 18th North Carolina open fire. Jackson's brother-in-law and other staffers call out, "Cease fire! You are firing into your own men!" Maj. John Barry of the 18th North Carolina shouts that this is a Yankee lie and commands his men to "pour it into them, boys!" These men are armed with smooth bore muskets, and at this range fire buck and ball.

In the darkness there is mass confusion. Several horses go down. Nearby, over on the turnpike some 80 yards away, Gen. A. P. Hill and his nine-man entourage, including Corps Chief Engineer James Keith Boswell, have also been fired upon by the North Carolinians. Boswell and two others are killed.

As the deadly volley is unleashed on Jackson's party, Jackson has raised his right arm into the air as if to ward off the bullets. A musket buckshot strikes him in the palm of his hand. A ball fractures his lower left arm, and another strikes his upper left arm, fracturing and shattering the bone. Jackson's horse, spooked by the fire, heads off through the thick undergrowth with Jackson in the saddle. A staff officer quickly reacts, following Jackson and his mount into the undergrowth, and manages to grab the reins of his horse and bring Little Sorrel to a halt. A second staff member arrives and assists Jackson in dismounting. Jackson tells them that he is badly wounded. They see that his face is sorely lacerated by the thick undergrowth as well. In the confusion and chaos, Little Sorrel strays into the Federal lines, but he is later found and is returned about six weeks later.

Initially, Jackson is in considerable pain, but it does not last long. I say that because of personal experience, having myself been shot four times in World War II; the severe pain does not last as shock sets in. Members of Jackson's staff stop the bleeding, and, seeing that Jackson has been seriously wounded, they seek to get him behind their lines for medical attention. They first try to walk him to the rear but they do not get far.

They then place him on a stretcher and begin the perilous journey to an aid station. As the party reaches the turnpike, Federal artillery opens fire with canister. A stretcher-bearer is struck by a deadly missile and goes down, but a staffer catches the litter's handle, and they ground the stretcher.

When they resume the journey, one of the litter-bearers trips, and Jackson is dropped. He moans as this causes more damage to his mangled left arm, and he begins to hemorrhage. Quickly, they stop the bleeding and get him back onto the stretcher and carefully work their way out of no-man's-land and out of harm's way. When they get behind the lines, Jackson asks for the corps' medical director, Dr. Hunter McGuire. He doesn't want one of the regimental surgeons to get ahold of him because of what he fears might happen. Jackson is placed in an ambulance with Col. Stapleton Crutchfield, his chief of artillery, who has been badly wounded in the leg. Both are taken to the field hospital back at the Wilderness Tavern. Crutchfield will lose a leg; Dr. McGuire amputates Jackson's left arm.

After the wounding of Jackson, his command is turned over to A. P. Hill. A shell concussion soon disables Hill. Although no blood is seen, it causes a severe contusion of the lower leg, which incapacitates him. He hands over command to Robert Rodes until they can find someone senior in rank to command the corps.

With Jackson and Hill down, the Confederate attack sputters to a halt in the dark. Jeb Stuart, although a cavalryman, is the only major general in the vicinity. He soon arrives and assumes command of Jackson's corps. He orders his cavalrymen to smite the Federals with everything they have at daybreak. His action is confirmed by General Lee. Hooker scrambles to consolidate his command; Lee anxiously seeks to reunite his forces, while the word from Fredericksburg is that the Yankees opposing Early are advancing. Both sides focus on Sickles's position on Hazel Grove. While the Union holds it, Lee can't unite his army; if the Confederates gain control of it, they will be able to emplace their artillery to support infantry attacks on the restored Union positions.

The Confederates know that the Union Army is throwing up breastworks confronting Jackson's corps along a north-south line throughout the night. The area is heavily wooded, so the Yankees make extensive use of timber in their construction, adding revetments and abatis. They clear brush for fields of fire. Three Union divisions are behind three lines of breastworks supported by Capt. Clermont Best's 26 artillery pieces at Fairview. All face west and will receive the initial blows of Stuart's attack on the morning of May 3, protected by earthen lunettes.

Henry Heth, who has replaced A. P. Hill, leads the division that spearheads the Confederate onslaught. Attacking on the Confederate right is James J. Archer's brigade. He strikes at Sickles's corps, which has returned to Hazel Grove. To Archer's left Heth has four brigades and one in reserve. In line behind Heth is Raleigh Colston's division. At Dowdall's Tavern, Rodes's division is re-formed and ready to constitute Stuart's ready reserve. Jackson had more than 29,000 soldiers when he began his May 2 flank march. Stuart now has only 24,000.

On the Union "side of the Hill," Meade's corps has been pulled from their entrenchments behind Mineral Spring Run and sent to the right flank. Reynolds's I Corps, making a late afternoon's march from Falmouth, has crossed the Rappahannock at U.S. Ford and takes position behind Hunting Run, its left tied into Meade's right and its right anchored in the Rapidan. Taking positions in the breastworks vacated by Meade are the re-formed divisions of the XI Corps. This is a good place for Howard because his corps holds an impregnable position. General Couch is missing one of his three divisions: General Gibbon's, of which we will hear more later. Couch has the division led by Hancock and Samuel Carroll's brigade of French's division behind breastworks facing east, covering the Chancellorsville crossroads; French's other two brigades face west, toward Stuart.

In the Union advance line south of the turnpike and facing west are soldiers of Slocum's XII Corps—150 yards deep into the woods. There is a second line of breastworks and then a third, constituting a defense in depth. The undergrowth is dense and low to the ground. You would not see large trees such as the ones there now. If you are a Confederate, you can expect high casualties due to poor visibility as you move through this undergrowth and suddenly come upon Yankee breastworks. There are cleared areas and an abatis, lines of brush piled with sharpened branches facing the enemy, in front of the log barricades where Union troops have felled trees. The Confederate attacks will come forward in successive battle lines. Employing a mid-20th-century military term, the Rebels will attack in human waves. They lose many men because they're going up against veteran Union troops posted behind breastworks.

Confederate attacks begin at daylight on May 3. It is incumbent that Lee reunite the two wings of his army. The combined number of men in Stuart's and Lee's wings is approximately 36,000. The Union force with Hooker is now concentrated, numbers more than 75,000, and is positioned between Stuart's and Lee's wings. If Sickles's corps remains at Hazel Grove, there is no way for Lee to reunite the army.

About 6 a.m. Sickles receives orders from Hooker's headquarters to abandon Hazel Grove. Hooker is concerned about Sickles's people posted in the apex of the Union salient. Sickles protests the order. In Sickles's mind, by giving up Hazel Grove, the Union Army will surrender to the enemy the battlefield's key artillery position. But when Hooker insists, Sickles acquiesces and pulls back. Archer's brigade of Stuart's wing, which had been repulsed in an earlier attack, now occupies Hazel Grove. The way is open to a linkup of the two wings of Lee's army.

The occupation of Hazel Grove enabled the Confederates to make use of this superb ground for artillery. Col. E. Porter Alexander, commanding Lee's I Corps reserve artillery, quickly assembles more than 40 Confederate guns on Hazel Grove. A terrific and terrible artillery duel ensues between the Confederate cannon and Captain Best's Fairview guns. Chancellorsville is one of the few battles in the Eastern Theater in which Confederate artillery overwhelmed the Union redlegs (artillerymen).

Following Jackson's mortal wounding on May 2, Lee temporarily appointed brilliant cavalry commander Maj. Gen. J.E.B. Stuart to take charge of Jackson's Corps.

Where is Hooker at this time? He is on the front porch of the Chancellor House. About 9 a.m. a shell fired by one of Alexander's cannon strikes the column that Hooker is leaning up against, splitting the column from end to end and throwing him to the ground senseless. If he is dead or disabled, that might solve everything and leave General Couch in charge. Hooker soon recovers consciousness and gives the order for Couch to pull back. Hooker's aides escort him around to the backside of the house. He lies down, trying to recover from the concussion to his head. While he is trying to shake off the effects of being knocked out, his aides move him again. When they do so, another shell comes in and hits the ground where he had been laying. If they had not moved him, that would have been the end of Hooker.

Many of Hooker's staff gather around Couch and urge him to take command. In their opinion, Hooker is incapacitated. Some are wondering if Hooker has lost his nerve. Some even feel that he may have been hitting the bottle again. Hooker is befuddled. But suppose Couch takes command and things go awry. What happens if things get worse instead of better, and he has taken over command of the army without first having Hooker certified by the army's chief medical officer as disabled? If the battle should further unravel for the bluecoats Couch could be accused of violating the articles of war. We all understand what the ramifications of that could be. As a result, Couch does not assume command and is compelled to carry out Hooker's instructions to withdraw the army to the newly prepared defense line anchored on "the apex" at the Chandler House.

Sam McGowan's and Jim Lane's brigades, advancing south of the turnpike, seize the first line of Union breastworks. McGowan is wounded and his South Carolina brigade cut to pieces in front of the second line of log breastworks. The Stonewall Brigade comes forward—and General Paxton is killed at the second barricade. Now Rodes's division surges to the front, and his Alabamians suffer the same fate as the South Carolinians. Rodes commits his freshest brigades, Stephen Dodson Ramseur's. The fighting is vicious as the Confederates press forward and finally overrun the second line of Union breastworks and assail the final Union defensive line manned by Brig. Gen. Thomas Ruger's XII Corps brigade. The fighting rages for what seems to be an eternity. Couch, implementing Hooker's orders, directs Captain Best to pull his artillery off Fairview. Slocum's and Sickles's infantry give ground, and Ramseur's North Carolinians climb the slope. Brig. Gen. Charles K. Graham is a Sickles crony, and his Pennsylvania brigade covers the retreat from Fairview at a fearful cost, suffering 750 killed, wounded, and missing, more than any other unit in the morning's fighting. North of the turnpike, Edward Thomas's Georgians and Dorsey Pender's North Carolinians hammer Hiram Berry's and French's Yanks, unmercifully gaining ground. Soldiers from the 13th North Carolina capture Brig. Gen. William Hays, one of French's brigade commanders. General Berry crosses the turnpike to check on the fight for Fairview and is shot by a Confederate sharpshooter. That is the end of

Hiram Berry. When Hooker learns of Berry's death, saddened by the words, he sheds tears. They had been longtime comrades.

Meanwhile, John Reynolds's I Corps has taken post behind Meade's on the Union right covered by Little Hunting Run. Thomas's Georgians gain ground but expose their left flank to a counterthrust by Meade. If Hooker had not been so preoccupied with a defensive posture, he might have capitalized on this situation. Meade and Reynolds could have been ordered to advance a short distance to the right and then turn south. They may have then overwhelmed Stuart's left wing while he was engaged in his front with Sickles's and Slocum's corps at Fairview. But, unfortunately for the Federals, Reynolds's and Meade's 30,000 men remain idle while Sickles's and Slocum's corps bear first the brunt and then crumble under the weight of Stuart's sledgehammer-like blows.

To shield the retrograde movement to their new position at the "Apex," it is mandatory that General Hancock and his people hold their ground covering the Chancellorsville intersection. Hancock is the ideal soldier to accomplish this task. He has the charisma and leadership qualities that all combat infantry of modern wars admire in an officer. He and his division hold the line. It is 10:30 a.m. when the last Yankees leave Chancellorsville and the burning tavern, set afire by Rebel shells about the time Hooker is disabled. Confederate soldiers surge across the clearing and accept the surrender of the 27th Connecticut before it can escape up the Ely's Ford Road. Lee arrives to the cheers of his veterans. But the supreme moment of his

OPPOSITE: *On May 3, Jeb Stuart, who succeeded the wounded Stonewall Jackson, launched a series of attacks against the entrenched Federals around Chancellorsville hoping to reunite his forces with Lee's. At 9 a.m., despite a gallant defense, Hooker ordered a withdrawal to new positions north of Chancellorsville. As the Confederates continued their assault during the late afternoon, Lee received word that Federal troops had broken through at Fredericksburg. Lee again divided his forces, and on May 4 the Confederates defeated the Federal VI Corps at Salem Church, forcing them to retreat across the Rappahannock at nightfall. On May 6 Hooker abandoned his position at Chancellorsville and withdrew across the river.*

Chancellorsville, II

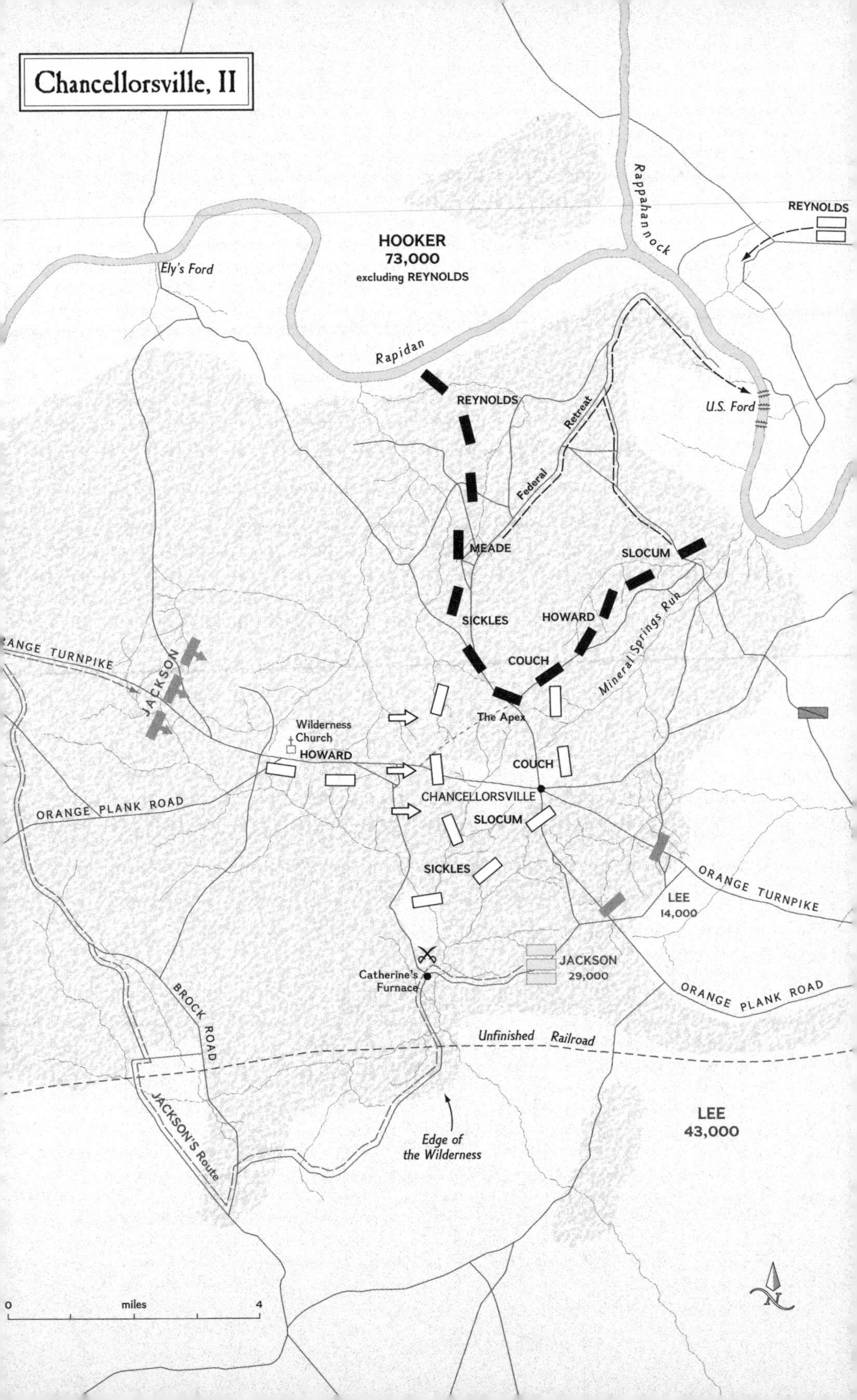

HOOKER
73,000
excluding REYNOLDS
REYNOLDS
Rappahannock
Ely's Ford
Rapidan
REYNOLDS
U.S. Ford
Federal Retreat
MEADE
SLOCUM
SICKLES
HOWARD
Mineral Springs Run
COUCH
ORANGE TURNPIKE
JACKSON
The Apex
Wilderness Church
HOWARD
COUCH
CHANCELLORSVILLE
ORANGE PLANK ROAD
SLOCUM
SICKLES
ORANGE TURNPIKE
LEE
14,000
JACKSON
29,000
Catherine's Furnace
ORANGE PLANK ROAD
BROCK ROAD
Unfinished Railroad
JACKSON'S Route
Edge of the Wilderness
LEE
43,000
0
miles
4
N

life as a soldier is interrupted and marred by bad news from Fredericksburg.

Though Lee has succeeded in reuniting his main force on May 3, he now learns that another Union force is threatening disaster.

Back on the night of April 28–29, Reynolds's and Sedgwick's corps had crossed the Rappahannock River downstream at Franklin's Crossing to hold Lee's attention while Hooker maneuvered against Lee's left flank. On May 2 Reynolds is withdrawn from the Fredericksburg area and marches west to join Hooker at Chancellorsville. That leaves Sedgwick near Fredericksburg with his three VI Corps divisions and Gibbon's II Corps division, some 28,000 strong, to confront Jubal Early's five brigades. On the afternoon of the second, before Jackson's flank attack, Hooker, still under the delusion that Lee is retreating, messages Sedgwick to storm the heights behind Fredericksburg and vigorously pursue the foe. That evening, after the rout of Howard's people, Hooker reiterates his orders for Sedgwick to seize the heights, but on doing so, he is to march west via the Orange Plank Road and come up in rear of Lee's army confronting Hooker's VI Corps at Chancellorsville. Because of problems with the military telegraph, Sedgwick does not receive the latter message until 11 p.m., when it is delivered by a mounted courier.

What does Jubal Early have available on the morning of May 3 to hold this front? Early's five brigades of infantry must defend a front that Lee held back in mid-December with 78,000 men. The brigades of Brig. Gens. Harry T. Hays and William Barksdale hold a two-mile line behind Fredericksburg reaching from Taylor's Hill on the river north of town, down along Marye's Heights, and on to the Howison House just below Lee's Hill overlooking Hazel Run. His remaining three brigades—Brig. Gens. Robert F. Hoke's, John B. Gordon's, and that of former Virginia governor Brig. Gen. William "Extra Billy" Smith—will guard the rest of the Confederate line from the Howison House to Hamilton's Crossing.

What does the opposing Union Army have available in Fredericksburg? It has the largest corps in the Army of the Potomac, the VI Corps, led by "Uncle John" Sedgwick. He is a soldier's soldier. His grandfather, also named John Sedgwick, was a major in Washington's army during the Revolutionary War. General Sedgwick commands four divisions—three led by Brig. Gens. William T. H. "Bully" Brooks, Albion P. Howe, and John Newton. A fourth light division follows Col. Hiram Burnham. On the north side of the Rappahannock River the Federals have two brigades of John Gibbon's II Corps division led by Col. Alfred Sully and Col. Norman Hall.

A thick fog envelops the Rappahannock Valley that morning, and it delays the Union troops as they seek to move into formation to attack Marye's Heights. Holding Marye's Heights is a brigade from McLaws's division, commanded by William Barksdale. He has five regiments—four Mississippi and one Louisiana—to defend a sector where four brigades were committed in December 1862. Supporting these regiments are seven guns on Marye's Heights, another four at Lee's Hill, and another eight in the Howison Hill sector.

Employing the town of Fredericksburg as a staging area, Sedgwick sends Newton against the Confederate lines between 8 a.m. and 10 a.m. Newton is a West Point graduate, a Virginian, a member of the Corps of Engineers, and a close friend of Meade's. Newton's first attack against the Confederate right on Hazel Run is repulsed. Newton's second thrust against the Confederate positions on the Sunken Road and on Marye's Heights is likewise turned back with little difficulty. John Gibbon's brigades attempts to skirt the base of Taylor's Hill to strike the Confederate left flank. Artillery fire from hastily assembled Confederate guns prevents his people from bridging the narrow industrial canal, forcing Gibbon to abandon efforts to outflank the Confederates northwest of town. Howe's division then goes forward and endeavors to turn the Confederate positions on Marye's Heights south of Hazel Run. His efforts also meet with no success. It is apparent to Sedgwick that the Confederate position on Marye's Heights is invulnerable to thrusts against its flanks. Hooker's insistence that the VI Corps hasten to the rescue of the army at Chancellorsville compels Sedgwick to risk a frontal assault.

By the time that the Federals launch their final attack against Marye's Heights this day, they have learned much since their December 13, 1862, debacle here. They recall that when A. A. Humphrey's division advanced, it did not go forward in line of battle, as was the standard practice. Instead, "Old Goggle Eye" led them forward by regimental column. Although men at the head of the column will suffer heavy casualties, it is felt that momentum will keep the formation moving ahead.

Sedgwick allots ten regiments to the assaulting columns—the 61st Pennsylvania heads the column of fours on the Orange Plank Road and the 7th Massachusetts on the Telegraph Road. Confederate artillery on the military crest of Marye's Heights and infantry in the Sunken Road open fire on the advancing columns. The head of each column melts away. The Yankees' attack is repulsed. A Union colonel sends forward a white flag and requests permission to remove the dead and wounded. Col. Thomas Griffin of the 18th Mississippi is naive. The Yankees come up under a flag of truce to gather up their dead and wounded and see that there aren't many Rebels holding the Sunken Road. They report this important information to their commanding officers upon their return to the safety of their lines.

The Federals, with seemingly unlimited manpower, resume their relentless assault. Troops are instructed not to stop to reload their rifles this time, but to continue to advance at the double-quick with bayonets fixed and overrun the hopelessly outnumbered Confederates in the Sunken Road. Savage hand-to-hand fighting occurs in the road, but numbers tell. The Confederates abandon their position, and the Federals surge upward and over the crest of Marye's Heights. By 11 a.m. they possess this key ground. Off to the south, General Howe's brigades overrun the Confederates on Lee's Hill. Early's defeated brigades retreat south via the Telegraph Road, which leads to Guinea Station, away from Lee and the Confederate Army at Chancellorsville.

Now that the Federals control the Fredericksburg heights, what should they do? Sedgwick has suffered heavy casualties in the fight to secure Marye's Heights, particularly in Newton's division. Sedgwick wastes about four hours bringing up "Bully" Brooks's fresh division before resuming the march toward Chancellorsville. During these precious hours Brig. Gen. Cadmus Wilcox and his Alabama Brigade set the stage to become Confederate heroes. Wilcox first sends his men east toward Marye's Heights and then toward the Salem Church, as his Alabamians fight a series of delaying actions along the Orange Plank Road.

Upon learning of the disaster at Fredericksburg, Lee responds to the emergency by splitting his army yet again and ordering four brigades under General McLaws to Salem Church. The question becomes who will reach Salem Church first, Lee's reinforcing brigades or John Sedgwick's laggard VI Corps?

It is 3:30 p.m. before the Federals near Salem Church. In advance is Brooks's division, some 4,000 strong. Behind Brooks are Newton's and Howe's divisions, and bringing up the rear Colonel Burnham's light division. Gibbon's division has been left in Fredericksburg to guard against a Confederate attempt to retake Marye's Heights. Confronting Brooks's Vermonters are 1,200 men in Wilcox's brigade and two cannon of the Pittsylvania Artillery. Wilcox, showing great initiative, selects excellent ground for fighting a delaying action. If General Lee does not send reinforcements, his choice of ground will be to no avail. Wilcox first deploys his brigade near a tollhouse a mile east of Salem Church. Later, he pulls his people back to take position along a north-south ridge at the church. Two regiments are north of the Plank Road and two south of it, with detachments of the Ninth Alabama inside the church building and schoolhouse. Artillery is unlimbered as Wilcox looks first at his watch with a concerned expression, then to the east, and finally the west, searching for signs of Lee's oncoming reinforcements.

The Federals approach and deploy into battle lines. Brooks positions Col. Henry Brown's New Jersey Brigade on either side of the road. Brig. Gen. Joseph J. Bartlett's brigade takes ground on Brown's left flank, with Brig. Gen. David Russell's brigade in support. When the Yankees advance, they drive in Confederate skirmishers. They continue pressing ahead until they reach and occupy the Salem Church. But just as they gain the church, the four reinforcing Confederate brigades arrive from the west. Approaching the church on the north side of the road and anchoring its right on Wilcox's left is Brig. Gen. Paul Semmes's brigade. Next in line on Semmes's left are Brig. Gen. William "Little Billy" Mahone's Virginians. Brig. Gen. Joseph B. Kershaw brings his South Carolina Brigade into line on the south side of the road on the right of Wilcox, and finally, on Kershaw's right, will be Brig. Gen. William T. Wofford's Georgians.

The Confederates have arrived in time to save Wilcox from destruction. Fighting around the church is savage. Brown loses more than 500 Federals and Bartlett's brigade more than 600. Their casualties are heavy, but the Confederates hold this vital ground, and Sedgwick's hammer is checked before it can smash Lee on Hooker's anvil.

What is General Lee going to do next? He decides to leave Jeb Stuart in command of the 23,000 men in Jackson's corps with orders to watch Hooker's 75,000 Union troops that are entrenched with their center anchored on the "Apex," with their left behind Mineral Springs Run, and their right behind Hunting Run. Lee will assemble all remaining Confederate troops in the vicinity of Salem Church and deal Sedgwick a crippling blow before he can escape with his corps back across the Rappahannock at Banks's Ford. He recalls Jubal Early's division from the area of the Cox House. McLaws will attack at the same time from the west and Anderson from the south. McLaws's division will lead off. When the other division commanders hear McLaws's guns, they are to advance. If they can coordinate their attacks, Lee hopes to drive Sedgwick back into the cul-de-sac formed by a bend of the Rappahannock at Banks's Ford and compel him to surrender.

On May 4 Sedgwick and his 25,000 bluecoats fight for survival. Confronting his command are almost 30,000 Confederates under Robert E. Lee's personal command. Stuart still watches Hooker in the Chancellorsville pocket. Sedgwick is in a tight spot.

But it is not to be a good day for the Confederates, particularly not for General McLaws in the Salem Church sector. Attacking as scheduled at 8 a.m., Early's division, spearheaded by John B. Gordon's Georgians, has reoccupied the high ground behind Fredericksburg by midmorning. Here Early waits in vain for the sound of McLaws's guns to the west. When General Lee arrives from Chancellorsville at 11 a.m., he is miffed to learn that Dick Anderson, with the three brigades that were to accompany him, is not up yet. Delay follows on delay, and soon Lee begins to fret, his ire centering on McLaws, who until Lee's arrival was senior officer present. Lee's staff officers present at the Salem Church command post recognize that Lee is angry. The signs are there as the back of their general's neck reddens and one of his ears twitches. Lee's ear will twitch a lot this afternoon as he waits for McLaws to act.

In the end, Lee's plans to hammer and destroy Sedgwick come to naught. On the night of the fourth the VI Corps troops, squeezed by the Confederates, use Scott's Ford to escape the trap Lee had forged for them south of the Rappahannock.

Disappointed that he could not gobble up one Federal force, Lee turns his attention once more to Chancellorsville.

Hooker expected Sedgwick to come to his rescue, but learning of Sedgwick's defeat at Salem Church, he must reevaluate the situation. He decides to hold his first council of war since the start of the Chancellorsville campaign. Hooker is heretofore so self-assured of his plans for victory that he has disdained advice from his subordinates and staff. He has kept his battle plans closely guarded secrets. But rapidly changing events on the battlefield over the past several days have shaken his self-confidence. By May 4, the self-assurance exhibited earlier in the campaign has vanished. At midnight of May 4–5, when the council of war convenes in Hooker's headquarters tent, Hooker has already decided what he is going to do following the unwelcome news of Sedgwick's failed attempt to rescue the army.

The council of war begins with most of the corps commanders present, including Couch (second in command), Reynolds, Meade, Sickles, and

Confederate dead lie in the Sunken Road at the foot of Marye's Heights at Fredericksburg. Federal troops of the VI Corps stormed the position on May 3, 1863.

Howard. Slocum has some distance to travel to reach army headquarters and arrives after the meeting has broken up. Sedgwick, understandably, is too busy to attend. Chief of Staff Dan Butterfield and Chief Engineer Gouverneur K. Warren are also present.

Hooker opens the meeting with a few remarks emphasizing the importance of protecting Washington. He makes disparaging remarks about the soldierly character of the men in the ranks and expresses apprehension regarding the want of steadiness in some of the units he has seen, demonstrated by unnecessary firing along some parts of the line. Having established a cautious atmosphere at the beginning of the meeting, he, along with Butterfield, leaves the corps commanders to consult among themselves. Dan Sickles takes the lead and speaks his piece. Butterfield and Sickles are Hooker cronies, and it is no wonder that Sickles supports Hooker's intentions. After Sickles delivers a short speech regarding the dire political consequences of another Union defeat and of voting to retreat, Meade, Reynolds, and Howard, in turn, make brief remarks and vote to remain and fight it out.

Couch is a bit reticent when it comes time for him to speak: He is disgusted with Hooker and his fumbling attitude regarding the battle. He votes in favor of retirement. Later he states that the Army of the Potomac did not deserve to be further sacrificed because of Hooker's incompetent leadership.

When Hooker and Butterfield return to the tent, Hooker asks each of his corps commanders for his vote. Meade, Reynolds, and Howard favor remaining and fighting it out. Couch and Sickles favor retreat. Hooker quickly intervenes, concluding that the vote was nearly even, so there doesn't appear to be overwhelming support for remaining south of the Rappahannock. It is probably best, he adds, if the army gets itself out of a hopeless, boxed-in situation and recrosses the river.

Retiring from the meeting, Hooker thanks his corps commanders for their opinions. Reynolds, following Couch out of Hooker's tent, echoes the sentiments of his fellow corps commanders: "What was the purpose in calling us together at this time of night when he intended to retreat anyhow?"

Hooker's decision to withdraw from his strongly fortified defensive position came just as Robert E. Lee was preparing to assault it. Perhaps Hooker was wise in forestalling disaster; it is even more likely, however, that Lee would have suffered a serious and bloody repulse. As it was, he could claim a bittersweet victory in what many scholars believe to have been his finest offensive battle during the war. Inflicting some 18,000 casualties at a cost of 12,800 men, he had rescued victory from the jaws of disaster, but it had deprived him forever of the services of Stonewall Jackson, who would die on May 10 of complications arising from his wounds. If Chancellorsville was Lee's masterpiece, it was a costly one.

6

GETTYSBURG

JULY 1–3, 1863

After the Battle of Chancellorsville Robert E. Lee turned back suggestions that he send some of his forces west, or go himself, to relieve Union pressure on Vicksburg and Middle Tennessee, deciding once more to cross the Potomac on a grand raid into Maryland and Pennsylvania. An invasion of the North would allow his men to forage liberally, taking the burden off the war-torn Virginia countryside, and perhaps leading to an opportunity to destroy the Army of the Potomac once and for all. Some observers will later claim that the defeat or destruction of the Army of the Potomac was his chief aim. Certainly a major Confederate victory on northern soil might lead to further demands by antiwar northern Democrats for a negotiated peace.

In addition, Lee and his chief, Jefferson Davis, both hoped that a triumph of Confederate arms would encourage France or Great Britain to recognize the Confederacy and intervene on her behalf. In mid-June the Army of Northern Virginia evacuated its earthworks behind the Rappahannock and slid west, then north, crossed the Blue Ridge, turned down through the Shenandoah Valley, and across the Potomac River. On the way north, Confederate forces captured Winchester and bypassed Harpers Ferry.

It is a restructured army of about 75,000 men that undertakes this invasion. After the death of Stonewall Jackson, Lee reorganizes his army into three infantry corps. James Longstreet will continue in command of

I Corps. Elevated to corps command and recently promoted to the rank of lieutenant general are Richard S. Ewell (II Corps) and A. P. Hill (III Corps). For Ewell, it's his first combat command in nearly a year, since his wounding in the Second Manassas campaign; Hill, an aggressive division commander, finds that corps command presents new challenges. Moreover, as he moves northward, Lee must contend with cavalry commander Maj. Gen. Jeb Stuart, whose ego is bruised after the Union cavalry embarrassed him in a pitched action at Brandy Station, the war's largest cavalry battle, on the eve of this campaign.

In the aftermath of Chancellorsville, the Union Army of the Potomac takes stock of itself. Regiments that had enlisted in 1861 reach the end of their service obligation and return home. Maj. Gen. Joseph Hooker contemplates responding to Lee's northward shift by striking at Richmond, but instead shields Washington from the invaders and feuds with General in Chief Maj. Gen. Henry W. Halleck about who should control various detachments. By the last week of June, President Lincoln has heard enough, and when Hooker offers his resignation, Lincoln selects Maj. Gen. George Gordon Meade, the commander of V Corps, as Hooker's replacement. Meade will have to take control of the army as he maneuvers against Lee.

On June 19, Ewell's vanguard begins to ford the Potomac River at Williamsport, and joined by the rest of the corps, crosses into Pennsylvania on the 22nd and occupies Chambersburg. Hill's and Longstreet's corps cross the Potomac on June 24 and 25, the former near Shepherdstown and the latter at Williamsport. Lee sends Jeb Stuart and three brigades of his cavalry to bypass the Army of the Potomac to the east and carry out "all the damage you can." Ewell's orders are to press on toward the Susquehanna River and Harrisburg and capture the state capital if possible. By the 27th the remainder of the Army of Northern Virginia is concentrated around Chambersburg.

Lee does not learn that the Army of the Potomac is north of the Potomac River until the night of June 28–29. He also soon finds out that the Union Army has a new commander, George G. Meade. Lee decides it's time to seek battle, and so he sends orders for his army to concentrate on Cashtown Gap, west of Gettysburg. By the evening of the 30th, he's with Longstreet's I Corps at Chambersburg, just behind A. P. Hill's III Corps at Cashtown. Just below the Susquehanna River, north of Gettysburg, is Richard Ewell's II Corps, stretched out between Carlisle and to the east of York. Remember, Lee doesn't begin to concentrate his army until the morning of June 29. It's a long way—35 miles up to Carlisle—to let Ewell know, and more than 50 miles over to York to apprise Early. The couriers carrying these messages are going to be pounding along on their horses. It's going to be late in the day on June 29 or in the early morning of June 30 before two of Lee's three corps commanders get their people in motion. Moreover, Lee doesn't know where the Yankees are, because Jeb Stuart is out of contact, having decided to ride around the Army of the Potomac, only to find that the Union Army is blocking his route of return.

Meade, after taking a day to get his bearings on June 28, moves up rapidly to take position to cover Washington and Baltimore and search for the enemy. He had accepted his new command reluctantly. He writes his wife that night and says, "I have been sentenced and convicted without a trial." It is an awesome responsibility that he assumes. Meade takes stock of his new command on June 28 and tries to appoint his own chief of staff, but three generals turn him down, and he's stuck with Hooker's man, Maj. Gen. Daniel Butterfield.

Heretofore, it was the Union leaders that had failed their men. This had led Lee to believe his army was invincible without realizing that extenuating circumstances made them superior, especially the awe in which the Union leadership held the Confederate Army of Northern Virginia and General Lee. One-third of the Union Army is from Pennsylvania. On the morning of June 30, men in I Corps, which has many Pennsylvania units in it, unfurl their colors. The bands break out their instruments and

Despite his misgivings, Maj. Gen. George Meade took command of the Army of the Potomac on June 28, 1863, less than one week before Confederate forces would converge on Gettysburg.

play as they cross into Pennsylvania. Down in Virginia women seemed of dour face and scowled. Up here they cheer and greet the soldiers. When they go by the convent at Emmitsburg, the nuns stand by the roadside ladling out buttermilk and water to the troops.

Lee does not want to fight a battle until his army is concentrated. Brig. Gen. J. Johnston Pettigrew takes his men forward from Cashtown to reconnoiter Gettysburg on June 30. Here they spot Union cavalry. Brig. Gen. John Buford, in command of the Union cavalry forces there, observes Pettigrew's men. Pettigrew comes back and reports what he's found. A. P. Hill makes a vital but flawed command decision: Instead of a brigade he will send two divisions to Gettysburg to find out who is there. I will argue that that's the worst decision any Confederate commander will make at Gettysburg. Lee prefers not to fight a battle until his army is concentrated, but Hill takes it upon himself to send out two divisions. In the lead will be the division headed by Maj. Gen. Henry W. "Harry" Heth, the bottom of the West Point class of 1847, supported by Maj. William "Willie" Pegram's battalion of artillery, to be followed up by Maj. Gen. William Dorsey Pender's division—a force of more than 14,000 sent to find out what and who is in Gettysburg.

Back in Gettysburg, Gen. John Buford and two brigades of cavalry await the Confederate advance. Heading north toward Gettysburg is Maj. Gen. John F. Reynolds's I Corps; not far behind is Oliver O. Howard's XI Corps. Buford will try to buy time for the infantry to arrive. He sends one brigade north of town to watch for Ewell, while a second brigade advances west along the Chambersburg Pike and throws out pickets to watch the roads north and west of Gettysburg.

Buford plans to fight for time to delay the Confederates. South of Gettysburg is Cemetery Hill and Cemetery Ridge, good terrain to hold if the Union opts to fight a battle here. His men move out about 5:15 a.m. on July 1. The Confederates are going to have to use artillery to support their skirmishers when they run into the Union cavalry. Buford's defense in depth buys time for the arrival of Reynolds's command. Buford forces the Confederates to burn up two hours before they even come within clear view of Seminary Ridge, west of Gettysburg. Buford is a West Pointer, class of 1848, one year behind his initial adversary, Harry Heth.

Buford establishes his main line of defense along McPherson's Ridge, a mile west of Gettysburg. Although he has 1,200 men, one-fourth of them are detailed as horse holders. Fighting dismounted,

On the first day of the battle, Federal I Corps troops under Maj. Gen. John F. Reynolds blocked A. P. Hill's attacking Confederates in the fields and woodlands of McPherson's Ridge.

armed with single-shot breech-loading carbines, Buford's men pop away, supported by an artillery battery. Heth's Confederates form into battle line to the west along Herr Ridge and advance eastward across Willoughby Run. They aren't quite sure what's ahead of them, and they have no way of finding out short of fighting. North of the Chambersburg Pike and the unfinished railroad grade, Brig. Gen. Joseph R. Davis, nephew of the Confederate president, deploys three regiments: the 42nd Mississippi, 2nd Mississippi, and 55th North Carolina. Brig. Gen. James J. Archer forms his brigade on the south side of the road. From right to left, he deploys the 13th Alabama, 1st, 14th, and Seventh Tennessee; the Fifth Alabama fans out as skirmishers.

If it looks like it's going to be Yankee cavalry versus Rebel infantry, it won't be that way for long. John Reynolds sets the I Corps on the road early in the morning. As he approaches Gettysburg from the south, Reynolds, riding with his staff up Emmitsburg Road, passes Big Round Top, Little Round Top, and Cemetery Hill, deciding the last is the best artillery position in the area. This is something Reynolds, a West Pointer, class of 1841, and an artillerist himself, can appreciate. He hears the firing of the artillery, "Boom, Boom!" He puts his staff officers to work tearing down the west fence alongside the road and then rides a short distance west across the fields toward Seminary Ridge, named for the local Lutheran Seminary perched on top. He looks up at the building's cupola, spots Buford, and asks what's going on. Buford replies, "The devil's to pay."

Reynolds evaluates the situation out front; he sees the Confederates, and he makes a decision. Can Buford hold on a while longer? Buford says he can. Reynolds sends two messages. One goes to Howard, directing Howard to close up. The other goes to Meade. Reynolds reports that the enemy is advancing in heavy force, and Gettysburg is a good place to fight a battle. He plans to hold this ground, and if driven from it, he'll fall back and barricade the streets of the town. He then returns to the Emmitsburg Road, where he'll meet the vanguard of Brig. Gen. James S. Wadsworth's First Division. He tells Wadsworth to hurry his men forward. He then rides back to the seminary to oversee the relief of Buford's men by the infantry. Buford's horse soldiers have accomplished their mission. They've held up the enemy for three hours.

Leading the way is Wadsworth's division. James Wadsworth is one of the wealthiest men in the United States. He had run as a Republican for governor of New York in 1862 and lost. In front is Brig. Gen. Lysander Cutler's Second Brigade, including the 76th New York, 56th Pennsylvania, and 147th New York. They'll take position north of a railroad cut just beyond the Chambersburg Pike. Moving into position south of the road are Cutler's 95th New York and the redlegged devils of the 84th New York—or, as they preferred to be called, the 14th Brooklyn.

The Confederates press forward. They are about to overlap Cutler's left. Reynolds hurries over and spots Brig. Gen. Solomon Meredith's "Iron Brigade" arriving: They have a band with them playing "The Campbells Are Coming." He directs them into line, and as he turns around, he's hit by a bullet behind the ear and is killed instantly. As his aides loosen his collar, they find two Catholic medallions hung around his neck. This is surprising because he is not Catholic, and none of them knows that he is seriously interested in any woman.

They carry Reynolds's body to the rear, with instructions to send it to his home in Lancaster after it is laid out in Philadelphia. And as they're laying him out on July 4, with his sisters there, a lady comes in. She is Katherine "Kate" May Hewitt. Kate has his West Point ring, and tells his sisters that they met on a boat from California to New York and that they're engaged. Reynolds was a Protestant, she a Catholic. That is why he had not told his family. The two agreed that if he was killed and they couldn't marry, she would join a convent. After he's buried, she will travel to Emmitsburg and join the St. Joseph Central House of the Order of the Daughters of Charity—the same order that had greeted the I Corps along its line of march the previous day.

With Reynolds's death, Maj. Gen. Abner Doubleday finds himself in command of I Corps and all the troops on the field. He needs help. Maj. Gen. Oliver Otis Howard arrives well in advance of his XI Corps, and goes up to Fahnestock's Observatory. About the time he arrives, the Union position north of the Chambersburg Pike collapses. The Confederates overlap the Union right wing by a considerable distance. The Confederate regiments are much larger—most of them far larger than I Corps regiments. The 55th North Carolina far overlaps the Union right, which causes the 76th New York and the 56th Pennsylvania to pull back onto Oak Ridge, leaving the 147th New York to fend for itself. The Confederates sweep around the New Yorkers' right flank. Their commander, Lt. Col. Francis C. Miller, is ready to give the command to retreat and he's wounded. Somebody yells, "Break for the rear," and

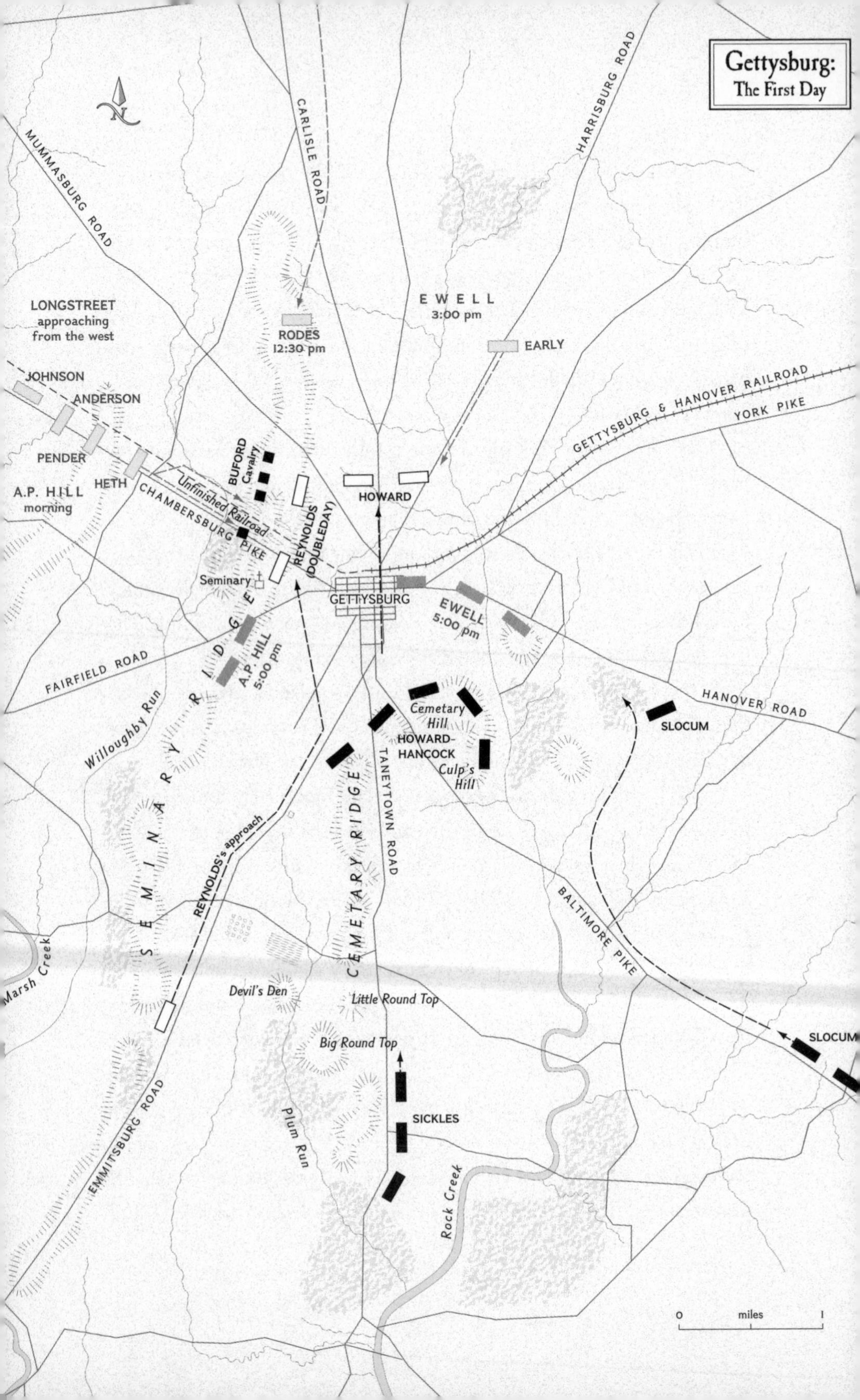

Gettysburg: The First Day
N
MUMMASBURG ROAD
CARLISLE ROAD
HARRISBURG ROAD
LONGSTREET approaching from the west
RODES 12:30 pm
EWELL 3:00 pm
EARLY
JOHNSON
ANDERSON
PENDER
HETH
A.P. HILL morning
BUFORD Cavalry
Unfinished Railroad
CHAMBERSBURG PIKE
REYNOLDS (DOUBLEDAY)
HOWARD
GETTYSBURG & HANOVER RAILROAD
YORK PIKE
Seminary
GETTYSBURG
EWELL 5:00 pm
A.P. HILL 5:00 pm
SEMINARY RIDGE
FAIRFIELD ROAD
Willoughby Run
Cemetary Hill
HOWARD-HANCOCK
Culp's Hill
HANOVER ROAD
SLOCUM
TANEYTOWN ROAD
CEMETARY RIDGE
REYNOLDS's approach
BALTIMORE PIKE
Marsh Creek
Devil's Den
Little Round Top
Big Round Top
SLOCUM
SICKLES
EMMITSBURG ROAD
Plum Run
Rock Creek
0 miles 1

the regiment breaks, and some of them flee into the streets of Gettysburg, arriving just as Howard enters the borough.

Howard decides to contact Meade, telling him, "Reynolds is dead. The I Corps has fled at the first shot," for which Doubleday never forgives him. I don't think anyone of I Corps forgave him either. Howard's messenger traveled almost as fast as Reynolds's to army headquarters at Taneytown. Reynolds's message arrives first. Meade reads it and he feels good about it. He likes the upbeat tone of Reynolds's message: "Just like Reynolds," he says to his staff. Within a half hour he reads Howard's harbinger of doom, reporting that Reynolds is dead and I Corps has fled at the first shot.

Meade knows that there's favorable ground near Gettysburg where the Union could accept battle, because Reynolds has told him so. He can't go to Gettysburg himself: He wants to wait for more information. So he turns to my "real hero of Gettysburg," Maj. Gen. Winfield Scott Hancock. Hancock's beginning to lose the "battle of the bulge." Charismatic, six feet two, a clean white shirt every day, and a booming voice. Meade tells Hancock to go to Gettysburg, make an estimate of the situation, and advise as to whether this is where Meade should concentrate and give battle. Hancock climbs into an ambulance, spreads out his maps, and heads to Gettysburg.

Back at Gettysburg, things do not look good for the Yankees. Joe Davis's brigade is bearing down on the Union right flank, driving the 147th New York before it. South of the Chambersburg Pike, James Archer's men are pressing forward.

OPPOSITE: *On the morning of July 1, two divisions of Confederates advanced to drive Federal cavalry from the town of Gettysburg. Against stiff resistance the Confederates pressed forward only to encounter infantry of the Federal I Corps, who drove the Rebels back from McPherson's Ridge. Other I Corps troops deployed west of Gettysburg, while the XI Corps moved into position north of the town. At noon part of Ewell's corps attacked the I Corps right; by afternoon the battle spread north of town, where Early's Confederates smashed into the XI Corps flank. At the same time, a fresh Confederate division attacked the I Corps on Seminary Ridge. By 4 p.m. the Federals retreated through Gettysburg to take positions on the high ground south of town.*

Archer is a cocky guy who was warned by Pettigrew to advance cautiously, but he does not. He's a Princeton man, not a West Pointer, but he is an old Army man who entered the military from civilian life. And he is going to be assisted initially by Davis's success. With the collapse of the Yankee line north of the railroad grade and the withdrawal of supporting artillery, the Federal regiments south of the pike are in a bad way with Rebels coming from two directions. Archer's people look up toward Seminary Ridge. The Iron Brigade has arrived on the field. Coming up in columns as they begin to deploy in line are soldiers in black hats. These Black Hats are the 2nd, and 7th Wisconsin and the 19th Indiana, joined by a new regiment, the 24th Michigan. The Confederates suddenly realize they aren't facing local militia; they are confronting the Iron Brigade.

The Yankees now overlap the Rebel right flank in the wooded area south of Herbst Woods and double them up like a jackknife. Alabamians and Tennesseeans flee. Pvt. Patrick Murphy of the Second Wisconsin is faster than poor James J. Archer: Murphy horsecollars him, and Archer has the privilege of boasting to his friends, I'm the first Confederate general captured in action since Bobby Lee took command of the Army of Northern Virginia. Doubleday encounters him: they knew each other in the prewar army. Doubleday runs up and sticks out his hand: Archer, damn glad to see you. Archer snaps back, Goddamn it, I'm not glad to see you. The Iron Brigade chases Archer's Rebels all the way back to and across Willoughby Run.

As the Iron Brigade drives back Archer, the attention of the Union forces shifts north across the Chambersburg Pike, where Joe Davis's brigade is bearing down on the unfinished railroad cut.

Davis has the ideal moment to strike what could be a fatal blow to Wadsworth's division. In my view, an experienced commander would have followed up on his initial success. As Davis advances he comes under fire. You remember the last time we saw the 14th Brooklyn, those "red-legged devils" and the 95th New York were facing west on West McPherson's Ridge. They've shifted position and are now behind a post-and-rail fence on the south side of the Chambersburg Pike fronting north. Not having reconnoitered the ground to his front, Davis orders a left wheel. That means the right-most soldier in the 42nd Mississippi will mark time, and every man to his left, shoulder to shoulder, will start turning like a door swinging open.

This is bad for the Second Mississippi because they are going to come up on this deep railroad cut. They are not going to know how deep this cut is until too late. The 55th North Carolina is not initially in big trouble because they are not going into the deep cut. Nor is the 42nd Mississippi. But for the Second Mississippi the cut is so deep and steep that a soldier can't fire out of it. It shows poor judgment on the part of Davis. Meanwhile, the two New York regiments are reinforced. Coming out of the edge of the timber at the seminary is the reserve regiment of the Iron Brigade, the Sixth Wisconsin under Lt. Col. Rufus Dawes. In addition to their 350 men, they have picked up the brigade guard, another hundred soldiers. Dawes takes position on the right of the 95th New York. Then the Yankees charge.

The Second Mississippi has no firebase. The people on their left—the 55th North Carolina—and right—the 42nd Mississippi—have a firebase but the people in the center are not firing. That means they had better get out of here. They're going to leave the Second Mississippi "holding the bag." Soon one of Lt. John H. Calef's guns, belonging to Company A, Second U.S. Artillery, is positioned and firing down the cut. Would you like to be in that railroad cut with a bunch of Yankees firing down on you? What are the Rebs going to do? They surrender. The Yankees capture more than 200, and Cpl. Francis Waller of the Sixth Wisconsin captures the Second Mississippi's colors. Dawes will later say that he had so many surrendered sabers he couldn't carry all of them in his arms.

Shortly after 11 a.m. on July 1 a lull settles over the battlefield. Even as the Union forces celebrate their victory in the railroad cut, more Confederates arrive on the field. This time it's the lead division of Richard Ewell's corps, commanded by Maj. Gen. Robert Rodes. They come from the north; Rodes observes the action in front of him from Oak Hill, a wooded area some distance to the north of the railroad cut.

Imagine what Robert Rodes and Dick Ewell think when they arrive here about noon. They see the entire battlefield in front of them. They look out and recognize that they have a splendid opportunity to strike the Union I Corps in the flank. There are no Union troops within hundreds of yards of them. So, without coordinating their movements what do they do? They order up two batteries of artillery, put them in position, and open fire, drawing to themselves the Yankees' attention.

Rodes's Confederates are to attack around 2:30 p.m., but it's not going to be coordinated. Brigade commander Col. Edward A. O'Neal advances first with three of his five Alabama regiments, not his full strength. They advance southward along the eastern slope of Oak Ridge, come under fire, and break. Next comes Brig. Gen. Alfred Iverson's four Tarheel regiments. They form in the low ground fronting the Forney Farm; they head southeast toward what they believe is the Union right in Wills Woods thrusting westward of Oak Ridge.

The problem with Alfred Iverson: He is a Georgian. According to Confederate law, if a brigade is composed entirely of regiments from one state it should be commanded by someone from that state. There is no doubt that these are all North Carolinians being led by this Georgia boy. He is not a West Pointer; he's gone into the Army from civilian life. He's the son of a former Georgia congressman. He has served in the elite First U.S. Cavalry. Iverson gives them a good fighting speech and away they go, toward the Union right … or so they think.

Brig. Gen. Henry Baxter's Federal brigade had reached Oak Ridge earlier and taken position on the right of I Corps, initially fronting the Mummasburg Road. From here, sheltered by a stone wall, they had savaged O'Neal's Alabamians. When they see Iverson's men come into view, Baxter redeploys his people at a right angle to the Mummasburg Road, behind another stone wall. Iverson's men are unaware of their presence. Baxter's front, the second rank-and-file closers, lie down and watch the Confederates come across the field. As the North Carolinians approach, the regiment on the left, the Fifth North Carolina, is closest to the Yankees. The 20th, 23rd, and 12th North Carolina extend the line southwestward—you want to be in the 12th. When the Confederates approach to within 50 yards of the Yankees, Baxter orders his men to fire. Rank after rank stands up and unleashes a deadly volley; then the bluecoats charge, capturing flags and taking prisoners as they go. Rebels wave white shirts or bandanas in an effort to surrender.

Back at the Forney Farm, adjacent to Oak Hill, Iverson shouts that his men are mutinying and going over to the enemy. His North Carolinians are repulsed with the loss of more than 500 men, 62 percent of their strength. A soldier later writes, "The widows and orphans of North Carolina from Piedmont to Tidewater must rue the rashness of that hour." Iverson's command is obliterated. His men are buried where they fall, including a group of bodies heel to heel. To this day some people claim this ground, known as Iverson's pits, is haunted.

Their ammunition exhausted, Baxter's brigade is relieved by Brig. Gen. Gabriel René Paul's brigade. Paul will be wounded and blinded for life in the desperate fighting here. The XI Corps' position to the northeast comes under severe pressure. Following a botched attack by Brig. Gen. Junius Daniel, the Confederates re-form and come at the Federals from two directions: Brig Gen. Stephen Dodson Ramseur's Tarheels from the north, and Daniel's from the west. Paul's brigade breaks: One regiment, the 16th Maine, stands fast to allow the others to escape. When the Maine regiment's colonel, Charles W. Tilden, sees time running out, he drives his sword into the ground and breaks it off at the hilt. His men tear up their colors as they retreat.

Earlier that day, as the Union XI Corps deployed two divisions north of Gettysburg, division commander Francis C. Barlow, seeing a rise in front of him, advanced his command to what will become known as Barlow's Knoll. It's higher ground, to be sure, but in moving forward Barlow loses contact with the remainder of the Union line. Moreover, he's so busy watching the Confederates to the northwest that he fails to be as observant about a new threat approaching from the northeast along the Harrisburg Road.

You will find on Barlow's Knoll that the ground to the north falls away quickly into Rock Creek, offering good cover to forces advancing from the north and northeast. In possession of the ground to the northwest are skirmishers from Confederate Brig. Gen. George Doles's Georgia Brigade—one of Rodes's five brigades. Barlow anchors his position with four guns of Lt. Bayard Wilkeson's Company G, Fourth U.S. Artillery, and the 17th Connecticut; he deploys three regiments around the knoll to the north and on each flank. There they are, when from the northeast, marching along the Harrisburg Road, approaches the division led by Lee's bad old man, Jubal Early. He has his artillery chief, Lt. Col. Hilary P. Jones, unlimber 16 guns north of Rock Creek. They blast away at Wilkeson's battery, wounding Wilkeson in the leg and knocking out his battery. Meanwhile, John B. Gordon leads his brigade forward. He'd been badly wounded at Antietam as colonel of the Sixth Alabama defending the Sunken Road. When he establishes contact with Doles's left, they're ready to attack. They will be joined by Brig. Gen. Harry T. Hays's Louisiana Tigers bearing down on the knoll from the northeast. You've got Gordon with his six Georgia regiments hammering Barlow's front, George Doles on his left, and Hays enveloping his right. Barlow's position collapses.

After the war Gordon spends much time preaching sectional reconciliation. He tells people that he came upon a badly wounded Barlow, who asks Gordon to send a message to his wife. Gordon agrees, and orders a soldier to look after Barlow. Then he rides away, thinking Barlow's a goner. In the meantime, a Confederate cavalry general, James Byron Gordon, had perished on the field of battle, so the story goes. Barlow thought that was the Gordon who had helped him. Years later Gordon encounters Barlow at a dinner party. Thus the two men meet, each thinking the other's dead, and they greet each other heartily—or so Gordon tells the story. Gordon forgets that they are both at Appomattox Court House and then embarked on public careers. Still, it makes for the sort of story people want to believe.

Wilkeson's fate offers a better story. His father Samuel is a newspaperman, representing the *New York Times*. He is with the army. This is going to be unfortunate for Meade, because the elder Wilkeson believes that his son's battery is placed too far out in front. When a shell explodes near the battery it all but severs the younger Wilkeson's right leg. The only thing that is holding his right leg to the rest of his body are the tendons. Wilkeson uses his pocketknife to amputate his lower leg—a personal amputation, and because of it he dies. Meade has made an enemy who will subsequently use his newspaper to unfairly criticize Meade.

As the Confederates swarm over Barlow's Knoll, the Union XI Corps breaks. It's about 4:30 p.m., and the corps retreats southward through Gettysburg. About that same time the Union I Corps also breaks, pulling back off Seminary Ridge and scampering through the streets of the town. As the Yankees rally on Cemetery Hill, just south of Gettysburg, the Confederates deliberate whether to launch another attack. As the XI Corps retreats, one Federal brigade, just north of town, attempts to check the advancing Confederates.

Popular legend blames Lt. Gen. Richard "Old Baldy" Ewell for Confederate defeat at Gettysburg due to his failure to carry out Lee's order to secure Cemetery Hill; a direct order was likely never issued.

In response to orders from General Howard, Second Division commander Brig. Gen. Adolph von Steinwehr contacts one of his brigade commanders, Col. Charles R. Coster, and says, "I want you to advance your brigade from East Cemetery Hill down into town and cover our retreat." As Coster approaches the "Diamond" (the term mid-19th-century residents of south-central Pennsylvania called the town square), he detaches the 73rd Pennsylvania. Coster advances his other three regiments, the 27th Pennsylvania, 154th New York, and 134th New York, and takes position behind a post-and-rail fence at Kuhn's Brickyard. Two Confederate brigades—Hays's and Avery's—charge, and after perhaps ten minutes Coster's men have had enough. They are driven through the town, a large number of them captured.

After the battle, on July 4, they're going to find an unidentified dead Union sergeant clutching an image of his three children. Newspapers publish the story and others circulate engravings made of the three adorable children. Finally, Philinda Humiston of Portville, New York, recognizes the faces as her children: The dead soldier was her husband Amos, of the 154th New York. The incident touched many hearts and led to fund-raising to establish an orphanage for children of the Union dead in Gettysburg, where the the Widow Humiston would later work. It opened in 1866; it's located on Cemetery Hill along the Baltimore Turnpike.

On Cemetery Hill, General Howard struggled ineffectively to reorganize the shattered Federal forces. When Winfield Scott Hancock arrived with orders from Meade to assess the situation, he displaced Howard and set about organizing a defense. By late afternoon, with the Federals falling back in disarray, it was time for the Confederates to decide whether to follow up on their previous successes.

Dick Ewell is trying to figure out what is going on. He informs Lee that he's willing to contemplate an attack. He can't form his command up in the streets of the town itself, he's got to deploy them east of the borough. He'd like to wait for the arrival of his third division under Maj. Gen. Edward "Old Allegheny" Johnson before attacking; he tells Lee, "I will attack if you will release to me Richard Anderson's division," which has just arrived west of town along the Chambersburg Pike. Lee responds, "No, no, I am not going to release Anderson. I have to keep him in reserve lest we face disaster here."

Notice that uncertainty in Lee's response? If you're Ewell, you are used to the vocal nuances of your commanding officer. What is Ewell to do? Unlike Stonewall Jackson, under whom Ewell had served as a division commander in 1862, Lee has given him a discretionary order twice repeated. You will exercise the discretion given to you, and that's what Ewell did. He decides he isn't going to attack and seize Culp's Hill on the evening of the first. Late that night a Confederate reconnaissance discovers that Union forces have occupied Culp's Hill.

Thus ended the first day of the Battle of Gettysburg. In future years Ewell will come under criticism for not attacking Cemetery Hill: His decision not to attack becomes one of the many what-ifs of the battle.

All through the night and into the next morning Union reinforcements arrive south of Gettysburg. They take up a line that resembles a fishhook, with the barb at Culp's Hill, the curve draped along Cemetery Hill, and the shank extending southward along Cemetery Ridge toward Little Round Top. By mid-morning the VI Corps has yet to arrive, and they are scheduled to appear during the day.

At his headquarters on Seminary Ridge, in the early morning hours of July 2, Robert E. Lee sets about making plans to renew his offensive.

Lee and Longstreet are in disagreement on what the Confederates should do. Longstreet believes that it would be best if the Confederates forced the Yankees to do the attacking: He remembers Fredericksburg. Lee, on the other hand, is anxious to attack: He remembers Chancellorsville. Lee finally breaks off the discussion, saying, "The enemy is there, and I am going to attack him." Longstreet responds, "If he is there in the morning that means he wants you to attack him—a good reason for not doing so." To which Lee replies, "I am going to whip them, or they are going to whip me."

Lee orders a reconnaissance of the Union left. He calls for Capt. Sam Johnston, the army's chief engineer. Lee tells Johnston, "I want you to take an escort with you and make a reconnaissance and see how far south on Cemetery Ridge the Union line extends. I want you to go up on the high ground." Johnston, accompanied by Maj. John J. Clarke of Longstreet's staff, makes his reconnaissance, and he sees that the Union line does not extend very far south (only to about the site of today's

Trusted adviser to Lee, Gen. James Longstreet (pictured in a postwar photograph) directed most of the fighting on the second day, recognizing the key strategic importance of Big and Little Round Tops.

Pennsylvania State Monument). He's back about 8:30 a.m. and makes his report to Lee and Longstreet.

Lee decides to order Longstreet to march his two divisions to a position along the Emmitsburg Road, deploy astride that road, and assail the Union left flank. At the same time, Ewell's corps will launch an assault on the Federal right at Culp's Hill. It will be Chancellorsville all over again, he believes. Longstreet tells Lee that he is missing one of his eight brigades—Brig. Gen. Evander Law's—and that he does not want to move out until Law joins. Lee gives him permission to wait for Law.

Now, where does Law have to march from? He has to come from New Guilford, Pennsylvania, more than 20 miles away. His men have been on the march since 2 a.m. After Law arrives, Lee envisions an attack unfolding from right to left, with the divisions of Maj. Gens. John B. Hood and Lafayette McLaws being joined by several of A. P. Hill's III Corps brigades, commencing with Maj. Gen. Richard Anderson's men. What kind of cooperation will there be between Hill and Longstreet? What is Anderson to do? If Anderson is to cooperate, is Anderson under Longstreet's command? Is Anderson under Hill? It's never spelled out who controls Anderson.

Anderson uses Brig. Gen. Cadmus M. Wilcox's big Alabama Brigade to extend southward along Seminary Ridge, opposite and more or less parallel to the Union positions on Cemetery Ridge. They make contact with Berdan's First U.S. Sharpshooters and the Third Maine in Pitzer's Woods. There's a sharp firefight, and Maj. Gen. Daniel Sickles learns that there are Confederates in his front, concealed in the woods. Sickles is not going to be hung out to dry in Chancellorsville style, so he begins moving his two III Corps divisions west to cover Emmitsburg Road and the Peach Orchard, leaving Little Round Top unoccupied by combat people. The Union left flank is not going to be where Lee thinks it is.

When Longstreet's people finally move out it is past noon. McLaws has the lead. The two divisions are supposed to work their way southward along a concealed route blocked from Yankee observation. There are two problems with this plan. First, no one has scouted out a route. Second, in the distance, atop Little Round Top, there is a detachment from the Union signal corps. Those men have a good view of the terrain west of Seminary Ridge; if the Confederate movement is detected, the entire operation may be endangered. As McLaws's vanguard prepares to cross Bream's Hill, the lead Confederates see the signal station, and they know that that means the signal station can also see them.

Longstreet calls for a countermarch. The countermarch costs valuable time, and the critics will ask why Longstreet didn't march all his men the way that Porter Alexander moves the 75 guns, the 150 limbers, and

75 caissons of the artillery—by avoiding crossing Bream's Hill and going around the hill. Instead, they countermarch, and it is not until 3 p.m. that the head of McLaws's column approaches Seminary Ridge, where he is to deploy astride the Emmitsburg Road.

Longstreet intends his men to attack in echelon—timing their blows in sequence from right to left. The intent of it is this: You hit first on the enemy's right. The enemy will shift men to check the attack. Then another advance hits to the left, and they may strike a weak spot. Sooner or later, if the attacker gets the enemy shifting units to the left, the enemy will leave a weak point as it scrambles forces to repel the echelon attacks.

Unfortunately for the Confederates, by the time McLaws and Hood are about to arrive at their jumping-off points, the situation has changed. The III Corps under Sickles was supposed to extend the line of the II Corps south along Cemetery Ridge to the vicinity of Little Round Top. But Sickles does not like his position. To the west he sees high ground, a site that looks ideal for artillery. When news comes back of the clash in Pitzer's Woods, he decides that if he waits in line he might find himself in trouble. So he advances his men, first to the Trostle Farm several hundred yards to the west, then several hundred yards more to Sherfy's Peach Orchard and the Emmitsburg Road. Union Brig. Gen. Andrew A. Humphreys deploys his division facing west along the Emmitsburg Road. David Birney struggles to cover the area between Trostle Lane and Sherfy's Peach Orchard and the foot of Little Round Top with three brigades, only to find that his line is divided by woods and farmland, particularly Rose Woods and a wheat field, west of Little Round Top.

Through midday George Gordon Meade appeared to be far more concerned about an assault against his right flank at Culp's Hill than a blow directed at his left. It is not until after 3 p.m. that he rides out to see what is going on. He is furious. Sickles's position may have some tactical advantages, but he has detached himself from the rest of the army and left the Round Tops undefended.

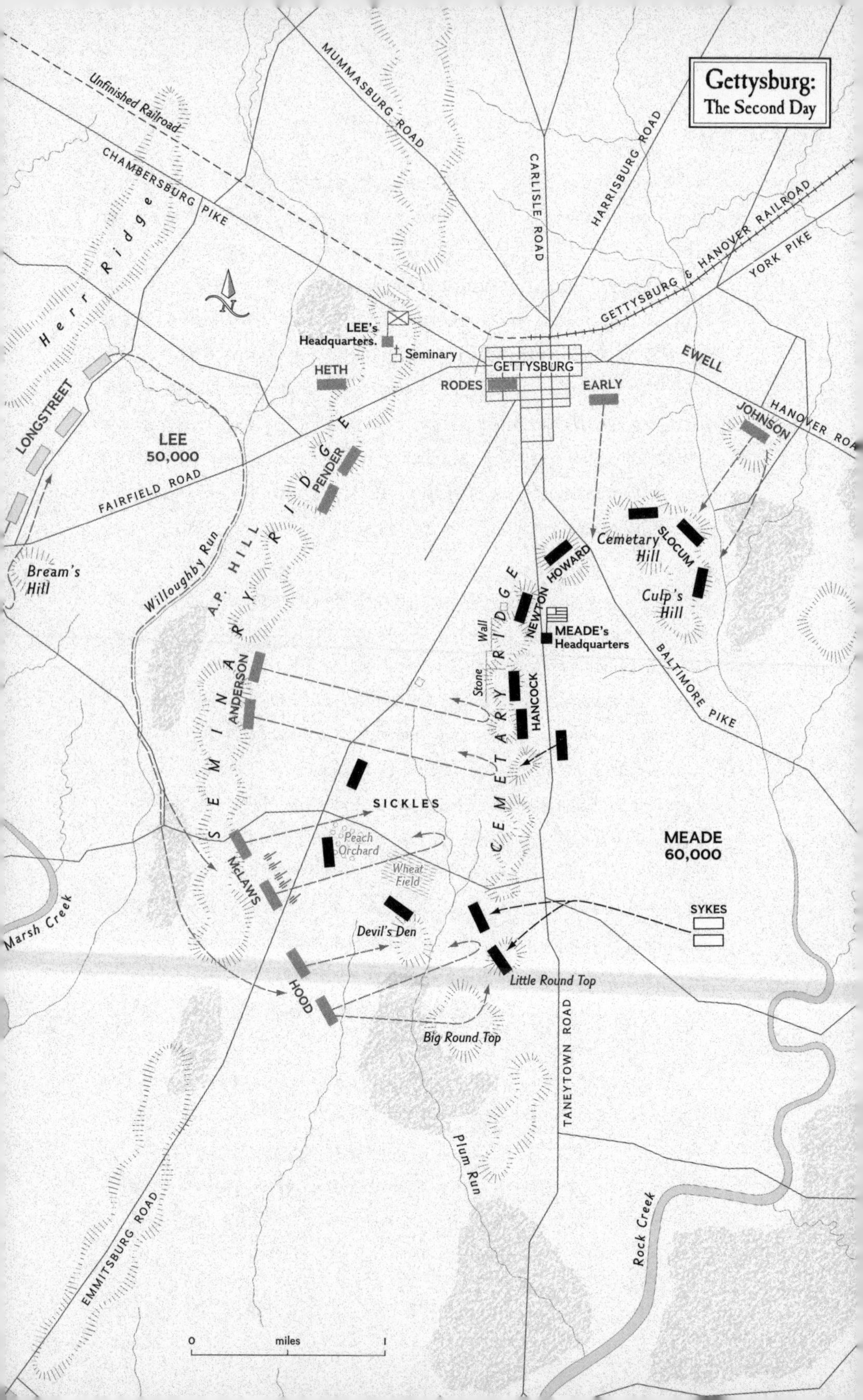
Gettysburg:
The Second Day
Unfinished Railroad
MUMMASBURG ROAD
CARLISLE ROAD
HARRISBURG ROAD
GETTYSBURG & HANOVER RAILROAD
YORK PIKE
CHAMBERSBURG PIKE
Herr Ridge
LEE's Headquarters.
Seminary
HETH
GETTYSBURG
RODES
EARLY
EWELL
JOHNSON
HANOVER ROAD
LONGSTREET
LEE
50,000
FAIRFIELD ROAD
PENDER
Bream's Hill
Willoughby Run
A.P. HILL
SEMINARY RIDGE
Cemetary Hill
SLOCUM
HOWARD
Culp's Hill
NEWTON
MEADE's Headquarters
BALTIMORE PIKE
Stone Wall
ANDERSON
HANCOCK
CEMETARY RIDGE
SICKLES
Peach Orchard
Wheat Field
McLAWS
MEADE
60,000
Marsh Creek
SYKES
Devil's Den
Little Round Top
HOOD
Big Round Top
TANEYTOWN ROAD
Plum Run
Rock Creek
EMMITSBURG ROAD
0
miles
1

The III Corps moves out 10,000 strong. As they make their final advance up to the Emmitsburg Road and to the Peach Orchard, Winfield Scott Hancock and his staff officers are impressed with the parade-ground precision Humphreys's men display. Hancock, being the realist that he is, remarks, "Just wait; they are going to come tumbling back much faster than they went out." Hancock is going to have to sacrifice to save Sickles by feeding in piecemeal five of his ten brigades to try to blunt the Confederate attack. Meade will also have to use three divisions of V Corps as he seeks to stall Longstreet's savage onslaught.

Longstreet may have been right in saying that the next three hours are going to show the finest fighting we've seen any soldiers do. Eleven Confederate brigades are going to beat up 15 Union brigades. It's going to be one of the few times in the Civil War when the attackers are going to lose fewer men than the defenders. One might even argue that this is the bloodiest single day of combat in the entire war, more so than Antietam, although the casualty returns cited for Gettysburg's three days are not broken down to enumerate the losses day by day.

The only person who is more surprised than General Meade as to the location of Sickles's corps is Lafayette McLaws, when he finds out where the Union left is posted. It isn't where he had been led to believe it would be. The Confederates are operating on out-of-date information. McLaws comes up on Seminary Ridge and sees lots of Yankee infantry and artillery to his front in the Peach Orchard and extending north along

OPPOSITE: *Meade held a fishhook-shaped position, with his right on Culp's Hill, his center along Cemetery Ridge, and his left near the Round Tops. Realizing that Meade's left was exposed, Lee ordered Longstreet to march south with two divisions to attack the Federal left. Longstreet's assault struck General Sickles's III Corps, forcing Meade to reinforce Sickles. After desperate fighting at the Devil's Den and in the Wheat Field and Peach Orchard, the Federal line collapsed. Earlier the Confederates attacked Little Round Top, where Federal forces arrived in time to block their advance. An attack by Ewell's corps on Culp's Hill on the Federal right came too late, and an attempt to storm Cemetery Hill at dusk also failed.*

the Emmitsburg Road to well beyond the Klingle House. They are not supposed to be there, so he's got big trouble. McLaws informs Longstreet of the situation.

Over on the far Confederate right flank is John Bell Hood's division. Holding down its right is Evander Law's brigade, which has been on the road since 2 a.m.

Hood moves into position, extending southward along the Emmitsburg Road. He doesn't like his situation. He would like to extend his flank and pass over and south of Big Round Top, a move somewhat like the one Longstreet urged on Lee twice, the previous day and that morning, before he had been overruled. Longstreet comes back short and sharp: "General Lee says we are to attack up the Emmitsburg Road, and we will attack up the Emmitsburg Road." Hood repeats his request and Longstreet repeats his reply. Hood makes a final appeal, employing a key member of Longstreet's staff to try to get him to change his mind. For the third time Longstreet points out that "General Lee says we will attack up the Emmitsburg Road."

Law's Alabamians will have marched at least 26 miles by the time they get into position. They're going to have the most difficult assignment of any Confederate unit, because they're going to be moving the farthest and they will be advancing across the roughest ground. Off to the east are two rocky hills: Big Round Top, 789 feet high and heavily wooded, and Little Round Top, 674 feet high, with its west face cleared. They know that's where the Union signal station is. Despite the fact that Hood's request to move to the left has been thrice rejected by Longstreet with a reminder of General Lee's order that they are to attack up the Emmitsburg Road, several of Hood's brigades immediately drift over toward the Round Tops and the jumble of boulders at their base called Devil's Den. Their advance seems as if by design.

A young Confederate soldier lies fallen among the boulders of Devil's Den.

Even before the Civil War, it was known as Devil's Den. It was a popular picnic place by day and at night a trysting place. Sickles's extreme left is here. Capt. James E. Smith unlimbers four cannon of the Fourth New York Battery on Houck's Ridge extending north from Devil's Den in support of the Orange Blossoms (the 124th New York). The Federals start off more than holding their own. But two Alabama regiments (the 44th and 48th) rush the 4th Maine, supported on the left by the Mozart Regiment (the 40th New York), as well as the 6th New Jersey and two of Captain Smith's cannon to the right.

Initially the Yanks check the Rebel surge, but the Alabamians soon prevail. The bluecoats abandon the Slaughter Pen and Devil's Den. The Triangular Field defended by the Orange Blossoms now becomes the focus of attacks spearheaded by the First Texas and Third Arkansas. Savage combat ebbs and flows as Confederates pour into the Triangular Field from the west. But there are too many Rebels. Four regiments of Georgians, Texans, and Arkansans storm forward and carry the position, capturing three of James Smith's four guns, and driving the Federals from Houck's Ridge.

While the fighting rages around Devil's Den, two of Evander Law's regiments approach the foot of Big Round Top.

One of Law's regimental commanders is Col. William C. Oates of the 15th Alabama. He has called for 20 volunteers to take as many canteens as they can and fill them up at a well. The cistern is not functioning, so they have to use the windlass. They fill the canteens, but by the time they return, Oates is gone. They wander around, and the Yankees are going to capture them along with the extra canteens, carrying the water Oates's people needed that hot July day.

When Oates reaches the summit of Big Round Top, he claims that he can see the Union supply train in the distance. He sends one company off to capture seven nearby wagons. That makes 110 men sent elsewhere as Oates directs the 15th Alabama to descend Big Round Top and head north to Little Round Top. The 47th Alabama follows, but it's becoming confusing in the woods, and the two brigades—Law's and Brig. Gen. Jerome "Aunt Polly" Robertson's Texans—intermingle. Had Hood been there, things might have been different. But he's down, hit in the left arm by fragments from a bursting shell near the Bushman Barn, and it takes some time to notify Evander Law that he is to take over for the fallen Hood.

While the two Confederate brigades close in on the Round Tops and Devil's Den, Chief engineer of the Army of the Potomac Brig. Gen. Gouverneur K. Warren ascends Little Round Top to take in the situation. Finding the summit unoccupied

Hastily constructed breastworks protected Federal soldiers from Confederate sharpshooters atop Little Round Top. In the distance, Big Round Top is visible.

by combat troops, Warren and his staff begin seeking troops to defend the spot. Off in the distance Warren sees Confederates advancing. There's no time to lose.

Warren and his engineer officers look for men just as elements of Maj. Gen. George Sykes's V Corps arrive on their march toward the Wheat Field. One aide rides up to Third Brigade commander Col. Strong Vincent, a lawyer, Harvard man, 26 years old. Taking in the situation instantly, Vincent, without waiting for orders, hurries his brigade to the south slope of Little Round Top, and then deploys it. On their right is the 16th Michigan. On their left is the 44th New York; on the New Yorkers' left is the 83rd Pennsylvania, and on the extreme left is the 20th Maine.

The first Confederate attack is launched against the 16th Michigan, the 44th New York, and the left wing of the 83rd Pennsylvania by three Rebel regiments: the Fourth and Fifth Texas and the Fourth Alabama. They fail and fall back. Fighting is also raging in the Slaughter Pen and Devil's Den at the foot of Little Round Top. The Confederates come back again and assail Vincent's three right regiments. They charge up in groups and are repulsed a second time.

By this time the Rebels hold the Slaughter Pen and Devil's Den. That means they have another regiment—the 48th Alabama—available for their next attack on Little Round Top. The 16th Michigan on the right is running low on ammunition; this time the Rebels roll them back from right to left and rush for the summit. Among the mortally wounded is Strong Vincent. Now arriving, coming in from the northeast, is Patrick O'Rorke's 140th New York, part of Brig. Gen. Stephen H. Weed's brigade of V Corps. O'Rorke's men come up in column. There's no time to deploy them into line. They charge in column with bayonets. The Rebels seem to be on the verge of crumpling Vincent's brigade from right to left and seizing Little Round Top.

Why is Paddy O'Rorke here? Warren did not see Vincent deploy, so he hurried down the northern slope of Little Round Top and encountered Weed's brigade. Warren knew the brigade because once it had been his own. Meeting Paddy O'Rorke, Warren tells him to hasten to Little Round Top. O'Rorke's a promising officer, top of the June class at West Point in 1861, and he goes off with his 140th New York, leaving his brigade commander to come up with the three other regiments. Warren also calls for Lt. Charles A. Hazlett to bring six guns of his Company D, Fifth U.S. Artillery, to the summit.

Weed has the best last words I've ever heard. A Confederate sharpshooter fires, and the bullet hits Weed under his right armpit, emerges through his left armpit, and severs his spine. As he falls he says, "Where is Hazlett?" Weed had once commanded Hazlett's battery; he wants to see his old comrade one more time. Hazlett goes over, having put his guns in position, and bends over Weed. As he is bending

Unlikely hero of Gettsyburg Col. Joshua L. Chamberlain, a college professor with little military training, led the 20th Maine in the defense of Little Round Top.

over Weed, a Confederate fires—maybe it's the same guy—and the bullet strikes Hazlett in the temple. Hazlett bathes Weed in his blood. He's dead. Now staff officers try to encourage Weed. They tell him that he's going to recover. And these are his last words: "By tomorrow morning I'm as dead a man as Julius Caesar." And he will be.

Even as O'Rorke and Weed secure the southwest approach to Little Round Top's crest, along the left front of Vincent's brigade, there's a new threat. Col. William Oates's 15th Alabama, supported by the 47th Alabama, is about to head straight for Col. Joshua Lawrence Chamberlain's 20th Maine, which forms the far left not only of Vincent's brigade on Little Round Top but of the entire Army of the Potomac.

Initially Chamberlain deploys in a straight line extending into the woods on the left of the 83rd Pennsylvania. He sends off Capt. Walter R. Morrill with Company B to check out the area to the southeast. Chamberlain later remembers that he's in position about ten minutes before the Rebels come. The Maine men repulse the first attack; then Oates and his Alabamians begin to work their way around the open Union flank. Oates pushes the 20th Maine's left flank back; Chamberlain extends his line as well. Before long the line has been bent back until it resembles a V. If Oates can close that V, that's the end of the 20th Maine and Joshua Lawrence Chamberlain.

It's been a long, hard, hot fight. Both regiments, as well as the 47th Alabama, are approaching the breaking point. The 20th Maine has probably marched seven miles this day. The 15th Alabama has already marched 26 miles. They've been going over more rugged terrain, and they've gone without water. So just as Oates attacks again, Chamberlain orders his men to fix bayonets and to sweep down on the Confederates like a door swinging open on their left flank. His men have the same idea, and just as the Alabamians pause, here come the Maine men, bayonets glistening, charging down. As the Confederates retreat, the boys from Company B, along with a score of the Second U.S. Sharpshooters, pepper their flank. Little Round Top is secure, and Chamberlain becomes a hero.

To the north of Devil's Den and west of Little Round Top is a wheat field bounded on four sides by woods. There's only one III Corps Union brigade available to hold the area; several Confederate brigades head toward it from the south and the west. In response, units from the Union II and V Corps arrive as reinforcements and will participate in some of the war's most confusing and bitter fighting, in an area that will eventually be known simply as the Wheat Field.

At the beginning of the action, there are only two Union regiments in place, because several others had been sent off to fight in Devil's Den.

Men of the 17th Maine, part of Col. P. Regis de Trobriand's Third Brigade of III Corps, know they're good, because they had received their diamond-shaped red corps badges before most other units. They are posted along and behind a stone wall. To their right is the 110th Pennsylvania; the other Yankee regiments are west of the Wheat Field on Stony Hill. There's a six-gun battery in support. Initially they're going to face an attack into this area by the Third Arkansas and the First Texas. The 17th Maine stands tall. They're behind a stone wall. It's going to give them a distinct advantage against the first assault, and they will repulse that. With the Confederate attack stalled, the Confederates commit a fresh brigade—Brig. Gen. George T. "Tige" Anderson's Georgians. The 17th Maine begins to give way.

Learning of the deteriorating situation, Winfield Scott Hancock rushes reinforcements to bolster Sickles's people in the struggle for the Wheat Field and Stony Hill. He commits Brig. Gen. John C. Caldwell's four-brigade division, including the Irish Brigade. Two divisions of V Corps, each minus a brigade (those of Vincent and Weed), appear as well. At the head of one of Caldwell's brigades is Col. Edward Cross. He's 31 years old. As we know, he has very little hair on the top of his head, and usually covers it with a red bandana. But on this day when he reaches for his bandana, it is black, which Cross reads as an omen. A veteran of the Mexican army, Cross has been wounded at Seven Pines, Antietam, and Fredericksburg. Hancock likes him. Hancock says, "This is your last battle without a star." Cross simply replies, "Too late, General, this is my last battle." And it was. To the west two more brigades, including the Irish Brigade, are committed to battle. Before the Irish Brigade advances, they kneel in front of Father William Corby, who grants them absolution before warning them that being cowards in the face of the enemy will deny them a Christian burial. No matter how many Yankees come into the Wheat Field, no matter how many times they drive the Confederates out, the Confederates come back for more.

By 6:30 p.m. they finally gain control of the field, which has become a maelstrom of death and destruction.

There has been savage fighting here, with nine Union brigades chewed up. Longstreet has committed two regiments of Robertson's brigade, one of Brig. Gen. Henry L. "Rock" Benning's brigade, Tige Anderson's Georgia Brigade, Brig. Gen. Joseph Kershaw's brigade, Brig. Gen. Paul Semmes's brigade, and finally Brig. Gen. William T. Wofford's brigade.

To the west of the Wheat Field, across the Rose Farm, is a peach orchard. The apex of Sickles's salient is found there in an area where artillery batteries make up for the lack of infantry. Even as Hood's division sweeps south of this position, Lafayette McLaws's division prepares to strike it.

It's 5:15 or 5:20 p.m. before McLaws sends in his first brigade. Out from the cover of the trees on Seminary Ridge emerge Joseph Kershaw's South Carolinians. They head for Rose Woods and the Wheat Field before they come under fire. Two regiments and a battalion break off from Kershaw's force and advance toward the Peach Orchard. Union infantry take position to check Kershaw's advance. Next out of the woods comes Paul Semmes's Georgia Brigade, and it fights its way into Rose Woods.

Meanwhile Brig. Gen. William Barksdale, in charge of a brigade of Mississippians, itches to get into action. He's a fire-eater, a former congressman, who back in 1858 got into a fistfight on the floor of the House with fellow Representative Galusha Grow of Pennsylvania. Elihu Washburne, Cadwallader Washburn, and John Potter, joined Grow in pummeling Barksdale. Potter sucker punched Barksdale from the rear, sending Barksdale and his toupee reeling. Barksdale forgot all about Grow and got down on the floor to search for his rug. Today Barksdale goes to McLaws not once but twice, "Are you ready for me to advance?" He has 1,700 Mississippians.

The third time he pesters McLaws, McLaws looks at Longstreet, who nods his head. Barksdale rides back and takes position between the 13th Mississippi and the 17th Mississippi. He orders his men to load and cap their pieces: They're going to double-time. They're going to come across that field as fast as they can, going on the presumption that if they cross that ground fast and with "the big momentum behind them," they will smash through the Yankees. And they do. Brig. Gen. Charles K. Graham and 700 men will ground their arms and surrender. The Confederates finally score a major breakthrough: They have shattered Sickles's angle. The Union batteries better get out of here fast. Meanwhile, three of Barksdale's regiments—the 13th, 17th, and 18th Mississippi—pivot to the left and open fire on the left flank of Andrew Humphreys's division. They are joined by Cadmus Wilcox's brigade, which surges out of Pitzer's Woods and closes on Humphreys's front.

Back by the Trostle Barn, Daniel Sickles watches his corps disintegrate. A cannonball strikes him in the right leg, midway between knee and ankle. They place him on a stretcher and begin to move him off the field. In an effort to reassure his men, he waves a cigar in the air.

Other Union soldiers soon follow. Capt. John Bigelow of the Ninth Massachusetts Battery, seeing his horses go down, orders his cannon to retire by prolonge—a tow rope used to attach a gun to its limber while it remains in firing position. Continuing to blast away, the men use the recoil to retire the guns in stages. That works fine until they reach a stone fence, where their route of retreat is choked off by a too narrow gap in the fence. Bigelow falls wounded; it's up to his bugler to rescue him from capture. His men save only one gun, but Bigelow has bought precious time by delaying Barksdale. More artillery unlimbers to the east of the Trostle Farm, waiting to hammer the advancing soldiers of the 21st Mississippi.

Andrew Humphreys's division gives ground. Humphreys seems to be everywhere. He later asserts that his men re-formed six times, and each time the Rebels break his line. When he finally rallies his division he can find fewer than 500 men, having started with well over 4,000. Barksdale and Wilcox have done well. They have smashed through Sickles's line. They now head for the thinly held Union center.

Awaiting them is Hancock "The Superb," who today of all days will more than live up to his nom de guerre. He sees Wilcox coming. He also sees the First Minnesota Infantry—262 men. Hancock rides up to Col. William Colvill and tells him that he wants Colvill to charge. Colvill sees that Wilcox has more than a thousand men. He's understandably reluctant, but when Hancock presses him, Colvill agrees to attack. He orders his men to load and cap their pieces. He wants them to advance at double time, carrying their weapons so the bayonets point toward the throats of the enemy.

The Alabama regiments can't believe it. They cannot believe that a force they outnumber four to one is coming at them. They are so stunned that they're too slow in responding. They let the Minnesotans close to within 20 or 30 yards. The Minnesotans halt and fire one volley and, with their bayonets, charge into the Alabamians. There is a wild melee. It may last five minutes. The Minnesotans lose some 80 percent of their command, but they blunt the Confederate onslaught.

Meanwhile, Hancock gathers more regiments—Col. George A. Willard's brigade, which today and the next will redeem its reputation and no longer be the Harpers Ferry cowards. He sends them forward to fill the gap in the Union front that has been opened east of the Trostle House by the collapse of Sickles's Peach Orchard salient, and drives back Wilcox and Barksdale. Barksdale's men have run out of gas; they finally give way under the force of this counterattack. As he leads his Mississippi brigade forward, Barksdale is riddled by bullets. He falls, and dies that night.

By 7 p.m. the Confederates continue to make headway. We've already spoken of the advance of Wilcox. Coming out of the woods and crossing the Emmitsburg Road in the vicinity of the white picket fence at the Rogers House site are the three small regiments of Col. David Lang's Florida

Maj. Gen. Winfield Hancock (center), commander of Federal II Corps, held key Union ground on July 1; by July 3 the "hero of Gettysburg" was in command of three-fifths of the Army of the Potomac.

Brigade, the Second, Fifth, and Eighth. As they cross those post-and-rail fences, they advance and pivot toward Humphreys. They help capture one Yankee gun belonging to Lt. John Turnbull's Companies F and K of the Third U.S. Artillery, and inflict more damage on Humphreys's infantry.

Finally, Brig. Gen. Ambrose "Rans" Wright's Georgians of Dick Anderson's division, cross the open fields and fence lines separating Seminary Ridge and Emmitsburg Road before hitting the Union position at the Codori House and outbuildings. They close on Gulian Weir's battery; three Union regiments break. It looks as if Wright is going to smash through the Federal position and win the day—except that as the Georgians look back, they see no one advancing on their left.

For a moment the Federal situation is desperate. Meade himself, along with his staff, scrounges up reinforcements in hopes of stopping Wright. Hancock rides over to Col. Francis Randall of the 13th Vermont and orders him to counterattack. Capt. John Lonergan's Company A lets go an "Irish yell" and surges forward. Crossing the Emmitsburg Road, Lonergan's people surround the Peter Rogers house and capture more than 80 Alabamans holed up on the property. Meade's headquarters guard is the Tenth New York, the National Zouaves. He goes to them and the 71st Pennsylvania and tells them "I want you guys to drive back the foe." Wright's men close on "the angle"—where a stone wall changed direction, jutting west some 260 feet. They're eyeball to eyeball with the 69th Pennsylvania. So far they've overrun three of the four guns of Lt. Gulian V. Weir's Company C, Fifth U.S. Artillery, and two Napoleons of Lt. T. Fred Brown's Company B, First Rhode Island Light Artillery.

Maybe it's all over for the Union. But that is not to be. The Yankees stand tall. Wright's men are driven back. The Yankees recover the two guns of Brown's battery, they recover Weir's cannon and the guns Lang's Floridians had captured. The mighty Confederate counterattack has run its course. The Union again has rallied troops under the fearless General Hancock, who today demonstrates the value of personal leadership—something lacking in Lee, Hill, and Anderson. No wonder Wright will say the next day, when he learns of another attack coming across this same ground, "I was there yesterday. The trouble is to stay there after you get there...."

As the Confederate attack on the Union left winds down, over on the Union right, on East Cemetery Hill and Culp's Hill, the action begins to pick up. Richard Ewell had been under orders to provide a diversion during Longstreet's attack. At first he did so simply by bombarding the Union lines opposite his corps. Now, with dusk approaching, he decides to turn his demonstration into an attack. Unknown to him, given the shift of Union forces to the left to stop Longstreet, he will face a weakened Union line, especially on Culp's Hill.

Union soldiers of Brig. Gen. George Sears Greene's New York Brigade of Brig. Gen. John W. Geary's division of XII Corps, deployed along Culp's

Hill, throw up breastworks: The ground is too hard to dig into, so there are few entrenchments. That work continues through the day on July 2 before word comes that help is needed on the left flank to contain Longstreet's attack. Brig. Gen. Thomas H. Ruger's division hustles over, leaving their former lines empty. As Longstreet's onslaught gains more ground, orders come for Geary to rush support to cope with Longstreet's increasing pressure, particularly with the loss of the Wheat Field. He marches off with two of his three brigades, leaving Greene to defend this entire XII Corps sector with his lone brigade of 1,400 men.

Greene's a crusty veteran. Born in 1801, graduated second in his class from West Point in 1823, he's an engineer who has no patience with the shoulder-to-shoulder tactics practiced by many officers who think they're Napoleon. He has his men throw up the best breastworks possible, despite the patronizing remarks of General Geary, to make up for his shortage of manpower. On his extreme right—the right flank of the entire Army of the Potomac—is Col. David Ireland's 137th New York, 423 men strong. Ireland's defending a front that is about three times as long as that held by Chamberlain's 20th Maine, although the two regiments are about equal in strength. He is going to be assailed by one of the largest brigades in this fight, Brig. Gen. George H. "Maryland" Steuart's unit, consisting of five regiments and a battalion. To help defend his position, where there's a depression between the two heights—the lesser and the greater—of Culp's Hill, Ireland has his men throw up a traverse, a breastworks that extends back from the main line, so that if the enemy breaks the line the defenders can pull back behind the traverse and grimly hold on.

"Old Allegheny" Johnson attacks with only three of his four brigades at dusk on July 2. Another brigade, the Stonewall Brigade, has to be detached to do what cavalry should be doing, watching the Confederate extreme left on Hanover Road. The Confederates sweep up Culp's Hill from Rock Creek, overrunning the vacated breastworks to Greene's right, and surge through the saddle. Ireland's people pull back behind the traverse. They're fortunate because two regiments from I Corps arrive at the same time as reinforcements—those redlegged devils of the 14th Brooklyn and the Sixth Wisconsin of the Iron Brigade. Other regiments shore up the Union position, and Greene holds fast.

As Johnson deploys his men to attack Culp's Hill late on the afternoon of July 2, to his right more Confederates prepare to advance against the apex of the Union position on East Cemetery Hill. Cemetery Hill is held by battered units of XI Corps along with several artillery batteries.

The gatehouse to Evergreen Cemetery, established in 1854, fronts on the Baltimore Pike. There's lots of artillery here on July 2. You figure that your infantry should have no trouble holding this ground. The Yankees send forward a skirmish line—the 41st New York and the 33rd Massachusetts, then set up a battle line behind a stone wall edging alongside Brickyard Lane, a road that runs along the lower slope. There's a gap in the line, just where the Confederates intend to go. What do you do? You've got a weak point, and since you're not worried about the area perpendicular to the Baltimore Pike and Brickyard Lane, you'll pull the 17th Connecticut out of there and send them down to plug the gap behind the stone wall fronting Brickyard Lane. So, you've closed a gap between the 75th Ohio and the 153rd Pennsylvania, but opened one between the 25th and 107th Ohio. What happens? The Louisiana Tigers come through the spot vacated by the 17th Connecticut.

The Confederate forces assigned to storm East Cemetery Hill are under Jubal Early, who likes to fight and hates Yankees. But he assigns only two of his four brigades—Harry Hays's Tigers and Col. Isaac E. Avery's Tarheels—to the attack. On the other side of the hill Robert Rodes takes one look at his bruised division and wonders whether he can do very much

Federal breastworks in the woods on Culp's Hill. Fighting on the Federal right flank along East Cemetery Hill and Culp's Hill closed the second day of battle at Gettysburg.

against the Yankee cannon and infantry up on West Cemetery Hill.

Early isn't worried, and when his men pour through that gap, the Union line gives way and the Rebels charge up the slope, overrunning one four-gun battery—Capt. Michael Wiedrich's Company I, First New York Light Artillery—and capturing two of the six cannon of Capt. Bruce Rickett's battery of Pennsylvania Light Artillery. It's a pitched battle, lots of hand-to-hand combat, but it's getting dark and the Confederates have no reserves with which to exploit their successes. Union reinforcements—including a II Corps brigade led by Col. Samuel "Bricktop" Carroll—rush to stabilize the Yankee line. The Yankees recover this position, recapture the six guns, and another serious threat has been dealt with. The Confederates again are left to muse about what might have been.

The fighting along East Cemetery Hill and Culp's Hill closes the second day of combat at Gettysburg. Although the Confederates scored impressive initial gains, in the end timely reinforcements, adroit use of interior lines, and inspired leadership save the Army of the Potomac. Lee and Meade contemplate their next moves. At first Lee plans for a renewal of his offensive against the Federal flanks, but the Union counterattack at Culp's Hill disrupts that plan. Meanwhile, at a small farmhouse that evening, Meade meets with his generals to discuss what to do next.

Meade has his headquarters at the Widow Liester's house from the morning of July 2 until the afternoon of the third. He has communication with Washington by courier. All of Meade's corps commanders, his two wing commanders, and a few other generals crowd into the cramped parlor, a dozen men in a room that measures 14 by 16 feet. The wisest man of all is Gouverneur Warren, who, nursing a neck wound, sits on the floor and nods off in the corner.

Meade asks his generals what they make of the situation, what they recommend to do next, and whether they should take the offensive. He's already told Washington that he intends to fight it out, but he wants to see what the others think. Basically, they agree with Meade's decision to fight it out. As the meeting breaks up, Meade turns to John Gibbon, in command of II Corps, and tells him that if Lee attacks on the third, it will be against the Union center along Cemetery Ridge, a position held by Gibbon's men. Odd thing about this conversation: There are no steps taken by Gibbon, Hancock, or Meade to strengthen the army's center.

On the morning of July 3, Robert E. Lee decides that he will indeed assault the Union center on Cemetery Ridge. He orders Longstreet to organize the attacking force, composed of the fresh division of Maj. Gen. George E. Pickett and the divisions of J. Johnston Pettigrew and Maj. Gen. Isaac Trimble. Ewell is to again attack the wooded heights of Culp's Hill. Lee hopes that Ewell's assault might force Meade to weaken his center by withdrawing troops to reinforce Culp's Hill. At the same time, Jeb Stuart, who had finally arrived on the field, will lead four brigades of cavalry in an attack beyond the Union right, with an eye toward getting in the Yankee rear, to spread panic and cut off the Army of the Potomac's line of retreat—the Baltimore Pike. But by noon, the Federals have bested Ewell's people in the fight for Culp's Hill, and there will be no action until that afternoon to support Longstreet's attack on Meade's center.

Longstreet protests the attack against the Union center. He will say to Lee, "I have been a soldier all my life. I have been with soldiers engaged in fights by couples, by squads, companies, regiments, divisions, and armies, and should know, as well as anyone, what soldiers can do ... [and] in my opinion no fifteen thousand men ever arrayed for battle can take that position." Whether he said it at that time or not, there are not 15,000 men to form up for the attack. Because of the heavy casualties suffered on July 1, there are about 12,600 men available. Lee will be shocked when he sees how many North Carolinians, Alabamians, Tennesseeans, Virginians, and Mississippians are going forward with wounds that would normally incapacitate them for the day's battle.

Although Longstreet places artillerist Colonel Alexander in charge of his corps artillery, Alexander does not have control over other Confederate Corps's artillery. The attack suffers as a result, because each commander does his own thing. For example, Brig. Gen. William Nelson Pendleton, Lee's chief of artillery, gives Alexander seven guns, all 12-pounder howitzers, double-charged with canister. When the advance begins these howitzers are supposed to go forward with the infantry, and when they close on the Emmitsburg Road, within 300 yards of the enemy, they will unlimber and open fire at point-blank range with canister. But nothing happens. The guns do not move forward.

At 1:10 p.m. Rebel cannoneers manning guns of Capt. Merritt B. "Buck" Miller's Third Company, Washington Artillery, open fire; these two rounds signal the beginning of what would be the war's best known

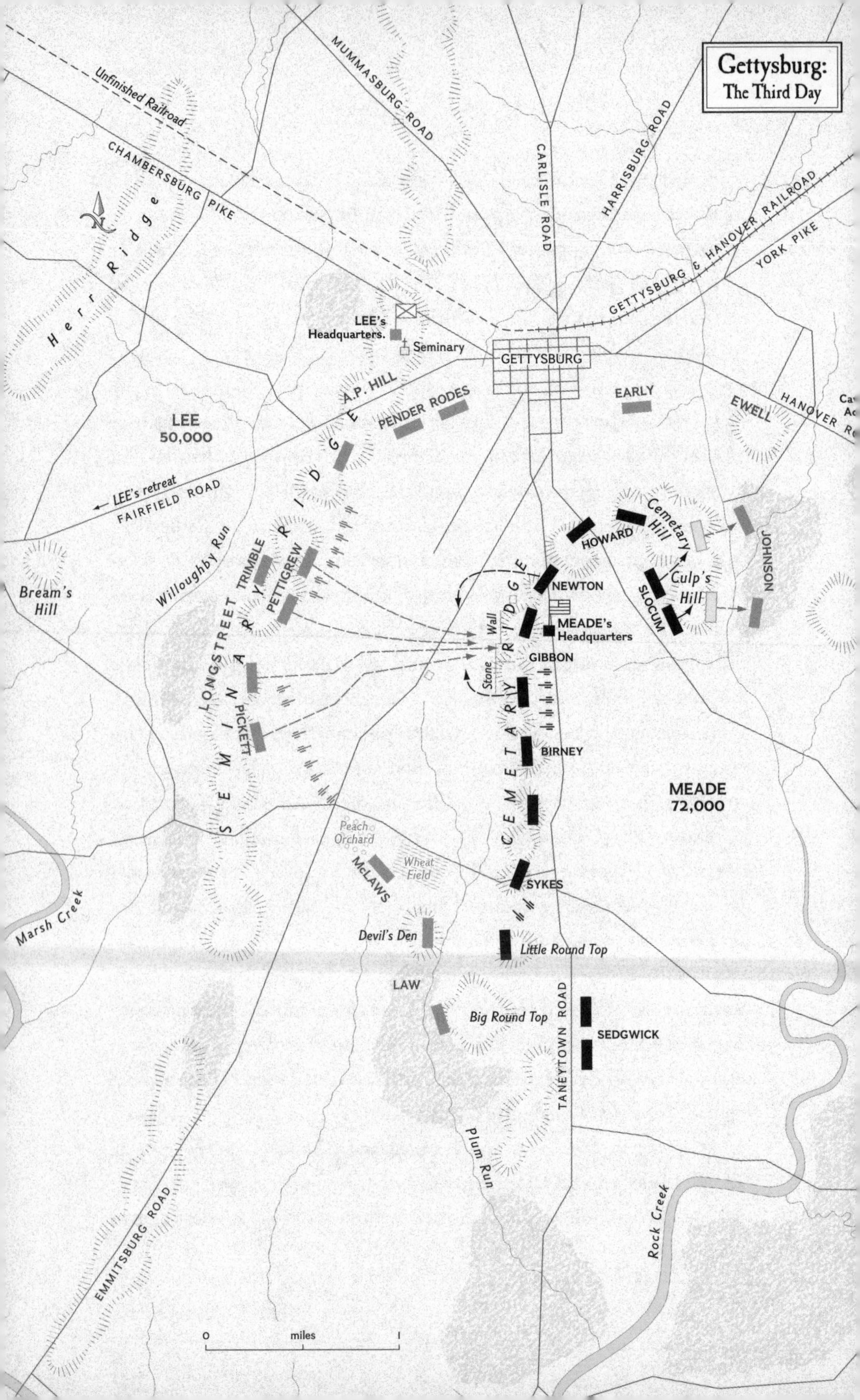
Gettysburg:
The Third Day
Unfinished Railroad
MUMMASBURG ROAD
CHAMBERSBURG PIKE
Herr Ridge
CARLISLE ROAD
HARRISBURG ROAD
GETTYSBURG & HANOVER RAILROAD
YORK PIKE
LEE's Headquarters.
Seminary
GETTYSBURG
A.P. HILL
PENDER
RODES
EARLY
EWELL
HANOVER
LEE
50,000
LEE's retreat
FAIRFIELD ROAD
SEMINARY RIDGE
Willoughby Run
Bream's Hill
LONGSTREET
TRIMBLE
PETTIGREW
PICKETT
Cemetary Hill
HOWARD
NEWTON
MEADE's Headquarters
Culp's Hill
SLOCUM
JOHNSON
Stone Wall
GIBBON
CEMETARY RIDGE
BIRNEY
MEADE
72,000
Peach Orchard
Wheat Field
McLAWS
SYKES
Marsh Creek
Devil's Den
Little Round Top
LAW
Big Round Top
TANEYTOWN ROAD
SEDGWICK
Plum Run
Rock Creek
EMMITSBURG ROAD
0
miles
1

cannonade, the distant roar of which was audible in Pittsburgh. Positioned along Longstreet's front extending from the northeast edge of Spangler's Woods to the Peach Orchard are 75 guns reporting to Colonel Alexander. To their left are 60 cannon manned by redlegs of A. P. Hill's corps, and on the Southern left, in one massed battery positioned on Oak Hill, are 24 guns of Dick Ewell's corps.

Initially many Confederate gunners use too much elevation and overshoot their primary targets: the Union infantry and artillery reporting to General Hancock posted behind the stone walls along Cemetery Ridge, extending from Ziegler's Grove on the north to beyond The Angle to the south. Defective fuses also plague the Rebels when they employ explosive shells and spherical case shot, or shrapnel.

Fifteen to 20 minutes elapse before 118 Union cannon emplaced along a two-mile front extending south from Cemetery Hill to Little Round Top return the enemy's fire. The rate of counter battery fire by Yankee redlegs is dictated by two forceful personalities, General Hancock and Chief of Artillery Brig. Gen. Henry W. Hunt. Hancock, an infantryman, calls for the Union artillerists along the II Corps front to fire as rapidly as possible. He correctly believes that this encourages his foot soldiers. Hunt, one of the Civil War's premier artillerists, calls for his gunners to limit their counter battery fire to one projectile per gun at two-minute intervals. He wants his people to conserve their canister, explosive shell, and spherical case shot to break the back of the Confederate infantry when and if they reach the Emmitsburg Road.

OPPOSITE: *After two days of fierce combat, Confederate attacks had failed to dislodge Meade's army. Determined to retain the initiative, Lee deployed his forces against the Federal center. The assault was to be made by the fresh division of Gen. George Pickett, supported by units of A. P. Hill's battered corps led by Gens. J. Johnston Pettigrew and Isaac Trimble. Lee placed the attack under Longstreet's direction. After a bombardment by massed Rebel artillery, Longstreet's divisions started forward at 3 p.m. Overlapped by Federal fire from both flanks, the Confederates suffered fearful losses but were able to briefly break through the Federal line before being driven back by Federal reserves.*

The three Confederate divisions wait and wait. J. Johnston Pettigrew has succeeded the wounded Harry Heth as commander of Heth's division. Arriving on the field in late morning is Isaac Trimble, 61 years old, a West Point graduate, an engineer, and a Yankee hater. He takes charge of Pender's men, Pender having been wounded on July 2. And then there's George Pickett. Wounded at Gaines's Mill, he did not return to duty until the Battle of Fredericksburg, where he saw little action. He was not at Chancellorsville. He's eager to fight. He's in charge of three brigades, commanded by Brig. Gens. Richard Garnett, James Kemper, and Lewis Armistead. Garnett had a run-in with Thomas "Stonewall" Jackson at the Battle of Kernstown in March 1862; eventually he transferred to Longstreet's command. Garnett's hurt: He will ride forward with his men, presenting an easy target. Kemper's a non-West Pointer, a veteran of the Mexican War. Then there's Lewis "Lo" Armistead, a prewar comrade of Hancock.

Longstreet has an out. If the bombardment does not suppress the Union guns, the assault can be called off. Longstreet delegates that decision to Alexander. At first, after the Union cannon open fire, they give as good as they receive. Alexander sends a message to Pickett and Longstreet that it looks like he is not going to be able to overwhelm the Union artillery. Then there's a lull in the action. Alexander sees what appears to be Union guns being bested; other guns are limbering up and withdrawing. It looks as if the bombardment may have worked. Alexander sends a message to Pickett, "For God's sake come quick. The 18 guns have gone. Come quick or my ammunition will not let me support you properly."

It is about 3 p.m. when Longstreet reads the message. Pickett, who commands the guide division, says, "Should I advance my division?" Longstreet can't bring himself to say "yes." But he bows his head, which Pickett assumes means "yes." Pickett rides back to his men, faces them, and commands: "Men of Old Virginia, prepare to charge the enemy!

A West Point classmate of McClellan and Jackson, Maj. Gen. George E. Pickett led the famous last-ditch charge against the Federal center on the third day of battle at Gettysburg.

Forward! Guide center! Quick time! March!" And so the line steps out, and as it does the other divisions see what's happening and they move forward as well. There are many swales and depressions in the fields where they advance, offering good cover; at times they can't even see Cemetery Ridge. But the silence of the Union artillery is short-lived, because Hunt was simply rotating batteries in and out of line; from Little Round Top Union artillery hits the advancing lines from the flank.

As Pickett's men approach the Emmitsburg Road they converge on Pettigrew's right. At the same time, however, Col. J. M. Brockenbrough's understrength Virginia Brigade on Pettigrew's left begins to give way, as the Eighth Ohio fronts south and fires into its flank. Kemper's men

Confederate dead gathered for burial near the Emmitsburg Road south of Gettysburg. The costly three-day campaign left more than 51,000 American men dead, wounded, or missing.

push toward Cemetery Ridge, and Brig. Gen. George Stannard's Vermont brigade moves out toward the Emmitsburg Road, wheels right, and fires into the flank of the advancing Rebels. Kemper is hit; his brigade gives way and crowds to the left, increasing the confusion in Pickett's ranks.

Pickett's men find when they come to the Emmitsburg Road that much of the sturdy post-and-rail fencing is standing, and climbing over it or through it or tearing it down takes time, leaving them terribly vulnerable to enemy fire. Union soldiers, taking deadly aim, chant "Fredericksburg! Fredericksburg!" Still the Rebels swarm forward toward the angle in the stone wall near a copse of trees in the center of the Union line. Garnett is hit; unhorsed, he falls, and his body is never recovered. (After a score of years his watch and sword show up in a Baltimore pawn shop.)

Pushing to the head of the mass is Armistead. He puts his hat on his sword. He's not riding a horse. He and a number of men come over the stone wall, overrunning Lt. Alonzo Cushing's Company A, Fourth U.S. Artillery. Cushing has been wounded four times. He will have two three-inch ordnance rifles pushed up here to the wall, and he orders double-charges of canister. As he pulls the lanyard and cries, "Fire!," a bullet strikes him in the mouth; that's the end of Alonzo Cushing. Winfield Scott Hancock rides along the Federal firing line during the bombardment accompanied by his II Corps flag-bearer. When a staff officer calls on him to dismount, he replied: "There are times when a corps commander's life does not count." He is struck down later with a serious wound.

The Confederates pour over the wall and advance. At first the Union line bends, and some bluecoats panic and flee. Then several regiments pivot and open fire while others rush up to seal the gap. Armistead falls; the Confederates find themselves faced with a choice between getting killed, wounded, captured, or getting out as best they can. Sometimes the choice is made for them. But it's over for Pickett's Virginians. To the north, some of Pettigrew's North Carolinians and Mississippians rush up to the wall and gain a temporary foothold in Bryan's barnyard, but they are soon cut down. And before long the attack is over, in far less time than in the epic 1993 movie *Gettysburg.*

As the dazed survivors of Longstreet's command drifted back across the fields, Robert E. Lee rode among them repeating, "It is all my fault." The grand Confederate assault has failed. At the same time, Jeb Stuart's attack on the Union rear failed. In a stiff action, Federal horsemen under Brig. Gen. George Armstrong Custer and Col. John B. McIntosh stood tall against the Rebel mounted arm, turning back Stuart's advance. Back on Seminary Ridge, Lee awaited a Federal counter-attack, but the only Union effort was an abortive and misguided cavalry charge on the Union left during late afternoon; Meade, in fact, contemplated an infantry assault, but decided against it. As darkness fell on July 3, Robert E. Lee began to consider his options and determined upon a withdrawal back into Virginia. The Confederate cause had reached its highest tide.

It rained on July 4. Lee pulled his army together, and by dusk had commenced making his way back to Virginia. Meade pursued, but was hesitant to attack given the condition of his command, with regiments and brigades battered and key officers dead or out of action. By the time Meade was ready to attack the Confederate bridgehead at Williamsport and Falling Waters, Maryland, on July 13 and14, Lee had managed to make his way back across the Potomac.

Gettysburg proved to be the bloodiest battle of the Civil War. Of approximately 97,000 Union soldiers, 23,000 became casualties; perhaps as many as 28,000 of Lee's 75,000 were killed, wounded, or captured. For the moment, Lee's invasion of the North had been a costly failure. Nevertheless, at best the Army of the Potomac had simply preserved the strategic stalemate in the Eastern Theater, for as summer gave way to fall the two armies once more faced each other in Northern Virginia.

7

THE VICKSBURG CAMPAIGN

MAY 18, 1863–JULY 4, 1863

Vicksburg, Mississippi, sits high atop a series of steep hills and bluffs on the east bank of the Mississippi River about 40 miles west of the state capital at Jackson. The city and its surroundings formed a natural citadel for the Confederacy, enabling Rebel forces there to contest Union control of the Mississippi River while maintaining communications with the trans-Mississippi Confederacy. A thriving prewar steamboat port, Vicksburg was linked by the Southern Railroad of Mississippi to nearby Jackson and rail connections to upper Mississippi, New Orleans, and the Deep South. With Federal Flag Officer David G. Farragut's capture of New Orleans in April 1862 and the advance of Federal amphibious forces from Cairo, Illinois, as far south as Memphis, Tennessee, Vicksburg remained as the South's key bastion blocking Federal plans to sever the Confederacy by gaining control of the entire Mississippi River. The city was so vital to the Confederacy that President Jefferson Davis referred to it as "the nailhead that held the South's two halves together."

Vicksburg had attracted the attention of Union military planners since the spring of 1862. Several early efforts to capture the river citadel had met with failure. An attempt by Farragut's deepwater warships and supporting ironclad gunboats of the "brown water" navy in June and early July 1862 to dash up-and downriver and seize Vicksburg failed to subdue the city. In December 1862, Maj. Gen. Ulysses S. Grant launched a two-pronged advance against Vicksburg—40,000 Federal troops under Grant advancing south through Mississippi along the Mississippi Central Railroad and a movement by water of 32,000 men under Maj. Gen. William T. Sherman against Walnut Hills on the Yazoo River to the north of Vicksburg. The campaign ended in a humiliating defeat.

Undaunted, Grant reunited most of his Army of the Tennessee at the west side of the river north of Vicksburg at Milliken's Bend and Young's Point and pondered how best to approach and capture Vicksburg, garrisoned by a large Confederate force under Lt. Gen. John C. Pemberton. From the beginning Grant realized that once spring came, he must move along the bayous, find dry ground, and cross the river somewhere to bypass the city's formidable river batteries and attack Vicksburg from the south.

Rejecting the advice of his trusted lieutenant William T. Sherman, Grant refused to take his army back to Memphis to try another overland advance southward. His reasons were not purely military; he realized that his senior corps commander, Maj. Gen. John A. McClernand, was doing all he could to supplant his superior as commander of the Army of the Tennessee. A retrograde movement northward would be interpreted as a retreat, and calls for Grant's displacement, already audible, would increase in volume and number.

Thus, as he awaited the advent of spring, Grant set his men to work on a series of projects, each looking to open another route to Vicksburg. Later he would claim that he did so merely to keep his men busy and healthy; in truth, however, he would take whatever opportunity came his way.

When Grant arrives at Young's Point, Louisiana, on the 30th of January, he takes active command of the campaign to capture Vicksburg and reorganizes the army into four corps, three in Louisiana and one, the XVI, under Maj. Gen. Stephen A. Hurlbut, back in Memphis. Figuring he has to humor the President, whose early experiences as a Mississippi flatboat man make him partial to the idea of digging canals, Grant breaks out the shovels and tells his men to get to work. They are going to furnish large working parties to work on this canal, soon to become known as "Grant's Canal." The canal had been started by Brig. Gen. Thomas Williams during Farragut's June-July expedition in an attempt to cut through the mile-and-a-half-wide hairpin bend peninsula at Vicksburg.

This would allow Federal forces to bypass the city out of range of its formidable batteries.

Sick lists grow. Death lists lengthen. After they get the canal cut through to a certain depth, they bring down four big floating steam dredges. They have steam pumps going to control the depth of water in the ditch. But on March 7, 1863, a massive crevasse opens in the Young's Point area and the Yankees find themselves perched on the levees like chickens in a flood, and the ground around is inundated. The high water soon begins falling, but by this time what are the Confederates doing? They quickly move their big guns downstream well below the South Fort area of Vicksburg's defenses onto high ground opposite the mouth of the canal. Even if you do run boats through the canal you are going to be sailing a mile and a half on a straight course with Confederate cannon commanding the canal's exit. That isn't going to be healthy.

In February a Federal force of 10,000 blasted their way through the levee at Yazoo Pass, 325 river miles north of Vicksburg, in an attempt to approach Vicksburg via the Tallahatchie and Yazoo Rivers, a route of nearly 700 miles. After fighting their way through high water past Confederate obstructions the Federals found their way blocked in mid-March by a force under Maj. Gen. William W. Loring, who had established Fort Pemberton 90 miles as the crow flies north of Vicksburg. An attempt in March to move an expedition 200 miles up Steele's Bayou to the rear of Fort Pemberton also failed.

Grant reevaluates his situation and decides to abandon the canal, along with his other interior waterway endeavors; he'll move his army down the west side of the Mississippi and find another place to cross.

The Mississippi is an alluvial river, and through the eons of time its course has shifted west of the bluffs to the west beyond Monroe, Louisiana. In its meandering path and along its different courses, it has built up natural levees. Many old channels remain as oxbow lakes

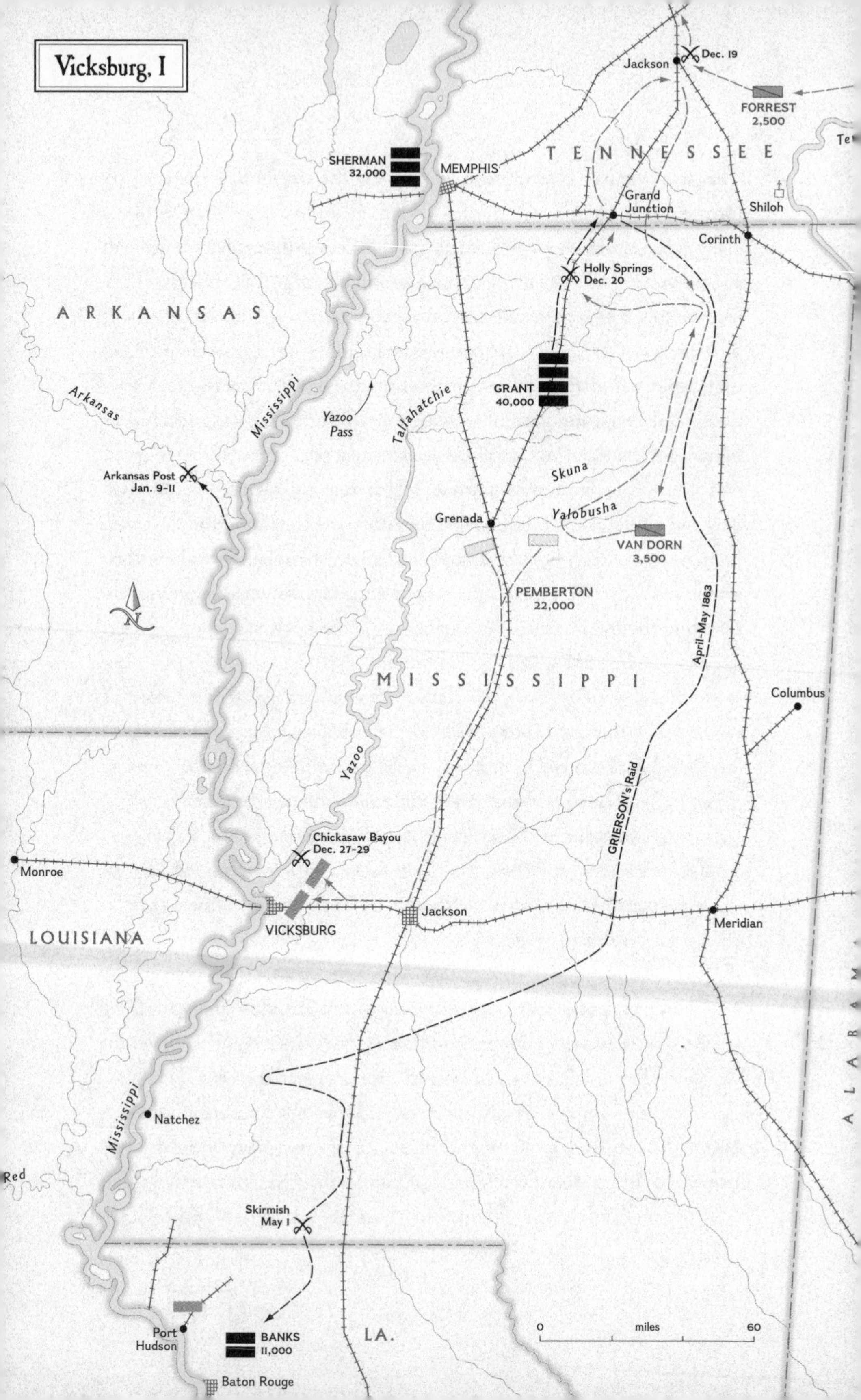

Vicksburg, I
Jackson
Dec. 19
FORREST
2,500
TENNESSEE
SHERMAN
32,000
MEMPHIS
Grand Junction
Shiloh
Corinth
Holly Springs
Dec. 20
ARKANSAS
Arkansas
Mississippi
Yazoo Pass
Tallahatchie
GRANT
40,000
Arkansas Post
Jan. 9-11
Skuna
Yalobusha
Grenada
VAN DORN
3,500
PEMBERTON
22,000
April–May 1863
MISSISSIPPI
Columbus
Yazoo
GRIERSON's Raid
Chickasaw Bayou
Dec. 27-29
Monroe
VICKSBURG
Jackson
Meridian
LOUISIANA
ALABAMA
Mississippi
Natchez
Red
Skirmish
May 1
Port Hudson
BANKS
11,000
LA.
Baton Rouge
0
miles
60

separated from the main channel. The land along these natural levees is higher than in the nearby swamps, fertile, and heavily cultivated by wealthy planters. The width of these natural levees seldom exceeds two miles.

On the last day of March, a Union column leaves Milliken's Bend to reconnoiter and open a road to New Carthage, 40 miles to the south by twisting waterways and 20 miles below Vicksburg in a straight line. But when they get to New Carthage the man-made levee fronting the river has crevassed. This slows the southward march as engineers search for and open a road along the Bayou Vidal natural levee.

To facilitate the movement of the tons of supplies needed to support the army, the Federals begin another canal linking Duckport Landing on the Mississippi with Walnut Bayou. The steam dredges are redeployed to the new project, but a rapid fall in the stage of the Mississippi dooms this undertaking.

By mid-April the Union buildup in the New Carthage area has reached the point where Grant calls on the navy. Rear Adm. David D. Porter is ready and eager to provide the muscle to get the army across the mighty river. The night of April 16 sees Porter successfully challenge the Vicksburg River batteries with eight gunboats and three steamboats. Although they take a hammering, only one vessel is lost. Six nights later, six more unarmed boats ran the gauntlet, with the loss of one. They bring with them a number of barges lashed to their sides.

OPPOSITE: *After several unsuccessful attempts to capture Vicksburg in the fall of 1862, Grant planned to shift his army to the east bank of the Mississippi to capture the city from the south. Vicksburg was guarded by two Confederate forces, one under Maj. Gen. Carter L. Stevenson in Vicksburg and a second around Jackson under General Pemberton. On the night of April 16, Rear Adm. Porter took his Federal fleet south past the Vicksburg batteries and ferried two Federal corps across the river on April 30. Between May 1 and 12, the Federals defeated Rebel forces at Port Gibson and Raymond and, on May 14, won a decisive engagement at Jackson, isolating Gen. Joseph E. Johnston, who had recently arrived from Tennessee. Grant defeated Pemberton at Champion Hill on May 16, forcing the Confederates to withdraw into the defenses of Vicksburg.*

Meanwhile, Grant's plan to stage his army at New Carthage has been scrubbed. He now proposes to embark his troops at Hard Times Landing on the lowland side and establish his Mississippi beachhead at Grand Gulf. Let us look at the Grand Gulf defenses. Since mid-March, the Confederates have rushed Brig. Gen. John Bowen's two-brigade division to Grand Gulf. They man two forts, Wade and Cobun—you don't want forts named after you, because it usually means you are dead.

By April 28, Grant's troops and Porter's fleet are ready to undertake what, for that time and place, is a formidable amphibious operation. That evening over at Hard Times Landing, four miles upstream, 10,000 men of John A. McClernand's corps board transports and barges. The unit you don't want to be with is the 67th Indiana. Lt. Col. Theodore Buehler and his men are in leaky barges, and they spend the night bailing to keep afloat. Porter and his seven ironclad gunboats have the mission of suppressing the fire of the Confederate forts. Porter has reconnoitered them from upstream. He knows where they are located. Grant, early on the morning of the 29th, boards the tug *Ivy* and takes station upstream well out of range of the forts' cannon. Behind him are 10,000 men waiting aboard vessels. At 7 a.m. on the 29th, signal flags go up: The gunboats cast off. They divide into two divisions, one consisting of four "city series" gunboats—the *Pittsburg, Louisville, Mound City,* and *Carondelet.* The other division includes the *Benton,* 16 guns, flying Porter's pennant. *Benton* is accompanied by the *Lafayette,* a new ironclad, and the *Tuscumbia.* The latter is a type of vessel that the Truman Committee would have investigated in World War II. It was a rip-off by the contractor. When he secured the armor plating to the timber backing, he fastened the spikes without having them secured by a nut to the opposite side. It isn't a shipshape vessel. This trio is to take out the upper battery, Fort Cobun. At 8 a.m. the ironclads come down the river in column. As they round Coffee Point, they open fire; first with their bow guns, then their port broadsides as they pass Cobun.

The *Pittsburg, Mound City, Louisville,* and *Carondelet* take position within a quarter mile of Fort Wade with their bows pointed upstream and their starboard 32-pounder guns bearing on the Rebels. Although each "city series" ironclad has 13 guns—they have three firing forward, four to port, four starboard, and two astern—meaning that the Yankees don't have four times 13 guns firing on Fort Wade. Only 16 guns at one time can bear on the fort. The other three ironclads engage Fort Cobun.

The Confederates reply with the four big guns emplaced in each fort. Col. William F. Wade of St. Louis is in charge of the lower battery. He probably should not have been walking back and forth, exposing himself, because a charge of canister will come toward him and he's going to lose his head, literally and figuratively.

By 10 a.m. the guns of Fort Wade are silent. One of the 32-pounders has burst. Mounds of earth have been torn up. But Porter's division doesn't silence Fort Cobun; the *Tuscumbia,* no match for the Rebs, is taken out of the fight. The other two ironclads, reinforced by the four "city series" gunboats, compel Fort Cobun to slow its rate of fire. About 1 p.m. Porter takes a break and confers with Grant. Between them, since Porter can't guarantee suppression of the Confederate fire, the decision is made to return the invasion armada to Hard Times Landing and march the troops across the base of Coffee Point. Somewhere south of there they'll cross the river.

Grant's soldiers march across Coffee Point during the late afternoon and night of the 29th. After dusk, the gunboats run downriver along with the transports and barges, successfully challenging the Grand Gulf gauntlet. On the morning of the last day of April, the navy begins embarking the Union forces at Disharoon's plantation to shuttle them across the Mississippi River downstream to Bruinsburg Landing, where Bayou Pierre flows into the Mississippi.

A Grant staffer, Lt. Col. James H. Wilson, had been in this area scouting out the ground. Grant romanticizes in his *Memoirs* that he learned about where to cross the Mississippi from a black informant. I'm sure he ran into the black refugee. I'm certain the refugee told him about the good road leading east from Bruinsburg toward Port Gibson, but I'm equally certain that Grant had other solid information besides what that fellow told him. When he starts south from Hard Times, he considers crossing at Rodney. If he goes to Rodney, he's going farther south, which would give the Confederates more time to concentrate to oppose his landing.

When General Pemberton learns from General Bowen, charged with the defense of Grand Gulf, that Grant is concentrating his army at Hard Times preparatory to crossing the Mississippi, he directs General Stevenson at Vicksburg to send 5,000 men to Grand Gulf, if practicable. But Stevenson is distracted by General Sherman's expedition up the Yazoo River, and he procrastinates for vital hours. Brig. Gen. Edward Tracy's Alabamians will not leave Vicksburg for Port Gibson until 7 p.m. on the 29th. Brig. Gen. William E. Baldwin will follow two hours later.

Grant crosses the Mississippi with McClernand's corps, some 16,000 strong, and two of Maj. Gen. James B. McPherson's three XVII Corps divisions, about 11,000 soldiers. Bowen has perhaps 4,200 defenders. Although Tracy and Baldwin are ordered to bring 5,000 men, they are going to have heavy straggling as they go south. Bowen will have 8,000 men and 12 cannon to battle 24,000 Yankees supported by 60 guns.

Having reached dry land on the east bank of the Mississippi, Grant's forces move inland. On May 1 they encounter John Bowen's Confederates south of Grand Gulf, four miles west of Port Gibson on the farm owned by A. K. Shaifer.

What can Bowen do? If he takes everyone down to Port Gibson, he leaves Grand Gulf in his rear open to attack by Porter's fleet. He holds half his men at Grand Gulf and sends Brig. Gen. Martin E. Green with his Arkansans and Missourians to Port Gibson. When Green gets there he goes west out of Port Gibson, two miles to the junction of the Rodney and Bruinsburg roads. He doesn't know whether the Yankees are coming from Bruinsburg or Rodney, so, upon arrival of Tracy's Alabamians, he splits his force. Green heads out the Rodney Road and posts his brigade near Magnolia Church, half a mile east of the A. K. Shaifer House; Tracy goes out the Bruinsburg Road and positions his men to cover a plantation road that links the Rodney and Bruinsburg roads. Tracy anchors his left at Point Lookout, commanding Bayou Pierre.

No one can improve on General Grant's description of the local landscape. He wrote in his *Memoirs,* "the country in this part of Mississippi stands on edge, the roads running along the ridges except where they occasionally pass from one ridge to another. Where there are no clearings the sides of the hills are covered with a very heavy growth of timber and with undergrowth, and the ravines are filled with vines and canebrake almost impenetrable."

Grant wants to get as far inland as he can before he fights a battle. He hopes to be on the high ground. He doesn't want to be like Billy Sherman in late December 1862, when he was down in the low ground fronting Chickasaw Bayou with the Confederates on the slopes of Walnut Hills and the high ground beyond. Brig. Gen. Eugene Asa Carr's division of the XIII Corps takes the lead as the army marches inland from Bruinsburg.

A West Pointer and former cavalryman, Carr assigns the lead to Col. William M. Stone's brigade. A future governor of Iowa, Stone employs the 21st Iowa and one cannon as his vanguard. A night march is called for, and the Rodney Road as it wends its way along the ridges and drops down to cross streams is as picturesque today as it was challenging to Grant's soldiers. The Hawkeyes find the Spanish moss that drapes from the trees romantic, but not the snakes and alligators.

Shortly after midnight on May 1 at the A. K. Shaifer House, the Iowans clash with a Confederate outpost and the first shots in the Battle of Port Gibson are fired. This initiates a nighttime firefight between Green's Arkansans and Missourians posted out by Magnolia Church and Carr's people. By 3 a.m. the fighting ceases as the blue and gray anxiously await the dawn to sort out where they are in a mazelike landscape.

Daylight reveals to the Federals that, in addition to Green's people to their front astride Rodney Road, Tracy's Alabamians are posted on a ridge to their rear. Along this ridge runs a plantation road linking the Rodney and Bruinsburg roads. How will Generals Grant and McClernand confront this situation? This is the only Civil War battle with which I am familiar where soldiers will advance in the opposite direction to get at the foe.

By 8 a.m. two more XIII Corps divisions have reached the Shaifer House staging area via Rodney Road. While Brig. Gen. Peter J. Osterhaus's division advances northwest up the plantation road, Carr's people, reinforced by newcomers of Brig. Gen. Alvin P. Hovey's 12th Division, thrust southeast down Rodney Road, intent on smashing Green's Magnolia Church roadblock. Although Osterhaus's division outnumbers Tracy's Alabamians more than two to one, its progress is slow. Among the Confederates killed is General Tracy; his men, now led by Col. Isham Garrott, stand tall, and Osterhaus calls for help.

Meanwhile, Carr and Hovey by 10 a.m. overwhelm Green's Magnolia Church roadblock, and send the Rebels skedaddling. The arrival of Confederate reinforcements—Baldwin's brigade from Vicksburg and Col. Frank Cockrell's Missourians from Grand Gulf—enables General Bowen to cobble together a force in the deep hollow where the confluence of the White and Irwin branches forms Willow Creek. Here the Rebels checkmate McClernand's corps.

By mid-afternoon the last of McClernand's four divisions—A. J. Smith's—and Maj. Gen. John A. "Black Jack" Logan's division of

At the outset of the war, Illinois Congressman John A. McClernand resigned his seat, raised a brigade of Illinois volunteers, and was made a brigadier general.

McPherson's corps reach the field. To break what is becoming an embarrassing impasse, Logan sends Brig. Gen. John E. Smith's brigade to assist Peter Osterhaus. The Yanks file off into the canebrakes and rugged ground separating Bruinsburg Road and Bayou Pierre. They soon turn the Alabamians' right flank, whose left had been earlier reinforced by Green. If they continue to fight, these Johnny Rebs will be cut off from Grand Gulf. Retreat is the order.

The Confederates disengage, and Garrott and Green head for Grand Gulf. Bowen's Confederates, who have checked the Yankees over on Rodney Road, are now in deep trouble. If they stay there, the bluecoats will sweep east along the Bruinsburg Road, capture Port Gibson, and these butternuts will get a free trip north to Union prison camps. So, what do they do? Col. Francis M. Cockrell takes his Missourians and heads for Grand Gulf; William Baldwin and his men retreat to and through Port Gibson.

By 6 p.m. Grant has won the Battle of Port Gibson. The fight has lasted from 1 a.m. until 6 p.m. The Confederates have fought a magnificent 17-hour delaying action by employing terrain skillfully to slow the Union forces. Hopefully, reinforcements are going to join them. They are on the way, but none of them will show up until the morning of May 3. By the third, it is too late. Grant has secured his bridgehead east of the Mississippi, and he isn't going to be driven back into the river. Through deception and diversion Grant has overcome the Confederate advantages of terrain and now holds the initiative. Grant orders McClernand to pursue the Confederates. The human toll as reported lists 60 Confederate dead, 340 wounded, and 387 missing, most of the latter captured. Union losses number 131 dead, 719 wounded, and 25 missing.

According to orders he receives from Washington, Grant is to entrench at Port Gibson and send a corps or go himself with a corps and join Maj. Gen. Nathaniel P. "Nothing Positive" Banks in the capture of Port Hudson. Grant knows that it takes at least two weeks to send and receive messages to and from Washington. He has also received word that Banks has taken a roundabout route by way of Bayou Teche to Alexandria and will not begin an attack on Port Hudson until at least May 10. Having finally secured a lodgment on the high ground, east of the Mississippi, he will not send a corps to cooperate with Banks. Instead he will pause, regroup, call down Sherman from Milliken's Bend and Young's Point, and then forge ahead.

Port Gibson and the occupation of Grand Gulf are significant achievements for Grant, although he would have wanted even more. Even as he grumbles about the performance of General McClernand, who chose a critical moment during the engagement at Port Gibson to deliver a stump speech to his men, Grant has more important decisions to make.

He decides to mass his three corps east of the Mississippi and move into the interior of the state, with the Big Black River on his left flank as he probes the Confederate positions between Vicksburg and Jackson. Grant hopes that by interposing his army between the Confederate forces at Vicksburg and Jackson, he can defeat each before they can combine against him. Aware that by advancing in that fashion he risks having Pemberton dash south to cut his supply line, Grant determines that his men will live partially off the land, with wagon convoys carrying medicine, certain rations, and ammunition. These trains will be escorted by parties of reinforcements departing almost daily from Grand Gulf for the front.

When Sherman arrives at Grand Gulf, Grant orders the army to move out. He now has his army of maneuver: McClernand and his four divisions, Sherman with two divisions, and McPherson with two divisions. With the coming of Sherman, Grant is at a point in his career where he has to make a key decision. General Loring is in field command of the Confederate troops then entrenching along a line extending from near Warrenton on the Mississippi seven miles below Vicksburg east to the Big Black River. The Confederates are dug in on bluffs looking south; they expect an attack against Vicksburg, coming north from Grant's Hankinson Ferry bridgehead on the Big Black.

Grant, however, decides on a daring move: a hook to the northeast, where he can threaten the state capital at Jackson and defeat and disperse the Confederate forces assembling there. Orders go out on May 7 and the Federals begin to move. At Reganton, on the ninth, Grant turns McPherson's XVII Corps into the Utica Road. McClernand, trailed by Sherman, follows the Natchez Trace from Rocky Springs to Cayuga and beyond. McClernand's people on the 11th halt to let Sherman pass as Grant now splits his army. As he closes northward on the vital railroad linking Vicksburg and Jackson, he will have McClernand on the left, Sherman in the center, and McPherson on the right. With Grant's army moving farther and farther northeast, the Confederates abandon the earthworks they are throwing up south of Vicksburg and change direction 90 degrees to front east.

The Confederates also rush troops toward Jackson. Pemberton, still uncertain as to what Grant plans, masses 20,000 men at Edward's Station about ten miles east of Vicksburg. Others come from as far off as Charleston, Savannah, Port Hudson, and Tullahoma but must pass through Jackson. Gen. Joseph E. Johnston boards a train on May 10 at Tullahoma, Tennessee, and hurries westward to take charge of these Jackson-bound brigades.

By May 11 McPherson's XVII Corps is preparing to march on Raymond, a small Mississippi town about 15 miles west of Jackson. Once one of Grant's staff officers, James Birdseye McPherson is a favorite with both Grant and Sherman; however, he has little experience as a combat commander. Among the Confederate brigades marching to the aid of Vicksburg is a force of 3,000 men under Brig. Gen. John Gregg. They had been ordered up from Port Hudson to Jackson and had been sent west toward Raymond to prepare for a possible strike at Grant's rear if the Federal commander made a move toward Vicksburg across the Big Black River. Gregg has been warned by Pemberton that there may be a Yankee feint toward Raymond, but he is not expecting the advance of a major enemy force.

Learning that there is a Union brigade at Utica, near Raymond, Pemberton orders Gregg to intercept it. Gregg arrives at Raymond on the afternoon of May 11. The "brigade" of Union infantry is actually six brigades of infantry and 22 cannon—12,000 men of McPherson's XVII Corps. Gregg understands that when he arrives he'll meet with Col. Wirt Adams's cavalry, who are to reconnoiter for him. So, when Gregg arrives, he is nonplussed to find no Adams, only some 40 horsemen commanded by Capt. J. M. Hall. Gregg sends Hall down the Utica Road to find out who's there.

Hall soon sends back word that Yankees are coming. Gregg, going on the assumption that the average Union brigade numbers 1,500 men, believes that with his command, 3,000 strong, he has no cause for worry. These men are Texans and Tennesseeans. They know what it is like being in Yankee prison camps—many had been captured at Fort Donelson back in February 1862. They will fight like hell. Gregg will act aggressively throughout most of the day. He's going to carry the fight to McPherson, who today will be far too cautious or, perhaps worse, timid.

What does Gregg do? He says to Col. Hiram Bronson Granbury, "Take your Seventh Texas and the First Tennessee Battalion and go out to the high ground commanding the junction of the Port Gibson and Utica roads, and put three guns into position." He tells Col. Calvin H. Walker, "Take your Third Tennessee and form them on the reverse side of that high ground rising northeast of the Fourteenmile Creek Bridge." To Lt. Col. Thomas W. Beaumont he says, "You go down the Gallatin Road, with your 50th Tennessee, supported by Col. Randal W. MacGavock of the 10th and 30th Tennessee." Gregg's plan is to engage the Yankees to his front and then order Beaumont and MacGavock to come down and turn the Union right flank. Good idea, if there are only 1,500 Yankees. Bad idea if there are 12,000 Yankees.

About 10 a.m. the Federals arrive on this high ground, known today as McPherson Ridge. McPherson is up here along with "Black Jack" Logan. They look out across the Fourteenmile Creek bottom. The Confederates see Yankees up here, and there come three puffs of smoke as Capt. H. M. Bledsoe's Missouri Battery opens fire. The lead Union battery is up front already. Captain Samuel S. DeGolyer of the Eighth Michigan Light Artillery unlimbers his six guns and duels with the Rebs.

Up comes another Union battery, Capt. W. S. Williams's Third Ohio Battery. Now there are 12 Union guns in action. Brig. Gen. Elias S. Dennis deploys his infantry brigade guiding on Utica Road, the 30th and 78th Ohio to the left, the 20th Ohio and 120th Illinois to the right. It is open ground until they close on Fourteenmile Creek, then they encounter woods. The Yankees move out. It is very dusty. The Yankee guns blast away. It looks good to Gregg. A Union brigade—that's just what he thought. There might, however, be a few more cannon than appropriate for a brigade. Gregg puts his plan into action. At noon, he orders Granbury to advance. The Texans surge into the woods east of the bridge and engage the Federals. The Yankees stop dead in their tracks. Meanwhile, Walker deploys his men in the lee of that ridge. McPherson looks to Logan. Black Jack calls up John E. Smith's brigade—four Illinois regiments and the 23rd Indiana. They come down off McPherson's Ridge and advance across open fields with the 23rd Indiana in front.

The Hoosiers cross Fourteenmile Creek, breaking formation to climb down and up the steep banks. They emerge, start dressing their ranks, and as they are doing so, the Third Tennessee comes over the ridge and smashes into them. The Indiana boys flee across the creek, the Tennesseeans in hot pursuit. As the Confederates come out of the woods and enter a field, two Yankee regiments—the 30th Illinois and 45th Illinois—are concealed in nearby trees. They open fire. The Confederates scatter and retreat into the timber. Up to this time the Seventh Texas and Third Tennessee have engaged nine Union regiments and fought them to a standstill.

Colonel Beaumont has gone out Gallatin Road to secure the high ground beyond Fourteenmile Creek where it is crossed by the road. If Gregg's estimate of the situation is correct, Beaumont once on the ridge will be beyond and well east of the Utica Road and positioned to envelop McPherson's Ridge and capture the guns of the three Union batteries now unlimbered there. But when Beaumont gains this vantage point, he sees through clouds of dust long columns of Union infantry marching up the Utica Road. Beaumont calls off his attack and sends a

Chief engineer to Grant during the Union advance through Tennessee, Maj. Gen. James B. McPherson commanded the Federal XVII Corps during the Vicksburg campaign.

messenger to tell Gregg what is happening. The courier does not get through. Beaumont recalls his regiment and Colonel MacGavock occupies the commanding ground (known today as MacGavock's Hill) with his consolidated 10th and 30th Tennessee. The former is an Irish regiment. Nearby on MacGavock's left is the 41st Tennessee.

By this time Logan has called up and committed Brig. Gen. John D. Stevenson's brigade. Two of Brig. Gen. Marcellus M. Crocker's three brigades are also on the field. More than 10,000 bluecoats demonstrate to the butternuts that their fire-eating politicians were in error when, as the secession crisis threatened breakup of the Union, they boasted that one Southerner could whip ten Yankees. Numbers now tell. McPherson, by 3 p.m., gets his act together after five hours. Soon Colonel MacGavock is dead, and the Rebels give ground, slowly at first and then rapidly. By four o'clock they retreat through Raymond, taking the road toward Jackson by way of Mississippi Springs.

McPherson marches into Raymond. First in are from the 20th Ohio of Dennis's brigade. The good ladies of Raymond have arranged on the courthouse square a super picnic lunch. They plan to feed the Confederates when they return victorious. The Rebels, however, do not pause, let alone stop, in Raymond to partake of the picnic laid out for them. The Buckeyes and friends make sure it does not go to waste. Union battle casualties are 68 killed, 341 wounded, and 37 missing; Gregg listed his losses as 73 dead, 252 wounded, and 190 prisoners.

Among Grant's senior officers, James McPherson combined intelligence, good looks, and loyalty. But of Grant's three corps commanders present with the army at Raymond, as later in the campaign, he will prove to be overly cautious and least willing to close with the foe. This is true whether discussing the May 22 Vicksburg assault, the October 1863 Canton expedition, or Georgia's Snake Creek Gap in May 1864.

News of McPherson's victory at Raymond causes Grant to change his plans. Instead of moving northward, he'll send Sherman and McPherson against Jackson, with orders to drive out the Confederates there, sever the area railroads, and destroy whatever manufacturing they encounter. McClernand will swing north and then east, keeping an eye on Pemberton at Edward's Station; once McPherson and Sherman finish their mission, they are to join McClernand and attack Pemberton. In Jackson on May 13, an exhausted and ill Joseph Johnston arrives to take command in the aftermath of Confederate defeats at Port Gibson and Raymond. Because Federal forces threaten northern Mississippi and Alabama, the ailing Johnston has had to take a 300-mile detour to travel from Tennessee to the front in Mississippi. With reinforcements he will have perhaps 12,000 men to face Grant's 20,000.

On the 13th, Union columns move out in accordance with Grant's new operational plan. Demonstrating flexibility—one of his strong points—Grant changes direction 90 degrees. He turns toward Jackson. On the morning of May 14, McClernand's corps concentrates in and around Raymond to guard Grant's rear. McPherson advances with two divisions down the Clinton-Jackson Road toward Jackson. Sherman bears in on the Raymond Road.

General Johnston arrives in Jackson at 6 p.m. on May 13. He takes a room in the Bowman House near the Mississippi capitol. He orders General Gregg, who is commanding in Jackson, to send everything of military value out of Jackson up the road to Canton, 30 miles northeast of Jackson. This will make it harder for Pemberton to combine his force with Johnston's. He also sends a message to Richmond couched in the stink of defeatism, "I am too late."

Brig. Gen. William H. T. "Shot Pouch" Walker, joined by Col. Peyton H. Colquitt, goes out and sets up a roadblock placing their two brigades on the Clinton road. Their people are far out in front of the Jackson earthworks, which Johnston says are improperly located.

Just as skirmishing starts at Colquitt's roadblock between the Confederates and McPherson's vanguard, clouds burst and rain pours down. So hard is the rain that men cannot open their cartridge boxes. Everything is suspended. This is positive for the Confederates, because they learn that Sherman is coming in on the Raymond Road. They rush Col. Albert Thompson and a small force of mounted infantry over there to stall Sherman.

It stops raining in the early afternoon, and the Yanks advance in overwhelming strength. The Confederates fight a delaying action to cover the movement of their trains north. By 5 p.m., the Rebels are out of Jackson and have retreated up the Canton Road. Grant establishes headquarters in the Bowman House, reputedly in the same room where Johnston had slept the previous night.

At the time the Federals capture Jackson, Pemberton's army is concentrated in the Edward's Station area. Johnston sends orders in triplicate to Pemberton telling him that four divisions of Federals are in Clinton, about ten miles west of Jackson. He has lost track of Sherman, who is at Mississippi Springs. With the enemy at Clinton and between them, Johnston directs Pemberton to march east, and he will close on Grant from the opposite direction with the Jackson Confederates. Pemberton gets his copy at Bovina on the morning of May 14. Some 12 hours before, an intelligence coup betrays into Grant's hands a copy of Johnston's orders.

Unknown to Grant, Johnston, on evacuating Jackson, marches north, halting for the night at Tougaloo, just north of Jackson. If he is seeking to join Pemberton, he is going in the wrong direction. On the 15th Johnston continues north as far as Calhoun, halfway to Canton, making the projected rendezvous with Pemberton more difficult.

Grant now turns west to confront Pemberton, who has come out toward him with a force of 23,000 men. The two armies meet at Champion Hill, seven miles east of the Big Black River.

Meanwhile, Pemberton has reached Edward's Station from Bovina. An acrimonious meeting ensues with his generals. Pemberton holds that Johnston's orders are contradictory to President Jefferson Davis's instructions that "to hold both Vicksburg and Port Hudson is necessary to a connection with the Trans-Mississippi." Pemberton wants to take position behind the Big Black with a bridgehead on the east side, and let the enemy assail him. We will repulse them, and then counterattack out of the bridgehead, he argues. His two senior generals—William W. Loring and Carter L. Stevenson—are unimpressed, and recommend that the army take the field in the morning, march southeast, and attack Union supply trains and reinforcements known to be en route to the enemy from

Grand Gulf. Pemberton, despite misgivings, buys into his generals' proposal. Orders are issued alerting the army to be ready to move out next morning, May 15.

There will be a five-hour delay while soldiers wait for rations and ammunition to arrive from Vicksburg and be issued. Two miles southeast of Edward's Station, the Raymond Road crosses Baker's Creek. The previous day's cloudburst has caused the creek to flood. No one had checked the crossing to see if it was passable for infantry and artillery. Wirt Adams's cavalry crosses on their horses, but when the infantry seeks to follow, the water is up to a tall man's crotch and to a short man's belly button. Pemberton is compelled to make a seven-mile detour by way of the Jackson and Ratliff roads to regain the Raymond Road east of the flooded Baker's Creek crossing. He then pushes on and halts for the evening at Mrs. Sarah Ellison's, where he and Loring spend the night. The long column halts along the road with the 400-plus wagon train bringing up the rear, parking at "the Crossroads" about daybreak on Saturday, May 16.

General Grant, on the 15th, moves to capitalize on his intelligence coup. Sherman remains in Jackson and wrecks the four railroads radiating into the town from the points of the compass. McClernand sends one division—Hovey's—to Bolton, about 20 miles west of Jackson. Two other divisions—A. J. Smith's (XIII Corps) and Frank Blair's (XV Corps)—march from Raymond, taking the direct road to Edward's Station, and McClernand with two divisions takes position on the Middle Road, midway between Bolton and Raymond. McPherson's corps, with Grant in attendance, hastens west from Jackson, one division—Logan's—halting near Bolton, and the other—Crocker's—at Clinton. Unlike the Confederates, the Federals make easy marches on the 15th and camp early.

On Saturday morning a courier sent by Johnston, upon his May 14 evacuations of Jackson, reaches Pemberton at Mrs. Ellison's with new instructions. Johnston reiterates his orders for Pemberton to pass to the north of Clinton and they will join forces and engage the foe. Time, however, is running out for Pemberton. Already east of Mrs. Ellison's, on the Raymond Road, Wirt Adams's cavalry supported by two infantry regiments has engaged the vanguard of one of Grant's three columns.

You hear the boom of artillery as the messenger gallops up. Pemberton, although he is in contact with the enemy, orders his army to countermarch. What are the Rebels going to do? They hope to march back to Edward's Station, where they will turn northeast into the Brownsville Road. The countermarch starts. It is a challenge to get the train turned around and start the wagons rumbling west escorted by Col. Alexander W. Reynolds's brigade.

Now as the Rebels move out, what are McClernand's orders? He is to advance cautiously and feel for the enemy. Grant does not want him bringing on a battle. The Raymond Road Yankees follow cautiously—A. J. Smith's division is in front followed by Maj. Gen. Frank Blair's two brigades. Confederate General Loring pulls back west of Jackson Creek and deploys his division on commanding ground on the Coker House Ridge. This is a good artillery position, clear gentle slopes in front, particularly if all the bluecoats are in that direction.

Then word comes from Champion Hill that the Yankees are also advancing on the Jackson Road. The Confederates are not prepared to meet this new threat. Brig. Gen. Stephen D. Lee—an Army of Northern Virginia veteran—sends a message to his division commander, Carter L. Stevenson, and tells him that he's taking measures to cope with this situation. Lee leads his men up Jackson Road to the crest of Champion Hill. Here, at the crest, is a ridge extending to the northwest. Lee's Alabamians file off and occupy this ridge.

Lee sees that the Yankees have reached Sid Champion's house and are deploying. First to arrive are Alvin Hovey's two brigades under Brig. Gen. George F. McGinnis and Col. James R. Slack. Artillery is unlimbered. Grant and McPherson come up from Clinton. Also reaching the area, at 10 a.m., is Black Jack Logan's division. Logan takes position at a right angle on Hovey's right with two brigades in advance. In reserve is John Stevenson's brigade. McPherson's other division, Crocker's, having spent the night at Clinton, will not arrive on the field till mid-afternoon.

The bluecoats advance about 10:30. The Confederates by now have moved a second brigade up onto Champion Hill. Three of Brig. Gen. Alfred Cumming's Georgia regiments take ground on Lee's right, forming a salient and supporting four cannon. The crest of Champion Hill is bald. Two of Cumming's regiments remain at the Crossroads faced east. They, along with four guns of Capt. James F. Waddell's Alabama Battery, have the mission of holding the Crossroads against McClernand's two divisions, who are cautiously feeling their way west, guiding on the Middle Road.

A second Georgia Brigade led by Brig. Gen. Seth Barton, accompanied by eight cannon, double-times into position on Lee's left. The three Rebel brigades occupy commanding ground with cornfields to their front.

Pemberton's three divisions as posted form a numeral "7." Carter Stevenson's three brigades on the left confront two Union divisions, and Bowen's and Loring's divisions on the right face four Union divisions who look to McClernand for orders. At this hour McClernand's orders from Grant are unchanged: Move cautiously, feel for the enemy, and don't bring on a battle. About noon Grant sends a staffer to McClernand with orders to attack. But instead of riding cross-country, the courier travels the roads, and more than two hours pass before McClernand learns that his mission has changed.

But the Confederates are in deep trouble long before McClernand receives his attack order. The Pennsylvania-born and -reared Pemberton carries lots of baggage. In the "Old Army" he had been a captain and Loring a colonel. Loring is "not a happy camper." He doubts Pemberton's capabilities. Brigade commander Brig. Gen. Lloyd Tilghman supports this view. The two sit around that morning making "ill tempered jests" about Pemberton, recalls Lt. William A. Drennan.

By noon the Confederate defense of Champion Hill has unraveled. The Union two-division attack on three Confederate brigades is long remembered, and for the Confederates it is a nightmare. On the right John Stevenson's reserve brigade is committed. Seth Barton's Georgians crumble and flee, and the bluecoats capture eight cannon. On the Union left George McGinnis's people guide on the Jackson Road. They reach the edge of the woods and halt less than 150 yards from the crest of the hill. Ahead is the salient held by Cumming's three Georgia regiments and four cannon.

McGinnis reconnoiters and passes the word to load and cap their rifles. "When I give the signal start forward, then I'm going to chop my sword downward. We will then drop to the ground and the Confederates, when they fire, will overshoot." It works! They come out of the woods, race forward, McGinnis chops his sword, and the soldiers go to ground. Confederate gunners pull their lanyards. Boom! Boom! Boom! Boom! The Yanks leap to their feet, race forward, rout the Georgia regiments, and capture the cannon.

What is S. D. Lee to do? The Yanks have turned his left; they have turned his right. By bold leadership he holds his Alabamians together, and they fall back, step by step, into the Jackson Road. Colonel Slack's men on McGinnis's left storm toward the Crossroads, scatter the 56th

OPPOSITE: *Approaching Vicksburg's defenses from the east and northeast, Grant launched two unsuccessful assaults on the city—on May 19 against the Confederate Stockade Redan and on May 22 against a three-mile sector of the front extending from the 26th Louisiana Redoubt to Square Fort. Grant determined Vicksburg could only be taken by siege. As the siege progressed into summer, the Confederates suffered from disease and starvation, and the city's residents were forced to seek shelter in caves and bombproofs from the daily bombardments by Grant's artillery and Federal gunboats and mortar scows. By July 3 Pemberton asked for surrender terms, and on the following day Federal troops entered Vicksburg.*

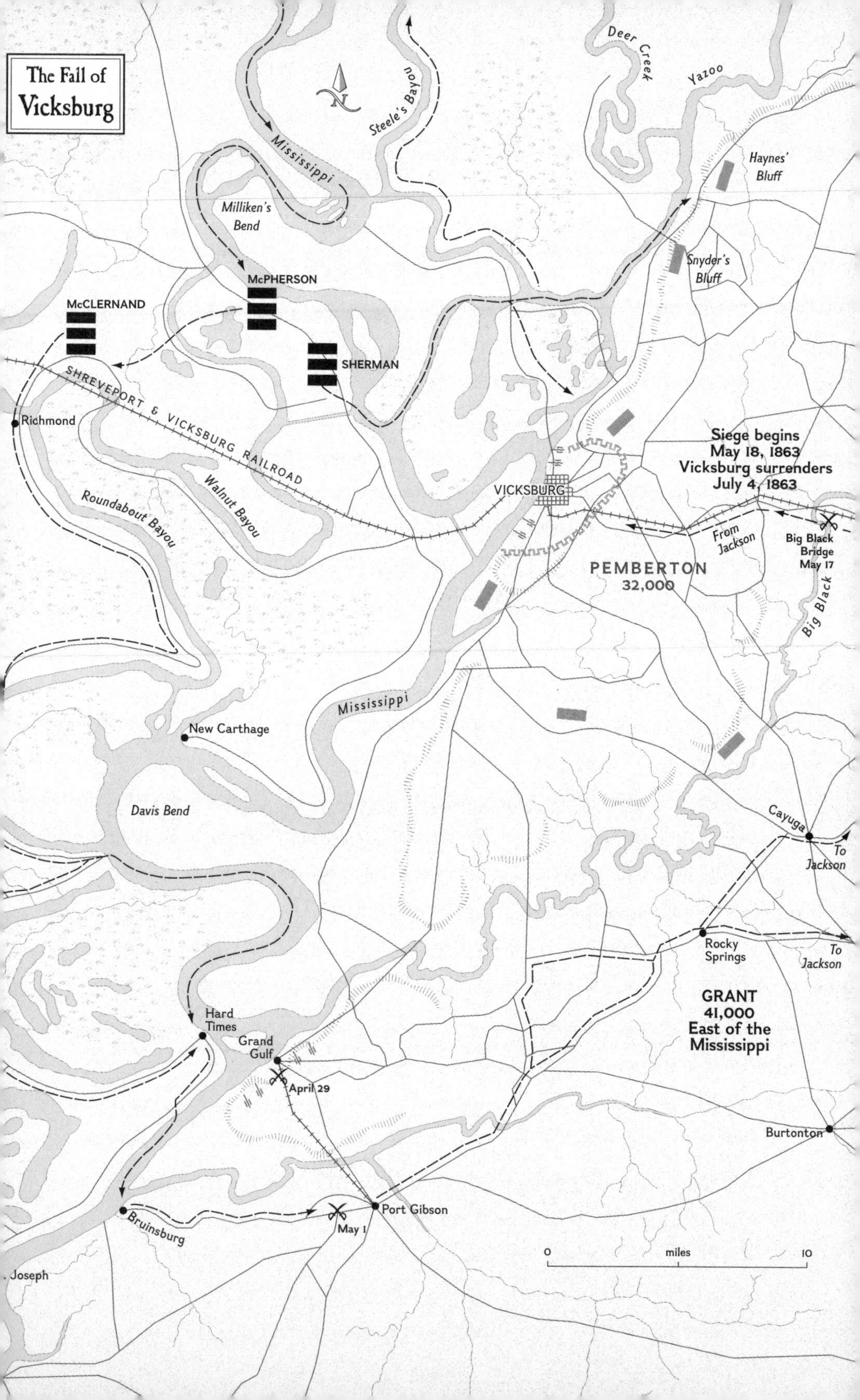

The Fall of Vicksburg
Deer Creek
Yazoo
Steele's Bayou
Mississippi
Haynes' Bluff
Milliken's Bend
Snyder's Bluff
McPHERSON
McCLERNAND
SHERMAN
SHREVEPORT & VICKSBURG RAILROAD
Richmond
Siege begins May 18, 1863
Vicksburg surrenders July 4, 1863
VICKSBURG
Walnut Bayou
Roundabout Bayou
From Jackson
Big Black Bridge May 17
PEMBERTON 32,000
Big Black
Mississippi
New Carthage
Davis Bend
Cayuga
To Jackson
Rocky Springs
To Jackson
GRANT 41,000 East of the Mississippi
Hard Times
Grand Gulf
April 29
Burtonton
Port Gibson
Bruinsburg
May 1
0 miles 10
. Joseph

and 57th Georgia, and capture Waddell's four cannon. General Grant at his Champion House headquarters, upon being apprised of this sweeping success, sends a message, "Go down to Logan and tell him he is making history to-day."

On the other side of the hill, Pemberton's initial steps to confront disaster are gut-wrenching. He sends orders by a staffer for Bowen and Loring to hurry to Stevenson's support. Bowen asks the aide, "What about the enemy to my front?" The staffer then questions Loring, and is told, "There are two Yankee divisions out there." Bowen and Loring do not know until mid-afternoon that McClernand's orders were to move cautiously.

Pemberton, on learning from his aide of the failure of his mission, rides off to see if he can get the two recalcitrant generals to respond to his orders to march to the left, where disaster threatens. Bowen responds to the crisis before Pemberton reaches him. He has pulled his two-brigade division off of the Jackson Creek line and is hastening to the Crossroads—the point of danger—via Ratliff Road. Bowen has waited almost too long. The situation is grim as Slack's people, having secured the Crossroads, brace themselves to forge ahead.

Bowen, however, is closing rapidly with his more than 4,500 veterans. His command includes Col. Francis M. Cockrell's Missouri Brigade. It has a combat record second to none. They lose more men in combat and fight in more battles than the famed Stonewall Brigade. As they come forward, Pemberton is a badly shaken man. I don't know how Cockrell does it, sword in one hand and a magnolia in the other. They deploy in echelon, Cockrell's brigade to the left of Ratliff Road; to the right of the road is Green's brigade, also in echelon. They strike Slack's men here, and his bluecoats skedaddle, headed north. Captain Waddell's four guns—and the Crossroads—are back in Confederate hands. Onward they go, closing on the crest of Champion Hill.

Capt. James Mitchell of the 16th Ohio Light Artillery has advanced and unlimbers two cannon here. Nearby, out of action, are the four captured Confederate cannon. Mitchell sees panic-stricken bluecoats coming toward him, fleeing for their lives. Next he hears Rebel yells and then he sees Bowen's people. The Buckeyes open with canister, but it is like trying to sweep back the tide with a broom. Storming forward, the grim Missourians and Arkansans kill Mitchell, capture his cannon, and send the Yankees in retreat down the north slope of Champion Hill. Grant, down at Sid Champion's house, is concerned and sends his wagon train to the rear.

Fortunately Union reinforcements are approaching. They belong to Crocker's division of McPherson's corps. Marcellus Crocker is an Iowan. Forced to drop out of West Point because of tuberculosis, he returns to duty as a volunteer. A daring fighter, he tells his Third Brigade commander, Col. George B. Boomer, to deploy his men astride the Jackson Road near and south of Grant's Champion House command post. This is difficult because coming toward them are frightened Yankees running for their lives. They break through Boomer's ranks, causing problems. Unfortunately for the Confederates, they are running out of ammunition. As Bowen approaches, General Hovey masses 24 guns in the fields east of the Champion House. The Rebels crash into Boomer's men, and the Yanks bend but do not break. Staggered and bloodied, the Confederates pull back. The bluecoats have met and mastered the battle's final crisis.

Slowly but surely John Bowen's dour fighters pull back. The crest of Champion Hill changes hands for a third and final time. As Crocker's men forge ahead, McClernand's bluecoats close on the Crossroads from the east. About 3 p.m. Loring belatedly starts for the Crossroads with two of his three brigades. Tilghman's brigade and two batteries pull back from the Coker House Ridge to the next ridge, one-third of a mile farther west. Here they redeploy. The Federals advance and occupy the high ground at the Coker House, and call up 12 cannon. An artillery duel ensues on the Raymond Road front during which Tilghman dismounts to help sight one of his guns. He is killed by an enemy shell. His men, since the Federals to their front hold their ground, keep up a bold posture until recalled to rejoin Loring.

Meanwhile, east of the Crossroads, McClernand's two Middle Road divisions finally receive Grant's delayed attack order. The Confederates now face defeat. Preceded by Carter Stevenson's shattered division, Bowen's mauled command retreats southwest cross-country and fords Baker's Creek at the Raymond crossing, the high water from the May 14 cloudburst having subsided. McClernand's people spearhead the pursuit via the Jackson Road. Troops cross Baker's Creek Bridge and turn toward the Raymond Road. They deploy and unlimber artillery and fire in a futile effort to intercept the Rebels as they head for Edward's Station.

Most of Loring's division does not ford Baker's Creek, and Loring declines to run the gauntlet of artillery fire. He recalls those who have crossed and, guided by a local, turns his column down into the Baker's Creek bottom. Several miles downstream Baker's Creek converges into east-west flowing Fourteenmile Creek. Although the flood has subsided, the river's bottom is boggy and the Confederates abandon 12 cannon, along with their caissons and limbers.

Early on Sunday, the 17th, Loring arrives at Whitaker's Ford, south of Edward's Station, and looking north, sees the glow of fires burning in the village. Loring decides to forgo rejoining Pemberton and heads for Crystal Springs.

Champion Hill is both the decisive battle and bloodiest engagement of the Vicksburg campaign. Union casualties number more than 2,400, while the Confederates list more than 2,800. This does not include the 3,000 stragglers lost by Loring's division on its roundabout marches to join Johnston's army.

Although Grant claims victory on May 16, he knows the campaign is far from over. He pushes westward, hoping to scoop up more Confederates before they make their way to the safety of Vicksburg's fortifications. The two armies will meet again the next day at Big Black Bridge, with the Confederates hoping to stem the Union tide.

At Big Black Bridge, the Jackson Road and the Southern Mississippi Railroad converge. East of the river, Pemberton's men had taken cotton bales and piled them up to build fortifications. Earlier Pemberton had wanted Grant to attack him here, so that he could counterattack out of the fortified bridgehead. Pemberton, on the morning of the 17th, has no idea about counterattacking. He doesn't know that Loring is heading for Crystal Springs as fast as he can go. Bowen's division, reinforced by Brig. Gen. John C. Vaughn's Tennessee Brigade, recently arrived from Vicksburg, is across the Big Black along with 18 cannon. McClernand's corps arrives in their front at 10 a.m. McClernand deploys three of his four divisions, from left to right A. J. Smith, Peter Osterhaus, and Eugene Carr.

Grant wants McClernand to pin the Rebels in position behind their breastworks east of the river; Sherman, who left Jackson on the 16th marching via roads parallel to and north of the railroad, will reach the Big Black at Bridgeport, north of the river's big bend, and cross the river there. With Sherman is the army's pontoon train. It is novel: Instead of wooden boats or canvas-covered collapsible craft, Sherman's pontoons consist of large, circular rubber tubes that, when inflated by a large traveling bellows, are anchored athwart the river to support the sleepers and planks that form the bridge. McPherson plans to cross the river midway between Bridgeport and the Big Black Bridge.

Something goes wrong with Grant's plan. The Union brigade commander on the right from Carr's division is Brig. Gen. Michael "Big Mike" Lawler from County Kildare in Ireland. He leads men from Iowa and Wisconsin. Lawler weighs well over 250 pounds, but it's all muscle. Big Mike, screened by trees, moves his men out toward the Big Black, which here flows through a deep trough between river and floodplain. Lawler puts them in that trough. Here they are invisible to the Rebels.

He forms them in assault columns. At 11 a.m. he digs his spurs into his horse's flanks and leads his Hawkeyes and Badgers out into the floodplain. The brigade sweeps forward and breaks the Confederate line. Colonel Cockrell looks up and sees what's happened and yells, "Devil take the hindmost. Get out of here."

The Confederates, in a matter of moments, break and run for the Big Black bridges. The Yankees capture 18 cannon; 1,700 to 1,800 cotton bales, which are salvaged and sent north; and more than 1,700 prisoners. Federal losses amount to 39 killed and 237 wounded. Prompt action by Confederate engineers, who torch the bridges, prevents McClernand's corps from crossing the Big Black until the next morning.

This is another dark day in the history of Pemberton's army. It was a mistake to await Loring's return. As he rides back to Vicksburg, Pemberton is heard to remark, "Just 30 years ago I received my appointment to West Point and today that career is ended in disaster and disgrace."

During the evening of May 17 and throughout the 18th, the retreating Confederates file into the nine-mile-long ring of fortifications guarding the land approaches to Vicksburg. Pemberton now has some 30,000 men to defend the city. Grant's army of 45,000 is close on their heels; one more blow might finish off the disheartened Rebs—or so the Yankees believe.

Just north of the center of the Confederate line, guarding the Jackson Road, is the Third Louisiana Redan; a mile to the north, at the northeastern angle of the Vicksburg defenses, is Stockade Redan.

The forbidding Third Louisiana Redan is one of nine major Rebel forts. It is on Jackson Road Ridge, the highest point on the battlefield, approximately 400 feet above sea level. A redan is a triangular-shaped fortification. If it is enclosed, it has three angles and an equal number of fronts. South of Jackson Road is Great Redoubt. A redoubt is a rectangular or square enclosed fortification. While Great Redoubt is fronted by a ditch, Third Louisiana Redan is not. Why is it called the Third Louisiana Redan? It is garrisoned by the Third Louisiana Infantry. The units posted in this sector are led by Brig. Gen. Louis Hébert, a Louisianian. His brigade belongs to Maj. Gen. John H. Forney's division. Forney's people, like most of Maj. Gen. Martin L. Smith's, have not engaged in the battles east of Vicksburg. Thus the Confederates who occupy the earthworks from Fort Hill, commanding the river on Pemberton's left, to the Second Texas Lunette north of the Southern Railroad of Mississippi, have not tasted defeat.

The nine major works are connected by rifle pits or trenches. Battery lunettes, crescent-shaped earthworks to protect cannon, are sited at commanding positions along and behind the defense perimeter. Timber has been felled in the ravines and hollows, creating extensive abatis. These works had been laid out during the fall of 1862 and early winter of 1863. They had not been revetted—reinforced by an interior facing of timber or logs—nor had their surface been covered by sod. Loess soil erodes rapidly when it is disturbed, and heavy spring rains had caused extensive erosion. When the Confederates manned the works, they had lots of work to do to put them into condition and to mount artillery in the forts and lunettes.

Grant approaches on the afternoon of the 18th. Closing via Jackson Road is McPherson's corps. Sherman follows Graveyard Road and McClernand's corps marches on Baldwin's Ferry Road. By evening only Sherman is in close. By late morning on the 19th, Sherman's men are the only ones that are in contact with Confederate pickets.

Union morale is sky high. They have beaten the Confederates in five battles in 17 days. On the 16th they mauled Pemberton's field army at Champion Hill. They routed the Confederates at Big Black Bridge. In these battles they inflicted more than 7,000 casualties on the foe; captured 65 cannon, and drove the Confederates back into Vicksburg, which seems ripe for plucking. The soldiers want to end it quick. Grant knows what a hot long summer on the river might do. Yellow jack—mosquito-borne yellow fever—or something equally atrocious might attack the Union forces. With scant preparation, Grant schedules an attack for the afternoon of May 19. The only serious fighting will be in the Stockade Redan section.

Stockade Redan is the strong point guarding the northeast approach to Vicksburg. Entering the Vicksburg works topping the ridge separating the headwaters of Mint Spring Bayou from the headwaters of Glass Bayou is Graveyard Road. Located here is Stockade Redan. Fronting Stockade Redan is a ditch or dry moat. Why is it called Stockade Redan? Across Graveyard Road is a poplar log stockade through which wagons can egress and ingress. To the west is the 27th Louisiana Redan, fronted by Mint Spring Bayou. Connecting the strong points are rifle pits. The Confederates here are fresh troops. They include the 36th Mississippi and 27th Louisiana.

Early on the 19th an event occurs that Sherman cites in his memoirs. When Maj. Gen. Frederick Steele's division advances and secures Bell Smith Ridge, bounding Mint Spring Bayou on the north, driving in Rebel skirmishers, they sight smoke of Union transports and gunboats on the lower Yazoo River. They yell, "Hardtack! Hardtack!" Sherman recalls that the soldiers are tired of their diet of freshly slaughtered meat. He'll turn to Grant and say, "You were right and I was wrong, because I thought you made a mistake when you marched south to cross the Mississippi rather than returning to Memphis and resuming the march down the railroad."

This day you don't want to be in Frank Blair's division. It's been a good division to be in so far. The men saw only skirmishing at Champion Hill, and they've seen no other action since their April 30–May 1 demonstration against Snyder's Bluff. Blair gives his orders to attack. They're going to have little or no artillery preparation. Col. Thomas Kilby Smith's brigade

Steamboats occupy the wharves along Vicksburg's busy waterfront. Vicksburg occupied a key strategic position on the Mississippi River for transporting goods between the Midwest and New Orleans.

guides on Graveyard Road. One of his regiments, the 55th Illinois, is led by Col. Oscar Malmborg, a heavy-drinking Swedish soldier of fortune. He's unpopular with his men.

On the ridges to the north Col. Giles A. Smith forms up his brigade. Among his units is a battalion of the 13th U.S. Infantry led by Capt. Edward Washington. The ravines where Mint Spring Bayou heads are filled with felled timber. Off to the northwest, on the far side of Mint Spring Bayou, there is the brigade led by Brig. Gen. Hugh Ewing, a friend of Stonewall Jackson back in today's West Virginia. His men are new to the western army. They include the 37th and 47th Ohio and 4th West Virginia, veterans who have seen much action in western

Virginia, and the 30th Ohio, which stood tall in the Antietam campaign. These newcomers with their kepis and paper collars are called "bandbox" soldiers by battered-hat wearing and raggedy-assed Westerners.

At 2 p.m. when Blair gives the word to attack, his men raise a "Huzzah!" They come forward in line of battle, elbow touching elbow. The second rank a step and a half behind the first, and then the file closers. As Kilby Smith's people come under fire, the men enter the abatis on the left and right of Graveyard Road. In the abatis they get hung up in the felled timber. They halt, re-form, and drive forward. They reach a spur and a handful of men—mostly from the 83rd Indiana—dash forward and jump into the ditch. Those on the spur are pinned down. Unable to advance any closer to the Rebel works, they volley fire.

In the 55th Illinois is Drummer Orion Howe, a 14-year-old from Waukegan. Howe is a musician, young and agile. The soldiers fire up their ammunition fast, and they send men to the rear for more. Howe is among these volunteers. While sprinting along Graveyard Road, the lad is struck in the leg by a minié ball. Undaunted, he continues on his hazardous mission. Staggering up to a mounted Sherman, Howe informs the general of the crucial shortage of cartridges at the front. Impressed by the lad's gallantry, the War Department awarded Howe the Medal of Honor on Sherman's recommendation. He thus became one of the youngest recipients of the nation's highest award for heroism.

Giles Smith's line of advance is at a right angle to Kilby Smith's. Surging first downward and then upward through felled timber, the bluecoats close on Stockade Redan's north face. Particularly hard hit is the First Battalion, 13th U.S. Infantry. Among those out front is Color Sgt. James E. Brown. He is mortally wounded, and four others will likewise be cut down as they seek to advance the national colors. Battalion commander Washington is mortally wounded. Capt. Thomas Ewing, a Sherman brother-in-law, and ten men reach the ditch fronting the redan, but this is the Regulars' high tide. Sherman calls the battalion's performance "unequaled in the Army," and authorizes the 13th to sew "First at Vicksburg" onto its colors.

The "bandbox" soldiers of Hugh Ewing's brigade charge the 27th Louisiana Lunette, and it "looked for a while as if they would stay." But in the end their battle line "went down in a windrow." Grant's May 19 assault has failed. Union casualties number 919, two-thirds of them belonging to Blair's division. Confederate losses may have reached 200. Grant and his soldiers, much to their surprise, found that the Confederates, fighting behind earthworks, had recovered their self-confidence. It is evident that Vicksburg will not be captured by a poorly organized and uncoordinated attack.

Grant is determined to break through the Confederate lines. He gives his generals two days to plan an assault with all their forces to be carried out on May 22. Grant secures the cooperation of Admiral Porter's gunboats, which will bombard the city's defenses from the river. The day's action will begin with a four-hour bombardment. As dawn breaks on the 22nd, the guns open fire.

Grant's May 22 assault takes place in three sectors in this order: McPherson's corps attacks north and south of Jackson road, Sherman's centering on Graveyard Road, and McClernand's south of the railroad. It will be an all-out assault. Grant has massed some 40,000 troops, and it will be up to the corps commanders how they will employ their soldiers. The plan is that at six o'clock in the morning all Union cannon will open fire. The bombardment will cease at 10 a.m. and be followed by the attack. Officers have synchronized their watches, perhaps a first.

On McPherson's front, General Logan attacks with two brigades. John E. Smith's forms in the ravine east of the Shirley House. The 23rd Indiana will lead the attack. When the artillery ceases fire, the Hoosiers come out of the ravine and onto Jackson Road in a column by eights.

The Yankees surge onward, and as they pass through the deep cut, 100 yards west of the Third Louisiana Redan, the Rebels open fire and they take cover in the hollow north of the road. The Indianans are staggered. The regiment following the Hoosiers, the 20th Illinois, hunkers down in the ravine south of the road, and Smith's attack is over. Out of Smith's five regiments, he has engaged two.

John Stevenson is made of sterner stuff; he deploys as skirmishers the 17th Illinois in the hollow fronting Great Redoubt. When the artillery ceases fire, these units are to form into columns of assault. In the right column, eight abreast, are the 7th Missouri and 32nd Ohio. The left column, 200 yards to their left, includes the 8th and 81st Illinois. They start up the slope. The Rebels open fire. Men drop and they recoil into the hollow. Union artillery again hammers Great Redoubt. The order forward comes, and screened by skirmishers, the two columns again move up the slope. Col. James J. Dollins of the 81st Illinois is shot down and the left column breaks and recoils.

The right column, spearheaded by the Seventh Missouri, seems invincible as the regiment climbs the slope. An Irish regiment, the Missourians carry an emerald green flag. The vanguard, with a final desperate lunge, leap into the ditch fronting the redoubt and discover that their scaling ladders are too short. An engineer had goofed estimating the height from the bottom of the ditch to the top of the superior slope as 12 feet when it is 17. Trapped in the ditch, their advance is turned back with heavy losses.

Brig. Gen. Isaac F. Quinby now leads Crocker's division, and he proves to be a timid soul. When his men cross a ridge 300 yards east of the Rebel works, they encounter a storm of canister and musketry and retire back having lost less than a dozen men. Of McPherson's 32 regiments present only 7 have been seriously engaged—underscoring that perhaps as a combat commander McPherson's leadership at Raymond had not been an aberration.

As it was on May 19, Sherman's XV Corps today is on McPherson's right. Less than 72 hours earlier the Confederates had savaged Blair's people in the abatis-choked ravines flanking Graveyard Road. So, Sherman comes up with a "better idea." A call goes out to Blair's division for 150 volunteers, 50 from each of his three brigades. They are designated the "Forlorn Hope." They will go forward carrying debris and scaling ladders. They will sling their rifle-muskets because they are going to come down the Graveyard Road eight abreast and they are not going to halt and fire. They will fill the ditch with the debris. The people coming behind are to charge over the debris and into the works. Following the Forlorn Hope is the brigade commanded by General Ewing in column by eights: the 30th Ohio, 37th Ohio, 4th West Virginia, and 47th Ohio. Behind them in the same formation are Blair's other two brigades. Behind them are Brig. Gen. James Tuttle's three brigades. You've got a battering ram that beats all battering rams. Almost 10,000 men, eight abreast, extending back along Graveyard Road for more than a mile.

The bombardment ceases at 10 a.m. Ewing looks at Capt. John Gorce, commanding the Forlorn Hope. Gorce bellows "Forward!" Pvt. Howell Trogden carries Ewing's headquarters flag, and down the road they come. The Confederate works are enveloped in dust and smoke. The Yanks hope that the artillery has solved everything. You hear the shuffling of their feet. When they reach the Graveyard Road cut, 100 yards from Stockade Redan, the dust and smoke clears, and a terrible sight appears: Rebels in two ranks come into view. They fire a crashing volley. Dead and wounded fall. Gorce and Trogden get into the ditch with a handful of men and plant Ewing's headquarters flag on the exterior slope.

Up comes the 30th Ohio. The Buckeyes see dead and wounded sprawled in the cut. They enter the cut and suffer a fate similar to the Forlorn Hope. Dead and wounded are cut down, and a handful of men surge onward and reach the ditch. Now comes the 37th Ohio, raised from in and around Toledo. The men enter the cut, see dead and wounded, freeze, and either go to ground or take cover in the ravines to the left and right. Col. Lewis von Blessing and Sgt. Maj. Lewis Sebastian, in a futile effort to get the attack moving, employ their swords upon the shirkers' backsides.

Sherman's attack is stymied. He has only committed the Forlorn Hope, and the 30th and 37th Ohio. Sherman will do nothing more until noon. Grant has joined him. Here Grant receives a message from General McClernand reporting, "We have part possession of two forts, and the stars and stripes are floating over them." Grant believes McClernand is exaggerating. But he can't let the opportunity pass. So he orders the attack renewed. General Quinby sends his division to reinforce McClernand at the Railroad Redoubt and the Second Texas Lunette, and Sherman will again assail Stockade Redan as well as the earthwork west and south of that salient angle, where the Missouri monument now stands.

Sherman launches four attacks during the afternoon. They are piecemeal and uncoordinated. At 1 p.m. Brig. Gen. Thomas E. G. Ransom's brigade, of McPherson's XVII Corps on Sherman's left spearheaded by the 14th and 17th Wisconsin and 72nd Illinois, charges up and out of the north prong of Glass Bayou. They close on the enemy's works but are thrown back. About a half hour later the brigades of Giles Smith and Kilby Smith are repulsed. Let's try what we did in the morning: Send another column down Graveyard road. Let's do it with Brig. Gen. Joe Mower, he's a helluva fighter, and commands the famed Eagle Brigade. "Old Abe," the Eighth Wisconsin's war eagle, is a much honored bird, but never soared above a battlefield because he is chained to his perch, which is carried next to the colors.

The brigade comes forward in column by eights. The 11th Missouri, Col. Andrew Weber commanding, leads off, followed respectively by the 47th Illinois, 8th Wisconsin, and 5th Minnesota. A handful of men accompanied by Colonel Weber of the 11th Missouri gain the ditch fronting Stockade Redan, and now two flags fly on the exterior slope of that work. Just as Old Abe enters the cut and is about to be blasted into eternity, Sherman looks at Mower, Mower looks at him, and they suspend the attack.

At four o'clock, at a point three-quarters of a mile west of Stockade Redan, General Steele finally gets his men into position. Up the steep slope they charge, but are repulsed. Sherman's May 22 attack has failed.

On McClernand's front to the south, the initial Yankee assaults against Second Texas Lunette and Railroad Redoubt fare better.

Railroad Redoubt juts out in front of the Confederate works. It is garrisoned by a detachment of the 30th Alabama, commanded by Col. Charles M. Shelley, one of five regiments in S. D. Lee's Alabama Brigade. Two cannon are emplaced in the work. To the north of the railroad, the Second Texas defends the lunette that bears the regiment's name.

McClernand has six brigades available for his attack. He places Eugene Asa Carr in command of the four brigades on the right. Carr assigns the brigades under Brig. Gens. Stephen Burbridge and William P. Benton to attack the Texans, and the two led by Mike Lawler and Col. William Landram to assail Railroad Redoubt.

Col. George Bailey's 99th Illinois heads Benton's column as it emerges from the ravine fronting today's visitor center and crosses Baldwin's Ferry Road. Bailey strides along in his shirtsleeves. Alongside him is one of his color bearers, Cpl. Thomas J. Higgins. Higgins rushes into the Rebel fire and doesn't look back. He goes into the foe's works and Texas Capt. A. J. Hurley pulls him in, grabs his chest, and inquires, "Are you wearing a bulletproof vest? My men are good shots. They were shooting at you." Higgins looks around. Where in the hell are his friends? He looks to the rear and sees that Bailey and the rest of the 99th have gone to ground.

But on come many more Yanks and after a desperate struggle finally gain the ditch fronting Second Texas Lunette. The lunette's interior traverses are bales of cotton and they catch fire. The Federals seek to crawl through the cannon embrasures. The Confederates throw them back. You've got bluecoats in the ditch and the Texans in the lunette. The Chicago Mercantile Battery under Capt. Patrick White, who along with five of his cannoneers become recipients of the Medal of Honor, push a brass six-pounder to within ten yards of the works. They begin pumping shots into the lunette.

South of the railroad a dozen Iowans led by Sgts. Joseph Griffith and Nicholas Messenger fight their way into Railroad Redoubt and drive the Rebels out. The Confederates counterattack. Hiding behind a traverse is Lt. J. M. Pearson and a score of Alabamians. Capt. H. P. Oden leads about 15 counterattacking Alabamians. As they enter the work, they see both Yanks and Rebels. The Johnnies are crouched down. Oden screams at Pearson, "Why in the hell ain't you fighting?" The Iowans fire. Oden and most of his men are killed or wounded in falling back. Pearson and his men ground arms and surrender.

The Iowans plant their colors in the redoubt and are soon reinforced by soldiers of the 77th Illinois. Unlike McPherson and Sherman, who have many men on the field but not in contact with the foe, McClernand and Carr have all their men engaged. They have no reserves to exploit the situation. The Confederates have reserves, the men of Bowen's division. Bowen sends Cockrell's Missourians to support the Stockade Redan defenders, and Green's brigade to bolster the Texans at the lunette. This leads to a stalemate on McClernand's front.

To break the impasse, McPherson sends Quinby's division. Instead of deploying the fresh division as a unit, McClernand breaks it up. Col. John C. Sanborn's brigade rushes to support Benton and Burbridge at Second Texas Lunette. Col. George B. Boomer is to reinforce Lawler and Landram at Railroad Redoubt. Col. Samuel Holmes goes to Square Fort to help Osterhaus's division.

It's 3 p.m. and yes, the Yanks still hold Railroad Redoubt and are in the ditch fronting Second Texas Lunette. The Confederates see Boomer forming his men. Brigade commander S. D. Lee knows he'd better drive those Yankees out of the Redoubt, or Boomer's bluecoats might punch through the Confederates' second line. He calls on Colonel Shelley for a counterattack, but Shelley refuses.

Now comes up a hero. Col. Thomas Waul had been a Vicksburg lawyer before going to Texas. He had raised Waul's Texas Legion and solicits for his Texans the honor of recapturing the Redoubt. Lee tells him to proceed. Two companies of Texans guided by Col. Edmund Pettus counterattack. They overwhelm the Yankees, capturing several flags. Down in the ditch fronting the works is Lt. Col. Harvey Graham with about 70 bluecoats. S. D. Lee rolls 18-pound shells down into the ditch. Soon Colonel Graham and his men ground their arms. The breach is sealed.

Too late, Boomer's men advance. The Confederates open fire and he's almost the first casualty. With Boomer mortally wounded his men drop to the ground. What's happening at the Second Texas Lunette? Up comes Sanborn's people. Burbridge's and Benton's troops have been here all day. As soon as the reinforcements come up, they pull out. To make a grim situation worse for Sanborn's newcomers, Green's Arkansans and Missourians sortie. Orders now come to retire. But before Sanborn does, Federal infantrymen help Captain White withdraw his brass six-pounder, which had been manhandled to within a few yards of the ditch fronting the lunette.

McClernand's soldiers are back where they were in the morning, the same as Sherman's and McPherson's. Losses on his front were much greater, though at one time his corps had secured part possession of Railroad Redoubt and gained the Second Texas Lunette's ditch. The great assault is over. There are 3,199 Union dead, wounded, and missing, of whom about 500 are prisoners. Five stands of colors are captured. Confederate losses do not exceed 500.

Thwarted in his efforts to take Vicksburg by assault, Grant decides to besiege the Confederate city. Union soldiers entrench; in various places they begin to dig approaches—zigzag trenches that push toward the Confederate fortifications.

Gen. Alvin Hovey's approach is directed against Square Fort. The Yankees position two sap rollers—huge wicker cylinders that can be rolled ahead of men digging a trench for protection against enemy fire. They dig two approach trenches that zigzag up these spurs. There are many Union sharpshooters. After May 22 you have a better chance to be killed or wounded if you are a Rebel. You ask, Why does that happen? The Rebs are entrenched. The Yanks aren't dug in as well. Where are the Confederates? They are on the high ground. Where do you expose yourself as a silhouette? On the high ground.

Where would you like to be if you are a Yankee marksman? You'd like to be on the low ground with sandbags in front of you or behind a tree, waiting all day until some Confederate exposes himself on the skyline. Because of optics, whether you are a Civil War soldier or a World War II combat infantryman, the human eye is such that if you fire down a grade your optic nerve tends to make you fire high. That is why the officers and NCOs when Civil War soldiers fought in line of battle kept yelling "Fire low. Fire low." If you fire at a man's knees you are probably going to hit him in the middle, if you aim high, the odds are that you will miss.

Particularly at risk are senior officers. Among those gunned down are brigade commanders—Col. Isham W. Garrott of the 20th Alabama is killed in Square Fort on June 17 by a Union sharpshooter, and Brig. Gen. Martin E. Green of Missouri on June 25. Subsequent to the two officers' deaths, Square Fort is designated Fort Garrott and a smaller work at the Missouri Monument Green's Redan.

Elsewhere the Yankees try other ways to breach the Confederate defenses.

Lt. Henry C. Foster of the 23rd Indiana gets revenge on the Confederates for what they did to his regiment on May 22 and earlier at Raymond. He and his men use railroad ties to construct a tower. The tower is built on commanding ground south of Jackson Road, adjacent to Logan's Approach, and is raised to a height sufficient to allow Foster to see over the Third Louisiana Redan's parapet. Foster, because of his marksmanship, became a terror to the Confederates. Among the Yanks in Logan's division, because of his coonskin cap, he became known as "Coonskin" Foster and his perch as "Coonskin Tower." He is visited here on one occasion by Ulysses S. Grant.

All the while the Federals continue digging and pushing Logan's Approach, which began in the hollow at the Shirley House closer to Third Louisiana Redan. As they dig, sappers push a railroad flatcar stacked with cotton bales ahead of them. In a successful effort to slow the Yanks, Col. Sam Russell of the Third Lousiana calls for smoothbore muskets. He then secures tow (refuse cotton), soaks it in turpentine, wraps it around small-caliber musket balls, and has his men fire these into the cotton bales. The sap roller catches fire and burns. But Logan's people improvise. What do they do? They get several 55-gallon barrels, nail two of them together, fill them with dirt, and then wrap them with cane. This gives them a mobile barricade ten feet wide and five feet high that is not flammable.

By June 23 the head of Logan's Approach has been driven to within 30 yards of the exterior slope of the redan. Now is time to extend a gallery from the head of the approach to extend under the redan. Volunteers with experience as miners are called for and soldiers of the 7th Missouri and

A warren of "bomb proof" shelters occupy the once beautiful grounds of Wexford Lodge, also known as the Shirley House. The dugouts in this photograph belong to the 45th Illinois infantry.

32nd Ohio respond. Within less than 48 hours the gallery has been completed and its head extends under the redan.

The Rebels hear digging. Men of the 43rd Mississippi start sinking countermines. They want either to tap into the Union gallery or, if they can get close enough, to place a barrel of powder in the countermine with a slow fuse, touch it off, and that's the end of the bluecoats working in the gallery. The Yanks hear the Mississippians digging. Confronted by what could be a crisis, the Federals place 2,000 pounds of black powder at the head of the gallery. At 3:30 p.m. on June 25, the fuse is lit and the Yanks hunker down. An explosion ensues; the ground shakes, a great geyser of dirt and dust ascends and then descends. Charging up Logan's Approach and into the crater is the 45th Illinois. But the Rebels, aware of what to expect, have thrown up a traverse—an interior earthwork—

across the gorge of the Third Louisiana Redan. Behind the traverse crouch the Louisianans. The Lead Miners of the 45th Illinois can't get out of the crater: They are pinned down. During the next 20 hours Union regiments, in a futile effort to break the stalemate, are rotated into and out of the crater. A Rebel counterattack is repulsed. Grant, seeing that McPherson's people are making no headway, cuts his losses and pulls his men out of the crater.

Grant is undaunted and so are his engineers. They immediately drive another gallery under the redan. When the siege commenced, Grant had requisitioned a hundred coehorn mortars—lightweight mortars that can be carried by four men—from the St. Louis depot, but in warfare you always have snafus. Although he has requisitioned them, the coehorns do not arrive. Logan's chief engineer, Capt. S. R. Tresilian, comes up with an ingenious idea. He takes three tree trunks, bores them out, one to take a 6-pound shell and two others sized for 12-pound shells. He bands them with iron and places them down in that ravine.

This time there isn't going to be an infantry attack following the detonation of the mine—1,800 pounds of powder. On the first day of July far more damage is done to Third Louisiana Redan than six days earlier. The mine explodes. A number of Confederates tumble down the bank, some are severely injured, and five of six blacks working on a countermine are killed. Tresilian's mortars open fire. During the next three days the wooden mortars inflict more Confederate casualties in this area than occurred from artillery fire in the previous 44 days.

Throughout June, Grant tightens the noose around Vicksburg. Reinforcements arrive, allowing him to fend off Johnston's relief efforts from the east and by the trans-Mississippi Confederates from the west with ease. Soon it appears to be only a matter of time before Pemberton will be compelled to give up. But the Confederate commander proves a stubborn foe. As July begins, Grant decides that unless Pemberton surrenders soon, he will mount an all-out assault on July 6. In the city,

On July 4, 1863, Confederate forces surrendered, ending the siege of Vicksburg. Federal forces raised the Stars and Stripes over the courthouse to mark the end of the long campaign.

civilians and soldiers alike suffer from lack of food and the incessant rain of Federal shells.

Finally, on July 3, Grant and Pemberton meet between the lines near the Jackson Road. At first it looks as if negotiations are going nowhere; by that night, however, an agreement is reached whereby Grant will parole Pemberton's command and enter the city. The next day, July 4, Union troops enter Vicksburg.

In the Jackson Road sector where Grant is, the Yankees don't celebrate. In Maj. Gen. Edward O. C. Ord's XIII Corps sector south of Fort

Garrott, it is different. One of the best Union diaries of this siege is that of Lt. Anthony Burton of the Fifth Ohio Battery. Burton writes that their chief of artillery says that they are supposed to fire a hundred-gun salute to celebrate the fall of Vicksburg, but adds, "the hell with blanks; we will fire blanks next year." There is cheering on the Union left. Up where Grant is, they keep a lid on cheering, but don't believe that all the Yankees sit there in silent respect to their gallant foe.

8

CHATTANOOGA

OCTOBER–NOVEMBER, 1863

After its defeat by the Confederates at Chickamauga, Maj. Gen. William S. Rosecrans's Army of the Cumberland found itself holed up in Chattanooga, Tennessee, with Gen. Braxton Bragg's Army of Tennessee holding the high ground of Lookout Mountain to the southwest and Missionary Ridge to the east. Other Confederate forces could interdict the Union supply lines, and it looked as if the Yankees would slowly starve to death or be forced to surrender if they did not break out. Bragg was so confident of eventual victory that he planned to detach Lt. Gen. James Longstreet's corps to move northeast toward Knoxville to drive out a Union force there—the Army of the Ohio, under the command of Maj. Gen. Ambrose Burnside.

Having lost faith in Rosecrans, the Lincoln Administration decided to reorganize its western command system by placing Ulysses S. Grant in charge of all Federal forces from the Appalachian Mountains to the Mississippi River with the exception of those along the Gulf Coast. Grant planned to replace Rosecrans with Maj. Gen. George H. Thomas; he then made his way to Chattanooga to take charge of affairs. By the time he arrived, Rosecrans, Thomas, and the chief engineer of the Army of the Cumberland, Brig. Gen. William Farrar Smith, had devised a plan to reopen the supply lines, and upon Grant's arrival the plan was implemented.

Chattanooga sits on the southern side of a bend in the Tennessee River. To the west the river curves into an inverted "S" with a major bend curling to the north around

Raccoon Mountain. The city is flanked on the east by a series of mountains that include Tunnel Hill and Missionary Ridge, and to the south loom the heights of Lookout Mountain. The town is the hub of four railroad lines: the Nashville & Chattanooga, Memphis & Charleston, Western Atlantic, and Chattanooga & Cleveland Railroads.

Rosecrans makes a major blunder on September 24 when he pulls his troops off of Lookout Mountain, giving the Confederates possession. Lookout Mountain itself is a wonderful observation point, and possession of Lookout Mountain allows the Confederates to control Lookout Valley, as well as the wagon road and Nashville & Chattanooga Railroad, making it very difficult for the Federals to supply Chattanooga. If Rosecrans is going to resupply his army, it has to be done principally by the Wagon Road as it crosses Walden's Ridge through Anderson's Crossroads and into Bridgeport—60 miles of hell. When the rains set in, it is particularly difficult to provision the army.

General Grant had serious reservations about General Rosecrans dating to the battles of Iuka and Corinth in the autumn of 1862. Grant rides down from Indianapolis with Secretary of War Edwin Stanton. Secretary Stanton is not an admirer of General Rosecrans and neither is his assistant, Charles Dana. Lincoln has made remarks about Rosecrans behaving like a duck that has been knocked in the head. Grant brings with him two official orders. He can use either one of them. One retains Rosecrans and one relieves him. He opts for relieving Rosecrans and promoting Maj. Gen. George H. Thomas. Then he sends a patronizing order urging Thomas to hold onto Chattanooga, and Thomas will reply, "We'll hold it until we starve."

Grant arrives here on October 23, 1863. He comes in with a pair of crutches over the pommel of his saddle, because he is still recovering from the injury that he suffered as a result of a mistake down in New Orleans. His error was in going to Gen. Nathaniel P. Banks's party. At Banks's party

Soaring more than 1,600 feet above the Tennessee River, Lookout Mountain occupied one of the highest—and most strategic—points in the Cumberland Mountains.

they probably had a little too much liquor. Afterward Grant was riding very, very rapidly; his horse shied when it saw an omnibus driving along the city streets. Grant's horse fell and the general ended up with a bruised leg. When Grant arrives at Chattanooga, he wonders why his subordinate commanders don't get up and greet him. They really are not that glad to see Ulysses Simpson!

The plan to reopen the supply line has already been worked out by William Farrar "Baldy" Smith—Baldy Smith has little hair. I have a certain respect for people with that nom de guerre. Grant approves the operation. The plan is to open up a new supply line so they can get the men off a diet of these damn "Lincoln" crackers, which are hardtack four inches square and accompanied by middlings of bacon. The Federal soldiers in Chattanooga claim that they can follow along behind the supply wagons and scavenge the corn that falls out through the bottoms of the wagon beds to subsist themselves.

The army is immobile because of the deaths of about 10,000 horses and mules. That's five times as many animals as had been killed in battle on the Union side at Chickamauga. Smith's plan is to open up a shorter line of supply—reduce it from 60 miles to a lesser journey of 27 miles by wagon and by boat.

Already under construction or nearly completed are 50 pontoons. These are flat-bottomed scows, blunt on both ends, which Federal engineers will drift downriver and use to construct a pontoon bridge. Key players include Baldy Smith and Maj. Gen. John M. Palmer, who is put in charge of two brigades. One will be Brig. Gen. William B. Hazen's; the other will be led by Brig. Gen. John B. Turchin.

In the early morning hours of October 27, they embark 24 men in each of the 50 boats. They cast off and drift downriver holding close to the right bank. They are going to drift by Confederate pickets. The Confederate pickets are not keeping a sharp watch as the Federals drift downstream around Moccasin Bend. The Federals pull into the west bank at Brown's Ferry just north of Lookout Mountain. At the same time, Turchin and his brigade, having crossed at a pontoon bridge up above Chattanooga, move across the peninsula formed by Moccasin Bend and are in position with the planking, anchors, and stringers, the bridging materials, when Hazen's people land on the river's opposite side.

Commanding the Confederates in the area is our old friend Gen. James Longstreet. He has in this area the brigade led by Brig. Gen. Evander E. Law, and guarding Brown's Ferry is the 15th Alabama of Little Round Top fame—or infamy, depending on your views. Downstream he has sharpshooters on Williams Island from the Fourth Alabama. But "they ain't" many Confederates available.

Having been told of the plan to open the Cracker Line, Maj. Gen. Joseph "Fighting Joe" Hooker will move from Bridgeport, Alabama, to Kelley's Ferry, then march through the gap separating Sand and

Raccoon Mountains to Brown's Ferry with a force of 17,000 men, consisting of the XI and XII Corps of the Army of the Potomac. The god of war is on the Yankees' side as the Federals drift down the river in the early morning hours of the 27th. They pull into the bank at Brown's Ferry, surprise the Confederates, and secure the bridgehead.

Col. William Oates of the 15th Alabama discovers what has happened and comes up with what would have been a good plan if he had had many men, but he doesn't. He is outnumbered about four to one. His men will take advantage of the mist and walk up until they get right up against the Yankees, and then throw their guns against them, pull the trigger, and blow them into eternity. Well, that is not going to work. The 15th Alabama is repulsed, and Oates is wounded.

In several hours Turchin's men build a bridge across the river. Soon they have a bridgehead on the west bank, but the Confederates have now been alerted. To compound the Rebels' problems, Hooker comes through a gap between Raccoon and Sand Mountains with two divisions of Maj. Gen. Oliver O. Howard's XI Corps, led by two good German boys, Brig. Gens. Adolph von Steinwehr and Carl Schurz. However, because Hooker and Maj. Gen. Henry W. Slocum can't work together, Hooker has only one of Slocum's two XII Corps divisions with him, for the other has been sent with Slocum to guard the railroad back to Murfreesboro, Tennessee. The division that remains is led by Brig. Gen. John W. Geary.

I like this guy. If you are going to organize a pro football team starting from scratch, and want a big, mean linebacker—overbearing, everything you think you would want in such a person—that is John Geary. If you are from San Francisco, you know him from Geary Street, named for him when he was mayor of San Francisco in the vigilante days of the 1850s. He's the fellow who puts the squeeze on "Bleeding Kansas" when he becomes the territorial governor. After the war he'll go on to be governor of his home state of Pennsylvania. He is—at least in his mind—the savior of Culp's Hill at Gettysburg. I, however, think he is exaggerating there, don't you?

When Hooker arrives on October 28, the Yankees have a strong force in Lookout Valley. Up there at the pontoon bridge are Howard's two divisions, led by von Steinwehr and Schurz; down in Lookout Valley, just around the bend at Wauhatchie, Geary halts and camps.

The Confederates decide to attack. You are going to have two great men up there at Sunset Rock that evening: Gens. Braxton Bragg and James Longstreet. They loathe each other by this time. They are each working out a plan, and when it fails, each is going to point a finger at the other. Who screwed up? Longstreet will claim that Bragg allows him to use only one division when he expected to employ two divisions against Hooker's Yankees.

That reduces him to the one division led by Brig. Gen. Micah Jenkins of South Carolina, a Longstreet favorite. The plan is for a night attack on October 28–29. We know that the late evening attack of Maj. Gen. Pat Cleburne on September 19 did not go well at Chickamauga. One can easily recall other examples of night attacks in the Civil War that end up in serious problems for the aggressor.

Awaiting the Confederates at Wauhatchie, just west of Lookout Mountain, is John Geary. Geary has with him Company E, Pennsylvania Light Artillery (also known as Knap's), in which his son serves as a lieutenant. He has with him, in my opinion, the regiment that does everything the 20th Maine does, and against larger numbers, and is not high profile at Gettysburg—the 137th New York. Unfortunately, its commander, Col. David Ireland, will die in September 1864. His official report on Gettysburg is very brief, and he never had the talents in writing that Col. Joshua Lawrence Chamberlain of the 20th did. But he does everything on Culp's Hill, with fewer men and against larger numbers, that Chamberlain does on Little Round Top. With Geary's force is a wagon train, and a number of horses and mules.

Brig. Gen. William F. "Baldy" Smith, shown here with his staff, oversaw construction of the pontoon bridge at Brown's Ferry that allowed Sherman and Hooker to come to the aid of Federal troops.

Jenkins's plan is to throw his old brigade against the Yankees at Wauhatchie and destroy the detached Union force. Two other brigades, one from Alabama and one from Texas, will block Yankee attempts to save Geary by keeping Hooker and Howard from coming to his aid. The Confederates gain the advantage of surprise. Unfortunately General Geary's son, other officers, and a large number of men in Knap's battery become casualties, but the bluecoats hold firm. The Confederates are checked in a confused engagement in which stampeding mules break toward the Rebels. Grant later remarked that he intends to make these mules brevet horses for their performance. Meanwhile, Howard's people bulldoze their way through Law's Alabamians and the Texas Brigade blocking force. Victory results in the Federals securing possession of Lookout Valley and opening the Cracker Line. With the use of steamboats and wagons they build up the health and welfare of the Army of the Cumberland invested in Chattanooga.

The Battle of Wauhatchie ends in more acrimony between Longstreet and Bragg. In fact, they get a divorce. They are mutually delighted when Longstreet with his corps, composed of Jenkins's and McLaws's divisions, entrains and starts toward East Tennessee, headed for Knoxville. There they hopefully will defeat and disperse Burnside's Army of the Ohio. Before long Longstreet is joined by Maj. Gen. Joseph Wheeler's cavalry. Bragg will soon start Brig. Gen. Bushrod R. Johnson and Maj. Gen. Patrick R. Cleburne to East Tennessee.

Even as Bragg detaches forces for an operation against Burnside at Knoxville, more reinforcements are earmarked for Grant's command, most notably a corps from the Army of the Tennessee led by Grant's successor as that army's commander, Maj. Gen. William T. Sherman.

Sherman has to send his men from Vicksburg to Memphis by boat; during that move Sherman's son Willie gets typhoid and dies. A lot of people will say this deeply moves Sherman, because Willie is his favorite son. General in Chief Henry W. Halleck directs Sherman to rebuild the railroad as he marches east from Memphis. This is an easy task around Corinth because the Yankees hold that rail center, but it's tougher as you move east because of Rebel raiders. Too bad for the Rebels that Maj. Gen. Nathan Bedford Forrest isn't there at this time, because he damn sure would have snared Sherman when Confederate cavalry raided the railroad at Collierville, Tennessee, on October 12. Where would Grant and the Union have been without Sherman?

But Confederate cavalry commander Brig. Gen. James R. Chalmers is no Forrest; he's injured early in the fight, and Sherman with a handful of men escapes capture at Collierville. Sherman then moves on to Corinth, where he has his men rebuilding railroads, and they are going slower than molasses in January. They finally reach Cherokee, Alabama. Grant, who has been at Chattanooga since October 23, wonders where in the hell is Sherman? He's just barely inside the Alabama line. Grant tells him to forget about rebuilding the railroad and get here as fast as you can. Detaching one division to rebuild the Decatur & Nashville Railroad, Sherman pushes on with the rest of his men and finally arrives at Bridgeport on November 13.

Grant's plan to lift the Rebel siege of Chattanooga calls for Sherman to take his four divisions, cross the Brown's Ferry pontoon bridge, move northward, and camp in the hills north of Chattanooga where the Rebels can't see him. He will then cross the Tennessee River downstream from the mouth of North Chickamauga Creek, which comes in from the north, and take position to assault the Confederate right along northern Missionary Ridge. General Hooker is to take possession of Lookout Mountain.

The Army of the Cumberland can look on. They are having a bad time; these bandbox soldiers from the East with their polished buttons and their celluloid collars are looking at them and they are laughing. Even worse are the guys in the Army of the Tennessee, who are sloppier looking than they are. These soldiers wear hats rather than kepis. They also brag, "We have never lost a battle." It is getting on the Cumberlanders' nerves.

On November 22, Lt. Col. Aquila Wiley of the 41st Ohio, part of Hazen's brigade, reports that he sees three columns of Confederates moving north along Missionary Ridge. Grant becomes concerned that the Rebels are detaching more men either to reinforce General Longstreet by rail or else they know that Sherman is hiding among the hills north of the river preparatory to crossing the Tennessee. What Wiley saw was Pat Cleburne's division withdrawing prior to entraining to join Longstreet. Other reports reinforce Wiley's observations. Grant decides he's got to disrupt any attempt to further reinforce Longstreet at Knoxville, so he decides to have Thomas press forward against the Confederate outer line along Orchard Knob, just west of Missionary Ridge.

Gen. George H. Thomas, the "Rock of Chickamauga," succeeded Rosecrans as commander of the Army of the Cumberland shortly before the Battle of Chattanooga.

On Orchard Knob the Confederates have no significant earthworks. Their defenses on the crest of Missionary Ridge are equally unimpressive and poorly sited. Rather, they've rested, content with digging a line of rifle pits at the foot of Missionary Ridge. The Federals determine to advance a strong skirmish line and conduct a reconnaissance in force to see what reaction they can get from the Confederates. Thomas designates two divisions of his IV Corps, headed by Brig. Gen. Thomas J. Wood and Maj. Gen. Phil Sheridan, to conduct the operation.

Wood's skirmish line takes the lead in advancing to drive in the Confederate skirmishers. Rebel pickets watch; they're not planning to stay there. It's quite a sight. The Confederates think they are watching a pass in review as the Yankees come out in front of their works. Bands are playing as the two divisions form up. Suddenly the bluecoats deploy skirmishers and start moving toward Orchard Knob. Since there is an overwhelming force of Federals advancing, the Confederate skirmishers fall back, abandoning Orchard Knob, and withdraw to their line of rifle pits at the base of Missionary Ridge. The Yanks are surprised. They've taken Orchard Knob; they are safe. They decide to hold it. The Union has scored an important success.

General Bragg is alarmed. He lacks significant earthworks up on Missionary Ridge. He'd better recall Pat Cleburne and fast. So the wages of sin are coming back to haunt Bragg. He has to spend all day and all night looking for a new place to establish his defensive line. He'll find out too late that the crest of Missionary Ridge is very narrow. At the top there may be 50 feet of level ground; in some places it's going to be even less. That means that on short notice he's not going to be able to select a good defensive position.

He has two options. The topographical crest is the highest point on the ridge. The military crest is that point on the ridge where you command the entire slope before you so there is no dead space. If you have your druthers you want to be on the military crest and not the topographical crest. But in many places the top of Missionary Ridge is so narrow that the Rebels will have to hold the topographical crest; a lot of ravines can't be seen from there, and as a result the artillery

OPPOSITE: *After Chickamauga the Federal Army of the Cumberland retreated to Chattanooga and the Confederates besieged the city. Grant united his forces and reestablished supply lines to the city. On November 23 the Army of the Cumberland took Orchard Knob and, on the following day, Hooker seized Lookout Mountain. On the 25th, Sherman attacked the eastern end of Bragg's line against stubborn resistance while on the left Hooker's advance was blocked by a wrecked bridge over Chattanooga Creek. At 3:30 p.m., Grant ordered Thomas to advance against a Confederate line at the base of Missionary Ridge. Without orders, Thomas's men stormed the ridge, forcing Bragg to order a retreat to Dalton.*

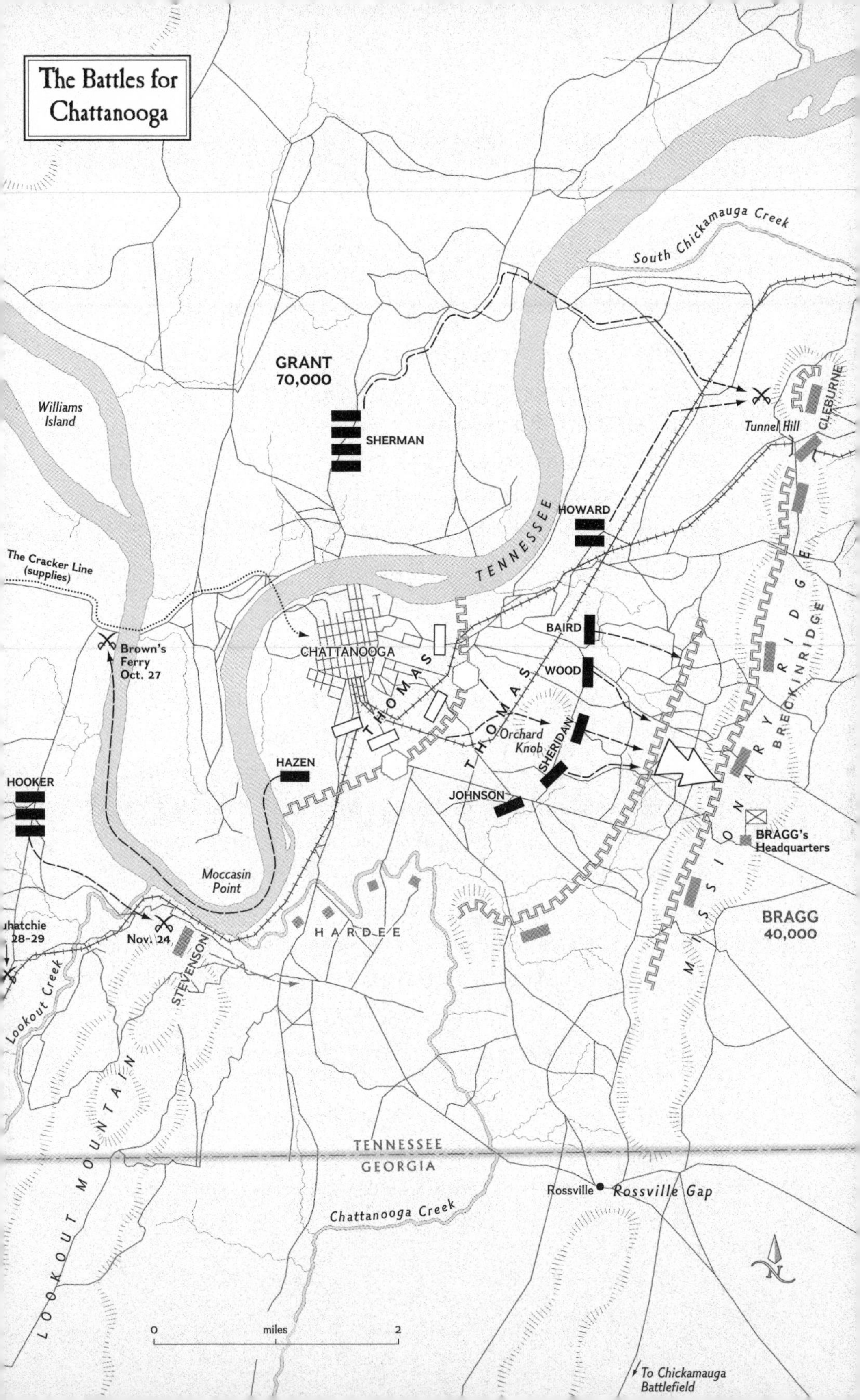

The Battles for Chattanooga
GRANT
70,000
SHERMAN
Williams Island
The Cracker Line (supplies)
Brown's Ferry Oct. 27
TENNESSEE
South Chickamauga Creek
Tunnel Hill
CLEBURNE
HOWARD
BAIRD
WOOD
SHERIDAN
JOHNSON
CHATTANOOGA
THOMAS
THOMAS
Orchard Knob
HAZEN
HOOKER
BRECKINRIDGE
MISSIONARY RIDGE
BRAGG's Headquarters
BRAGG
40,000
Moccasin Point
HARDEE
Nov. 24
STEVENSON
Lookout Creek
LOOKOUT MOUNTAIN
TENNESSEE
GEORGIA
Rossville
Rossville Gap
Chattanooga Creek
miles
0
2
N
To Chickamauga Battlefield

cannot be placed to the best advantage to control the slope. So that's part of the problem.

The other part of the problem is that Bragg doesn't like to call his people together. He doesn't like Maj. Gen. John C. Breckinridge in particular. But Breckinridge commands three divisions posted at the army center. Nor does Bragg value B. Franklin Cheatham. He breaks up Cheatham's Tennessee division, and sends his reconstituted division to reinforce the Rebel left on Lookout Mountain and in Chattanooga Valley. Cheatham is one helluva fighter as well as one helluva drinker, but he is on Bragg's purge list. So the Confederates have a lot of troop movement going on during the night of November 23.

The following day, November 24, Hooker embarks on his assault up Lookout Mountain.

But Lookout Mountain is not impregnable. The flat-topped mountain rises to a height of 2,200 feet above sea level and 1,600 feet above the Tennessee River. Near the crest there is a steep rock escarpment 50 to 60 feet in height, through which there are few passages giving access to the crest. About two-thirds of the way up to the escarpment on the northeast front of the mountain is a five- or ten-acre plateau, the site of the Robert Cravens Farm and his white house. The slopes of Lookout Mountain up to the escarpment from the Cravens Farm Plateau are steep but climbable. Access to the top of the mountain for the Rebels is by a wagon road connecting with Chattanooga Valley.

The morning ushers in a foggy, drizzling day. General Geary's reinforced division inaugurates the day's action. His troops cross Lookout Creek at Light's Mill, east of Wauhatchie, and work their way up the west face of Lookout Mountain. His right flank brigade—Col. George A. Cobham's—anchors its right on the escarpment, with Ireland's on his left, and Col. Charles Candy's on Ireland's left.

Whitaker's brigade of Charles Cruft's division is in reserve. Hooker's command today constitutes a diverse force: Geary's Army of the Potomac people, being joined by Cruft's Army of the Cumberland Division and Brig. Gen. Peter Osterhaus's division of the Army of the Tennessee, which was stranded here when there were delays crossing at Brown's Ferry when the bridge broke.

As Geary's men advance, pivoting on the escarpment, driving a handful of Confederate skirmishers before them, they uncover a crossing of Lookout Creek used by two of Cruft's brigades, 800 yards upstream from the ruins of the railroad and railroad bridge. They eventually uncover the area south of the bridge ruins to allow Osterhaus's men to cross. Like a gate, the bluecoats round the mountain, anchoring the right flank on the palisade. Down on Orchard Knob, where the Union high command is, they hear the firing and occasionally see the flash of an exploding shell. Quartermaster General Montgomery Meigs is there and calls the engagement the "Battle Above the Clouds."

As Geary's men come around the point of the mountain and approach the Cravens Farm Plateau, they encounter Confederates behind breastworks. There are too many Yankees, and they push the Rebs back by the Cravens House and beyond. The Confederates bring up reinforcements. The Federals run short of ammunition. They send Brig. Gen. William P. Carlin's brigade, of the Army of the Cumberland, up there. By late afternoon the Confederates are driven from the Cravens Farm Plateau.

Bragg has been focusing on what Sherman is doing. Sherman by midmorning has crossed the Tennessee with two divisions. He squanders four hours waiting for Brig. Gen. Hugh Ewing to get his division across. Bragg has a difficult choice. Do you leave Maj. Gen. Carter L. Stevenson with the rest of his division up on Lookout Mountain or do you abandon Lookout Mountain? The decision is to abandon Lookout Mountain, and that means pulling off the three brigades that have been fighting there. Bragg pulls the men off the top of the mountain, and they retreat across Chattanooga Creek, botching the job of destroying the bridge before falling back to Missionary Ridge.

All this makes it easy for a team from the Eighth Kentucky to go up to the top of Lookout Mountain on the morning of the 25th and unfurl the U.S. flag, which the Army of the Cumberland can see—particularly the important people up on Orchard Knob. This has a tremendous psychological impact and causes Union morale to soar. The mountain has been engulfed in fog and clouds until now. Officers and men—particularly the Cumberlanders—knew fighting was under way here. They could see exploding shells but they didn't know who was in possession of the crest of Lookout Mountain until the clouds broke and they saw Capt. John Wilson unfurl the colors of the Eighth Kentucky.

On the Union left, William T. Sherman prepares to advance against the Confederate line on north Missionary Ridge.

On the night of November 23–24 Sherman crosses the Tennessee below the mouth of North Chickamauga Creek. By 6:30 a.m., two of Sherman's divisions, led by Brig. Gens. Morgan L. Smith and John E. Smith, are across. But Sherman doesn't do anything. He stays there until noon waiting for Ewing's division to get over. Then he moves forward. He advances against what he believes to be the northern end of Missionary Ridge. By dusk the Yankees are atop Billy Goat Hill, overlooking the Western & Atlantic Railroad at the northern end of Missionary Ridge. At first the Yankees do not realize that there is a deep gorge between Billy Goat Hill and Tunnel Hill to the south. Tunnel Hill gets its name because at this point the Chattanooga & Cleveland Railroad passes through a tunnel. Sherman has reached Billy Goat Hill, but it is too late: Pat Cleburne's elite division, having been recalled by Bragg at the last moment, has reached Tunnel Hill ahead of Sherman.

What are Grant's plans for November 25? His plan calls for General Thomas and his army to have a supporting role. Grant and Sherman have little confidence in the Army of the Cumberland. They see it as a force they have come to rescue, an army that had been defeated at Chickamauga and driven back into Chattanooga. Sherman's men have had to come all the way from Vicksburg to relieve them.

Thomas's troops, during the day, will form from left to right with Brig. Gen. Absalom Baird's division, then Thomas J. Wood's, then Philip Sheridan's, and last but not least the division led by Brig. Gen. Richard Johnson. They will form up, but all they are going to do is focus the Confederate attention on their lines, while Sherman assails the Confederates, drives them from Tunnel Hill, and rolls them up from the Rebel right to the left. Hooker will press forward from Lookout Mountain, cross Chattanooga Valley, and seize Rossville Gap.

If you were teaching terrain appreciation, you would fail the Union leadership here, particularly Sherman and Baldy Smith. There is a deep ravine between Billy Goat and Tunnel Hills, and they are unaware of its existence. Once he gets on Billy Goat Hill, Sherman assumes all he has to do is march southward and roll up those Rebels. When Sherman realizes he isn't on Tunnel Hill, it's too late on November 24 to do anything about it.

Opposite Sherman on Tunnel Hill are Pat Cleburne's men, along with a battery of artillery, six 12-pounder Napoleons of the Warren County Mississippi Artillery, supported by Brig. Gen. James Argyle Smith's Texas Brigade, with another brigade in support. Remember, Sherman is center stage. If we were at an opera, all lights would be on him. He has three divisions of the proud Army of the Tennessee who think they are the best the Union has. He has one division of the Army of the Cumberland, led by Brig. Gen. Jefferson Columbus Davis, and access to Howard's corps. So he has what you would call an overwhelming force.

On November 25, 1863, forces under Thomas and Grant stormed up this slope to the summit of Missionary Ridge, routing Bragg's defending Confederate Army.

Sherman, a cautious combat leader, decides not to commit an overwhelming force. When the Yankees attack, they will have to come across that deep gorge, up a steep grade, and then across open ground against James A. Smith's boys supported by Lieutenant Shannon's six guns. They are going to attack twice, and they are going to be repulsed twice. Three later attacks suffer the same fate.

By early afternoon Sherman "ain't" doing well. His attacks are piecemeal, and he only commits two brigades of his own command in the morning and three brigades in the afternoon. That is about a third of his force. Hooker moves slowly also. He has trouble rebuilding the bridge across Chattanooga Creek. Finally, by late afternoon, he approaches Rossville Gap.

On Orchard Knob, Grant is getting very, very nervous. He's got reports that the Confederates are rushing reinforcements to Tunnel Hill—pure baloney! The Rebels are not sending any reinforcements up here to bolster Cleburne, but we have to go on what Grant thinks. So he decides to have a demonstration. He directs Thomas to advance his four divisions—21,000 men—and drive in the Confederate skirmishers, who are out about 200 yards in front of the line of rifle pits at the base of Missionary Ridge. What's supposed to happen next is unclear. Some people, particularly in Wood's division, think that that will be only step one. People in other divisions, Johnson's and Baird's, say later that no one gave them a clear idea of what to do after they took those rifle pits, so they conclude they'll halt there. So there is a poor understanding of what they are going to do.

As Thomas's men get ready to move, Grant is unhappy. He looks over and sees IV Corps commander Maj. Gen. Gordon Granger sighting a cannon. Granger thinks he's back in the artillery, where he'd been a lieutenant. Grant goes over and chews on Granger awhile. Now, the signal guns will fire the salvo. Boom! Boom! Boom! Boom! Boom! Boom! That is the signal, and Thomas's men advance. Among the Confederates is Maj. Gen. James Patton Anderson's division, some of whose brigade commanders understand that when the enemy advances, they are to fall back onto the main line of resistance atop Missionary Ridge. Others believe that they are to fight like hell in the rifle pits at the foot of the ridge.

The Union troops advance. They have little problem until they come out of the woods about a half mile before they hit the Confederate rifle pits at the base of the ridge. Now, Rebel skirmishers are falling back on the rifle pits. Rebel cannon open fire. You see Yankees falling. But, on they go. Now, as they get closer, Tennesseeans of Brig. Gen. Otho F. Strahl's brigade stay in their rifle pits and let the Yankees come on and on. And they'll battle the Yankees in the rifle pits. Soldiers of the Florida Brigade to their right have not understood their mission, and

Federal troops of Company B, 9th Pennsylvania, atop Lookout Mountain. While the summit held little tactical value, "the Battle Above the Clouds" inspired dramatic stories and art.

they retreat up the mountain. Before long the Yankees carry the pits. Grant now feels better. That's what they are supposed to do.

The rank and file in the Army of the Cumberland feel patronized. They have been in a supporting role. They have heard remarks about the Army of the Tennessee having to come to their rescue, and their popular leader General Rosecrans was unceremoniously sacked. They halt, maybe five minutes, perhaps ten minutes, and then they start up the slope. Sheridan, as he looks to his left, sees Wood's men moving out first. Sheridan reaches into his vest, pulls out his decanter, and, as he puts it up to his lips, a shell bursts nearby. He then takes his flask and hurls it toward the Confederates. Now he can start fighting.

Back on Orchard Knob, watching what's going on, Grant is beside himself. He's concerned that the advance up the steep ridge will end in a repulse when Thomas's brigades get up to the Confederate main line of resistance. He turns to Thomas and asks, "Thomas, who ordered those men up the ridge?" Thomas responds, "I don't know, I did not." Grant inquires of Granger, "Did you order them up?" "No," Granger assures, "they started without orders. When those fellows get started all hell can't stop them." This is one the troops have done on their own. Grant will want to see what happens to Thomas's Cumberlanders. The decision to go on is made by the soldiers, the people who must make the ultimate sacrifice.

They are not going to come up in lines of battle. Usually the color guard and the colors are out in front along with certain junior officers, like 18-year-old First Lt. Arthur MacArthur of the 24th Wisconsin, carrying its flag and shouting to his men, "On Wisconsin." The Confederates who choose to fight are overwhelmed and start running up the slope, forming a shield that prevents many of their comrades from firing at the upcoming bluecoats. The Yankees, using the folds in the terrain and screened by retreating Rebels, find that many of the Confederates entrenched at the top of Missionary Ridge can't fire downslope. Too many of them are posted on the topographical crest. The Yankees surge upward in scores of "flying Vs."

A number of Union commanders claim that they are first to reach the crest. Handsome Col. Charles Harker, one of Sheridan's brigade leaders, gains the top near Bragg's headquarters. He reports, "though officers and men were constantly falling, the command moved forward taking advantage of every depression in the ground—or tree or stump—to rest for an instant and then reload." With a surge the Yanks storm ahead and capture a battery whose "gunners were still at their posts." In the excitement Harker sprang astride the hot tube and then off even faster.

To Harker's left the Second Minnesota of Baird's division vied with Harker's brigade for the honors of being first up and captured several hundred prisoners. To the Minnesotans's left skirmishers of the Eighth Kansas of Wood's division closed to within a dozen yards of the enemy breastworks, when the foe "broke in wild confusion and fled."

Bragg grabs a flag in an effort to rally his men, calling, " Here's your commander." The men flee past him, some of them shouting and jeering with epithets such as "General, here's a mule for you!" The collapse runs along the line beginning in Anderson's division. The Confederate right stands firm. Cleburne and W. H. T. "Shot Pouch" Walker are confident that the Confederates down here at Bragg's headquarters on Missionary Ridge are going to repulse the Yankees just like they have on Tunnel Hill. But the line is crumbling. Making things worse is the arrival of Hooker's force in the Rossville Gap sector. The Confederate left and center give way; finally the right follows suit. The only Union soldiers that will pursue, and will pursue a very short distance, are General Sheridan's.

The Federals have won the Battle of Chattanooga. Bragg has lost only 6,000 men out of 50,000, far fewer than Lee suffered at Antietam, but the army is in much worse condition. Any confidence the soldiers had in Bragg is gone. After a half-hearted pursuit, Grant dispatches Sherman to rescue Burnside at Knoxville, only to find that, by the time Sherman arrives, Burnside has already beaten Longstreet back.

So Union arms have reversed the tide in the West that had seemingly turned against them in their bitter Chickamauga defeat. What would have happened without Thomas and his brave Cumberlanders here we don't know. But in Washington they're looking for a new general in chief for the Union Army. General Halleck has proved himself a good clerk, nothing more. The road that began for Grant at Fort Donelson, continued on to "Bloody Shiloh," on to Vicksburg, and then to Missionary Ridge and Chattanooga, will lead to the position of general in chief of the Union Army. Ulysses S. Grant receives his third star as lieutenant general on March 9, 1864, and from there the road will lead through bloodier campaigns and ever lengthening casualty lists of dead and wounded before ending in Wilmer McLean's parlor at Appomattox Court House on the afternoon of April 9, 1865, at 3:30 p.m.

1864

On March 9, 1864, Ulysses S. Grant was promoted to the rank of lieutenant general, and given stewardship of the Armies of the United States. Grant understood that it would be necessary to defeat Lee's army if he was to end the war. As a result many of the final battles of the war would play out in Virginia. In June of 1864 at Cold Harbor, outnumbered Rebels entrenched themselves in strong earthwork fortifications, and rode out each successive Yankee assault. More than 10,000 Union soldiers were lost in the fighting along the Cold Harbor line between May 31 and June 12.

9

THE WILDERNESS

MAY 5–6, 1864

On March 9, 1864, President Abraham Lincoln handed Ulysses S. Grant his commission as a lieutenant general, and within days Grant took command of the armies of the United States. The President had decided to place Grant in overall command in the hope that the hero of Fort Donelson, Vicksburg, and Missionary Ridge could crush the rebellion—or at least achieve sufficient success to guarantee Lincoln's reelection—so that the war would be fought to ultimate victory.

Grant decided to turn over command of operations in the West to his trusted subordinate Maj. Gen. William T. Sherman. He planned to stay in the East and oversee the operations of the Army of the Potomac and other forces against Robert E. Lee and the Army of Northern Virginia. For the spring of 1864 he had mapped out an offensive plan on four fronts. One Union army, 8,900 men under Maj. Gen. Franz Sigel, would advance southward up the Shenandoah Valley; another would operate in southwestern Virginia; a third force, the Army of the James under Maj. Gen. Benjamin F. Butler, would travel up the James River toward Richmond and threaten the Confederate capital, looking either to capture it or cut it off from the Confederate heartland. Grant would accompany Maj. Gen. George G. Meade's Army of the Potomac and direct the operations of Maj. Gen. Ambrose Burnside's separate IX Corps. Grant employed more than 116,000 men against his target, the 65,000 men of Robert E. Lee's Army of Northern Virginia.

After Gettysburg, Union and Confederate armies had continued to maneuver against each other, sparring around Culpeper and the heavily fortified Confederate lines behind Mine Run, a tributary of the Rapidan. Neither side could gain the advantage, and both armies settled into an uneasy truce for the winter. In September 1863, Lee had sent Lt. Gen. James Longstreet with two divisions of his corps west by rail to reinforce the Army of Tennessee. Longstreet's men fought at Chickamauga and Knoxville before returning to Virginia in mid-April 1864. The Army of Northern Virginia spent the winter south of the line of the Rapidan River in the Virginia Piedmont; the Yankees remained north of the river with their winter camps located in Culpeper County and around Warrenton.

Grant proposed to cross the Rapidan, march southeast through the Wilderness, and then turn west to confront Lee, forcing him to fight on open ground. He looked for Sherman to commence his operations in northern Georgia the same week. So once more, as in years past, a new Yankee commander would match wits with Robert E. Lee, who had yet to lose a campaign conducted on Virginia soil. The Wilderness is a 60-square-mile region of played-out tobacco land, cut over in the 18th and early 19th century. The region had grown up in dense scrub, and brush-choked fields were intersected by tangled, wooded creek bottoms. Roads and a few hardscrabble farm fields provided rare openings in an otherwise impenetrable landscape. Grant planned to use the Wilderness to shield his movements, but hoped to march through it quickly before confronting Lee.

The Union Army broke camp at dusk on May 3. They marched southeast to cross the Rapidan River; three-quarters of the Army of the Potomac's 116,000 men and thousands of horses and mules will cross at Germanna Ford. In front is a cavalry division under Brig. Gen. James H. Wilson, a Grant protégé who has been promoted and transferred from staff to line; it clears away the few Confederates in the area and secures the crossing. The engineers arrive and commence positioning two pontoon bridges. They'll also build two bridges down at Ely's Ford, five miles downstream, and one at Culpeper Mine Ford.

Troops of Maj. Gen. John Sedgwick's VI Corps cross the Rapidan River at Germanna Ford on May 4, 1864, advancing into "the Wilderness," a stretch of tangled brush and woods west of Chancellorsville.

Wilson's cavalry pushes on to the Wilderness Tavern, located at the crossroads of the Germanna Plank Road and the Orange Turnpike. Behind him the infantry commences crossing the river. First to cross is Maj. Gen. Gouverneur Kemble Warren's V Corps. By early afternoon on May 4 the last man of V Corps is across. They are followed by VI Corps. Grant and Meade establish their command posts on the high ground near the ford. It will be May 5 before Gen. Ambrose Burnside's IX Corps marches all the way from Warrenton Junction to cross the river. They'll then take up one of the pontoon bridges, leaving the other in place.

As Warren's men cross, soldiers see Elihu Washburne traveling with Grant's staff. The Illinois congressman wears severe black clothes. The soldiers speculate that this is going to be a bad campaign, because he looks like Grant's personal undertaker. One of Meade's aides, Lt. Col. Theodore Lyman, wonders if every man that crosses those bridges who is to become a casualty in the next six weeks would wear a badge, what would it look like? If so, nearly half of those men who are crossing here would have a badge. In six weeks, half of those men will become casualties.

Maj. Gen. Winfield Scott Hancock's II Corps is crossing downriver at Ely's Ford. A portion of Grant's supply trains also crossed at Ely's while other wagons crossed at Culpeper Mine Ford, between the two wings of the Federal forces. But the wagon trains cannot cross in an expeditious manner. So nightfall on May 4 finds Warren camped at Wilderness Run and Ellwood, 12 miles short of Spotsylvania Court House. Hancock, with his vanguard, has reached Chancellorsville, where the gaunt walls of the Chancellor House stand, fire-blackened from the conflagration that destroyed it just one year earlier on May 3, 1863. Hancock's here by 10 a.m. with the vanguard, but they can't move on. Grant's plan to get through the Wilderness in one long day's march has unraveled. They cannot leave the more than 5,500 wagons. They're part of the army's trains and can't get across the river that day, and responsible Federal officers are worried that Rebel cavalry may sweep down on and maul the wagon trains. If you put all those wagons on one road, the line would reach from Richmond to Washington, D.C. It's a logistician's nightmare.

Lee is already responding. Approaching along the Orange Turnpike, seven miles west of Wilderness Tavern, is Lt. Gen. Richard S. Ewell's corps. About 12 miles off, along the Orange Plank Road, is Lt. Gen. A. P. Hill's corps, with Lee present. They march east to intercept the Yankees. Think of the Union columns as twin snakes moving southeast through the Wilderness; Lee wants to strike the columns and cut them in two. Longstreet has the farthest to go. He has marched at noon from Gordonsville and is still more than 25 miles away on the night of May 4. If Ewell's people reach Wilderness Tavern and get astride the road, he will cut the Federal snake in two; if Hill reaches the intersection of the Orange Plank and Brock roads first, that snake will be cut into three parts.

As morning dawns on May 5, Grant intends to continue moving southeast, hoping to get through the Wilderness before turning west to face Lee. The general in chief decides to establish headquarters near Wilderness Tavern. Some two miles away to the west Federal skirmishers spot Ewell's advance.

Saunders Field is one and a half miles west of Wilderness Tavern astride the Orange Turnpike. It is owned by an absentee landowner, Horatio Allen from New York City. Saunders was his tenant, but he has not raised a crop here in two years. The turnpike was much narrower then than it is now. It is a macadamized or gravel road.

On May 4, Wilson's Union cavalry rides west along the turnpike to Locust Grove, several miles away. Instead of leaving a strong force here to guard the turnpike, Wilson takes his division south to Parker's Store and beyond. Approaching on the turnpike are 17,000 Rebels led by Edward "Allegheny" Johnson's division. Headed east on the Orange Plank Road to the south are about 22,000 eager Confederates of A. P. Hill's corps spearheaded by Maj. Gen. Henry Heth's division. If Grant keeps moving through the Wilderness, he will have his army cut into three parts. If Longstreet comes in on the Catharpin Road, which parallels the Orange Plank Road to the south, it could be severed into five parts.

That morning, Warren starts V Corps, spearheaded by Brig. Gen. Samuel Crawford's division, down a country road that leads from Ellwood by the Chewning Farm to Parker's Store. He is to be followed by the divisions of Brig. Gens. James S. Wadsworth and John C. Robinson. Before Robinson can move out, word is received that the Rebels are approaching via the Orange Turnpike in force. These are the men of Ewell's corps—the divisions of Maj. Gens. Edward Johnson, Jubal A. Early, and Robert E. Rodes.

Trigger-tempered Brig. Gen. Charles Griffin is ordered to take his First Division, some 5,000 strong, and march west along the turnpike to engage and block Ewell. When he reaches the east side of Saunders Field, the Confederates have gained the west edge of the field and are deploying. He asks for instructions and is told to attack; he is promised by Warren that Maj. Gen. John Sedgwick's VI Corps will provide support on the right. Sedgwick has turned the head of his column off the Germanna Plank Road and is cutting southwest, marching along the narrow Culpeper Mine Road, which runs into the Orange Turnpike, but Sedgwick is a long way off and isn't going to get into the area until late afternoon. His march will be slowed by Rebel skirmishers and cavalry.

Griffin's division attacks the Confederates to his front, and it isn't going to be enjoyable. It starts as fun for the Yankees, but it turns into a disaster. Brig. Gen. Romeyn B. Ayres's brigade deploys north of the pike. Out in front is the 140th New York along with seven battalions of regulars. In support are the 146th New York and the 91st and 155th Pennsylvania. Like the 140th New York, these three regiments wear variations of the Zouave uniform. South of the road is everybody's favorite regiment, the 20th Maine. It is in Brig. Gen. Joseph J. Bartlett's brigade, along with the 83rd Pennsylvania and 44th New York. Like many of Ayres's men, they are veterans of the struggle for Little Round Top. Two other regiments also join the group. They are supported by a third brigade, Col. Jacob B. Sweitzer's.

Griffin knows the Rebels are in the woods entrenching. He protests to Warren his attack orders. Warren reiterates his orders, which he got from Meade, to assail the enemy to your front. He again promises Griffin that he'll be supported on the right by Sedgwick and on the left by the Iron Brigade of Wadsworth's division. So Griffin advances. Col. George Ryan of the 140th New York loses his sword as he dismounts and uses his hat to gesticulate as he leads his men forward. They surge through a swale angling across Saunders Field; confronted by thickets, the regulars diverge to the right, opening up a gap in Ayres's line.

Five hundred and twenty strong, the New Yorkers ascend the slope and attack the Confederates on the west edge of Saunders Field. For 30 minutes they cling to a foothold in the woods, but they lose half their men—killed, wounded, or captured. Then the second wave comes forward—the 146th New York and 91st and 155th Pennsylvania. Like the 140th, they are repulsed because they have no support on their right. Sedgwick, as promised by Warren, has not come up.

The Confederates have thrown up breastworks back about 20 yards in the woods along the western side of the field. Johnny Rebs move up to the edge of the woods to fire at the bluecoats. When the New Yorkers top the first rise beyond the midfield swale, the Rebels really give them hell. First the 140th and then the 146th New York give way. To their right the regulars and the two Pennsylvania Zouave regiments are hammered by Brig. Gen. George "Maryland" Steuart's brigade of Virginians and Tarheels and by Brig. Gen. James A. Walker's Stonewall Brigade. By 2:30 p.m. the only Yankees left in Saunders Field are dead and wounded. The rest retreat back into the woods to the south and east, abandoning two cannon manned by redlegs of the First New York Artillery, Company D, as they flee.

News for the Federals is not much better south of the turnpike, where Bartlett's brigade attacks Brig. Gen. John Marshall Jones's Virginia Brigade.

The Confederates are positioned along high ground south of the turnpike, entrenching, when Bartlett's brigade breaks hard-drinking Jones's brigade, killing Jones, and sweeping everything before them. But

OPPOSITE: *On May 4, 1864, the Army of the Potomac crossed the Rapidan River into the Wilderness and collided with Lee's forces on May 5, leading to a day of fierce but inconclusive fighting in the tangled thickets. At dawn on May 6 the Federals renewed their attack, but by the end of the day the Confederates had checked the Federal assaults. Grant continued his advance on May 7, moving around Lee's right only to be blocked by the Rebels on May 8 at Spotsylvania Court House, beginning two weeks of brutal combat. On May 21, Grant broke off the fight and continued his advance on Richmond.*

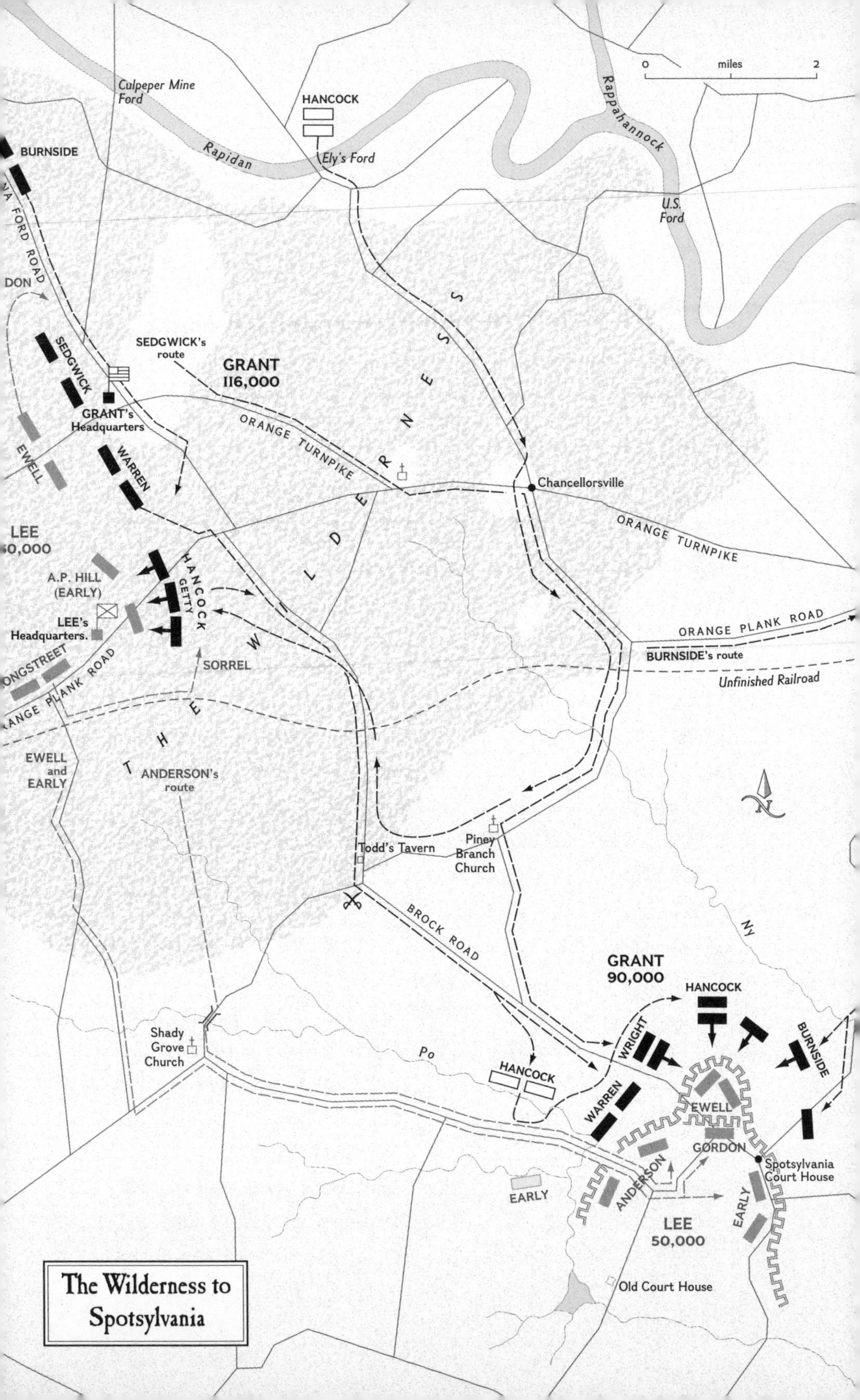

Culpeper Mine Ford
Rapidan
HANCOCK
Ely's Ford
Rappahannock
U.S. Ford
miles
0
2
BURNSIDE
DON
SEDGWICK
SEDGWICK's route
GRANT 116,000
GRANT's Headquarters
EWELL
WARREN
ORANGE TURNPIKE
THE WILDERNESS
Chancellorsville
LEE
A.P. HILL (EARLY)
HANCOCK
GETTY
LEE's Headquarters.
SORREL
ORANGE PLANK ROAD
BURNSIDE's route
Unfinished Railroad
EWELL and EARLY
ANDERSON's route
Todd's Tavern
Piney Branch Church
BROCK ROAD
Ny
GRANT 90,000
HANCOCK
WRIGHT
BURNSIDE
Shady Grove Church
Po
HANCOCK
WARREN
EWELL
GORDON
Spotsylvania Court House
ANDERSON
EARLY
EARLY
LEE 50,000
Old Court House

The Wilderness to Spotsylvania

as they advance, they find that Ayres's repulse has left their right flank vulnerable to fire from north of the turnpike. Worse, some 300 yards on the far side of a ravine to their front is Brig. Gen. Cullen A. Battle's Alabama Brigade. These are the first people of Gen. Robert E. Rodes's division to come up to reinforce Johnson's lead division. Bartlett believes they are carrying everything before them as they press onward, driving Jones's men before them like chaff. They then run into a counterattack. Ayres has been bested, two cannon abandoned, and the Alabamians are on their flank. Worse, Wadsworth's division, with the Iron Brigade in front, on its left has encountered more of Rodes's units—Brig. Gens. George Doles's and Junius Daniel's brigades. Bartlett is isolated; his brigade collapses and flees into the woods east of Saunders Field. The situation looks bleak for V Corps.

Griffin is beside himself. No support on his right. Where is Sedgwick? Griffin has received preemptive orders to attack and he has met disaster. He rides to the rear blazing with anger. As he rides up to army headquarters, he speaks harshly of decisions such as this. He denounces General Warren because he's the guy who gave him the orders. His rage bounces up the command chain. Dismounting, Griffin ignores Grant. Addressing Meade, he curses Warren and Sedgwick for their actions. Meade does not respond, and Grant's chief of staff, John Rawlins, shakes his head as Griffin turns his back and walks away.

Grant is shocked and inquires of Meade, "Who is this General Gregg? You ought to put him under arrest." Meade, known as "Old Snapping Turtle," is the only cool officer present. He sees that Grant's coat is unbuttoned. He steps up to Grant, buttons his coat, and says, "His name is Griffin not Gregg, and that's only his way of talking." That momentarily calms the passions that have been aroused at Grant and Meade's headquarters.

About a mile south of Saunders Field, at the Higgerson Farm, savage fighting has erupted. One of the Confederates' advantages is that they know the terrain, including the lay of the land, the ground cover, and ways to get around quickly. If they can find and get on the Union flanks, they can shatter the Yankees.

General Wadsworth is a non-West Pointer from Genesee, New York, and one of the wealthiest men in the North. He has three brigades. North of Wilderness Run in the woods is a popular unit both then and now, the Iron Brigade, commanded by Brig. Gen. Lysander Cutler. Moving through the Higgerson Farm, somewhat unable to keep abreast of Cutler on their right, are Col. Roy Stone's four Pennsylvania regiments. They're beating their way through the underbrush bounding a branch of Wilderness Run. On their left, moving faster, is Brig. Gen. James C. "Crazy" Rice's brigade.

The Confederates send two brigades from Rodes's division into this area. North of Wilderness Run, confronting the Iron Brigade, are Doles's Georgians; south of the creek, Daniel's North Carolinians attack Rice. From Jubal Early's division, the Confederates rush a brigade, six regiments of Georgians, led by Brig. Gen. John Brown Gordon, to engage Stone.

Permelia Higgerson is unhappy when the bluecoats come through her garden, and she threatens retribution. Retribution comes soon. Gordon's men strike the Union center, held by Stone's Pennsylvanians. The Federals break. That exposes Rice's men on Stone's left and the Iron Brigade on his right. The situation is critical. General Crawford at the Chewning Farm is ordered to send four of his Pennsylvania Reserve Regiments through the woods to try to plug the gap that has been ripped in the Union line.

Now, we get a great human-interest story. As the Yankees pull back, the Seventh Pennsylvania Reserves is isolated in a thicket. Maj. James D. Van Valkenburgh of the 61st Georgia, who had been captured by the Pennsylvania Reserves at the Battle of Fredericksburg and then exchanged, is maneuvering with just one company of men. He doesn't know who is in front of him, but he demands that unit's surrender. Realizing they are isolated, but not cognizant that they are confronted by fewer than 35 or 40 Confederates, the Seventh Pennsylvania, almost 300 strong, surrenders. The poor folks in the Seventh Pennsylvania aren't very lucky. Grant has issued an order ending the exchange of prisoners; they are fated to be sent to that "wonderful rest camp" in Georgia known as Andersonville. There 270 of them will see more than 90 of their comrades die.

The news for the remainder of Samuel Crawford's division, a mile south of the Higgerson Farm at the Chewning Farm, is not much better.

Samuel Crawford is in charge of the Pennsylvania Reserves; they are advancing toward Parker's Store, located to their south on the Orange Plank Road, where James Wilson left the Fifth New York Cavalry when his division rode south to scout the Catharpin Road. Near Parker's Store the cavalrymen soon find themselves confronting the advance of Henry Heth's division, five North Carolina regiments commanded by Brig. Gen. William Kirkland, spearheading A. P. Hill's corps.

What is Crawford going to do? He is isolated. He has several options if he is a great general. One is to attack the Confederates in the flank, or he can reinforce the Fifth New York Cavalry. He opts for the latter, but sends only one regiment: the 13th Pennsylvania Reserves, armed with repeating Spencer rifles. Spencer rifles might be useful, but they are not that good when one's outnumbered more than five to one. He could also pull back. He stays at Chewning's, and soon finds himself in a difficult situation. He gets a call to rush reinforcements to the fight at Higgerson Farm. Next Wadsworth warns Crawford that he is in danger of being cut off unless he withdraws to Ellwood, which he does.

With Crawford no longer threatening their left flank, A. P. Hill's men march east along the Orange Plank Road. If they reach the intersection of Brock Road, they'll occupy ground between the Yankee V and II Corps and split the Union Army in two. Hancock turns and races north from Todd's Tavern toward the junction to prevent that. So does Brig. Gen. George W. Getty, a division commander in Sedgwick's VI Corps.

It looks bleak for Meade's Army of the Potomac. The Fifth New York Cavalry is pushed back by Kirkland's Tarheels, and there are many more Confederates behind them: Henry Heth's division, 6,000 strong, is backed by Maj. Gen. Cadmus M. Wilcox's division. Arriving at the intersection of Orange Plank and Brock roads on a march from Wilderness Tavern are three VI Corps brigades led by Brig. Gen. George W. Getty. Getty rides up with his staff; they dismount and strive to buy time until their division comes up. Finally the brigades appear. Col. Lewis A. Grant's Vermont Brigade anchors the left flank fronting along Brock Road south of the Plank Road; the other brigades—Brig. Gen. Frank Wheaton's and Brig. Gen. Henry L. Eustis's—are posted north of the Plank Road. Getty gets his people in position just in the nick of time and keeps the Confederates from occupying this crossroads and cutting the Union Army in two. But General Grant wants more men at this key point, having resolved to fight Lee in the Wilderness.

Hancock's four-division corps has marched via the Plank and Catharpin roads from Chancellorsville en route to Shady Grove Church, about six miles west of Spotsylvania Court House. By early afternoon he has reached two miles beyond Todd's Tavern. Here he is halted and ordered to countermarch back to the Brock Road, and follow that road north to its intersection with the Plank Road.

Hancock's men are the "Bully Boys" of the Army of the Potomac. They not only think they're good—they know that they're good. It's mid-afternoon when they begin arriving at the strategic crossroads. Wilson's

Confederate breastworks in Saunders Field, located along the Orange Turnpike west of Wilderness Church, site of a major engagement during the Battle of the Wilderness.

cavalry is left near Todd's Tavern to guard the intersection of the Shady Grove Church and Catharpin Roads. First up is Maj. Gen. David Birney's division. Brig. Gen. Alexander Hays's brigade goes into position north of the road. You do not want to be in Hays's brigade. He will lose more than half his men here. Hays is a Grant favorite. The friendship goes back to West Point, Hays being one year behind Grant. Hays is big, even then. Grant is small. Grant owes him a few favors from West Point for protecting him from bullies.

Now, there are two schools of thought regarding Hays's character. His old II Corps people think he is great. The men who have been integrated into Hancock's corps from the disbanded III Corps view him as a loud-mouthed drunk and braggart. Meanwhile, Brig. Gen. Gershom Mott's Fourth Division comes up and takes position south of the Orange Plank Road to bolster the Vermont Brigade. The bluecoats now have numbers on their side: One division of VI Corps, two divisions of II Corps, and soon Brig. Gen. John Gibbon arrives with another division.

Hays leads his men in, brandishing his sword, and a bullet strikes him in the temple. Grant takes his death hard. The fighting ebbs and flows. Wilcox's four brigades enter the battle in support of Heth. Slowly the Yankees begin to gain the upper hand. Numbers tell. Moving south from Ellwood is General Wadsworth. He has re-formed his V Corps division. Here fortune smiles on the Confederates.

As Wadsworth brings his men forward he bears in on the Confederate left flank. Lee's only reserve is the Fifth Alabama Battalion, 250 strong. But, in the woods, you don't know whether they are 250 or 2,500. The Fifth Alabama Battalion strikes Wadsworth's men in the flank, inducing caution. By nightfall, the Confederates in the Orange Plank Road struggle have had it. They disengage and fall back to where they have been told Longstreet will relieve them when he arrives sometime during the night. They don't bother to entrench. Exhausted, they fall asleep.

Meanwhile, north of the Orange Turnpike, John Sedgwick finally gets VI Corps into action.

It's about 5 p.m. when troops of VI Corps advance against the Confederates posted behind the earthworks, which are anything but formidable. The Confederates have had little time to throw up breastworks. Desperate fighting ensues. Among the casualties is Brig. Gen. Leroy Stafford, commanding a brigade of Louisiana boys 1,200 strong. He is shot through the body, the ball lodging near his spine, and within a day he is dead. Also badly wounded is Brig. Gen. John Pegram, in charge of a brigade in Early's division.

The Union is unable to prevail in the turnpike sector, nightfall comes, and here the Confederates work like beavers throughout the night to strengthen their position. Four hundred yards away the Yankees do the same thing—entrench. At Gettysburg you see few field fortifications. Here you see the transition that has occurred in less than a year. Soldiers now do not move any distance without entrenching. The idea to entrench comes from the bottom up, not from the top down, because the bottom people realize that if they entrench there is a better likelihood of returning home.

Thus the fighting comes to an end on May 5. Lee has offered battle, and Grant has eagerly accepted. The Confederates have had the better of the fight to this point, but Grant is not yet done. He plans to renew the attack by sending Hancock's II Corps, reinforced by elements of V and VI Corps, to smash A. P. Hill's front and left flank. Ambrose Burnside's IX Corps, which has finally arrived in position on Hancock's right late that evening, will strike south into Hill's rear.

At five o'clock on the morning of May 6, Hancock's reinforced II Corps resumes the attack, crashing into Hill's corps along the Orange Plank Road at dawn. Hill's men have failed to throw up breastworks because they are under the impression that Longstreet's corps would arrive during the night to relieve them. Staffers say the Confederate line at that time is like a Virginia worm fence. In the tangled Wilderness there is no continuity between regiments. Some face southeast, others front northeast; they have not entrenched.

Longstreet pushed his men hard on May 5. Lee opines that Longstreet will be here long before daybreak. But Longstreet realizes his men are getting tired and hungry and has called a halt. He would rather have them fresh the next morning than arrive during the night with exhausted men. So he's not here on the morning of May 6. The Union Army is spearheaded by Meade's best combat commander on the field. Hancock has readied a sledgehammer-like blow. He masses three brigades under Getty, and two brigades each under Birney, Mott, and Gibbon for an attack guiding on the Orange Plank Road. Wadsworth with three V Corps brigades is to attack from north to south. The Yankees assail the Confederates with more than 30,000 bluecoats. After subtracting casualties, Heth's and Wilcox's divisions number less than 10,000 rank and file, giving the Yankees a three to one bulge on this front.

Grant had ordered the attack to begin at 4:30 a.m. Meade tells him he can't be ready by then, so Grant agrees to delay the attack 30 minutes. When the Federals advance, the Confederate troops yield slowly at first. Ninety minutes later they are fleeing across Widow Tapp's farm. Lee and his staff ride out. In front of them are 16 Confederate cannon of Col. William Poague's battalion. As soon as the infantry are out of the way, Poague's men open fire. Lee looks south toward the Orange Plank Road and sees Brig. Gen. Sam McGowan's South Carolina Brigade retreating. Lee calls to McGowan, "Is this splendid brigade of yours running like a flock of geese?" McGowan replies, "These men are not whipped. They only want a place to form, and they will fight as well as they ever did."

The situation is grim. Longstreet has had his men on the road since 3 a.m.; the head of his column has reached Parker's Store, where a side road links the Catharpin and Orange Plank Roads. As Longstreet's men advance, one column marches on the north side of the road. It is Maj. Gen. Charles Field's division spearheaded by the Texas Brigade commanded by Brig. Gen. John Gregg. Lee does not know Gregg, who took charge of the brigade while Longstreet was in East Tennessee. On the south side of the road, stepping along parallel with them, is a brigade of South Carolinians under Col. John W. Henagan; in support of the Texans are Henry "Rock" Benning's Georgians. As the Rebel reinforcements arrive, the Yankees are coming across the Widow Tapp's field, seemingly irresistible as Poague's cannon boom. Lee rides out, and the first man he encounters is General Gregg. Lee asks, "Who are these men?" and Gregg says, "The Texas Brigade." Lee reportedly shouts, "Hurrah for Texas." That must be bad for the morale of the

Third Arkansas boys, also members of the famed brigade. Taking off his hat, Lee waves it and orders: "Go and drive out these people."

Gregg addresses his brigade, "Men from Texas and Arkansas prepare to advance and engage the enemy. The eyes of General Lee are upon you. Forward march." As they start to move out, who has joined them? Robert Edward Lee, mounted on Traveller, with lots of Yankees to his front. Seeing Lee the soldiers raise the cry, "Lee to the rear! Lee to the rear!" Lee continues to sit his horse, until a tall Texas sergeant comes up and grabs Traveller's reins and leads Lee off to the rear. This will be the first of four "Lee to the rear" incidents that occur before May 13.

The Confederates then surge forward, and a titanic struggle ensues. They advance across the widow's field, and slowly but surely drive the Federals back into the woods. Within two hours the tide of battle has turned. Longstreet's two divisions, soon joined by Maj. Gen. Richard H. "Dick" Anderson's unit—Hill's other division, which has also arrived on the field—push the Union troops back to the area near today's Hill-Ewell Drive. What had looked like an overwhelming Union success at 8 a.m. has turned into a Union repulse followed by a stalemate.

Lee and Longstreet look for ways to break the bloody stalemate. Lee's chief engineer, Maj. Gen. Martin L. Smith, is out reconnoitering, and he discovers the unfinished railroad grade in the woods south of the Orange Plank Road. The road and railroad grade diverge as they lead eastward. He returns and briefs Lee and Lt. Col. Moxley Sorrel, Longstreet's chief of staff. He explains that there are no Yankees posted on or near the grade. Here is an opportunity to send a column east along the grade and position the men perpendicular to the enemy's battle line. It's a similar situation to the one Jackson occupied and exploited vis-à-vis the XI Corps at Chancellorsville on his famed march on May 2, 1863. Only this time the foe is not XI Corps people. These are elite units of the Union Army: II Corps and one division each from V and VI Corps.

Lee meets with Longstreet and determines to attack. Sorrel guides three brigades: Brig. Gen. William "Little Billy" Mahone's Virginians, Brig. Gen. George T. "Tige" Anderson's Georgians, and Brig. Gen. William Wofford's Georgians—some 3,500 soldiers—through the woods and onto the unfinished railroad. The three brigades march eastward until they are both astride and overlap Hancock's left flank. The bluecoats are oblivious that Confederates are out there. At 11 a.m. the Rebels strike, first assailing Mott's division. They advance along a broad front against Union troops that have no flank protection. They hit them where they are not anticipating an onslaught.

One of the first brigades the Confederates encounter, facing west with its flank toward them, is the Excelsior Brigade from New York. It is like rolling up a wet blanket as they double up the Union troops from left to right. At the same time, attacking from west to east are soldiers of Field's division, joined by two of A. P. Hill's divisions under Dick Anderson and Cadmus Wilcox. Hammered on the flank, assailed in front, eight Union brigades collapse. General Wadsworth tries to rally his troops north of the Plank Road, and he is shot through the back of the head. He falls from his horse, but never recovers consciousness. He is carried to Kershaw's field hospital. Here a local farmer, Patrick McCracken, whom Wadsworth had befriended when he was military governor of the District of Columbia, calls at the field hospital. McCracken takes custody of Wadsworth's watch and a number of his personal effects, and after he dies, sends them to the general's family in New York State.

It's a great moment for Lee and Longstreet. They have the Union troops on the ropes. Longstreet prepares to continue the attack. He rides from west to east along Plank Road with Micah Jenkins's South Carolina Brigade following in a column of fours. Jenkins, 27 years old, No. 1 in his class at the Citadel, is a handsome individual. His men are dressed in new shell jackets that have a bluish cast. Out in front rides Longstreet,

Jenkins, Joe Kershaw, and their staffs. On the north side of the road are about 150 men of the 12th Virginia. Most of Mahone's Virginians, who up to now have swept all before them, are south of the Plank Road. Through the smoke they see the mounted cavalcade, riding eastward along Plank Road.

Soldiers of the 12th Virginia fire a crashing volley into the column. Longstreet is shot. The bullet slams through his right rear shoulder blade and emerges from his throat. The force of the minié ball all but lifts him out of the saddle. Jenkins is shot through the head. Two of his staff officers are dead. Amid confusion, staffers help Longstreet drop from his horse. They put him on a stretcher and everything comes to a stop on the Confederates' part. They cover his face with his hat to conceal his identity and protect him from the sun. Rumors soon spread, Longstreet is wounded—no, he is dead. To reassure his people that he is only wounded, Longstreet raises his hat with his left hand, indicating that he lives. Cheers go up. He will not return to duty until the fourth week of October 1864.

At 4 p.m. the Confederates resume their offensive against Hancock's new and reinforced position. From the time of Longstreet's wounding there has been a hiatus along Hancock's front. Union troops have entrenched behind three lines of breastworks covering the intersection of the Brock and Plank Roads and extending north and south for more than a mile. Lee now wears two hats. He is commanding Longstreet's corps as well as the Army of Northern Virginia. He also has Anderson's division of Hill's corps at his disposal.

Ground fires have broken out. Why? Because it is very dry, and there are dead leaves blanketing the ground. When you fire a muzzle-loader, you first tear the paper cartridge, pour the powder down the bore, and then wad the paper. Next you place the lead projectile on the wad and use your ramrod to seat the projectile. When you fire the projectile, you have both the lead and the wadding coming out of the bore. The wadding is smoldering. If the wadding falls into dry leaves and you have wind, you can have a ground fire. A fierce fire fronting the Union breastworks starts about 300 yards south of the Plank Road. When it reaches a man who can't move because of a broken hip or femur, he is in serious trouble. When the fire reaches his cartridge box, it cooks off the rounds and they sound like a string of firecrackers—Bang, Bang, Bang! It makes for a horrible sight.

The Confederates advance; the flames and smoke, driven by a west wind, screen them as they press ahead. Henagan's South Carolinians and Tige Anderson's Georgia Crackers gain the Union breastworks. The bluecoats at some point need to stand back because of the heat and have to shoot through the flames at the Rebels.

The Confederates attack; the flames are leaping up and the wind is blowing. With Micah Jenkins dead, the senior colonel, John Bratton, has taken over the brigade. Covered by the fire the Rebels rush into the Yankee works, and they're up on top of the works. It looks like there may be a breakthrough. Fresh Union troops of Hancock's corps, led by "Old Bricktop," Col. Samuel Sprigg Carroll, and Col. Daniel Leasure of Burnside's corps, seal the breach. At other points the Confederates are stopped in their tracks. Lee's veterans vainly pound away for another hour; the fires continue to burn, and the Rebels pull back.

Checked along the Plank Road on the Federal left, General Lee rides over to the Orange Turnpike to see if there is a chance yet to garner victory out of this long and terrible day. Throughout the morning and afternoon of May 6 there is relatively little combat along and north of the Orange Turnpike. In the morning John Sedgwick is supposed to attack at the same time as Hancock, but Ewell anticipates the thrust and advances first. Within hours the fighting here ebbs.

About noon, Gen. John Brown Gordon, out reconnoitering, sees that the Union extreme right, held by Brig. Gen. Truman Seymour's division of Sedgwick's corps, is hanging in the air. Like Howard's XI Corps at

Haunting reminders of the fierce fighting that took place here, skeletons of soldiers killed during the Battle of the Wilderness are visible in this 1865 photograph.

Chancellorsville, it's neither anchored nor resting upon an impassible barrier. Gordon reports this to Jubal Early. Early does not believe that the Yankees can make the same mistake they did at Chancellorsville a year and four days earlier. He brings the situation to the attention of corps commander Richard Ewell.

Ewell is, as they say, dominated by petticoats, but his wife and his stepdaughters aren't here. So that means he can be bullied by Early, a self-confident and profane individual. Early is over six feet, but he has rheumatism and both walks and stands with a stoop. He chews tobacco. His beard is turning salt and pepper and it is stained yellow around his mouth from tobacco spit. Ewell and Early pass the buck back and forth until late in the day when General Lee arrives and will finally rule in favor of an attack. When the attack is made, Gordon will commit two brigades: his own Georgians and Brig. Gen. Robert Johnston's North Carolinians. They file out to their left to get farther north of the Union lines and well beyond Seymour's right flank. They deploy, facing south; Johnston is on the left and Col. Clement A. Evans with Gordon's Georgians is on the right, and they sweep toward the Union flank.

Seymour's people hear them coming. A quarter of a mile away, they hear high-pitched Rebel Yells. Soon they see their comrades running toward them, pursued by Confederates. Had the Yankees refused their line, they probably could have checked the attack. Instead the butternuts scoop up hundreds of prisoners and two brigadier generals—Truman Seymour and Alexander Shaler.

The Confederate attack first slows and then stalls. The Yanks stabilize their line; it's growing dark. Supporting Confederates on Gordon's right make no headway. Gordon lacks men to exploit his gains. Meanwhile, the Union calls up reserves and forms a new front at a right angle to oppose Gordon.

There is panic at Union headquarters. It's rumored that Sedgwick has been killed or captured. Confederate success is exaggerated. There are wild rumors: the Confederates have reached the Germanna Plank Road, cutting communications with Germanna Ford. When Grant hears this he caustically remarks, "I am heartily tired of hearing about what General Lee is going to do. Some of you always seem to think he is going to turn a double somersault and land in our rear and both of our flanks at the same time. Let's start talking about what we can do ourselves and not what General Lee can do." Grant asserts himself again to show he is going to get more involved in providing overall guidance for the Army of the Potomac. In Grant's staff officers' minds, Meade is beginning to lose operational control of his army.

On the morning of May 7, VI Corps reestablishes its line on the right by pulling back and entrenching. The Confederates occupy the abandoned Union fortifications and reface them fronting southeast and paralleling

Sedgwick's. It's been a bloody battle. Union casualties for the two-day battle number more than 17,600, and for the Confederates about 11,000. Grant now shows his will. If he had been a General Hooker or General Burnside or General Meade he would have gone back across the Rapidan on the night of the sixth. Instead he will head to Spotsylvania Court House to continue the fight. When the Union troops, after all those losses, find out they're not going back across the Rapidan, there is tremendous cheering that evening. All the Confederates, except General Lee, think that they've won the battle and that the Yankees are going back across the river. Lee is the only one in authority in the Confederate Army who is convinced Grant will resume the march through the Wilderness. Napoleon Bonaparte said that a successful general has to look into the enemy's eyes and know what he is thinking. Lee has looked into Grant's eyes and knows what he is going to do.

10

SPOTSYLVANIA

MAY 8–21, 1864

The Battle of the Wilderness, fought May 5 and 6, 1864, resulted in a bloody tactical draw. If Grant did not deal Lee a decisive blow, neither did Lee force Grant to retire back across the Rapidan River. By choosing to advance, Grant showed that he would not allow his strategic plan to be upset by tactical setbacks. Grant intended to keep contact with his enemy, Robert E. Lee, and to allow the Confederates no opportunity to break contact and gain the advantage of maneuver. Grant employed his superiority in manpower to grind down the Army of Northern Virginia. The Union advance also signaled the continuation of what became a nearly continuous moving battle, in which the opposing armies either were fighting or preparing to fight nearly every day for the next six weeks.

The objective of the Union march was Spotsylvania Court House, about ten miles southwest of Fredericksburg. It was a county seat and a hub of roads going out to all points of the compass. It was also on open ground, where the Union could use its superior numbers and artillery. By moving to Spotsylvania Court House, Generals Grant and Meade could establish the Army of the Potomac's forward supply depot at Fredericksburg. If it's at Fredericksburg, supplies can reach the army by boats ascending the Rappahannock River to Falmouth, just above Fredericksburg. Federal engineers restored service over the Richmond, Fredericksburg & Potomac Railroad southward from Aquia Landing—on the Potomac downstream from the present Quantico Marine Corps Base—to Fredericksburg. They also opened a major supply depot downriver at Belle Plain near the mouth of Potomac Creek.

Army wagons and transports at the lower landing at Belle Plain, Virginia, a major supply depot for Federal forces near the mouth of Potomac Creek on the Potomac River.

Grant hopes to beat Lee to Spotsylvania. On May 7 Chief of Staff Andrew A. Humphreys distributes orders for a movement that night. As soon as it gets dark, Maj. Gen. Gouverneur K. Warren, whose V Corps is concentrated in and around Wilderness Tavern, is to march his men southeast along Brock Road. Brock Road will carry them through and beyond the intersection with Orange Plank Road, where II Corps is positioned behind lines of earthworks—as ground fires still rage. Warren will continue through the intersection to Todd's Tavern, then on to Spotsylvania Court House. At some point south of Todd's Tavern, Warren is expected to encounter two divisions of Federal cavalry charged with clearing any Confederate cavalry out of the way.

Maj. Gen. John Sedgwick, commanding VI Corps, is to leave the area northwest of Wilderness Tavern, taking the Orange Turnpike. He is to follow the turnpike as far as Chancellorsville and turn south, employing the local road network to gain the Piney Branch Church Road and trail Warren to Spotsylvania Court House. Taking the same route will be Maj. Gen. Ambrose E. Burnside with his IX Corps, who, when he passes beyond Alrich's place, will follow a series of roads and eventually turn onto the Fredericksburg–Spotsylvania Court House Road. To relieve Burnside's feelings of outranking Meade but having to serve under him, Burnside will continue to report directly to Grant's headquarters.

As soon as the roads are clear, Maj. Gen. Winfield Scott Hancock is to take his II Corps and follow the route pioneered by Warren. Brig. Gen. James Harrison Wilson's cavalry division will swing east to Fredericksburg, take the road from Fredericksburg to Spotsylvania, and be at the courthouse when Warren arrives. The army's trains are to roll along the Orange Turnpike and into Fredericksburg.

Meanwhile, at Confederate headquarters, Lee decides that Grant will break contact with the Army of Northern Virginia and probably head for Spotsylvania Court House. He calls in Chief of Artillery Brig. Gen. William Nelson Pendleton and tells him to take the pioneers and open a road from the Orange Plank Road to Catharpin Road west of Todd's Tavern. This will give the Confederates an alternate route—the Shady Grove Church Road—by which they can hopefully reach the courthouse first.

So what is the situation at midday on May 7? The burial parties are hard at work interring the Wilderness dead. They're recovering the wounded and sending them to hospitals—if you're a Yank, to the Fredericksburg area; if you're a Confederate, to Orange Court House or Gordonsville. The wounded General Longstreet ends up at the former, getting faster service than other people being sent to hospitals.

The Confederates have a number of new people in key leadership positions. With Longstreet wounded, Lee names Maj. Gen. Richard H. Anderson of South Carolina to lead "Old Pete's" corps. He had been Longstreet's West Point classmate, a steady division commander, but with a rumored drinking problem. Lee discovers that another corps commander, A. P. Hill, is too sick to exercise command. He settles upon Maj. Gen. Jubal Anderson Early, a confirmed bachelor, as Hill's replacement. Don't get ideas that he's not a ladies' man—he has two families and doesn't marry either woman.

Early turns over his II Corps division to Brig. Gen. John Brown Gordon; Brig. Gen. William "Little Billy" Mahone takes over Anderson's III Corps division. Mahone has the most elaborate headquarters of any senior officer in the Army of Northern Virginia. They call him "Old Porte" because he reminded everybody of an Ottoman Empire sultan when he went into the field.

At Spotsylvania, the important features are two rivers. The Ni flows from northwest to southeast. It cuts across the Fredericksburg Road about two miles northwest of the courthouse. The Po flows easterly until it approaches the area two and a half miles west of the courthouse, where it makes a sharp bend and flows southward and into a horseshoe bend about two miles before resuming its eastward course. The Po and Ni join near Guinea Station to form the Poni River.

Between May 8 and May 20 Spotsylvania sees a series of battles. On May 8 combat centers on Laurel Hill, northwest of the courthouse. The fighting on Laurel Hill continues through May 9 and 10. On May 10 there's a fight at the Po River, west of Block House Bridge. Then there are two all-out assaults on the Confederate salient south of the Ni on May 10 and 12, followed on May 14 by fights at Myers Hill east of the courthouse, and three days later on Lee's "Final Line" at the Harrison House, closing out on the 19th at the Harris Farm. Grant started the campaign with about 116,000 men; he's now down to 100,000. Lee had about 65,000, but some of his losses have been offset by reinforcements. He now has around 55,000.

The bloodshed is forcing commanders to consider new tactics. Earlier Civil War generals had embraced Napoleonic tactics, with shoulder-to-shoulder advances and mass assaults with artillery pushed forward to within 800 yards of the foe. These were good tactics when the standard weapon of the infantryman was a smoothbore musket with an effective range of 60 to 70 yards. This meant you closed on the enemy, providing he didn't have any artillery, fired a few rounds, and then a bayonet charge would decide the issue. When the Civil War got under way, a technological revolution had outdated these linear tactics.

In 1849, Capt. Claude E. Minié of the French Army developed a new type of bullet for use with the rifled muzzle-loaders then being introduced into warfare. This bullet was a conical-shaped projectile with a concavity in its base that expanded into the helical grooves of a gun barrel's rifling when fired. This gave what was soon known as the minié ball a spin that reduced the projectile's air resistance, flattened its trajectory, and provided an effective range of 200 to 250 yards—and a killing range of up to 500-plus yards.

The old tactics of moving men forward shoulder to shoulder in linear formation were now flawed. The learning curve began at the bottom with the rank and file, not the generals. It was the common soldier who became as efficient as engineers at selecting favorable ground and proficient in throwing up earthworks, which made it all but suicidal for the enemy to advance in line of battle. By this point in the war, if you gave soldiers eight hours they would have an all but impregnable position. You're going to need three- or four-to-one odds to carry that position, and in the process, you will probably suffer prohibitive casualties.

It is dusk on May 7 when Warren's men move out from the Wilderness battlefield. Expecting to turn left and retreat back down the Germanna Plank Road, they instead turn right and advance. Near the Plank and Brock Road intersection they see Grant riding along. They cheer. The Confederate rank and file first wonder and then begin to realize what this means. The Union Army is not turning back across the river following the Battle of the

Wilderness. Soon joining the columns are Grant and Meade and their staffs. They travel together but don't intermix. Meade and his people are in one group, Grant and his staff in another. Events on May 7 and 8 will cause Grant to reconsider his hands-off relationship with Meade as to tactics and personnel.

Grant from his youth has had a stubborn streak. Once he turned into a road going someplace, he never liked to admit he was wrong and turn back. As the cavalcade rides south down Brock Road, Grant inadvertently turns right at a fork into what is today known as the "Jackson Trail West." If they keep going along that road, Grant, Meade, and their staffs might blunder into the Confederates. Unknown to Grant and Meade, General Lee has divined Grant's plan and has started Anderson's corps on a forced march to Spotsylvania Court House. Anderson leaves the Wilderness battlefield via the road opened by General Pendleton and the pioneers. Fortunately for the Union, Grant's staffers hear the noise of people up ahead. They have a hard time convincing Grant he'd better turn back, but they succeed. Otherwise, Grant and Meade may have blundered into Anderson's column and been killed or captured.

Meanwhile, Anderson moves his corps along the road cut by Lee's pioneers and races forward toward Spotsylvania. Along Brock Road to the north, Warren's Federal V Corps finds its way blocked beyond Todd's Tavern. For most of the day on May 7, two divisions of Federal cavalry seek to drive back Maj. Gen. Fitz Lee's Confederate cavalry, which block the Federal advance on Spotsylvania Court House.

Warren gets to Todd's Tavern about 11 p.m. on May 7, only to find the Federal cavalry there in bivouac and the road to Spotsylvania blocked by Confederate cavalry. Meade discovers that the Federal cavalry is also without orders from Sheridan and decides to order David M. Gregg's division west on Catharpin Road to screen the Federal movement and Wesley Merritt's division to clear the courthouse road. Merritt's horse soldiers encounter a series of roadblocks manned by Rebel cavalry led

Cavalry commander Maj. Gen. Philip Sheridan and his staff. During the Spotsylvania campaign Sheridan led cavalry operations against Confederate forces defending Richmond.

by Fitz Lee. Merritt is compelled to dismount and deploy to break the roadblocks. Valuable time is lost as the Rebels slow and stall Merritt. Warren's column moves at a snail's pace.

Anderson, marching along the Shady Grove Church Road, crosses the Po and reaches the Block House, two miles west of the courthouse, about 8 a.m. on May 8. Wilson's horse soldiers come down the road from Fredericksburg, charge into Spotsylvania Court House, and run Tom Rosser's Confederate cavalry out of the village. But Wofford's Georgians, rushed there by Anderson, drive out Wilson's horsemen and reclaim control of the courthouse road hub.

An hour later Anderson gets word that Yankee infantry are approaching south on the Brock Road; in response, he heads toward Laurel Hill, a mile north. He beats Warren to Laurel Hill; now his challenge is whether he can hold this ground in the face of a slashing enemy onslaught.

The struggle for Laurel Hill begins in earnest on the morning of May 8.

When Warren's lead division, commanded by Brig. Gen. John C. Robinson, arrives via Brock Road just beyond the Alsop Farm, the Yankees look up and across the Sarah Spindle Farm to their south and see that Confederates have won the race to Laurel Hill and are tearing down and piling up fence rails, anything they can get their hands on, to throw up breastworks. The Yankees are too late. It will be a long day from 8:30 a.m. until 6 p.m. as V Corps, 20,000 strong, battles Anderson's 12,000 Rebels. But the men in butternut hold the blue back.

Robinson has three brigades, but none of them makes any headway. Among the casualties is Robinson, shot out of his saddle at a range of 50 yards. Warren's First Division commander, Brig. Gen. Charles Griffin, commits his division piecemeal, brigade by brigade. The Yankees have a big bulge in numbers, but the Confederates work like Trojans, constantly strengthening their earthworks while beating off repeated attacks. Brig. Gen. Romeyn B. Ayres's Union brigade, which opened the fighting at the Wilderness, appears with several regiments—what's left of his Zouave brigade. In a failed effort to break the stalemate, Warren throws in the divisions of Brig. Gens. Lysander Cutler and Samuel W. Crawford. The entire V Corps sees combat during the day at Laurel Hill, but Anderson doesn't drive worth a damn.

Today nothing has gone right for the Union Army. When Warren fails to storm Laurel Hill and is stopped less than two miles from Spotsylvania on the evening of May 8, the Union leadership is in turmoil. Meade and cavalry commander Maj. Gen. Philip Sheridan have a heated discussion. Both are hot-tempered individuals. "Old Snapping Turtle" Meade is cantankerous and bespectacled. Sheridan at this time is about 110 pounds and five feet four. He had been suspended from West Point for one academic year for fighting.

There were only two changes to the leadership of the Army of the Potomac that Grant made as general in chief. He brought Sheridan in from the West to take over the Cavalry Corps; Brig. Gen. James H. Wilson was given a mounted division. So far in the campaign the latter has been a disappointment. Sheridan had complained to Meade: Your infantry leaders are not using the mounted arm right. We ought to employ our cavalry as a striking force to carry the fight to the enemy and not be the infantry's handmaiden. Why don't I use our horse soldiers to go after the enemy's cavalry? Today Meade tells Sheridan that his cavalry has failed and the Federals would have been at Spotsylvania Court House if the cavalry had carried out their mission. Sheridan heatedly counters, "You should have used the cavalry to engage the enemy's horsemen and not see their strength dissipated doing the infantry's work scouting and as couriers. If you would let me use my cavalry like I want to, I'll go out and beat Jeb Stuart."

Meade is shocked that a subordinate talked to him in such a manner, and they take up their dispute in Grant's presence. This is where Meade begins to lose his effectiveness in the army's day-to-day operations. Meade, as senior, expects Grant to side with him. But Grant comes down on Sheridan's side, and after learning of his boast about taking care of Jeb Stuart and his cavaliers in gray says, "Did Sheridan say that? Well he generally knows what he is talking about. Let him start right out and do it." Meade shrugs his shoulders. Orders are drafted giving Sheridan authority to take all of the cavalry except one brigade and see if he can draw Stuart into a fight well away from the army. On the morning of May 9, 10,000 horse soldiers ride east via the Orange Turnpike; near Fredericksburg, they turn south on the Telegraph Road heading toward Richmond. Stuart pursues with half his cavalry.

Lt. Gen. Richard S. Ewell's Confederate II Corps arrives at dusk on May 8. They go into position on Anderson's right. The soldiers, moving out without any guidance from their engineers, occupy the high ground separating the Ni and Po watersheds. As they dig they create a salient soon to be known as the "Mule Shoe," because of its shape. Lee debates getting rid of the salient. He knows a salient takes more men to defend, and it can become the target of converging fire. He concludes, however, that it will damage morale to give up this ground.

It's a new kind of war. Heretofore the armies paused and went into camp between battles. Antietam and Fredericksburg were three months apart. Fredericksburg and Chancellorsville were five months apart, Chancellorsville and Gettysburg, two months. Now, they're in contact every day. Grant's objective is to wear Lee down. He will use superior numbers and economic power to outmaneuver and overwhelm Lee's Army of Northern Virginia. He can succeed provided he and his way of war retain the confidence of President Lincoln and the electorate.

By May 9 both armies have concentrated at Spotsylvania Court House, and Grant looks to find a weakness in Lee's lines. John Sedgwick's VI Corps deploys to the left of V Corps, within sight of Laurel Hill but facing southeast.

"Uncle John" Sedgwick had been commandant of cadets at West Point. He is popular with his troops. But he is not a favorite of the secretary of war and the administration. He is the last McClellan loyalist and avowed Democrat in the Army of the Potomac's senior command. Today, May 9, he's inspecting a position some 500 yards in front of Laurel Hill, where a Massachusetts battery has placed its guns. The Yankees are throwing up earthworks; skirmishers are out. Confederate sharpshooters watch the Union forces dig in. Soldiers are moving about, and there is a crack! One of the Union soldiers throws himself to the ground. Sedgwick remarks, "Why my man, I am ashamed of you, dodging that way," and taps him with the toe of a boot. A staffer recalls that his general, to reassure his people, says in jest, "They couldn't hit an elephant at that distance." The soldier scrambles to his feet and takes off. There is another crack followed by a splat. Blood appears under Sedgwick's left eye. He is dead by the time he hits the ground. His body will be sent to Cromwell, Connecticut, his home, to be interred.

He has a handsome statue at the United States Military Academy's Trophy Point, looking out over the Hudson. If you are a senior cadet having trouble in mathematics, you rub the right spur before you go for your final examination.

Maj. Gen. Horatio G. Wright, an engineer, and Sedgwick's choice to succeed him, becomes the VI Corps commander.

Thwarted in his efforts to drive the Confederates off Laurel Hill on May 8, Grant looks for new ways to crack Lee's line and plans an all-out attack for May 10. Late on the afternoon of the previous day, Maj. Gen. Winfield Scott Hancock with three of his four divisions crosses the Po River with orders to maneuver against Lee's left flank, hoping to find a weak spot.

They plan to push southward, strike the Shady Grove Church Road, seize the Block House Bridge, recross the Po, and turn Lee's left. The Confederates successfully counter Hancock. Early's corps, on May 9, had marched out of the Wilderness. On reaching Spotsylvania, Early posted his troops on Ewell's right, fronting east and guarding the sector between the courthouse and the Mule Shoe. During the night Lee is apprised of Hancock's movement against his left and rushes two of Early's divisions under Mahone and Maj. Gen. Henry Heth to counter this move. Hancock, on the morning of May 10, finds Early waiting and entrenched.

Grant now orders Hancock to join Warren in front of Laurel Hill. The Confederates have different ideas. They don't want to let Hancock re-cross to the Po's north side. They want to punish him. Early's people cross the Po downstream from Block House Bridge and hope to pocket Hancock between the Shady Grove Church Road and the Po. Hancock withdraws two of his divisions under Maj. Gen. David B. Birney and Brig. Gen. John Gibbon and leaves a third division, that of Brig. Gen. Francis Barlow, as rear guard.

Barlow has a difficult task to get his men across the Po with a strong Confederate force to his front. The Rebels come on hard and strong, hoping to drive Hancock's men into the river. Up to this day men of II Corps have boasted that they haven't lost a cannon since June 1862. But today that becomes "trash talk" as Barlow's people are fortunate to even escape across the Po, but they are compelled to leave a cannon behind.

Meanwhile, several senior officers of VI Corps preparing for their role in the May 10 all-out attack ponder whether there might be an alternative to yet another deadly frontal assault in the traditional style.

Brig. Gen. David A. Russell, who now commands Horatio G. Wright's old division, reflects on past experiences. He recalls that at Fredericksburg, division commander Andrew Humphreys did better than anyone else in the assault on Marye's Heights in December 1862. When Humphreys sent his last brigade forward, the troops were ordered not to cap their muskets. They were to try and go over the Confederates' stone wall in a rush without stopping to fire. They didn't get over, but they got nearer than any other unit. So, the senior officers think, maybe we shouldn't halt and fire as we advance against the Confederate earthworks at Spotsylvania.

Capt. Ranald S. Mackenzie, No. 1 in the West Point class of 1862, was assigned by General Wright the task of reconnoitering just where to assault the Confederate line, which might be critical to the attack's success. Col. Emory Upton, West Point class of 1861, commanding a brigade in Wright's old division, is not even consulted until the decision has been made to make the attack. Generals Russell and Wright inform Upton that he will lead the assault, that 12 regiments, the best in the corps, have been made available. The ideal site selected for the attack is on the west face of the Mule Shoe, the salient held by Brig. Gen. George Doles's Georgia Brigade.

The only Confederate cannon nearby are two 3-inch rifled guns and two 12-pounder Napoleons posted on Doles's left. Yankee skirmishers have driven in the Confederate pickets. When he returns from reconnoitering, Mackenzie explains, "If we're careful and shield ourselves in the woods, we can place our men within 200 yards of the enemy. If we don't make any noise and nobody sees us, our attack will come as a surprise.: Col. Martin T. McMahon a staffer, tells Upton that General Russell had selected him to lead the attack, and if he fails, not to come back. If you're successful, McMahon says, you will be a brigadier general.

Upton's regiments will advance by regimental column. Instead of forming ten companies in line, a regimental column forms two companies in line. Behind them another two companies until you have accounted for ten companies. They line up three regiments abreast. Upton posts his brigade in front. The 12 regiments number 5,000 men. The men are told to load their weapons, but only the front line are to cap their muskets. They shuck everything except their canteens, cartridge boxes, and cap pouches.

Upton will not move out alone. Brig. Gen. Gershom Mott's division from Hancock's corps, posted three-quarters of a mile to Upton's left, will attack in support, then link up with Upton to exploit the expected success. Hancock and Warren can either pin down potential Confederate reinforcements being rushed to Doles's salient by attacking Laurel Hill or shuttle regiments to reinforce the point of Upton's attack.

Upton will advance on a narrow front. His men are to keep a low profile and remain silent to facilitate surprise. The artillery is to open fire at 5 p.m., followed by the assault ten minutes later. Upton's columns are to charge at the double-quick; the officers will not say anything until they break out of the woods. Then the officers will chant the order again and again, "Forward! Forward!" That's how it is supposed to work.

Then things start to go wrong. Hancock has trouble extracting Gibbon, Birney, and Barlow from south of the Po River. Warren gets nervous and perhaps, in his heart, wants his corps to score the success that had eluded him on May 8. He dons his dress uniform and at 4 p.m. attacks Laurel Hill, but is repulsed. Hancock now arrives and throws his men in at 5 p.m. and doesn't do any better. Because of their Laurel Hill fiasco, Hancock and Warren cannot support Upton.

Because of what has happened at Laurel Hill, Upton's attack is postponed one hour. No one tells Mott about the revised time schedule. Mott is separated by V and VI Corps from Hancock and the remainder of the II Corps. Communications with Hancock are arduous, and other senior generals also send requests seeking support from the orphaned division. Mott attacks at 5:10 p.m., unsupported, with about 3,500 men. He seeks to cross more than half a mile of open ground against a Confederate position, the point (the north face) of the Mule Shoe, defended by more than 20 cannon. He advances about 400 yards before he is stopped by artillery fire.

The Confederates are oblivious to what is about to happen in front of Doles's western side of the salient. In Maj. Gen. "Allegheny" Johnson's division they're on a high after seeing Mott easily repulsed. They hear the sounds of heavy fighting coming in from the direction of Laurel Hill. They are getting good vibes from what is happening at Laurel Hill. They also know that Burnside's thrust against their right down the Fredericksburg Road and across the Ni has bogged down.

What was to have been a ten-minute artillery bombardment has been extended for another hour in conjunction with the delay of the main assault. About 6:10 p.m. Upton leads his men forward. He is riding on the right of the 121st New York, his old regiment—the only mounted man in the assault column. They move up as "quiet as a mouse" to the edge of the woods. Then it's forward at double-time for 120 yards.

The only hindrance Upton's men face involves breaking through an abatis about 40 yards in front of the Confederate works. An abatis is the Civil War equivalent of barbed wire. Usually it is felled trees fronting the earthworks with the sharpened branches fronting the enemy. At most Doles's Rebels get

On May 10, Col. Emory Upton, shown here as a major general, led an assaulting column of 12 regiments in an attempt to storm the Confederate salient at the Mule Shoe.

off two volleys. They gun down a number of Federals. But, with successive waves coming in hard on the heels of the front ranks, the Yanks break through.

The first wave overruns the earthworks of the 44th Georgia and opens a breach, then turns both left and right to widen the gap. The right of Upton's force wheels right and heads for the Confederate cannon manned by Third Company, Richmond Howitzers, commanded by Capt. Ben H. Smith. Smith's men get off one or two rounds, but Upton's bluecoats capture their four guns. The Confederates, however, make off with their loading implements and friction primers. The Yanks don't have the means of servicing the guns. Doles pretends he is dead; thus he escapes a trip to a Union prison camp. But his brigade suffers more than a thousand casualties.

Another wave of Federals, led by the Fifth Maine, crashes through the Rebels' reserve line. They have punched a gap in the Confederate line, which Upton "guesstimates" at a quarter of a mile in width. He looks for Mott. Where is Mott? He's already been repulsed. No one told Upton that Mott had not been apprised of the one-hour delay and that he had already attacked and been thrown back.

The Confederates respond rapidly because no one rushes to Upton's support. The Stonewall Brigade under Brig. Gen. James A. "Stonewall Jim" Walker folds back its left wing and takes position perpendicular to Upton's line of advance. With Burnside checkmated, Brig. Gen. George "Maryland" Steuart's brigade, posted on the other side of the salient, faces about to repel Upton's surge. General Lee rushes artillery and infantry to seal the breach. There is another "Lee to the rear" incident, this time involving Brig. Gen. Robert Johnston's North Carolina brigade. Brig. Gen. Cullen A. Battle's Alabamians and Brig. Gen. Junius Daniel's Tarheels recover the four captured cannon.

Upton, Russell, and Wright want help. They send a message to General Warren. Warren says we have lots of trouble ourselves over at Laurel Hill. They're sent a preemptory order from Meade to reinforce, but by this time the Confederates are counterattacking.

Upton pulls out, but when he gets back to headquarters, Grant is impressed by what he had accomplished. Since he carried the works, albeit temporarily, and comes back despite admonition, Grant, likes his "new style of fighting,"and gives him a spot promotion that night to brigadier general.

What had started as a spectacular success turns into defeat because of a failure to follow through. But Grant doesn't see it that way. He sees it as a lesson on how to end the stalemate and break the enemy line. Maybe when he does it again the supporting players will perform their roles correctly. Instead of 5,000 men, the next time he will employ 20,000 men in a bold attempt to shatter Lee's line. Where a division went, Grant will say, a corps can go. The next day Grant sends his patron Illinois Congressman Elihu Washburne back to Washington, bearing his ringing words, "I propose to fight it out on this line, if it takes all summer."

On May 11, Grant shifts forces in preparation for a grand assault on the morning of May 12. His primary target will be the Mule Shoe salient at the center of the Confederate line. If he can replicate Upton's attack on a larger scale, commence an assault in the early morning hours so that he will have plenty of time to exploit opportunities, and commit all his men either to the main attack itself or in support of it, he believes Lee's line must break somewhere.

Along the Confederate line at the Mule Shoe are 22 cannon. With these guns Allegheny Johnson easily repulsed Mott's advance on May 10. But he is not going to have these 22 cannon on the night of the 11th and 12th. Why not?

Lee, who usually can read his enemy's intention, having a talent for looking into their eyes and knowing their thoughts, has read the Federals wrong. Reports of movement behind the Union lines lead him to believe that the Union Army is preparing to move around to his right. If that happens Lee wants to be ready to sweep out fast to intercept and engage the enemy. He orders Brig. Gen. Armistead L. Long, chief of artillery of II Corps, to withdraw the guns. Twenty of the 22 pieces are limbered up and sent to the rear.

The scheme worked up by Grant and Meade calls for Burnside to attack at the eastern neck of the Mule Shoe with IX Corps. This time two of Grant's staff officers will make sure that he does what is expected of him. Warren will have his V Corps people ready to either attack the enemy to his front on Laurel Hill or reinforce Hancock. Wright is to pull two of his three divisions out of the works and have them prepared to support Hancock.

Hancock with his four divisions will spearhead the onslaught. On the evening of May 11 it starts to rain and the temperature falls. It's a cold, miserable rain. Capt. George Mendell, the staff officer who is to identify the jumping-off points for Hancock's divisions, becomes disoriented. An impatient Francis Barlow finally snaps, "For heaven's sake, at least face us in the right directions, so that we shall not march away from the enemy and have to go around the world and come up in their rear."

Barlow's division is to advance in regimental column by company front. The other three divisions are to attack in different formations. On Barlow's right is David Birney's division, which will attack in line of battle. He is to be supported by Mott's and Gibbon's divisions. The Union troops are on the ground by 2 a.m. on May 12. They wait to step off at 4 a.m. But, because of the darkness and fog, Hancock postpones the attack 30 minutes.

Meanwhile, Allegheny Johnson is getting nervous. Despite the storm, his pickets hear suspicious noises out in front, and Johnson sends a message to corps commander Ewell to ask Lee to return the 20 guns to the Mule Shoe. Lee orders the artillery to come up, but this time it's the Confederates who are unlucky. At 4:35 a.m. the Yankees move out. The Rebels can't see Barlow's people through the mist and fog until they close to within 50 yards.

Barlow's columns become so intermingled that they appear to be a mob. The Confederate skirmish line is under orders to delay the enemy, but their ill-fortune continues. Many Rebel soldiers have loaded and capped their rifled muskets. Water has seeped into the bores and the cartridge boxes. Many of them find that when they squeeze the trigger, the cap pops but there is no mule-like kick into the shoulder nor a sharp crack as their piece misfires. The pickets fall back before the enemy. Barlow, as he closes on the Rebel works, comes in at an oblique angle and crosses them at the "Apex."

About the time the Federals arrive, the Confederate artillery comes up. Using whip and spur, the Rebel redlegs arrive, but they are too late. Only two cannon are unlimbered at the Apex. These get off a round or two before the Yankees are over the works. Allegheny Johnson is hitting slackers across the backsides with the cudgel that also serves him as a cane. He also strikes out at the Yankees. But it is too little and too late. Twenty-two cannon—20 still limbered—are captured. The Federals also capture about 3,100 Confederates. They all but destroy Johnson's division, capturing Johnson and one of his brigade commanders, Maryland Steuart. But the Yankees do not press on. They are almost as disorganized by their success as the enemy is by their disaster. There are too many men hunting flags—if you get a flag it's an almost automatic Medal of Honor. Too many men are looking for souvenirs. There is lack of leadership in reorganizing Barlow's division and his supporting II Corps units to press on and exploit their success. They give the Confederates a respite.

When the Confederate prisoners are escorted back to the Brown House, the Yankee headquarters, Johnson is greeted by Hancock. Old Allegheny is a jovial and convivial sort, and Hancock and his staff will soon be passing a bottle to him, extending a cigar, and Johnson will ride into captivity at Belle Plain. When Maryland Steuart shows up, Hancock extends his hand, and Steuart says, "Under the circumstances I decline to take your hand." Hancock responds, "Under any other circumstances I should not have offered it." No whiskey, no cigar for Steuart. He has to walk to Belle Plain.

Although Barlow has scored a breakthrough, Hancock fails to capitalize on the success. Piling in on top of Barlow's people are Gibbon's and Mott's. When Birney comes forward with his two brigades, they move into and occupy the Rebel works between the Apex and the west angle of the Mule Shoe, a place soon to be known as the Bloody Angle. No one takes charge or urges the Yanks to press ahead deeper into the Mule Shoe. This gives the Confederates much needed time to recover from their disaster. Lee takes corrective action. He turns out his pioneers to continue work on a reserve line south of the Harrison House at the base of the Mule Shoe. He has been overseeing this project since May 10 to meet just such an emergency. Staffers ride out to bring up troops from other points. Meanwhile, the Confederate reserve division is responding. It is commanded by John B. Gordon and consists of three brigades, Robert Johnston's four North Carolina regiments, Col. John Hoffman's five Virginia regiments, and Gordon's old brigade, six Georgia regiments under Col. Clement A. Evans.

This is a critical moment for Lee. Barlow's men, supported by Birney, Gibbon, and Mott, have destroyed Edward Johnson's division. The beginning of what will prove to be a long day of crises is at hand. Lee rides up and tells Gordon that we must drive those people back. Lee almost always refers to the enemy as "those people." Gordon replies that his men have never failed him. Lee pulls away and starts riding toward the enemy. Sgt. William A. Compton of Hoffman's brigade dashes up, grabs Traveller's reins, turns him aside, and leads Lee to the rear. Again, for the third occasion since May 6, the cry of "Lee to the rear" is raised by the Confederate rank and file.

Johnston, Hoffman, and Evans advance toward the Apex; the Union threat there is nullified. The battle shifts toward the Bloody Angle.

Southeast of the Mule Shoe, despite the presence of two Grant staffers, Burnside's contributions to Union success are scant. He is unable to get started before Brig. Gen. Jim Lane's North Carolina and Brig. Gen. Edward R. Thomas's Georgia brigades arrive at the choke point of the salient east of the Harrison House. In the afternoon, the defenders again stop Burnside in his tracks.

Barlow's men overwhelm Johnson's brigades to the right and left of the Apex about 5 a.m. The fighting is going to continue until after midnight, some 20 hours. From 8 a.m. until after 10 p.m. combat of a most savage character rages for possession of the Bloody Angle. The Confederates must hold tight while their pioneers continue work on the line of earthworks south of the Harrison House to their rear.

Wright's VI Corps surges toward the Bloody Angle at 6 a.m. But, by the time Wright commits himself, Lee has responded and sent in first Brig. Gen. Stephen Dodson Ramseur and then Daniel's Tarheel brigades of Robert Rodes's division. Bad luck for Daniel because he is killed. Lee will pull men out of Billy Mahone's division, Alabamians under Brig. Gen. Abner Perrin, then Mississippians under Brig. Gen. Nathaniel Harris. Perrin soon numbers among the slain and Harris's people again raise the call "Lee to the rear!" Lee feeds brigade after brigade into the western sector of the Mule Shoe.

The Federal VI Corps does likewise. The bluecoats are outside of the works, and the Rebels are inside. It has been raining for eight hours. The Yanks wheel up two cannon. There is no recoil mechanism built into the carriage of a Civil War cannon, so when the guns are fired, the wheels soon sink up to their hubs in the mud. You're going to have these two cannon mired here from 10 a.m. till midnight. You're not going to fire many rounds. Lewis Grant's Vermonters seek to bolster Hancock's right flank. They are answered by Lee when he commits Brig. Gen. Sam McGowan's South Carolinians.

Here, at a slight bend in the Mule Shoe, is the most savage of the day's fighting. Yanks get atop the works and use their bayoneted rifles as javelins to hurl down into the Confederates. Men fire down into the Rebel works. Others pass loaded weapons forward for men in the front rank to use. It continues to rain. It's muddy, and the water has a red tint. Wounded men drown, pressed head-down in the mud-filled "hog pens." Some Yankees reach down and grab Confederates by the collar (or their "stacking swivel," in World War II Marine Corps lingo) and pull them out of the works. Rebs pull Yankees down into the works and either beat them to death or send them to the rear as prisoners. The Confederates fight from "hog pen to hog pen" in a futile struggle to recover the Mule Shoe's Apex. Their task is to buy time so that the Harrison House line can be completed and manned.

The struggle goes on. Everybody wonders when the slaughter will end. It does not end until 3 a.m., when Lee receives word the Confederates have completed work on the Harrison House line. Only then do the butternuts pull back, and the most terrible, prolonged fighting of the Civil War ends. It involves 20,000 men from II Corps and 10,000 VI Corps soldiers. The Confederates employ about 15,000 men, but lose about 8,000. This is a bad day for the Confederates. Union casualties for the fight may have exceeded 9,000.

The fighting at Spotsylvania on May 12 is arguably the most severe of the war—so heavy that at the Bloody Angle, rifle fire felled a tree 22 inches in diameter. It is only one of many trees felled by the sleet of lead and iron. Despite suffering terrible losses, however, Lee hangs on; not to be deterred, Grant seeks new opportunities.

On May 13 the soldiers rest after a horrible night. A Rebel band strikes up "The Dead March" from Handel's *Saul.* A Union band answers with "Nearer My God to Thee."

Warren's and Wright's Federal corps on the night of May 13–14 shift to the left, crossing the Ni. Their attack the next day at Myer's Hill is repulsed by Early's corps. Grant is sure Lee is looking to protect his right, so he schedules an attack against the Confederate center at the Harrison House for the morning of May 18. He will employ Wright's and Hancock's corps at that point, while Burnside's will again attack the salient's eastern face. This time the Confederates have felled timber in front of them, and their cannon are dug in and sighted. It is not going to be a happy day for the Union. When the Yanks come, Ewell's and Early's infantry are only lightly engaged, while Confederate cannon savage the attackers. Imagine what would have happened if those 22 cannon had been in position in the Mule Shoe on May 12. This is not a happy day for Grant. The only thing good about it for the rank and file is that Grant calls off the attack before he is too deeply committed. Even so his casualties exceed 1,500. Confederate losses are slight. Grant now decides to leave Spotsylvania.

By noon on Thursday, May 19, Meade has redeployed the Army of the Potomac east of the Ni, with his right flank refused. Hancock's corps is encamped at Anderson's Mill, ready and eager to take the road toward Massaponax Church and beyond. That afternoon Ewell, seeking to determine Grant's intentions, undertakes an unwise reconnaissance in force across the Ni. This brings about a bitter fight at Harris Farm, initially with Brig. Gen. Robert O. Tyler's numerically strong division recently arrived from the Washington area. Tyler's men are heavy artillery regiments, garrison troops from the capital's defenses. The heavy artillerists, fresh from months of "soft duty," became instant combat infantry. They stand the test. Ewell loses his cool, and General Lee has to step in and withdraw the Confederates. The last of the Spotsylvania battles ends in a Rebel repulse in which they "accomplished very little, whilst we lost some good men."

Grant may have pledged to "fight it out on this line if it takes all summer," but when he made that statement he was operating under the assumption that the other Virginia Union offensives he has set in motion—Gen. Benjamin Butler's advance along the James River and Franz Sigel's thrust up the Shenandoah Valley—were proving successful, and that he could best assist them by pinning Lee down and landing a telling blow. Within days he learned that Butler and his Army of the James had bogged down at Bermuda Hundred on the James between Richmond and Petersburg and that Sigel had been defeated at New Market. He now knows he will have to rely upon his own skills to bring Lee to heel.

Even as Grant and Lee battle at Spotsylvania, Philip Sheridan acts upon his pledge to go out and defeat the Confederate cavalry. In the process, he deprives Grant of the use of cavalry for reconnaissance and probing that might have turned the tide in the second week of May. But Sheridan would rather pitch into Jeb Stuart and his horse soldiers and on May 11, at Yellow Tavern, he gets his chance.

On May 8 Meade had drafted orders directing Sheridan to take whatever force he thinks requisite and make a dash toward Richmond. The hope is that he can draw Stuart's cavalry into battle, defeat the "Plumed Cavalier," and, if he can catch the Confederates unaware, dash into Richmond. On the morning of May 9, 10,000 Union cavalrymen head east toward Fredericksburg before turning south. By evening they have reached the North Anna River. Brig. Gen. George Armstrong Custer's brigade lunges across the North Anna and, at Beaver Dam Station, captures two trains and releases some 275 Union prisoners, most of them captured in the Laurel Hill fighting on the previous day.

Stuart learns that Sheridan is out and about. He assembles about half his cavalry and starts in pursuit. By evening of May 10, Sheridan's men have reached the South Anna, about 20 miles from Richmond. Stuart thunders ahead, steals a march on Sheridan, and arrives at Yellow Tavern first. He posts his horsemen parallel to and east of the Telegraph Road to threaten the Union rear. Sheridan responds by attacking. This is what he has boasted he can do. In the ebb and flow of the fighting, the Fifth Michigan Cavalry charges. A number of the Yankees are dismounted, and as they are running back to their lines, they look to their right and see a group of people sitting their horses near some Confederate guns.

One is a large man, well mounted, with a bushy beard—he is firing his pistol at them. It's Stuart. Pvt. John A. Huff of the Fifth Michigan turns and snaps off a round. The bullet hits Stuart in the abdominal area and penetrates his liver. As he is carried off he speaks to Fitz Lee: "Fitz, I had rather die than be whipped." He is placed in an ambulance and taken to his brother-in-law's house on Grace Street in Richmond, where he dies the next day. On the morning of May 13, Lee receives word that Stuart has died. His eyes well up with tears, and his voice chokes as he says, "He never brought me a piece of false information."

Ulysses S. Grant, center, leans in to examine a map held by Gen. George Meade outside Massaponax Church on May 21. The men are seated on pews removed from the church.

While Stuart's death is both demoralizing and damaging, the Confederates block Sheridan's efforts to approach Richmond, and eventually he decides to link up with Butler's army before returning to Grant. That means that Grant will be without most of his cavalry for two weeks, at a time when he could use it to assist his operations against Lee. Grant decides it's time to slide around Lee's right and head south.

11

NORTH ANNA, COLD HARBOR, AND PETERSBURG

MAY 20, 1864–JULY 30, 1864

Stalled at Spotsylvania, Ulysses S. Grant decided that he would continue to press southward around Lee's right flank. The Confederate capital at Richmond was only 50 miles away. Lee had no choice but to follow.

On the night of May 20, Grant disengages and commences another swing around Lee's right. General Hancock takes the lead with his once-powerful corps, which has been badly weakened in the fighting of the previous three weeks. They move out toward Guinea Station, where Stonewall Jackson died a year earlier. Army of the Potomac commander Meade advances Hancock as bait, hoping that Lee would move out of his formidable Spotsylvania works and attack him. If Lee does not choose to come out and assail Hancock, Lee will be flanked out of his position, and compelled to fall back.

Lee does not go for the bait. He holds his position until May 21, when he learns from his cavalry that Federals have mauled one of his infantry brigades at Milford. The Rebels throw forward skirmishers, and find that the Union Spotsylvania lines east of the Ni have been weakened. There is fighting along the sector of the Union works held by Wright's VI

Corps, which will be the last of Meade's army to move out of Spotsylvania County and head south. Lee realizes what Grant is doing and puts his army in motion for the North Anna River. The Confederates win the race to the North Anna and arrive there on the morning of May 22 and take position with Ewell's corps on the right and Richard Anderson's corps, when it comes up, in the center. The last corps to arrive is A. P. Hill's, and it's posted on the left. Coming from the Shenandoah Valley is Maj. Gen. John C. Breckinridge's division, which had defeated Gen. Franz Sigel at New Market on May 15. Breckinridge reports directly to Lee: He is held in reserve. Also arrived is George E. Pickett's division from Richmond, where his people fighting under Gen. P. G. T. Beauregard have helped best Butler's Army of the James at Drewry's Bluff on May 15–16.

Grant moves up rapidly on May 23. On the north side of the river the Confederates leave a small force to hold Henagan's Redoubt. Hancock arrives first, and one of his division commanders, David Birney, throws two brigades against the redoubt, overwhelms it, and next morning crosses the North Anna. Meanwhile, upstream some five or six miles, at Jericho Mill, Warren's corps has reached a point where it finds the ford unguarded and crosses there. A. P. Hill moves forward to attack the Union forces, using only Wilcox's division. They throw back a reconstituted Iron Brigade, and the Yankees give ground. However, Hill neglects to support the attack, and Warren calls up reinforcements and Wilcox disengages. Lee will chide Hill, saying, "Why did you not do what Jackson would have done—thrown your whole force upon these people and driven them back?"

On the morning of May 24 Hancock's corps crosses the North Anna and begins moving immediately to the high ground to the south. The Confederates hold Ox Ford with "Little Billy" Mahone's division of Hill's corps. Entrenched on Mahone's left are Hill's other two divisions, the left of Heth, anchored on Little River. Anderson's corps on Mahone's right fronts the North Anna, while Ewell's corps and Breckinridge's division guard Lee's right, covering the vital Hanover

Soldiers of Company B, 170th New York Volunteers, play cards, read, and smoke in this undated photograph. They would suffer heavy causalities in fighting at Spotsylvania and the North Anna.

Junction railroad crossover. The Confederate line forms a V with its strongest point at Ox Ford, where Hill on the left and Ewell on the right can promptly reinforce each other as the situation warrants.

Lee succeeds in placing Grant in an embarrassing situation. To reinforce his left with his right or his right with his left, he has to bypass Burnside's troops at Ox Ford and cross the river a second time. In describing Grant's dilemma, Confederate Brig. Gen. Evander M. Law wrote, he "had cut his army in two by running it upon the point of a wedge."

But Lee has leadership problems. Ewell has been plagued by declining health, lack of mobility because of his leg amputation, and perceived loss of judgment at critical times during the Spotsylvania fighting, particularly at Doles's salient on May 10 and again at Harris Farm nine days later. At the latter he got more than 900 soldiers killed or wounded in an ill-advised reconnaissance in force. Hill, beginning at Gettysburg, then at Bristoe Station, and again at Jericho Mill, has proven to be an ineffective corps commander. Anderson is new to corps leadership, and Lee is ill.

Lee seeks to run his army from an ambulance and his tent, but he is unable to get anything to jell and take advantage of Grant's gross tactical error. Nothing happens and Lee declares, "We must strike them a blow—we must never let them pass us again—we must strike them a blow." Even so, it would be difficult to drive Hancock's corps, already throwing up breastworks, back into the North Anna. In addition to the day's skirmishing along Hancock's front, a blunder at Ox Ford by Burnside brigade leader James H. Ledlie costs his command dearly. A heavy drinker, "full of Dutch courage," Ledlie sends his troops to be slaughtered against formidable works defended by Mahone's people. As too often happens, Ledlie will soon be promoted to lead a division, where we will hear more about him on July 30, at Petersburg's Crater.

On the afternoon of May 24, Sheridan's cavalry corps rejoins the army on the North Anna from the road that had taken it to Yellow Tavern and beyond. With the return of Sheridan, and checked on the North Anna, Grant by the 26th is ready to move on. He again, as he had on the march to Spotsylvania and again to the North Anna, sends Meade's army on a wide jug-handle swing to get around Lee's right flank. He transfers his supply base from Port Royal on the Rappahannock to the head of steamboat navigation at White House Landing on the Pamunkey, back where McClellan had been in his Peninsula campaign two years before. "Harry" Wilson's cavalry will try to keep Lee in his position behind the North Anna as long as possible and then follows along behind the army as it heads southeast. Lee on May 27 throws out patrols and finds the Yankees gone. Lee marches across the chord, so he travels a shorter distance. He moves out and masses his army in the Ashland area, where he will be positioned to intercept Grant wherever he crosses the Pamunkey River and strikes southwest toward Richmond. Ewell has for some time been in poor health, and Lee urges him to take a long sick leave, which Ewell is reluctant to do, but

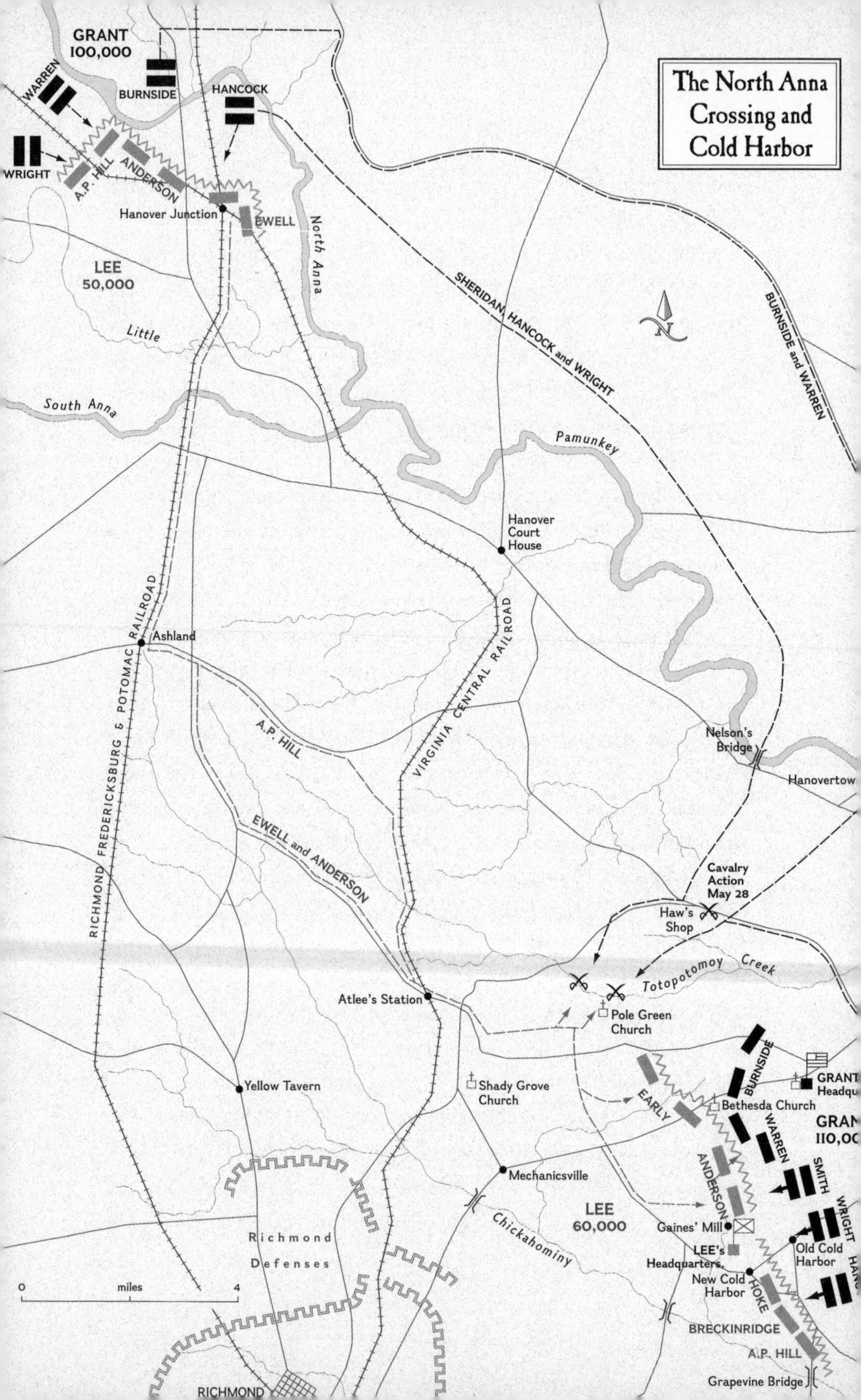
The North Anna Crossing and Cold Harbor
GRANT
100,000
BURNSIDE
HANCOCK
WARREN
WRIGHT
A.P. HILL
ANDERSON
Hanover Junction
EWELL
North Anna
LEE
50,000
Little
South Anna
SHERIDAN, HANCOCK and WRIGHT
BURNSIDE and WARREN
Pamunkey
Hanover Court House
RICHMOND FREDERICKSBURG & POTOMAC RAILROAD
VIRGINIA CENTRAL RAILROAD
Ashland
A.P. HILL
EWELL and ANDERSON
Nelson's Bridge
Hanovertow
Cavalry Action May 28
Haw's Shop
Totopotomoy Creek
Atlee's Station
Pole Green Church
BURNSIDE
GRANT Headqu
Shady Grove Church
Yellow Tavern
EARLY
Bethesda Church
GRAN
110,00
WARREN
SMITH
ANDERSON
WRIGHT
Mechanicsville
LEE
60,000
Gaines' Mill
Old Cold Harbor
LEE's Headquarters
New Cold Harbor
HOKE
HANC
Chickahominy
Richmond Defenses
0 miles 4
BRECKINRIDGE
A.P. HILL
Grapevine Bridge
RICHMOND

Lee insists. He names Jubal Early to command the II Corps. Early had had experience earlier leading Ewell's corps. He had led it in the Mine Run campaign in the fall of 1863 when Ewell became too sick to command, and he had led III Corps during most of the fighting at Spotsylvania, when, as so frequently happens, Hill reports himself sick.

Escaping from Lee's trap at the North Anna, Grant swings south once more across Lee's right flank. For several days the two armies race southward, clashing in a series of sharp fights at Haw's Shop (May 28), Totopotomoy Creek (May 29–June 1), Bethesda Church (May 30), and other places. On the afternoon of May 31, Sheridan's cavalry in a bitter fight bests Fitz Lee's horse soldiers and takes possession of a crossroad at a place called Old Cold Harbor. Satisfied that Lee's army is on its last legs, Grant decides to deliver one more blow. To help, he has ordered the transfer of William F. 'Baldy" Smith's XVIII Corps from Butler's Army of the James.

On the morning of June 1, an effort by Lee's infantry to recover Old Cold Harbor misfires. A late afternoon attack by Smith's corps and Horatio G. Wright's VI Corps ruptures the Confederate line held by Kershaw's division of Anderson's corps and Clingman's Tarheels of Robert Hoke's division north of the Cold Harbor Road and west of today's national cemetery. Rebel reinforcements are called up; Field's people rally, and seal the breach. When nightfall ends the day's fighting, the Federals count more than 2,100 casualties, but they have captured more

OPPOSITE: *On May 31, Federal cavalry seized the crossroad at Old Cold Harbor, turning back an attack by Confederate infantry. Confederate reinforcements arrived and dug in. Late on June 1, Federal infantry reached Cold Harbor and assaulted the Confederate works. By the following day both armies had arrived, facing each other on a seven-mile front between Bethesda Church and the Chickahominy River. At dawn on June 3, a massive Federal assault was repulsed with heavy casualties. On the night of June 12 Grant abandoned his entrenchments and shifted his forces by the left flank toward the James River.*

than 750 prisoners. These gains encourage Grant and Meade. Hancock's corps, posted along the Totopotomoy, is called upon to make a night march and take post on the left of Wright's VI Corps astride the headwaters of Boatswain Swamp, paralleling the Dispatch Station Road. Hancock's men, because of poor maps and confused orders, are exhausted by their march, and Grant twice postpones his June 2 attack order.

As Grant's aide Horace Porter wanders around that night, he will tell us in his memoirs, he notices a number of men taking off their coats, and he wonders if they are repairing their clothes or searching for and crushing lice. He looks closely and can see that a number of them are pinning their names onto their clothes. The soldiers realize what is coming even if Grant and Meade do not. There were no GI dog tags in the Civil War, although you could buy them from sutlers.

Commissary sergeants issue two days' rations to the troops, and they draw their full units of fire. Horatio Wright deploys the three divisions of his VI Corps with Russell on the left, Brig. Gen. James B. Ricketts in the center, and Brig. Gen. Thomas H. Neill on the right. Skirmishers will be out in front, and again, like it was on the first, their axis of advance will be the Mechanicsville Road that leads west to New Cold Harbor. On his right is "Baldy" Smith's corps. Smith and Wright are both engineers by training, and Smith asks Wright, "what are you going to do?" Wright says, "my orders are to pitch into the enemy and not to pay any attention to what is going on to my right or to my left." Smith is incensed by Wright's words, and he explodes to his staff that the attack is "simply an order to slaughter my best troops." He examines the ground in front of him. The ground is quite level, but there are some elevations that have enabled Confederate engineers to lay out an intricate system of works, fronting which are few areas not covered by fire. Smith noticed that a watercourse draining west into Powhite Creek would give his men some cover from enemy fire; he plans to use it as he advances.

The Confederates take care of Wright quickly. Wright's men attack straight ahead. Within a very short time, VI Corps will grind to a stop with relatively light casualties compared to the other two attacking corps. Wright reports his men pinned down, no further gains possible. Some of the Confederates are sorry for the Yanks. Others are not.

On the left, Hancock attacks on a two-division front—Barlow on the right, Gibbon on the left. He has not reconnoitered. And as Barlow's people advance Col. John R. Brooke leads his men forward across a level area fronted by what has been a swamp. The Confederates pulled their pickets out of there because it had been raining most of the night. The Yanks storm forward, penetrate the Rebel works, and capture three cannon, one stand of colors, and 200 men of Edgar's 26th Virginia battalion. Brooke is shot down. Off to his left Nelson Miles's men likewise reach the Rebel works. To the counterattack comes Joe Finegan's Florida Brigade up from the reserve. All good Irishmen will be delighted with Finegan and his Floridians. With their leadership shattered, crowding up on Brooke's and Miles's brigades is Richard Byrnes at the head of the Irish Brigade. He's killed. Barlow's Yankees, having suffered a loss of more than a thousand men, fall back several hundred yards. They dig in with their mess gear and anything else they can lay their hands on.

Gibbon's division, as it presses ahead on Barlow's right, finds its front divided by a hollow formed by Boatswain Creek, which deepens and widens as it nears the Confederate earthworks. On the right, Brig. Gen. Robert Tyler, north of Boatswain Creek, is shot down and wounded as he leads his men forward. Pressing forward behind them is Boyd McKeen's brigade; McKeen will go down, and Frank Haskell will take over the brigade and seek to lead it onward, only to be mortally wounded. The 164th New York Zouaves storms forward south of Boatswain Creek, Col. Martin T. McMahon leading them. He plants the colors on the Rebel works, where he dies. Gibbon pulls back and, like Barlow, reports more than a thousand casualties.

Baldy Smith commits two of his three divisions—William T. H. "Bully" Brooks's and John H. Matindale's—to the onslaught. They advance on a narrow front by columns of divisions separated by Middle

Ravine, which, like Boatswain Creek, drains to the west. As they surge forward, first Brooks's people on the left and then Martindale's on the right find themselves pocketed by "Tige" Anderson's Georgians on their left and Evander Law's Alabamians on their right. The latter recalled his men's morale was sky high—laughing and talking as they "fired" at the oncoming bluecoats. He was taken aback by what he saw: United States and regimental colors being advanced, and then several puffs of dust as minié balls struck chests, and the foe fell like a row of dominos. Law, a veteran of the killing grounds of Second Manassas and Fredericksburg, recalled that this "was not war, it was murder."

Smith's attack stalls and, like Wright and Hancock, he reports no gains and heavy losses. Grant encourages Meade to continue the attack: Meade tells the corps commanders to continue to push ahead without reference to the units to their left and right. If they do so and the corps to their left and right don't gain ground, they will find themselves in a salient and get shot to pieces. They send back for further orders. The orders are to continue the attack. Capt. Thomas Barker, leading the 12th New Hampshire, is angered by such foolishness and shouts, "I will not take my men into another charge if it was an order from Jesus Christ." Men lie on the ground and fire into the air. Although the orders are to continue the advance, they're not going to. They will hold where they are. By noon orders come down from Grant through Meade to cease the attack. "Dig in and hold the ground."

Grant and Meade do not realize the full impact of what has happened. Grant telegraphs to General Halleck that afternoon and reports the attack. He notes that his men have gained positions close in to the Rebel lines, and that losses in the Confederate and Union armies have been modest. It hasn't struck him what has happened, nor does Meade realize the full impact of what it implies when soldiers go to ground and refuse to charge a second and third time when ordered. Meanwhile, Union soldiers entrench along the ridge line to hold the ground they have gained. The first trenches are farthest to the east. Between June 3 to June 12, they'll inch their trenches ever closer to the Confederate lines, while Grant ponders his next step.

Meanwhile, fighting breaks out on the Confederate left along the Shady Grove Road when soldiers of Burnside's IX Corps, supported by Warren's, assail Early's corps. The Confederates, again fighting behind earthworks, hold their own—the Federals in this fighting lose another 1,200 men. Added to the 4,500 cut down in the Old Cold Harbor sector, Union casualties for the day number 6,000.

Lee at first does not realize how disastrous for the Federals the repulse has been. At the end of the day he reports that they again turned back the Federals, and with the blessing of God they've won a success. On the field, in the Middle Ravine, along either side of the Cold Harbor Road, and north and south of Boatswain Creek, dead and wounded Union soldiers lie in great numbers. Many Confederates do not realize a major attack had been made. Later on in the afternoon there is some heavy firing as each side advances skirmish lines. Grant orders a systematic approach. Wounded Yankees, the ones closest to the lines, are taken back to aid stations. You can hear in the evening the pitiful wails of "water, water" rising. Out in front, in no-man's-land, more and more of the wounded die—the bodies turn black and bloat. Finally, on June 7, when Grant finally makes a tacit acknowledgment of defeat, there is a brief truce, which enables the Federals to come out, recover and bury their dead, and succor any wounded still alive out there.

The Battle of Cold Harbor is a disaster for Grant. Although reports that some 7,000 men fell in less than 30 minutes are highly exaggerated, the truth—that perhaps 4,500 men fell in a few hours—is bad enough. Other generals launched costlier assaults at Gettysburg, Fredericksburg, and Franklin, to name but a few, but it would be Cold Harbor that would forever give Grant the reputation of being a butcher.

Yet the setback at Cold Harbor proved only temporary. Grant immediately contemplated a new operation. This time he eyed Petersburg, Virginia, as his target. Due south of Richmond, on the Appomattox River, Petersburg was a key strategic point, for if the Union captures it, Richmond would be virtually cut off from the rest of the Confederacy. To get there, however, would require skill and daring, for along the way Grant would have to cross the James River, all the while making sure that Lee did not seize an opportunity to deal the Yankees a serious and perhaps decisive blow while they are astride the river.

Petersburg was Virginia's second city in 1860, with a population of 18,000. Petersburg is known as the "Cockade City" because of its support for the War of 1812. It is important as a tobacco processing and cotton milling center and county seat. Because of its railroads, it is the gateway to Richmond from the South. Small deep-draft steamboats cannot reach Petersburg, which is located at the fall line of the Appomattox River. Coming into Petersburg are several railroads. From the east at City Point is the City Point Railroad. Coming into Petersburg from the south and a little to the east is the Petersburg & Norfolk Railroad, continuing on to Norfolk. Coming into Petersburg from the south is a very important railroad, the Weldon Railroad. The Weldon Railroad connects Petersburg with the blockade-running center at Wilmington, North Carolina, and with the North Carolina railroad system. Coming into Petersburg from the west, on the south side of the Appomattox River, is the South Side Railroad, which leads from Petersburg to Lynchburg, where it ties into the Virginia & Tennessee Railroad and the Orange & Alexandria. About 50 miles west of Petersburg is Burke's Station, modern-day Burkesville. At Burke's Station, the South Side Railroad crosses the Richmond & Danville Railroad coming out of Richmond. The final railroad leading north out of Petersburg is the Petersburg & Richmond.

Petersburg was vulnerable in the summer of 1862, when General McClellan thought of attacking it in the aftermath of the Seven Days' Battle and his retreat to Harrison's Landing. Since then there have been changes. It is no longer an unfortified rail center. The Confederates have laid out what became known as the "Dimmock Line," and it guards all of the Petersburg approaches from south of the river. The Dimmock Line began on the Appomattox River two miles downstream from Petersburg at Battery No. 1. It then circled Petersburg, staying at a distance of about 2.5 miles from the important rail center. It anchored on the right on the Appomattox River two miles upstream from Petersburg. It consisted of 55 batteries with a connecting line of earthworks. This is what is going to confront Grant when he crosses the James River and moves west. When the first Federals cross the river on the night of June 14–15, there are less than 3,100 Confederate troops to occupy the ten-mile perimeter.

Following the bloody June 3 attack at Cold Harbor, Grant sends Sheridan with two cavalry divisions on a raid into piedmont Virginia. Sheridan is to wreak havoc on the Virginia Central Railroad, go on to Charlottesville, and establish contact with Maj. Gen. David "Black Dave" Hunter's army, which has advanced far up the Shenandoah Valley. Learning of the departure of Sheridan, General Lee bites the bullet. He selects Wade Hampton to succeed Jeb Stuart as his chief of cavalry. Hampton is sent in pursuit of Phil Sheridan; he will fight and best him at the Battle of Trevilian Station, with heavy losses on both sides. Sheridan returns without completing his mission. Hunter has been raising hell with the Confederates in the Shenandoah Valley. He defeats the Confederate defenders of the valley at Piedmont on June 5 and occupies Staunton the next day. Lee responds by sending General Breckinridge and his small division back to the valley. But Hunter, now reinforced by a Union column from West Virginia, takes Lexington on June 11 and torches the Virginia Military Institute. Lee is forced to detach Jubal Early's corps to put a stop to Hunter's rampage. That leaves Lee on June 13 with just two corps, commanded by Richard Anderson and A. P. Hill, plus Robert Hoke's division on loan from Beauregard's command.

On June 12 Grant breaks contact with Lee and starts for the James River, the first obstacle on his way to capture Petersburg, the back door to Richmond. He assigns a major role in the operation to Baldy Smith. Grant had thought highly of Smith since the autumn of 1863, when he played a major role in establishing the "Cracker Line," the initial step on the road to Union victory at Chattanooga. He had indicated to Smith that the latter would replace Meade. After meeting Meade, however, Grant changed his mind. Instead, he decided to assign Smith to duty under Benjamin Butler in the Army of the James. When Meade's Army of the Potomac crossed the Rapidan River, Butler moved the Army of the James, consisting of two army corps, by water up the James River and occupied Bermuda Hundred. Butler sought and failed to break into Richmond from the south. He then pulled back into Bermuda Hundred, where he was bottled up by Gen. P. G. T. Beauregard's smaller army.

Grant's plan evolves as follows: Meade gradually pulls back his right wing and it entrenches. He then extends his left wing out to the Chickahominy River. Under cover of darkness on the night of June 12, Smith's corps departs the Cold Harbor line and marches back to White House Landing and boards transports. By nightfall on the 14th, having gone down the Pamunkey and York Rivers, by Hampton Roads, and up the James River, Smith's people land at Bermuda Hundred. Meanwhile, Warren's V Corps, on the extreme right of the Army of the Potomac, having gone into reserve, crosses the Chickahominy River at Bottoms Bridge and advances on Richmond via the Long Bridge Road to Glendale. Warren is accompanied by Harry Wilson's cavalry division.

It's all ruse—and Lee falls for it. He redeploys his army south of the Chickahominy and takes position south of White Oak Swamp and north of Malvern Hill fronting east. Here Lee's people skirmish with Warren and Wilson. Lee is certain Grant is going to attack through that area. Meanwhile, the remainder of the Union Army, composed of Burnside's IX Corps, Wright's VI Corps, and Hancock's II Corps, disappears from the Cold Harbor battlefield and crosses the Chickahominy River downstream from Bottoms Bridge. The army trains cross the river farther downstream near Williamsburg at Jones Bridge. General Hancock's II Corps is a ghost of its former self. Since crossing the Rapidan in early May, it has suffered 16,000 casualties. The casualties have been replaced as to numbers, but missing are the "old breed," so the quality is down. Many of the newcomers are recruits, bounty jumpers, conscripts, and the "heavies," people that have been manning the heavy guns in the Washington fortifications. Hancock himself is not his old self. The wound he received in the groin at Gettysburg is bothering him. A Confederate minié ball had crashed into the pommel of his saddle and had driven through seven inches of flesh and lodged against his tailbone. The bullet had been removed, but there is shattered bone in the wound, which develops into osteomyelitis. There are splinters of broken saddle framing in his wound as well. In those days you rode a horse. And, as the campaign continues, he is going to get very sore, and by June 17 his wound is going to break open and start draining puss and blood.

By midday of June 14, Beauregard knows he is in serious trouble. Where are Beauregard's men? He has sent Robert Hoke's division, his biggest, to Cold Harbor with General Lee. Bushrod R. Johnson is holding the Bermuda Hundred line with 4,000 men opposing the Army of the James's X Corps. General Butler is there still, neatly corked in a bottle. Holding the Petersburg perimeter, ten miles in extent, are the 2,400 men of Henry Wise, ex-governor of Virginia, who has no use for those damn West Pointers. An ascerbic personality, he is General Meade's brother-in-law. Beauregard also has James Dearing's 800 cavalrymen and the militia.

Grant is in an excellent position to score a knockout blow to the Petersburg Confederates. Beauregard is at Petersburg with about 3,200 men. Johnson is holding the Howlett line. General Early is heading toward the Shenandoah Valley as fast as he can march. Wade Hampton, with his and Fitz Lee's divisions of cavalry, is en route from Trevilian Station, having checkmated Sheridan. Rooney Lee's cavalry and Hill's and

Federal engineers constructed a pontoon bridge across the James River in a matter of hours. The bridge stretched close to half a mile across the river, and withstood the river's strong currents.

Anderson's infantry are north of the James River, protecting Richmond from Warren's infantry and Wilson's cavalry, which, unknown to "Marse" Robert, no longer constitutes a threat to the Confederate capital.

As darkness falls on June 14, Hancock's columns arrive at Wilcox's Landing; throughout the night, they're ferried across the river and land on the south side of the James. There is a snafu. The problem is an order drafted at army headquarters. The staffers order Hancock across the river with three divisions, about 20,000 men. Hancock is to provide rations for the troops before moving out. It will be 10:30 a.m. on the 15th before the men draw their three days' rations. They then march toward Petersburg. The map Hancock is using has two streams confused. They are to go to a point near Petersburg on Harrison's Bed (bed is a name used locally for streams or runs), where the Confederates have an earthwork. There are two Harrison creeks. The one that shows on the Union headquarters map is at Baylor's Farm. The one that Hancock's men are to march to is behind the Dimmock Line. Thus, Hancock has bad information, and he is not told that there is any need to hurry.

Windmill Point, several miles downstream below Charles City Court House, is the narrowest place on the James between Hampton Roads and City Point. Here the engineers construct what is then considered a miracle—a long pontoon bridge across a tidal river. They have their bridging equipment down at Hampton Roads. They come up the river on June 14 and, at dusk, they unload 101 pontoons and, during the next eight hours, they lay the bridge across the river—2,200 feet, or almost half a mile in length. There is a strong tidal ebb and surge, so they have to secure scows at various points to anchor the lines that hold the bridge in position. Also, they cannot close the river to traffic because of the passage of gunboats and transports. The center section of the bridge has to swing. It is quite an engineering task to build this bridge, equal in complexity to bridging the Rhine in March 1945.

Grant meets with Butler and Smith at Bermuda Hundred. He will send Smith with two—Martindale's and Brooks's—of the three divisions that had accompanied him to and from Cold Harbor across the Appomattox River. He will have attached to him a division of blacks that has been landed at City Point since June 5. They are led by Massachusetts-born Brig. Gen. Edward W. Hincks. They will be accompanied by August V. Kautz's cavalry division.

Smith's two infantry divisions cross over from Bermuda Hundred on a pontoon bridge at Pocahontas. They are expected to be in position to carry the Confederate defenses by 10 a.m. The first engagement takes place at Baylor's Farm between Kautz's cavalry and 600 Rebel horse soldiers supported by three cannon of the Petersburg Artillery. The Confederates will check Kautz's cavalry, and then the Fifth Massachusetts Cavalry appears. They charge the Rebels, and get favorable publicity because the periodicals feature sketches of the blacks bringing in a captured cannon. It is a shot in the arm for black recruiting, but Kautz has squandered valuable time.

When Smith's two white divisions approach Petersburg, they are on a broad front: Martindale is on the right; moving along the railroad is Brooks. On Brooks's left will be Hincks's black division, and on Hincks's left is Kautz's cavalry. The Federals by early afternoon have positioned 15,000 soldiers fronting the Rebel works, from Battery No. 1 on the north to Battery No. 20 on the south. Hancock is en route and closing with another 20,000 men. Opposing them, Beauregard has Wise's 2,200 men to defend Petersburg with another 3,200 confronting Butler at Bermuda Hundred. Lee is north of the James with more than 40,000 men. The only Union troops in front of Lee from June 13 to the 14th are Warren's V Corps and Wilson's cavalry. Lee made several errors during the war, and this is one of them. Lee's admirers do not like to spend much time on this period in his military career.

Smith and Kautz, however, dawdle. It is 7 p.m. before Smith, now overly cautious because of his experience in attacking Confederate breastworks at Cold Harbor on June 1 and 3, sends a reinforced skirmish line drawn from Brooks's division forward. The Yanks encounter sharp small-arms fire but carry the salient defended by Battery Nos. 4–6, capturing several hundred prisoners and four cannon. Hincks's division attacks at the same time that Smith is attacking Battery No. 5. Hincks's black regiments crack the Confederate line, capturing Battery Nos. 7, 8, 9, 10, and 11. Each of these batteries emplaced one to two guns. The Union forces have now breached the Confederate lines over the distance of a one-mile front.

It is a moonlit night. Smith hears locomotives chuffing. Beauregard has requested the return of Hoke's division, loaned to Lee. Hoke had arrived with his men at Cold Harbor on May 30 in the nick of time and had remained north of the James with Lee until 5 p.m. on June 14. Hoke's division marches to Drewry's Bluff, crosses the James River pontoon bridge, and entrains. The first cars cross the Appomattox into Petersburg about 7:30 p.m., carrying Johnson Hagood's South Carolinians. They are followed by other troops of Hoke's. The Federals detect this movement from signal towers.

Smith is dismayed by this news. He goes to Hancock, who is finally on the field. Smith asks Hancock to relieve his Army of the James people. It is 11 p.m. before the II Corps troops complete the relief of Smith's men. While Hancock and Smith posture and procrastinate, more of Hoke's units reach Petersburg by rail and are quick-timed out to the danger point.

By morning on June 16, the Confederate forces available to Beauregard for the defense of Petersburg have been increased from 3,200 men (not counting the home guard) to more than 10,000 men. The Union has wasted many hours. Hancock's men are ordered to attack, but it is almost noon before his corps launches its first attack, led by David Birney's division. Col. Thomas W. Egan's brigade spearheads the attack against the Confederate lines and captures Battery No. 12. Egan is badly wounded. Later in the day, the division attacks again. You do not want to command the Irish Brigade. This is a brigade consisting of the 63rd, 69th, and 88th New York and the 28th Massachusetts. At Cold Harbor on June 3, Col. Richard Byrnes had been killed leading the brigade. Today, Col. Patrick Kelly will be killed. In the afternoon attack the bluecoats storm Battery Nos. 13–16. As the crisis deepens, General Beauregard messages both Lee and the Confederate War Department that he must pull Bushrod Johnson out of the Howlett line, because of the continued Union buildup in front of Petersburg with the arrival of Burnside's IX Corps from Windmill Point. With Johnson's departure for Petersburg, Beauregard warns, the cork will be out of the bottle and Butler will be free to sweep west and, again as he had in mid-May, sever the railroad and pike linking Petersburg and Richmond.

By nightfall on June 16, Beauregard, with the arrival of Johnson, has more than 14,000 men in Petersburg. The Federals' increases during the day boost their strength to 55,000. Although they move slowly, on the evening of the 16th Butler's troops occupy part of the trenches Johnson abandoned on the Howlett line. The timely arrival of Pickett's division, rushed to the danger point by Lee, followed by a savage counterattack, drives Butler's men out of their Howlett line toehold.

The Federals have missed a once-in-the-war opportunity, which condemns thousands of men on both sides to death, disabling wounds, and a long, hard winter before Petersburg eventually falls. The Yanks have Petersburg within their grasp on the evening of June 15 and again the next night, but each time irresponsible leadership lets it slip away.

Smith is not the only Union commander to forfeit an opportunity on June 15 and 16. To his left one of his divisions, composed of black regiments under Edward Hincks, scores some early successes.

The vanguard of Burnside's IX Corps by 10 a.m. on June 16 is posted on the left of Hancock. At dawn the next day, Brig. Gen. Robert Potter's division storms forward. Depending on the bayonet, the Yanks take the Confederates of Johnson's division by surprise, and capture more than 600, many of them asleep. In addition to carrying the Rebel works at the Shind House, Potter's people also seize four cannon and five stands of colors. Attacks later in the day by Burnside's two other white divisions, supported by II Corps troops on their right, yield minor gains before being checked by Brig. Gen. Archibald Gracie's Tennessee Brigade, and again success has eluded Grant and his generals.

Beauregard wonders when and if Lee will cross the James and rush south to aid in the defense of Petersburg. He instructs his chief engineer, Col. David B. Harris, to lay out a new defense line covering the eastern approaches to the Cockade City. The Confederates have lost the defenses of the Dimmock Line from Battery No. 4 to Battery No. 16. His two divisions—Hoke's and Johnson's—have fallen back and entrenched on the west side of Harrison's Bed. Harris selects a new defense line on commanding ground a mile east of Petersburg. His engineers walk and stake out positions where the troops are to dig in. Under cover of darkness on June 17–18, the Confederates abandon their temporary line behind Harrison's Bed, and fall back to the new line anchored on Battery Nos.

1, 2, and 3 and extending southward to Colquitt's Salient and beyond to Rives's Salient. This new line is fronted by Taylor's Branch from Rives's Salient to the Hare House. The Confederates are prepared for an all-out Federal attack slated for the morning of June 18.

The June 18 fighting is often overlooked. If you were a soldier in the Army of the Potomac or the Army of the James, you would rather be at Cold Harbor from May 31 through June 4 than at Petersburg between June 15 and 18, because you would have a better chance of getting killed, wounded, or captured at the latter. The Petersburg assaults do not get the same press and publicity as those at Cold Harbor.

By morning on June 18 Wright's VI Corps has arrived from Windmill Point, taking position on the right of the Federal line. Hancock is incapacitated by his Gettysburg wound, and turns command of the II Corps over to General Birney. On Hancock's left is Burnside; on Burnside's left is Warren. Almost 67,000 Union troops close on the new Confederate defense line guarding Petersburg. They come upon the old Confederate defense line where they find abandoned rifle pits, huts, stragglers, and fresh graves. They press onward to encounter stiff resistance from the Rebels, who by morning had been reinforced by General Lee with two divisions of his Army of Northern Virginia veterans, in their new defensive positions. The fighting is more bitter, if possible, than it was at Cold Harbor. Between June 15 and 18, the Federals will lose more than 11,000 troops killed, wounded, and missing. When the II Corps is ordered to advance later in the afternoon on the 18th, they refuse to go forward. Instead, they lie upon the ground and fire their weapons into the air. They have reached a point—they are not going to participate in any more frontal assaults. This is a very critical time for Meade's Army of the Potomac, which has lost more than 65,000 men since crossing the Rapidan River in early May. Their opponents have lost more than 40,000 men.

June 18, 1864, is a terrible day for the Union Army. Several examples will suffice. The First Maine Heavy Artillery Regiment had been in the army

Some of the vast network of earthworks erected by defending Confederate soldiers at Petersburg, Virginia. The siege of Petersburg would last until the closing days of the war.

since late summer 1862, manning artillery in the Washington Defenses. They came to the front when Grant called upon the heavy artillery regiments for combat duty in mid-May. Seeing their first serious combat, they go forward elbow to elbow in line of battle, some 900 strong, to face death and destruction at the hands of the well-entrenched Rebel defenders of Colquitt's Salient. Six hundred thirty-two Maine men are killed, wounded, or missing in action in minutes. It's the heaviest loss for any regiment during the Civil War. Other regiments will lose greater percentages, but no other unit will lose that many men in a day's action during the war.

Joshua Chamberlain, now leading a V Corps brigade against Rives's Salient, is gravely wounded when cut down by a Rebel minié ball that strikes him in the pelvis, twice penetrating his bladder. He will recover from this life-threatening wound and be a major player at the Appomattox Court House drama.

The Confederates, posted behind breastworks, suffer far fewer casualties in the day's fighting. The Army of the Potomac has reached, momentarily, the end of the line. Grant realizes that he has a serious morale problem among the troops. The esprit of the army's frontline soldiers is at an all-time low. Grant decides it is senseless to continue to assault enemy earthworks and breaks off the attacks. He will not again send Meade's people against earthworks until the Battle of the Crater, which is an aberration. Instead, he moves farther west into open country, seeking to cut the remaining Confederate rail lines entering Petersburg from first the south and then the west.

For the next month Grant and Lee find themselves stalemated outside Richmond and Petersburg. Lee tries to break the siege by ordering Jubal Early to follow up his victories over David Hunter in the Shenandoah Valley and threaten Washington, but Grant's rapid redeployment of VI and XIX Corps heads off disaster. It being an election year, Grant is not content to sit and wait. But it is left to a regiment along Burnside's front to devise a possible solution to his problem.

At one point the Confederate line comes very close to the Union trenches: That area is at Elliott's Salient. Brig. Gen. Stephen Elliott commands a brigade that has been brought up from South Carolina. Holding the center of the line here are the 18th and 22nd South Carolina along with four cannon of Pegram's Virginia Artillery. You would not want to be in those units, because your days on Earth are numbered.

Belonging to Robert Potter's IX Corps division is Lt. Col. Henry Pleasants. He leads the 48th Pennsylvania, which was raised in and around Schuylkill County. These men are all experienced anthracite coal miners. Knowing this, Pleasants comes up with an idea of how to break the stalemate that's developed since June 18 and the failure of the

Wilson-Kautz cavalry raid and the II and VI Corps' muffed opportunity to break up the Weldon Railroad and the Jerusalem Plank Road.

Pleasants plans to drive a gallery underneath the Confederate line. The gallery will be five feet high, four feet wide at the base, and two feet at the ceiling. The army engineers do not think much of the plan, and they refuse to give Pleasants's people mining shovels to do the work. So, they use ordinary shovels, cutting the handles down to make them shorter. They improvise wheelbarrows. They plan to dig a gallery a distance of 511 feet.

The soldiers begin digging. At a hundred feet they reach a point where they need to ventilate the gallery. They construct a wooden tube eight inches square; as they dig toward the Confederate line they lay the duct on the floor of the tunnel. They next drive a vertical shaft to the surface and place an airtight bulkhead between where they are digging and the bottom of the gallery. Then they start a fire next to the vertical shaft, and as the heated air rises to the surface it draws fresh air into the tunnel through the duct.

The Confederates hear the miners as the tunnel gets closer to their lines. Brig. Gen. Porter Alexander becomes suspicious of what the Yankees are about. He decides to have his men sink vertical countermines to locate the gallery. If they hit the gallery, they can employ charges of black powder to destroy it, along with the Union miners. But the Confederates have bad luck. Before Alexander can take countermeasures, he is wounded. His fellow Confederates fail to appreciate the danger. When they finally focus on the threat and sink four countermines, it is too late.

Pleasants's people began work on the gallery on June 25; by July 23 they have reached the area under the Confederate works. They dig two lateral galleries perpendicular to the main tunnel, in which they will place the explosive charges. These lateral galleries are dug for a distance of 40 feet on each side of the main tunnel. Each lateral contains four magazines. They place a thousand pounds of powder in each magazine. They have difficulty again when they fail to obtain 8,000 pounds of first-grade powder. Nor are they given continuous fuses, so they have to splice ten-foot lengths of fuse.

During the siege of Petersburg, Union forces employed "the Dictator" or the "Petersburg Express," a 13–inch, 17,000–pound mortar, to shell the city from over two miles away.

Burnside has four infantry divisions. The three white divisions have pulled heavy duty in the trenches, losing an average of 30 men per day. Burnside plans to use the black division commanded by Brig. Gen. Edward Ferrero in the attack. Ferrero's men spend several weeks practicing what they will do when the mine explodes. The first thing is to move forward immediately, to take advantage of the shock and confusion created by the initial explosion. And they are to stay out of the crater created by the blast. They are to pass to the north and south of the crater, avoiding it at all costs, as they press ahead. Their mission is to seize the high ground and secure a lodgment on the Jerusalem Plank Road.

On July 28, the mine is ready. Burnside notifies headquarters. It is the first Grant and Meade have heard of his plan. Grant prepares a diversionary attack to draw the Confederates' attention away from this sector of the front by sending Sheridan's cavalry and Hancock's corps north of the James River to attack Deep Bottom. When Meade learns details of Burnside's plan, he becomes concerned about what will happen if the attack fails and the black division is slaughtered. If disaster ensues, he believes he will be accused of sending the blacks to certain destruction. He refers the situation to Grant, who on reviewing it sides with Meade. That means the men who have been training to lead the assault are not going to. Burnside makes an even worse decision by allowing James Ledlie's white division to have the lead. The choice is made by drawing straws. Not only is Ledlie the most incompetent division commander in IX Corps, experience has shown that he is the poorest choice for the critical mission in the Armies of the Potomac and the James.

The Union high command alerts all parties on July 29 that at 3:30 the next morning they will detonate 8,000 pounds of powder under Elliott's Salient. Hancock's men, returning from north of the James, take position on the right of Burnside's corps; Warren's corps on Burnside's left is alerted to be ready to join in the attack. Union artillery is massed and ready to hammer the area north and south of the crater. Ledlie's men move up and take position just behind the Union picket line, going to ground concealed from the Rebels' view. Ledlie's two brigades are led by Col. Elisha Marshall and Brig. Gen. William Bartlett. Bartlett is my favorite because he will lead his men into action with one cork leg. He has lost his right leg between the hip and the knee. The men have not been issued scaling ladders nor have they been given any specific instructions as to what to do when the mine explodes. In short, nothing has been done to properly prepare Ledlie's division to spearhead the assault once the mine detonates.

With the troops in position and ready to go, Colonel Pleasants enters the gallery and lights the fuse. After lighting the fuse, Pleasants comes out of the tunnel, and the Union troops anxiously wait for the big explosion. Everyone looks at their watches. Over in the 14-gun battery, Burnside waits. Crowded into the nearest approach trench, or sap, eight feet wide and six feet deep, is General Potter's division. In the south

Maj. Gen. William "Little Billy" Mahone helped block the Federal assault during the Battle of the Crater after the Federals exploded a mine under Confederate fortifications.

approach trench, in a ravine 500 feet farther south, standing four abreast and extending back hundreds of yards, is Brig. Gen. Orlando Willcox's division. The blacks of Ferrero's division, who were supposed to lead the attack, are some distance to the rear.

The generals look at their watches; 3:30 a.m. comes and nothing happens. At 4:15 a.m. Pleasants calls for volunteers to enter the gallery and see what has gone wrong. Sgt. Henry Rees and Lt. Jacob Douty respond. They enter the gallery crouched low and discover that the fuse has gone out. They splice the fuse and relight it. It is supposed to ignite the 8,000 pounds of powder 15 minutes from the time they relight the fuse. They come out of the tunnel and wait. At 4:40 a.m. there is a huge explosion. The Earth seems to shake as a great geyser of earth, men, and artillery pieces are hurled into the air. Great clods of earth and debris rain down upon Ledlie's people. They, unlike Ferrero's blacks, have not been properly trained for what to expect when the explosion occurs. They do not do anything but stare in awe and amazement at the spectacle of devastation before them for some ten minutes. Finally the men move forward. Ledlie will not go with his men. Instead, he retreats to the protection of a bombproof and pulls out his bottle and begins to indulge.

When the mine explodes it devastates much of Elliott's Salient, kills or maims 280 Confederates, wrecks four cannon, and creates a Crater 170 feet in length north to south, 30 feet deep, and 60 feet wide. The Crater has been partially filled in and the landscape molded and sodded in the years since.

Unlike the Union leadership, General Lee and key Confederate subordinates are not paralyzed by what could for them have been a disaster. Lee rides to the area and takes position on high ground near the Jerusalem Plank Road. From here he can see the scene and call up reinforcements and throw them into the fight when and where needed. Col. John T. Goode's 59th Virginia to the south takes position facing the Crater. Supporting Goode's Virginians and Elliott's South Carolinians who have survived the blast are the cannoneers of Davidson's Virginia Artillery from a position 400 yards south of the Crater. A similar distance to the north are sited four cannon manned by Wright's Virginia Artillery. The gunners hammer the ground between Ledlie's jumping-off point and the Crater with a storm of canister and spherical case shot. The Confederates, like they had at

OPPOSITE: *After Cold Harbor, Grant crossed the James River and moved against Richmond's rail center at Petersburg. The initial Federal attempt to break into the city on June 15 failed, and Lee by June 18 shifted his army to reinforce Beauregard in the formidable Confederate works ringing the city. Grant was forced to begin siege operations. On July 30, 1864, Union forces attempted to break into the city by exploding a mine under part of the Confederate works, but the battle ended in a bloody repulse for the Federals. Throughout the summer and fall Grant extended his left to the south and west to sever Lee's supply lines, forcing the Confederates to extend their fortifications westward. Siege operations lasted through the bitter winter of 1864–65.*

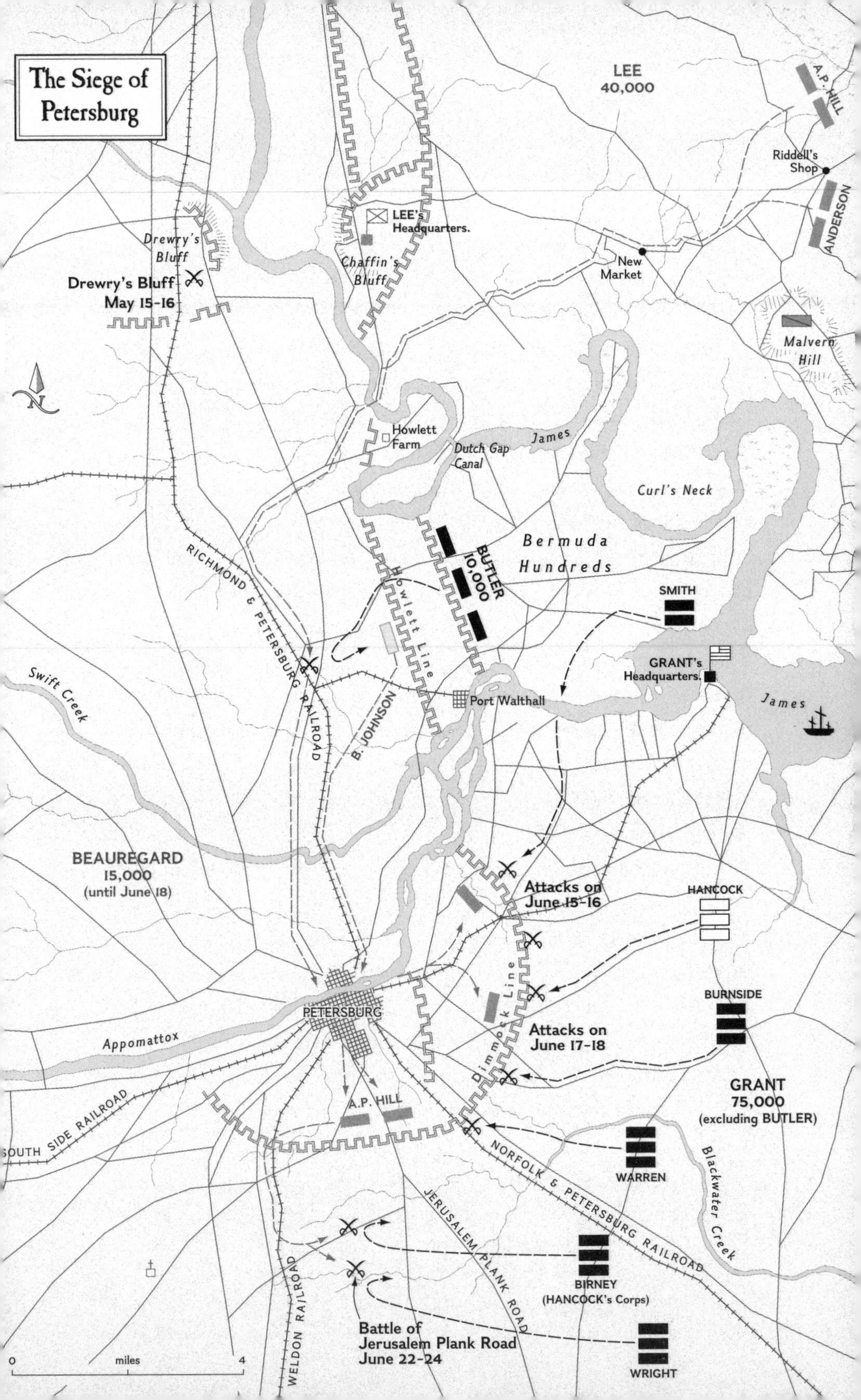

The Siege of Petersburg
LEE
40,000
A.P. HILL
Riddell's Shop
ANDERSON
LEE's Headquarters.
Drewry's Bluff
Chaffin's Bluff
Drewry's Bluff
May 15-16
New Market
Malvern Hill
Howlett Farm
Dutch Gap Canal
James
Curl's Neck
Bermuda Hundreds
BUTLER
10,000
Howlett Line
RICHMOND & PETERSBURG RAILROAD
SMITH
GRANT's Headquarters.
Swift Creek
B. JOHNSON
Port Walthall
James
BEAUREGARD
15,000
(until June 18)
Attacks on
June 15-16
HANCOCK
Dimmock Line
BURNSIDE
PETERSBURG
Appomattox
Attacks on
June 17-18
GRANT
75,000
(excluding BUTLER)
A.P. HILL
SOUTH SIDE RAILROAD
WARREN
NORFOLK & PETERSBURG RAILROAD
Blackwater Creek
JERUSALEM PLANK ROAD
WELDON RAILROAD
BIRNEY
(HANCOCK's Corps)
Battle of
Jerusalem Plank Road
June 22-24
WRIGHT
0
miles
4

Spotsylvania on May 10 and 12, have taken action to shore up the flanks of the gaping hole in their fortifications torn by the explosion of the mine.

The Yankees approach the Crater and are mesmerized by what they see. They haven't been warned by their officers and NCOs to avoid the Crater. They should have been told to pass the Crater to the north and south and press on to the Jerusalem Plank Road as quickly as possible. But leaderless without their division commander, they crowd into the Crater. Some good Samaritans rescue partially buried Confederates. Some duck for cover from the small-arms and artillery fire that is beginning to be brought down upon them from Confederates ensconced on either side of the Crater.

Moving up in support is Bob Potter's two-brigade division. They crowd in upon Ledlie's people. Few soldiers attempt to pass around the terrible pit. Willcox's division comes forward to suffer a similar fate. Soon, there are thousands of bluecoats milling about in the Crater. Too late, Burnside commits Ferrero's division, composed of Col. Joshua K. Sigfried's and Col. Henry G. Thomas's brigades. They seek to do what they were trained to do: Pass to the north and south of the Crater. By now the Confederates have had two hours to recover from the shock of the explosion. Col. John Haskell has arrived with two 24-pounder coehorn mortars, a high-trajectory weapon; his men arch shells into the Crater from point-blank range.

Arriving on the scene is the first of the Confederate reserves that Lee has rushed. They belong to William Mahone's III Corps division. "Little Billy" Mahone is an 1849 graduate of VMI and weighs 110 pounds. He had been a journeyman soldier in the Confederate Army of Northern Virginia until 1864's Overland campaign. A hypochondriac, he travels with a cow and chickens so he can have milk and eggs daily. He counterattacks, first with his former brigade of Virginians now led by Brig. Gen. David Weisiger, a Petersburg native. There is more flagrant killing of blacks by whites and whites by blacks than there was at Fort Pillow.

It is bloody combat of the worst kind. Mahone now sends in Brig. Gen. Ambrose "Rans" Wright's Georgians, who charge into the Crater.

About this time Grant and Meade arrive on the scene, and they see what is happening. They are unhappy with the way Burnside is running the show and order him to withdraw his men. Meanwhile, General Ferrero has joined Ledlie in the bombproof, and they both imbibe "John Barleycorn" as their men are cut to pieces.

By noon, boyish-faced Brig. Gen. J. C. C. Saunders's Alabama Brigade arrives. There are now too many Rebels surrounding and pummeling the Yankees hemmed in and around the Crater. They charge the Federals. The Union troops break. General Bartlett's cork leg is shattered by a Confederate shell, and he cannot escape. It is a grim day for the Union cause. There are more than 4,000 Union casualties, with 1,100 men killed outright and 2,900 either wounded or captured. This will be the last frontal assault Grant will undertake against the Petersburg and Richmond defenses until Sunday, April 2, 1865.

The Confederates reoccupy the Crater and throw up a new line of earthworks to its rear. If the Union troops had reached the Jerusalem Plank Road, Petersburg might well have fallen that day. The war would probably have soon ended and the lives of thousands doomed yet to fall saved.

For the next seven months, Grant will probe north and south of the James River, stretching Lee's lines, looking for weak spots. Several times it seems as if he might prevail at last; each time Lee hangs on, and in some cases delivers a punishing counterblow. The two titans have battled each other to a draw, but Grant has pinned Lee to the Confederate capital, effectively taking him out of the war. In the past, the Confederate commander could be counted on to do something daring. Now he finds himself sitting and waiting.

1865

Three days after Robert E. Lee's surrender to Ulysses S. Grant at Appomattox on April 9, 1865, Confederate infantry proceeded down what would become known as Surrender Avenue to lay down their battle flags and stack their rifles and accouterments and receive parole; many proceeded to walk home, as it was their only means of transport. Weary Union troops gathered at either side of the road silently to honor the Southern forces and to accept their submission. "The war is over," Grant told his troops shortly after the surrender. "The Rebels are our countrymen again."

12

SHERMAN'S CAROLINAS CAMPAIGN

JANUARY 11, 1865–APRIL 26, 1865

On November 15, 1864, Maj. Gen. William T. Sherman provisioned his army with 20 days' hard rations and abandoned the devastated city of Atlanta. Behind him he left wrecked railroads, leveled fortifications, and a city in flames. His new target was Savannah, Georgia, about 225 miles to the southeast, on the Atlantic coast. Marching in two wings, Sherman's army of 62,000 men advanced against light opposition from Confederate Maj. Gen. Joseph Wheeler's cavalry and the Georgia Militia, cutting a 60-mile-wide swath of destruction through the heart of Georgia. After a savage fight at Griswoldville (November 22), lesser engagements at Ball's Ferry and Sandersville, and running cavalry fights in and around Waynesboro, Sherman arrived at the gates of Savannah on December 11, 1864. To facilitate a linkup with the Federal fleet, Sherman sent Brig. Gen. William B. Hazen's division to capture Fort McAllister on the Ogeechee River. The fort fell on December 12. Unable to hold the city, Lt. Gen. William J. Hardee evacuated Savannah on the night of December 20, marching his troops across a series of pontoon bridges built on rice barges appropriated from nearby plantations. On Christmas Eve, President Lincoln received a telegram from Sherman: "I beg to present you, as a Christmas gift, the city of Savannah, with 150 heavy guns and plenty of ammunition, and also about 25,000 bales of cotton."

Sherman is troubled by the messages he gets from Ulysses S. Grant apprising him of Washington's desire for Sherman to leave a small force to hold Savannah and transport the rest of his army to City Point, Virginia, by ship and join Grant's "army group" operating against Lee. Now Sherman has to carry out a long-distance debate with the War Department and General Grant to sell his program of marching his army through the Carolinas, rather than playing it safe by leaving a small force to hold Savannah and moving his army by water to join Grant's army group in Virginia. He wishes to bring fire and sword to South Carolina. "I do sincerely believe," he states, "that the whole United States, North and South, would rejoice to have this army turned loose on South Carolina to devastate that State, in the manner we have done in Georgia." South Carolina is a state in which Sherman had been stationed for nearly four years. His years at Fort Moultrie were pleasant. He knows South Carolina as well as northwest Georgia. This remarkable man has an almost photographic memory for topography as well as an inquiring mind. He seems to know the geography of both Georgia, where he spent little time, and the Carolinas, particularly South Carolina, better than most of the opposing Confederate generals. In Georgia this is particularly galling to Gen. Joseph E. Johnston, a former topographical engineer, who has spent more time in the state than Sherman.

But Sherman has to sell his program to the Lincoln Administration. A strong issue in his favor is that it would take almost two months to assemble the shipping and to transport his army from Savannah to the Richmond and Petersburg area. And that's a lot of time. He also argues that a march through the Carolinas will bring the war home to the Southern people and particularly to the Southern troops—especially the Carolinians serving in Robert E. Lee's army—the same as he had brought it home to Lee's Georgians on his march from Atlanta to the sea.

After the war, Sherman, in speaking about his two great marches, believed the one through the Carolinas was far more challenging. Not since the armies of Julius Caesar had there been such an army as Sherman led on the 500-mile march from Savannah and Port Royal Sound to Goldsboro, North Carolina. Half men and half alligators, his

Ruins of a train depot destroyed during Sherman's departure from Atlanta. In November 1864, Sherman began his destructive march through the heart of the Confederacy to Savannah.

soldiers during February and the first three weeks of March bridged eight rain-swollen rivers—the Savannah, Salkehatchie, Edisto, Saluda, Broad, Wateree, Great Peedee, and Cape Fear—flowing southeast to the sea. They corduroy miles of roadways across swamps deemed by the foe to be impassable during the worst season of the year for campaigning. They foraged for rations "from a poor and wasted countryside," and as Sherman would later boast, reached "our destination in good health and condition."

Let us look at the situation faced by Confederate armies as they enter the new year. Sherman and his army group is in and around Savannah with another strong force, supported by the Navy, holding the Port Royal Sound enclave. Sherman's "March to the Sea" has been a disaster for the Rebels. Before leaving Atlanta, Sherman sends two corps and Maj. Gen. George H. Thomas back to Middle Tennessee to guard against Gen. John Bell Hood and his gallant Army of Tennessee. Hood strikes out for Tennessee as Sherman heads in the opposite direction toward the sea. Despite head-shaking in Washington and loss of nerve on Grant's part, Thomas successfully copes with Hood. On November 30 at Franklin, Maj. Gen. John M. Schofield's bluecoats savage Hood's frontal attacks, and at Nashville in mid-December, Thomas routs Hood.

As the defeated Rebels cross the Tennessee River on December 26–27, the dispirited soldiers sing a parody of the "Yellow Rose of Texas" as they trudge southward—"Gallant Hood Played Hell in Tennessee." Hood retreats to Tupelo, Mississippi. There he asks to be relieved of his command, and on January 17, his request is accepted. Within a short time the once formidable Army of Tennessee scatters—one division goes to Mobile, while the three corps, mere shadows of the army they had once been, start for the Carolinas. There they will be part of the force that will fight Sherman at Bentonville in mid-March. Many discouraged veterans go home, on either furlough or "French leave," not to return. Bedford Forrest and his horse soldiers will finally meet defeat at Selma, Alabama, on April 2 at the hands of James Harrison Wilson, who has learned a lot about cavalry fighting since his bad days in the Wilderness, 11 months before.

In the Trans-Mississippi, Maj. Gen. Sterling Price's formidable mounted command that had advanced deep into Missouri has likewise run into disaster. Defeated at Westport (October 23), routed at Mine

Creek (October 25), and chased out of Missouri at Newtonia (October 28), Price does not halt his retreat until he crosses the Red River.

The Shenandoah Valley, the Union vale of disaster, has finally been neutralized. After the defeat of Lt. Gen. Jubal Early's Confederates at Cedar Creek on October 19, 1864, the Federals leave Maj. Gen. Philip Sheridan in the valley with two cavalry divisions, and both sides redeploy most of their infantry. Maj. Gen. Horatio Wright, with VI Corps, returns to Petersburg. Jubal Early, discredited, remains in the Valley with a small force. Maj. Gen. John B. Gordon, having replaced Early, rejoins Lee at Petersburg with a much reduced II Corps. The threat posed by Sherman's advance into South Carolina causes Lee to rush Wade Hampton to his home state with a cavalry division and an infantry brigade he can ill afford to spare.

In the siege lines around Richmond and Petersburg there is still a stalemate as Sherman prepares to move north. It's been a grim winter for the Confederates, but particularly for the Carolina and Georgia boys in Lee's army. Many of them know what is about to occur there. Georgians know what has happened in their home state. They know that the Confederate government, for whom they are fighting in Virginia, is unable to do much to protect the "home folks," permitting Sherman to go wherever he wants. Railroads are cut, supplies grow short, and Brig. Gen. Lucius Northrop, a favorite of President Davis, retains his office as chief of the Confederate Commissary Department. He is undoubtedly the most incompetent of any senior staff officer holding a key position in either the North or the South.

The only place where you can look for any solace at the end of the year, if you were a Confederate, is the temporary success at Fort Fisher scored over a mighty Union amphibious force led by Maj. Gen. Benjamin F. Butler and Rear Adm. David D. Porter.

Fort Fisher was the massive earthen fortification that guarded the port of Wilmington, North Carolina, the South's last major gateway to the outside world. In early December 1864, Grant ordered General Butler to capture Fort

After completing his march to Savannah, Sherman, pictured here astride his horse at Atlanta, turned north, wrecking a path of destruction through the Carolinas meant to force the South to surrender.

Fisher. With a force of 6,500 men on transports, Butler sailed from Virginia and joined Porter's fleet in North Carolina.

Butler, as always, has a scheme. He has read an article about an explosion on two barges loaded with powder in England that leveled nearby warehouses. He gets an abandoned ship, the *Louisiana,* and packs it with 215 tons of gunpowder. Butler and Porter despise one another, but upon reflection Porter decides that Butler may be onto something, and the Navy takes over when foul weather compels

Butler's convoy to put into Beaufort. The Army not being present, Porter's tars on the night of December 23–24 position the *Louisiana* off Fort Fisher. At 1:40 a.m. the fuse is lit and the volunteers abandon ship.

Porter and the absent Butler are certain that the force of the explosion will level the fort and kill or paralyze the defenders. But what they had planned to be the Civil War equivalent of the Hiroshima atom bomb proves to be a dud. After the debris settles, Porter's waiting armada opens fire. The bombardment makes a lot of noise but the Rebels stand tall.

Porter and Butler point fingers at each other, holding the other responsible for the bomb's failure. Butler is understandably livid when he returns from Beaufort and his soldiers come ashore on Christmas Day. A nor'easter roars in. Butler, despite a reconnaissance that gives promise of a successful attack, pulls his troops off the beach and heads back to Hampton Roads, whereupon Porter informs Grant that before the Navy returns to Fort Fisher, "Butler has to go!" Grant has put up with Butler's shortcomings for some time, and before the Federals return Butler will be relieved of his command.

In January 1865, a new commander, Brig. Gen. Alfred Terry, assumed command of land operations against Fort Fisher. Terry organized a force at Bermuda Hundred on the James River and transported it by sea to join Admiral Porter's North Atlantic Blockading Squadron for another try at Fort Fisher. Backed by the 594 guns of Porter's 58 warships, Terry's 9,000 infantry and artillery landed near the fort on the morning of January 13, 1865. After a massive two-and-a-half-day naval bombardment in which the ships expended almost 30,000 rounds, the Federals prepared to assault Fort Fisher on January 15.

Fort Fisher sits on a peninsula, known before the war as Federal Point. The garrison of Fort Fisher under Col. William Lamb numbers about 1,300 men, but Lamb gets some 350 reinforcements early on the day of the attack. Gen. Braxton Bragg has Maj. Gen. Robert Hoke's 6,000-man division posted at Sugar Loaf four miles north of Fort Fisher. The fort, known as the Goliath of the Confederacy, is a massive L-shape work, consisting of a short land face and a long sea face. The latter is anchored on the land face at the Northeast Bastion and on the right by the Mound Battery. Commanding New Inlet and the wharf is Battery Buchanan. Twenty big guns are positioned in 16 gun chambers on the land face and larger numbers on the sea face.

Working together, Porter and Terry coordinate plans for an all-out onslaught scheduled for mid-afternoon of January 15. The Navy's landing force consists of three battalions of sailors 1,600 strong, armed with cutlasses and revolvers, and one battalion of 400 marines with rifled muskets. The bluejackets are to charge down the beach and storm the Northeast Bastion, and the marines are to pin down the defenders with their small-arms fire. Brig. Gen. Adelbert Ames's army division, led by Col. N. Martin Curtis's brigade deployed in battle line, is to sweep down the Wilmington Road and fight its way into the fort through the riverside Sally Port, known as the Bloody Gate. North of the fort, a division of black troops is posted to hold Hoke's division at bay should he seek to assist Lamb and his defenders.

At 3:25 p.m. the warships blow their steam whistles—the attack is about to begin. The warships redirect their fire from Fort Fisher's land front south to its sea front. Hoping to reach their goal first, the sailors surge forward to meet a short but costly repulse.

The brigade led by six-foot-seven-inch Colonel Curtis takes up the attack. The pioneers use their axes to widen gaps made by naval fire in log palisades. After a desperate struggle, soldiers of the 117th New York gain a toehold in Battery Shepherd and seize the Bloody Gate. Union reinforcements come forward and the tide turns against the Rebels. Within 30 minutes after the battle opens, more than 4,000 Yankee soldiers have either entered Fort Fisher or are seeking to do

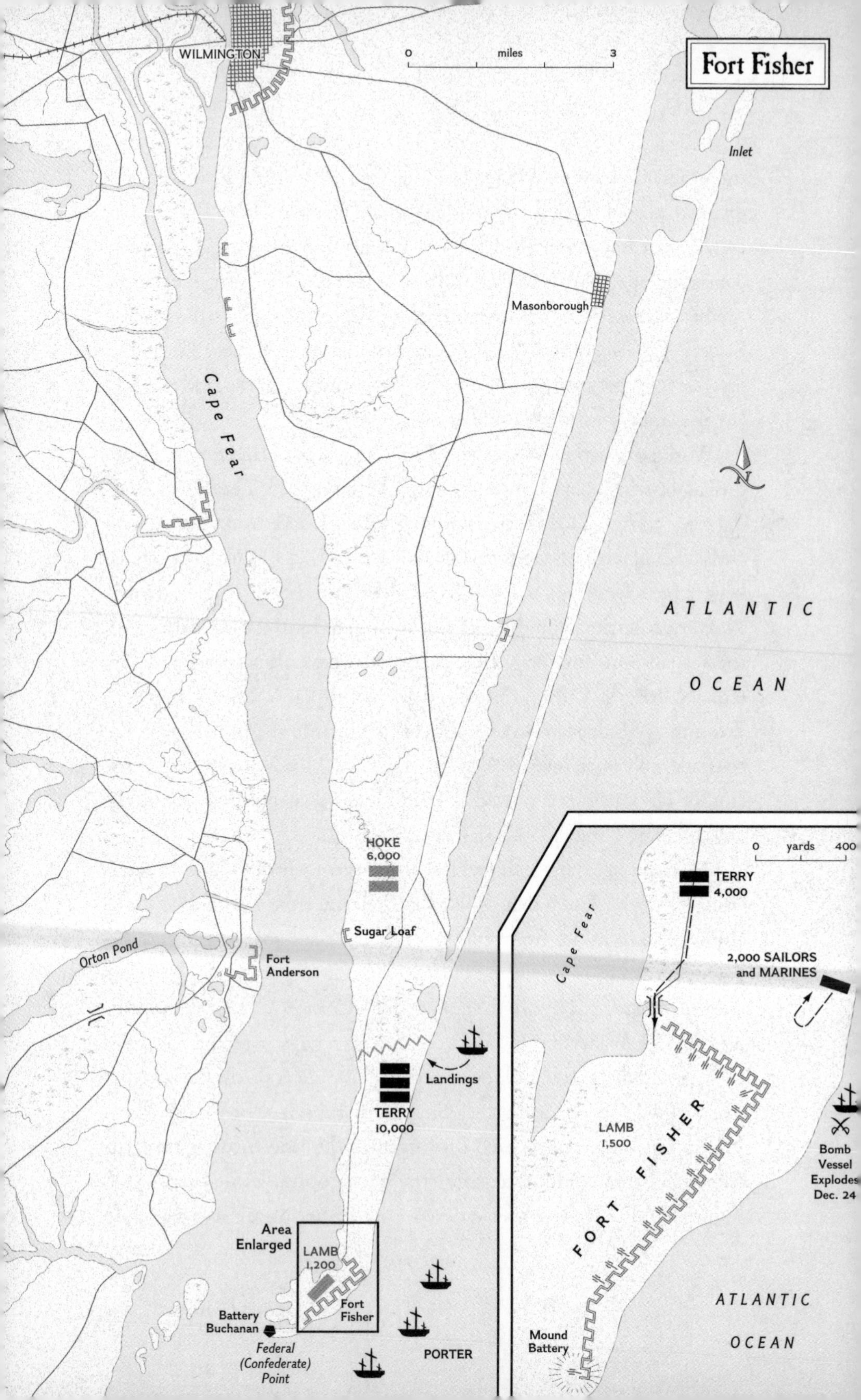

Fort Fisher
0 miles 3
WILMINGTON
Inlet
Masonborough
Cape Fear
ATLANTIC
OCEAN
HOKE
6,000
Sugar Loaf
Orton Pond
Fort Anderson
Landings
TERRY
10,000
Area Enlarged
LAMB
1,200
Fort Fisher
Battery Buchanan
Federal (Confederate) Point
PORTER
0 yards 400
TERRY
4,000
Cape Fear
2,000 SAILORS and MARINES
LAMB
1,500
FORT FISHER
Bomb Vessel Explodes Dec. 24
ATLANTIC
OCEAN
Mound Battery

so. Among the desperately wounded Confederates is Colonel Lamb. The struggle continues until the bluecoats overrun the last gun chamber on the land front. Efforts by the Confederates to re-form for a last-ditch stand at Battery Buchanan are frustrated when Rebel sailors and marines desert their post. The only option remaining to the handful of defenders is surrender.

The storming and capture of Fort Fisher costs the Union Army 955 casualties and Porter's Navy 383. The Confederates lose about 500 killed or wounded and more than 1,000 prisoners. The Federals also close off the mouth of the Cape Fear to blockade runners.

Next Mr. Lincoln's Army and Navy focuses its attention on Wilmington. To do so, the War Department transfers General Schofield and his XXIII Corps by rail and boat from Tennessee to the coast of North Carolina. When the Federals take the offensive, Terry's troops advance north from their toehold on Federal Point and their Fort Fisher base, while Maj. Gen. Jacob D. Cox's XXIII Corps division crosses the Cape Fear and advances on Fort Anderson.

The Rebels evacuate Fort Anderson on the night of February 18. The loss of Fort Anderson uncovers Sugar Loaf, and it is evacuated to be immediately occupied by Terry's troops. The twin battles of Town Creek west of the Cape Fear and Forks Road on the Wilmington side of the river render the largest city and port of North Carolina untenable. The Confederates evacuate Wilmington, and the civil authorities

OPPOSITE: *Fort Fisher protecting the mouth of the Cape Fear River and the Confederate port of Wilmington, North Carolina, was a formidable earth-and-sand fortification with a mile of seacoast earthworks armed with 22 heavy guns emplaced in protected batteries. On December 24 a Federal amphibious expedition under Maj. Gen. Benjamin Butler arrived. Butler planned to level the fort using a bomb ship loaded with 215 tons of gunpowder, but the vessel was detonated too far offshore. On Christmas morning, following a bombardment by Federal warships, Butler landed his forces north of the fort. They approached to within 50 yards of the fort before Butler, learning of the approach of Confederate reinforcements, called off the expedition and returned to Hampton Roads.*

Maj. Gen. Henry W. Slocum, commander of the Union Army of Georgia under William T. Sherman

surrender it on February 22 to General Terry. Meanwhile his black troops march in lustily singing "John Brown's Body." After securing Wilmington, Terry's troops turn and advance up the Weldon Railroad, heretofore one of General Lee's lifelines, repairing the railroad as they close in on Goldsboro. At the same time, Cox's division is redeployed by boat to New Bern on the Neuse River. New Bern has been in Union hands since mid-March 1862. Cox's mission is to rebuild the railroad leading by way of Kinston to Goldsboro. When and if Sherman reaches Goldsboro he will find friends and two railroads linking Piedmont North Carolina to the coast.

Sherman, meanwhile, having sold his proposed campaign to Grant, completes preparations. A XIX Corps division is transferred from the Shenandoah Valley and will hold the Savannah enclave when Sherman's Army group again takes the field. As on the March to the Sea, Maj. Gen. Oliver O. Howard's Army of the Tennessee constitutes the right wing. Maj. Gen. Peter J. Osterhaus, a popular and competent soldier, has been replaced as commander of the XV Corps by Maj. Gen. John A. Logan. A former Douglas Democrat, Logan, a popular stump speaker, has spent the weeks preceding the general election on the campaign circuit rallying voters for the Lincoln-Johnson ticket. One of the most able of the political generals, Logan's nom de guerre is "Black Jack" because of his jet-black hair, walrus mustache, and eyes. Frank Blair, like Logan a former congressman and son of an influential father, continues to lead the XVII Corps.

Maj. Gen. Henry W. Slocum retains command of the left wing, the Army of Georgia. An 1852 West Point graduate, he resigned his commission in 1856 and became a lawyer in upstate New York. He led a regiment at First Manassas and was wounded. A senior corps commander in the Army of the Potomac at Chancellorsville and Gettysburg, he went west in September 1863 with General Hooker, whom he respected neither as a general nor as a gentleman. The Army of Georgia's XIV Corps looks to Brig. Gen. Jefferson C. Davis, a career soldier, as its leader. He is not a West Pointer, having enlisted at 18 and served as a sergeant in the volunteers during the Mexican War. Davis possesses a hair-trigger temper and a grim visage. He is anti-black, able, and ambitious.

Commanding the XX Corps is Brig. Gen. Alpheus S. Williams. A Yale graduate, lawyer, and Mexican War soldier, he had been postmaster of Detroit. Although they call him "Pop," he is only 54 years old. He has served both in the East and the West, and is deemed a good, solid soldier.

Sherman's chief of cavalry is Brig. Gen. Hugh Judson Kilpatrick, West Point class of 1861. Kilpatrick is a would-be playwright, a widower, and a womanizer. Frequently referred to as either "Little Kil" or "Kil-Cavalry," he attracts controversy like honey does flies. In November 1864 Sherman states, "I know that Kilpatrick is a hell of a damned fool, but I want just that sort of a man to command my cavalry in this expedition."

Sherman's force numbers about 60,000 strong—some 5,000 artillery and cavalry, the rest infantry. Strange to say, the Army has a huge wagon train, because travel will be more difficult in the Carolinas than on the Georgia march. There are more than 2,500 wagons and 600 ambulances. The wagons carry ammunition to suffice for one major battle, 7 days' forage, and 20 days' rations. On a good road the trains, if passing along a single route, would extend more than 25 miles. Each corps accordingly travels a separate road.

Although Sherman is not apprised of it as he begins his march, President Lincoln and Secretary of State William Seward on February 3 meet with three high-ranking Confederates headed by Vice President Alexander Stephens aboard the presidential yacht *River Queen* anchored in Hampton Roads. The meeting intended to end the war comes to naught. Lincoln demands the preservation of the Union and the Confederate representatives insist on the South's independence.

Sherman, preparatory to again moving out, redeploys Howard's right wing from its Savannah camps to Beaufort. Most of the troops make the trip by water. On January 20 Slocum's left wing leaves Savannah by roads many of the troops had traveled on the March to the Sea. They are en route to Sister's Ferry, 40 miles away. The next day Sherman takes a steamboat to Beaufort, and the Carolinas campaign is under way. But is it? Heavy rains and terrible roads slow Slocum's march, and it is January 29 before the last of his columns cross the Savannah River at Sister's Ferry and enter South Carolina.

Sherman, as he had on his earlier march, hopes to keep the Confederates in the dark that Columbia is his immediate goal. Thus,

Abandoning his initial plan to defend Charleston, Gen. P. G. T. Beauregard decided instead to evacuate the city and move his Confederate forces to Cheraw, South Carolina.

by sending Howard to Beaufort, General Hardee, who now commands at Charleston, will believe that the "Citadel of the Confederacy" is the enemy's initial destination. Advancing by way of Sister's Ferry, Slocum seems to be heading toward Augusta, where Gen. P. G. T. Beauregard watches and waits.

The worst rains in 20 years beat down, drenching the columns and turning the roads into ribbons of mud. The first serious resistance is encountered and mastered by Howard's wing at Rivers Bridge across the Salkehatchie Swamp on February 2–3. By the ninth both wings, though slowed by swollen rivers and creeks and washed-out bridges and impassable fords, have reached the Charleston & Augusta Railroad on a broad front from Midway to Blackville. While the soldiers wreck the railroad, twisting rails into "Sherman neckties," Kilpatrick's cavalry on February 11 gallops into Aiken and has a shoot-out with Wheeler's cavalry in the town's streets. This is as close as the Federals get to Augusta. By that day much of the lower part of the state is a smoldering ruin, and Union soldiers jest that the town of "Barnwell was now Burnwell."

General Beauregard, the commander of all Confederate forces in South Carolina, ordered Hardee to evacuate Charleston and move his forces up the Northeastern Railroad to Cheraw. While the Confederates evacuated Charleston, Howard's wing marched through Orangeburg and headed toward Columbia, the capital of South Carolina. Sherman's other wing, under Slocum, moved parallel with Howard to the west, marching via Duncan's Bridge and Lexington.

The Confederates had planned to defend Charleston, but Beauregard becomes convinced that if he does so, Hardee's 10,000 troops will be lost along with the city. There are signs that the Confederates are pulling out, and the Union fleet, accordingly, feigns a landing at Bull's Bay, north of Long Island (today's Isle of Palms). Hardee orders evacuation on the night of February 17–18. For several nights prior to the evacuation, supplies and equipment are sent off by train. Many Charlestonians flee the city and become refugees. There is an exodus of people—refugees as well as troops head for Florence and beyond. On February 17th Sherman marches into Columbia. With the fall of both Columbia and Charleston on the 17th, it is a grim night for the Confederacy.

On the morning of February 17 the vanguard of Howard's right wing crosses Broad River and enters Columbia. The mayor and other

By the end of the Civil War, much of the once beautiful port city of Charleston lay in ruins.

officials ride out to meet the invaders and surrender the city. The Yankees remain until the 20th, and on the first night of their occupation, the night turns into noonday. Much of the city's downtown area is torched; listed as fire-gutted and destroyed are six churches, 11 banks, Hunt's Hotel (Columbia's best), Evans & Cogswell, where much of the Confederacy's currency was printed; and the Ursuline Convent and Academy.

Who is to blame is still debated. Was it Union soldiers who marched in singing, "Hail Columbia, Happy Land. If I don't burn you, I'll be damned?" Was it whiskey, stragglers, and misfits? Was it cotton bales fired by Confederates to prevent them from falling into Union hands? Perhaps all of these, but in Sherman's mind the last was the most important factor. To which Confederate Lt. Gen. Wade Hampton, whose nearby mansion Millwood was burned, took strong exception. Even today this is a subject that generates hot words. Whatever the cause, high winds quickly spread the flames across the city. After destroying the railroads in the vicinity of Columbia, Sherman resumes his advance.

Upon leaving Columbia, Slocum's left wing marches north and then east, crossing the Great Peedee at Sneedsboro, while Howard, after passing through Winnsboro, crosses the Wateree at Peary's Ferry. On March 4, the right wing battles Hampton's cavalry at Cheraw before crossing the Great Peedee River. Prior to entering North Carolina, Sherman issues orders to afford the Tarheels gentler treatment. The "bummers" will be leashed, and foraging soldiers will no longer be permitted to enter dwellings under any circumstances.

As the wings close on Fayetteville, Little Kil and two of his cavalry brigades bivouac at Monroe's Crossroads, right in the path of Wade Hampton, who now commands Wheeler's cavalry as well as his own. On March 10, Hampton's dawn attack takes the Yanks by surprise in what becomes known as "Kilpatrick's Shirttail Skedaddle." Kilpatrick's embarrassment causes a few chuckles, but it does not slow Sherman's march.

On the 11th the Union vanguard enters Fayetteville too late to prevent Hardee's retreating column, composed of the two divisions that had accompanied the general on his retreat from Charleston, from destroying the Cape Fear River Bridge. Sherman makes a 26-mile ride to arrive in Fayetteville. The Arsenal's quartermaster, a friend of his from the "Old Army," meets with Sherman. Sherman makes caustic remarks to him about turning his back on the Union, but he details men to guard his house, the only building the Yanks don't burn on the Arsenal grounds.

The most welcome things the troops find at Fayetteville are the steamboats, which have come up the Cape Fear River from Wilmington. The first item landed is the mail, and mail is always all-important to a soldier. It's another reason why the soldiers liked Sherman. They appreciate officers who look after their welfare, officers they can see, officers they know are not back in a bombproof somewhere in the rear.

On January 22 President Jefferson Davis signed into law an act passed by the Confederate Congress providing for the appointment of a general in chief of the Confederate armies. The man Congress had in mind for this position was Robert E. Lee. Davis wasted more than two weeks before appointing Lee to this rank. On February 22, Lee used his new authority to recall Joseph E. Johnston to duty and place him in overall command of the forces arrayed against Sherman. While Johnston attempted to concentrate his scattered and reeling forces, Union General Cox, advancing along the railroad toward Kinston from New Bern, collided with Rebels under Gen. Braxton Bragg at Southwest Creek on March 8. Part of the Federal force was overrun and captured, but the rest of Cox's force dug in during the night. Bragg's and Cox's forces skirmished the next day, and on the tenth, the Confederates launched a frontal assault and were repulsed. Apprised of the arrival of Union reinforcements, Bragg retreated across the Neuse and evacuated Kinston, falling back first to Goldsboro and then joining Johnston at Smithfield.

Johnston continues his efforts to assemble the scattered units that will constitute his army as he prepares to engage his antagonist from the Atlanta campaign. Both he and Sherman know and respect each other. As yet all the fragments of Johnston's Army of Tennessee, making their way willy-nilly across Piedmont North and South Carolina, have not reported.

On March 15 Johnston assigns Hardee's infantry and Hampton's cavalry the vital task of buying time for him to call in more troops and organize his heterogeneous units into an army. Outnumbered as he is, Johnston must attack one wing of Sherman's army and beat one or the other before it can be reinforced. And with Terry's and Cox's

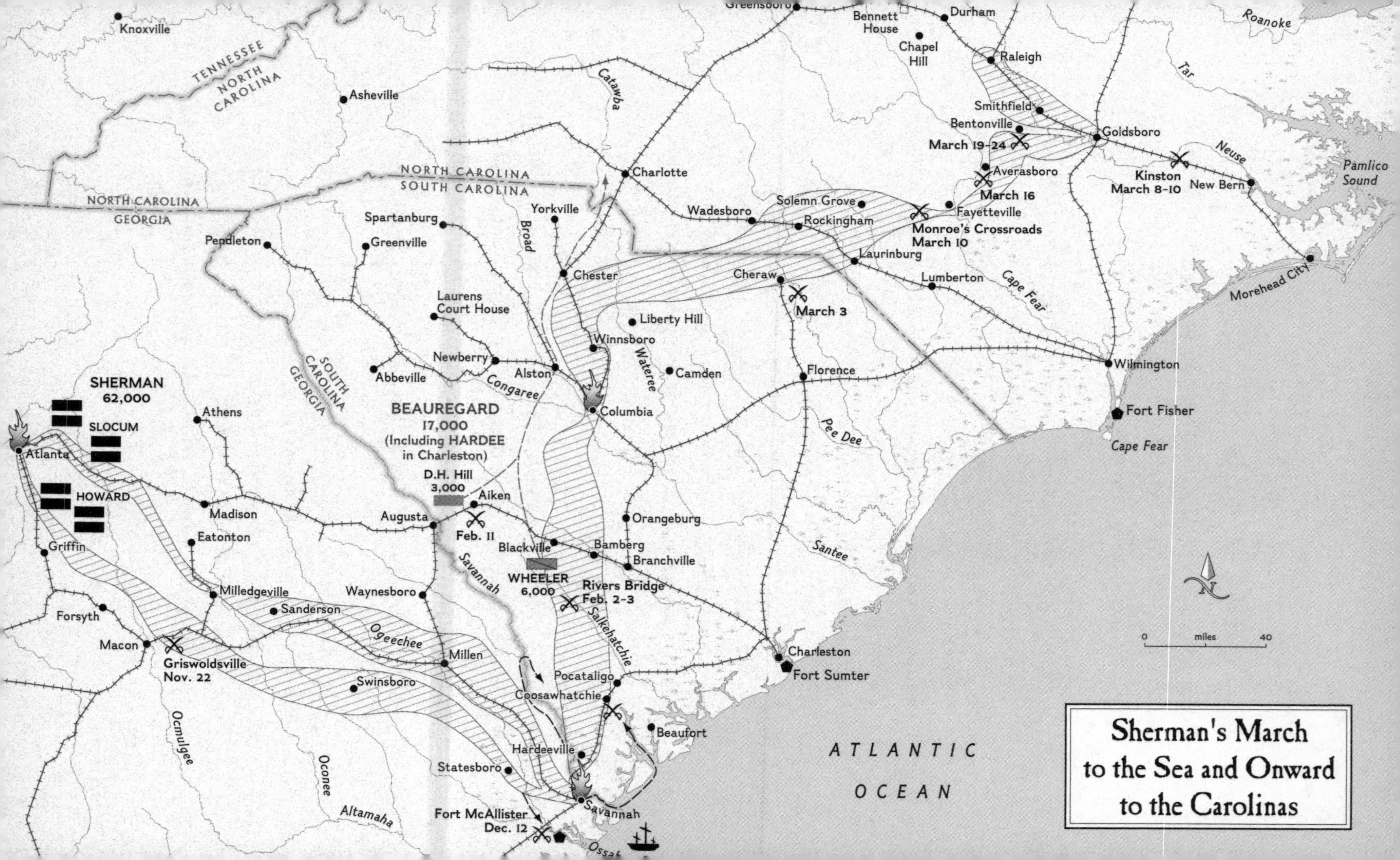
Sherman's March
to the Sea and Onward
to the Carolinas
ATLANTIC OCEAN
SHERMAN
62,000
SLOCUM
HOWARD
BEAUREGARD
17,000
(Including HARDEE
in Charleston)
D.H. Hill
3,000
WHEELER
6,000
NORTH CAROLINA
SOUTH CAROLINA
NORTH CAROLINA
GEORGIA
SOUTH CAROLINA
GEORGIA
TENNESSEE
NORTH CAROLINA
Knoxville
Asheville
Greensboro
Bennett House
Durham
Chapel Hill
Raleigh
Smithfield
Bentonville
March 19-24
Goldsboro
Averasboro
March 16
Kinston
March 8-10
New Bern
Fayetteville
Monroe's Crossroads
March 10
Solemn Grove
Rockingham
Wadesboro
Laurinburg
Lumberton
Charlotte
Yorkville
Chester
Cheraw
March 3
Liberty Hill
Winnsboro
Camden
Florence
Wilmington
Fort Fisher
Cape Fear
Cape Fear
Morehead City
Pamlico Sound
Roanoke
Tar
Neuse
Catawba
Broad
Wateree
Congaree
Pee Dee
Santee
Salkehatchie
Savannah
Ogeechee
Ocmulgee
Oconee
Altamaha
Spartanburg
Greenville
Pendleton
Laurens Court House
Newberry
Alston
Abbeville
Columbia
Athens
Atlanta
Madison
Eatonton
Griffin
Forsyth
Macon
Griswoldsville
Nov. 22
Milledgeville
Sanderson
Waynesboro
Augusta
Aiken
Feb. 11
Blackville
Bamberg
Branchville
Orangeburg
Rivers Bridge
Feb. 2-3
Millen
Swinsboro
Pocataligo
Coosawhatchie
Beaufort
Charleston
Fort Sumter
Hardeeville
Statesboro
Savannah
Fort McAllister
Dec. 12
0 miles 40

columns rapidly closing on Goldsboro, Johnston's window of opportunity is narrowing. When Sherman crosses the Cape Fear, there might be such an opportunity.

Sherman moves out on March 15. Kilpatrick's cavalry has the lead as the army crosses the Cape Fear River. Followed by Slocum's left wing, the horse soldiers turn into the Raleigh Plank Road. Kilpatrick and Slocum are feinting due north toward Raleigh to keep Johnston guessing as to Sherman's objective, which is Goldsboro. Paralleling the road to the west is the Cape Fear, and a few miles to the east is the Black River. Ahead is the community of Smithfield, where Hardee has been camped since the evening of the tenth. Howard's right wing, accompanied by two divisions of the Army of Georgia, as well as Slocum's "nonessential wagons," takes a more direct Goldsboro Road. Sherman travels with Slocum because that is where he expects to encounter the foe. Apprised of Kilpatrick's approach, Hardee, familiar with the terrain, posts his men behind three parallel lines of breastworks, the first held by Col. Alfred Rhett's brigade, the second by Stephen Elliotts' brigade. These two brigades comprise Taliaferro's division, longtime Charleston defenders. The third line is held by Maj. Gen. Lafayette McLaws's division. In the initial fighting Kilpatrick's people, armed with breech-loading carbines, hold their own, and among the Rebels captured is Colonel Rhett, a Harvard-educated Charleston dandy and son of archsecessionist Robert Barnwell Rhett.

OPPOSITE: *Abandoning Atlanta, Sherman advanced into Georgia with four army corps marching in two major columns about 60 miles apart. The two armies marched largely unopposed, facing only sporadic opposition from Confederate cavalry under Gen. Joseph Wheeler. By December 11 Sherman's troops reached Savannah, where they faced an entrenched Confederate force under General Hardee. Sherman captured Rebel Fort McAllister south of the city, and Hardee, fearing that his forces might become trapped, retreated on December 20. After taking Savannah, Sherman moved into the Carolinas, burning the state capital at Columbia before entering North Carolina the first week of March. Sherman defeated General Johnston's forces at Bentonville on March 19–21. Johnston surrendered his troops on April 26, 1865.*

The next morning, March 16, Kilpatrick's cavalry opens the fight by engaging Rebel skirmishers. Two XX Corps divisions arrive from the vicinity of Bluff Church, and Brig. Gen. William Ward's division deploys on the left. Three Union batteries unlimber 12 cannon near Oak Grove, the John Smith house, and hammer Rhett's men posted behind breastworks to their front with shot and shell. A charge into the Confederate right flank by Col. Henry Case's brigade shatters Rhett's former command, causing one of the Yanks to boast, "I was never so pleased in my life as I was to see the rebs get up and try to get out of the way. I tell you there was a good many of them bit the dust."

Although Slocum commits more troops, Hardee makes skillful use of the terrain to fight a delaying action as rain continues to beat down. By dusk Confederates of McLaws's division still hold the third line of breastworks where they had begun the day. Hardee has stalled Sherman for 24 hours and gained an extra day for Johnston to concentrate his army. But the Confederates remain uncertain as to the enemy's destination—is it Goldsboro or Raleigh? Union losses at Averasboro, as the battle is called, number 682 and the Confederate 500.

After reaching Averasboro Slocum's wing turns east toward Goldsboro. Nightfall on March 18 finds its lead division halted on the Goldsboro Road two miles north of Blackman Lee's store, where the advance of Howard's right wing camps. During the day Slocum's vanguard has clashed frequently with Hampton's cavalry, but Union bummers complain that the Rebels didn't drive worth a damn. Hampton, satisfied that the open ground near the Willis Cole plantation, two miles south of the rural village of Bentonville, is the place to fight Slocum, relays this information to Johnston. Johnston orders his troops to assemble there, many of them making a forced march. Johnston hopes to overwhelm Slocum's 20,000-man wing before Howard can come to his assistance. Unaware of Slocum's danger, Sherman joins Howard on the morning of the 19th confident that the day would see no battle.

By 10 a.m. the vanguard of Davis's XIV Corps—Brig. Gen. William Carlin's division—finds its way barred by Bragg's command facing west and Lt. Gen. A. P. Stewart's hard-core Army of Tennessee veterans fronting south. Carlin probes Stewart's right and Bragg's left, only to be beaten back. Both Slocum and Johnston up the stakes, calling up reinforcements. "Little Jimmy" Morgan's XIV Corps division goes into position south of the Goldsboro Road on Carlin's right. When Hardee's corps, slowed by poor maps and confused guides, arrives on the field, Johnston posts Taliaferro's people on Stewart's right and rushes McLaws's to Bragg's left.

A slashing attack by Army of Tennessee troops and Taliaferro's Charleston defenders overwhelms Carlin's people, capturing three cannon and many bluecoats. General Carlin, who is wearing his dress uniform, narrowly escapes capture. Demonstrating they are fleet of foot, one of Morgan's brigades counterattacks Stewart's flank north of the Goldsboro Road, which slows and then stops the Confederate surge. Morgan's people then stand tall in the "Bull Pen." They are first assailed from the front by Bragg and then the rear by four undersized Army of Tennessee brigades.

The 3 p.m. arrival of Williams's XX Corps, which had spent the night of the 18th ten miles in rear of the XIV Corps bivouacs, gives Slocum a much needed boost, and Ward's and Brig. Gen. Nathaniel J. Jackson's divisions take position on the Reddick Morris Farm in support of Morgan's people, who continue to hold out in the Bull Pen south of the Goldsboro Road. In a final effort to build on his successes at the expense of Carlin's division, Johnston hurls Taliaferro's and then Maj. Gen. William Bate's Army of Tennessee boys against the Union strongpoint on the Reddick Morris Farm. Supported by six batteries manning 21 cannon, the Federals repulse four desperate Confederate attacks. Whereupon the Confederates pull back and entrench on the ground from which they had launched their initial attack more than seven hours earlier.

Slocum has messaged Sherman several times that Johnston has turned on him and that his troops have given ground. By the time the first of these communications reaches Sherman, Howard's nearest corps has halted for the night near Cox's Crossroads at the intersection of the Goldsboro and New Goldsboro Roads. The crisis had passed, but this is unknown to Sherman. It catches "Uncle Billy" in his long-handled underwear, and as he strides about puffing on cigars, he orders Howard to march to Slocum's aid.

The first right wing troops reach the Bentonville area and establish contact with Slocum by midday on the 20th. Johnston, apprised of their approach, pulls back his right and left flanks and entrenches. There is continuous skirmishing on Johnston's left as first the XV and then the XVII Corps arrive, press in the Rebels, and dig in. Johnston establishes a bridgehead south of Mill Creek on the 21st, which chances fate. Late that afternoon Maj. Gen. Joseph Mower, a fighting general, assails and routs the cavalry holding Johnston's extreme left. Disaster threatens the Confederates. Hardee launches a slashing counterattack in which his only son, 16-year-old Willie Hardee, is mortally wounded, and a cautious Sherman recalls Mower. That night Johnston abandons the field, and, under cover of darkness, retreats to Smithfield.

The Confederates gone, Sherman resumes the march to Goldsboro. Here he links up with Schofield's columns under Cox and Terry on March 23. Bentonville is the last battle between Sherman's and Johnston's armies. Union casualties in the three-day fight number 1,527 and Confederate, 2,606.

But this would not be the two commanders' last wartime meeting. The next time they would meet as peacemakers.

In the fourth week of March President Lincoln comes to City Point on the *River Queen* to meet with General Grant. With the Confederacy on its last legs, Sherman soon departs Goldsboro by rail and boat for

City Point and a meeting with far-reaching implications. At City Point, Sherman meets with President Lincoln, Grant, and his old friend from Vicksburg days Admiral Porter. Their gathering takes place on March 28 aboard the *River Queen,* and their discussion centers on strategy for ending the war and putting the nation on the road to peace and reconciliation. Sherman's desire that Sheridan's formidable cavalry corps join him in North Carolina is discussed. Concerns are voiced that if Sherman comes north and flushes Lee's army out of the Petersburg lines, it could cause postwar political problems between the East and West. It is decided to trust the fate of Lee's army to Grant and his army group and the offensive that he has scheduled to begin the next day. Sherman returns to Goldsboro and plans to have his troops ready to move against Johnston on April 10. Although no notes were taken, Sherman comes away from the meeting believing that Lincoln's intent was that once the Rebel armies had laid down their weapons, the Southern people "would at once be guaranteed all the rights" as citizens. Sherman is back at Goldsboro on March 30.

As planned, Sherman's army breaks camp at Goldsboro on April 10 and advances on Smithfield. Johnston immediately withdraws from Smithfield, pulls back to Raleigh, and then retreats westward to Hillsborough. The Federals enter Raleigh on the 13th. Jefferson Davis and senior members of his government flee Richmond by train on Sunday night, April 2, en route to Danville. They pause there for a week before learning of Lee's Appomattox surrender and move on to Greensboro, North Carolina. In Greensboro Johnston and Beauregard meet with Davis and his Cabinet on the 13th, and Johnston is empowered to meet with Sherman. Sherman agrees to meet with Johnston and approves the Confederate's request for an armistice limiting troop movements and establishing a truce line. Their meeting will take place on the Bennett Farm, five miles by railroad west of Durham Station on April 17. Before starting out that morning

Sherman receives a coded telegram advising him of Lincoln's assassination. After swearing the clerk to secrecy, Sherman heads west. The two generals and their escorts meet at the home of James Bennett, a farmer. Once inside, Sherman shares the telegram with Johnston. They then turn to the subject that brought them together. Sherman states that as Lee has surrendered Johnston could do likewise "with honor and propriety." Johnston agrees, and the two generals expand their discussion to the possibility, if President Davis would agree, of the surrender of all Confederate forces in the field. Sherman later recalls, "It did seem to me that there was presented a chance for peace that might at least be worth the few days that would be consumed in reference." They agree to return the next day after Johnston had consulted Davis.

Fearing the worst when his soldiers learned of the President's assassination, Sherman takes stern measures to keep the troops in their camps, away from whiskey, and off the streets. He is successful and there is no rioting or burning in Raleigh.

Having gained Davis's reluctant acquiescence, Johnston, accompanied by Confederate Secretary of War John C. Breckinridge, returns to the Bennett Place as scheduled. Carried away by his role as peacemaker, Sherman's peace terms—called the "Memorandum or Basis of Agreement"—go far beyond what Davis or Johnston expect, or what the authorities in Washington will authorize. In addition to providing for the surrender and disbanding of all Confederate forces, the President of the United States was to recognize existing state governments when their officials took an oath of allegiance to the United States, and so on.

Needless to say, President Andrew Johnson rejected Sherman's "Memorandum." Secretary of War Stanton even branded Sherman's terms as treasonous. But the furor over Sherman's agreement soon died down in the North, and he was once more a hero. When Sherman next met with Johnston on April 26. They signed a surrender document including terms similar to those agreed upon by Lee and Grant at Appomattox Court House. The number of Confederate troops—more than 89,000—embraced by the Bennett Place surrender far exceeded those paroled at Appomattox Court House.

13
FROM FIVE FORKS TO APPOMATTOX COURT HOUSE

MARCH 29, 1865–APRIL12, 1865

In the aftermath of the brutal series of battles that marked his Overland campaign—the Wilderness, Spotsylvania, North Anna, Cold Harbor—Lt. Gen. Ulysses S. Grant ultimately recognized that his successive attempts to turn the right flank of Robert E. Lee's Army of Northern Virginia had been to no avail. In mid-June 1864, Grant shifted his line of operations to the south side of the James River, crossing the river on June 14–17 with the intention of seizing the city of Petersburg, south of Richmond, to sever the Confederate capital's communications with the South.

Following the failure of Maj. Gen. Benjamin F. Butler's Army of the James to capture Petersburg by coup de main on June 9, Grant ordered a renewal of the attack. Between June 15 and 18, forces of the Army of the James and Maj. Gen. George G. Meade's Army of the Potomac again fail to capture the city, and Grant determined to begin siege operations. For nearly nine wearying months the armies dug trenches, constructed batteries and mines, and suffered the unpleasant life of static siege operations. Despite constant fighting on the flanks—in the Shenandoah Valley and north of the James at Deep Bottom, New Market Heights, and Fort Harrison, and to the south and west of Petersburg at Weldon Railroad, Peebles Farm, Reams's Station, Burgess Mill, and Hatcher's Run—the stalemate remained.

As March 1865 drew to an end Ulysses S. Grant worried that, with the arrival of spring and dry roads, Robert E. Lee would abandon Richmond and Petersburg and march to unite his forces with Joseph E. Johnston's command in North Carolina, with an eye to taking on first Sherman and then Grant. Hoping to forestall Lee and possibly turn him out of the Petersburg defenses, Grant ordered Maj. Gen. Philip H. Sheridan to take his cavalry—three divisions, 9,000 horsemen—as well as Maj. Gen. Gouverneur K. Warren's V Corps and swing westward around the Confederate right below Petersburg and head for the South Side Railroad, the last remaining rail link between Petersburg and the Confederate heartland. The offensive would be supported by operations against Lee's right by II Corps. If Sheridan succeeds, the Confederates would find themselves in serious trouble, and it would be difficult for Lee to make his way to North Carolina unimpeded.

Lee, too, was active. In an effort to threaten Grant's vital supply base at City Point, east of Petersburg at the mouth of the Appomattox River, he ordered an attack on Fort Stedman, located just east of Petersburg, on March 25. The seizure of part of the Federal line might cause Grant to have to abandon some of his efforts west of the city. Although at first the Confederates enjoyed some success, the attack was repulsed; it failed to deter Grant from moving out against the Confederate right. After turning back the Confederates in a series of small clashes, Sheridan, on April 1, approached a road junction known as Five Forks, well aware that if he took it he would be able to make his way to the South Side Railroad.

On March 31, Lee orders Maj. Gen. George E. Pickett to hold Five Forks at all costs with his 10,000 infantry and cavalry. Pickett attacks the Federals first. Throughout the day of March 31, fighting in driving rain and on muddy roads, Confederate attacks drive back the advancing Federal cavalry. By evening Confederate cavalry and infantry have nearly pushed the Yankees back to Dinwiddie Court House. That night, Federal forces march and countermarch to reinforce Sheridan. Sheridan hopes that Warren's V Corps will be in position to press the issue. Sheridan is a profane man, and he is using strong language in referring to Warren and his absence on the field. Later, he will charge Warren with wishing the sun to go down before he is prepared to attack.

Warren's infantry finally arrives after having fought a bitter battle on White Oak Road with Rebel forces on March 31. The Confederates have fallen back to Five Forks by about 8 a.m. on April 1; the Union cavalry under Sheridan reaches the area in front of the Confederates at Five Forks about noon. Out in front of the Confederates is Brig. Gen. Thomas C. Devin's division of cavalry as well as the division commanded by the ladies' favorite cavalryman, Brig. Gen. George Armstrong Custer. The Union cavalrymen have dismounted and have called numbers, and every fourth man is holding the horses while the others skirmish with the Confederates, keeping them pinned down behind their breastworks.

The Confederates deploy defensively along White Oak Road, covering the Five Forks intersection where the Dinwiddie Court House Road converges with several other roads. East of the junction the Confederates refuse their line north of the White Oak Road in what is called "the Return," so the Confederate line looks like the capital letter "L," with the long part resting along White Oak Road. The Rebels fortify their line, digging in and throwing up fence rails to protect themselves. Pickett screens the mile gap between the Return and Hatcher's Run with dismounted cavalry of Thomas Munford, and the four-mile interval between Five Forks and Lee's fortifications at White Oak Road with the understrength Tarheel mounted brigade led by William P. Roberts. But they don't expect the Federals to attack this day.

Maj. Gen. Fitzhugh Lee and Pickett have been invited to a shad bake by Maj. Gen. Thomas Rosser; they leave the front lines without telling anyone where they are going. I would lay down money that there never has been a shad bake in Virginia at which whiskey was not available. They have not told Col. Thomas Munford or any of the brigade commanders where they are going, because they are certain that the Federals will not attack.

At the angle in their line the Confederates have positioned four guns of Capt. W. M. McGregor's Virginia battery, with Brig. Gen. Matthew Ransom's North Carolina Brigade in support. Brig. Gen. William H. Wallace's South Carolinians are positioned on the right of Ransom. McGregor's four cannon have been sighted to face east, and the timber has been removed from in front of the guns. Brig. Gen. George "Maryland" Steuart's brigade of Virginians man the defensive line that parallels White Oak Road from Wallace's right all the way to Five Forks. At Five Forks, there are the three guns of Col. William J. Pegram's battalion, and Col. Joseph Mayo's and Brig. Gen. Montgomery Corse's brigades are on the other side of the intersection, three more of Pegram's guns, along with Maj. Gen. William H. F. "Rooney" Lee's cavalry division on the far right. Covering the left of the Confederate line is Tom Munford, wondering where Fitz Lee might be.

Coming up via the Dinwiddie Court House Road and then turning into the Gravelly Run Church Road is Warren's V Corps. Warren has about 12,000 men with him. He arrives about 4 p.m. and is soon joined by Sheridan and his chief engineer, Maj. George Gillespie. Gillespie sketches a map in the soft ground based on the Confederate line being located a half mile farther to the east than it actually is. He does not know where the Confederate left flank is anchored.

Sheridan wants Warren to form his corps so that Brig. Gen. Romeyn B. Ayres's division is placed on the left side of Gravelly Run Church Road. It is numerically the weakest division in Warren's corps. He wants Brig. Gen. Samuel Crawford's division to be placed on the right side of the road; it is numerically the largest division in Warren's corps. Brig. Gen. Charles Griffin's division will take position in echelon to the right rear of Crawford's division. As the three divisions advance, they are to keep the sun over their left shoulders. By doing so, this will ensure that when Ayres's division goes forward it will strike the west front of the Confederate angle, and Crawford's division will swing around the Confederate left flank and get into their rear. It is a good plan, provided that the Confederate left flank is a half mile farther to the west.

Warren has difficulties getting his divisions into the formation that Sheridan wants. Finally, at 4:30 p.m., he has his divisions in line ready to advance and they move forward. Where is this line of advance going to take

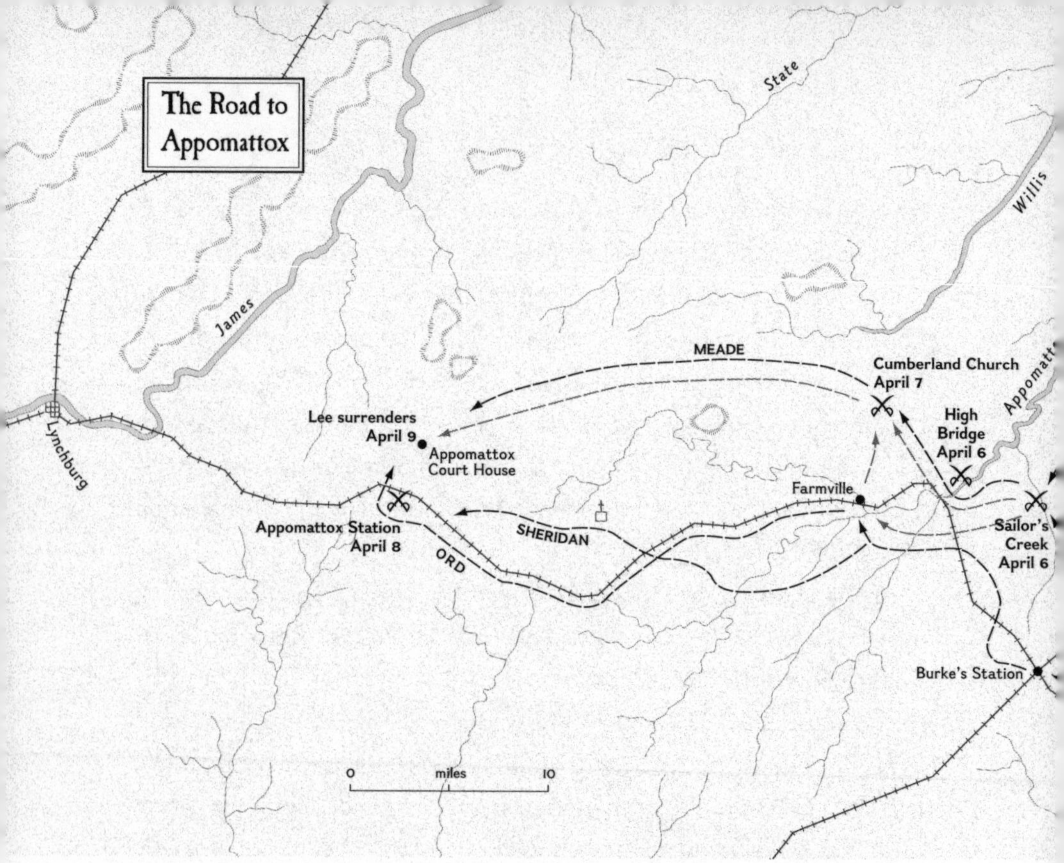

them? Ayres's division expects to approach White Oak Road and find the Rebels directly in front of them. Relying on Gillespie's defective sketch map, Ayres's division crosses White Oak Road a third of a mile to the east of the Return instead of striking it head on as planned. As they cross the road, they come under artillery and rifle fire. This throws Ayres's people into confusion. Col. Frederick Winthrop, one of Ayres's brigade commanders, is mortally wounded by the Confederate fire.

Sheridan gallops up and tries to restore order to the confusion and tells General Ayres to shift the direction of his advance by changing front from north to west. He looks for Warren and cannot find him. Warren and his staff have ridden off to locate Crawford's and Griffin's divisions, which seem to have moved off into a never-never land and become lost.

Sheridan grabs a cavalry guidon and leads Ayres's men forward. This is indicative of his personal style of leadership. Warren is a low-key individual: He is not outgoing, and he does not have a good personality when dealing

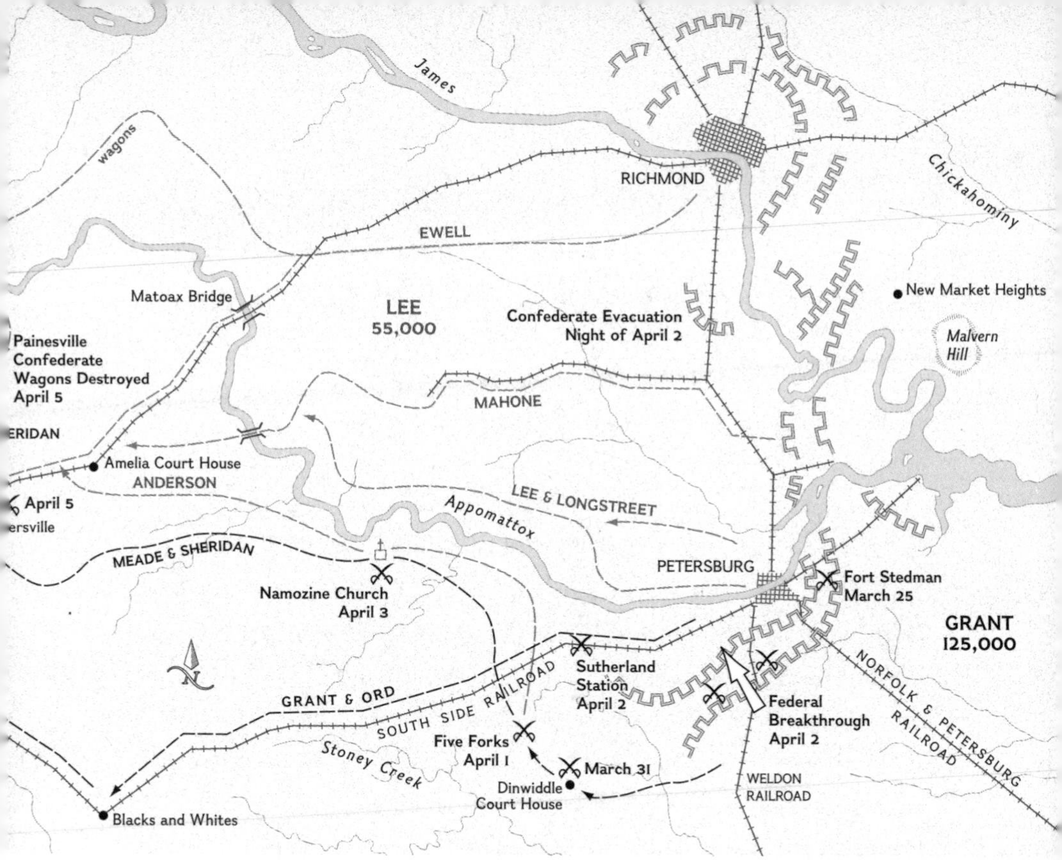

ABOVE: *After Sheridan's victory at Five Forks, Federal forces broke through the weakened Confederate defenses at the Boydton Plank Road and Fort Gregg. Lee was forced to abandon Petersburg and Richmond on April 2 and marched west hoping to link up with Johnston in North Carolina. His corps marched by several routes converging on Amelia Court House. When provisions failed to arrive, Lee's hungry troops resumed their march on April 5. Grant sent his forces in pursuit, pushing Federal cavalry forward to slow Lee's advance. Amid continuous fighting Lee pressed on, losing a quarter of his forces at Sailor's Creek on April 6. Turning toward Lynchburg, Lee found his way blocked at Appomattox Court House and surrendered his army on April 9.*

with subordinates. He also has difficulty in making decisions. He has been on Meade's "s——" list almost since the beginning of the 1864 Overland Campaign. In mid-June1864, Meade was ready to relieve Warren of his command. Grant has already heard several bad stories about Warren, and undoubtedly Sheridan has heard the same ones. Sheridan has gotten permission from Grant to relieve Warren of his command if he does not measure up to expectations. He is already unhappy with today's performance.

Warren soon finds Crawford's staff, and he informs them to tell Sam Crawford to change the direction of his division and march west. He meanwhile sees Charles Griffin and tells him to do the same. But Sheridan sees none of this.

Elsewhere things are going about as badly for George Pickett as they are for Gouverneur Warren.

The shad bake is going well. Because of an acoustical shadow and convivial conversation over drinks, the participants at the shad bake are unaware of the fighting taking place at Five Forks. Soon a messenger arrives with startling news about combat at Five Forks, and they now hear firing off in the distance. Pickett sends two staffers to find out what is happening. One staffer soon comes galloping back and reports that the Yankees have broken the defenses at Five Forks and are sweeping west and soon will reach the South Side Railroad. Pickett and his staff quickly mount their horses and barely avoid capture as Crawford's division storms across the road leading to Ford's Depot. The Confederate situation at Five Forks is bleak.

For George Pickett, already immortalized for his actions at Gettysburg, Five Forks will prove a disaster. The story of the ill-fated shad bake haunts him for the remainder of his life. Nearly a week later Lee, though unaware of the shad bake incident, relieves him of command; soon thereafter, spotting Pickett's distinctive profile, he growls, "I thought that man was no longer with the army."

The famous Partisan Ranger Col. John Singleton Mosby tells a story about a meeting he attended with Pickett and Lee after the war. Pickett still holds a grudge against Lee, and he is rather angry about the manner in which Lee had received him. As they leave the meeting with Lee, Pickett turns to Mosby and says, "That old man destroyed my division at Gettysburg." Mosby replies: "Yes, what you say may be true, but that 'old man' made you famous as well."

The climax of the afternoon's action takes place at Five Forks, where the Dinwiddie Court House and White Oak Roads intersect. The Confederates have thrown up earthworks running east and west along White Oak Road, covering the crucial intersection; cavalry and infantry shield both flanks, with the Confederate left draped in a north-south line north of White Oak Road about a mile and a half east of the junction.

Gouverneur Warren finally catches up with Griffin and changes the direction of his advance. They are now moving in a southwest direction to get into the rear of the Five Forks Confederates. Ayres's division is surging west toward the intersection at Five Forks, guiding on the road and rolling up the Confederate line as he advances. Griffin's infantry emerges from the woods and moves into Sydnor's Field. Crawford's division is advancing on their right much closer to Hatcher's Run.

Sheridan, leading the charge, sinks his spurs into the flanks of his horse, Winchester, and leaps over the Confederate earthworks, carrying the cavalry guidon with him. The other men of Ayres's division follow him into the Confederate works; they capture McGregor's four guns and a large number of Ransom's and Wallace's men. The remainder of the Confederates flee to the rear, pursued by Ayres's division.

The Confederate line along White Oak Road is rolled up from east to west by Ayres's division. Coming up on Ayres's right is Griffin's division, spearheaded by Brig. Gen. Joshua Chamberlain's brigade. Crawford, having overshot his mark, swings southward, coming in on Griffin's right. Advancing northward through the woods south of White Oak Road are the dismounted cavalrymen of Devin's and Custer's divisions.

The Confederates fall back to the position at the Five Forks intersection. Col. Willie Pegram has three guns positioned there. The bespectacled young artillerist sits astride his horse calmly directing the fire of his three cannon against the advancing Yankees. A Union minié ball strikes him in the chest, mortally wounding him. The shattered

Confederate prisoners captured at Five Forks on their way to prison camps in the North.

survivors of the brigades commanded by Steuart, Mayo, Wallace, and Ransom re-form across the road.

Union forces converge on the intersection and overwhelm the Confederates. With the way to the west blocked by Custer's cavalry, the Confederates flee from the battlefield in confusion in a northwesterly direction. They have lost six cannon and approximately 2,500 troops. About half of the Confederates involved in the battle are killed, wounded, or missing.

To give you an idea of the kind of personality Sheridan has and the electric effect he has on his men, there is the story of a soldier who has been severely wounded in the neck. Sheridan rides along and sees him lying on the ground and tells him to get up and charge the enemy. The badly wounded soldier barely drags himself to his feet and makes an attempt to charge forward when he collapses and dies on the battlefield.

It is now 7:30 p.m. and Sheridan has arrived at the Five Forks crossroad, and he is asking, "Where is General Warren?" Sheridan turns to a staff officer and tells him to go find Warren and to tell Warren that he is relieved of command and that he is to turn his corps over to Charles Griffin. Warren is shocked. He rides to Sheridan a broken man and asks if he will reconsider in light of what has transpired on the battlefield. Sheridan uses harsh profanity and refuses to listen to Warren's plea. He then tells him to report to Grant for his next assignment. Broken and downtrodden by the strange course of events, Warren reports to Grant, undoubtedly looking for some sympathy and hoping to salvage his situation. Grant supports Sheridan's decision to relieve Warren; eventually, Grant will put him in charge of the defenses of City Point and Bermuda Hundred.

Warren spends the remainder of his life seeking exoneration for his performance at Five Forks. Years later a court of inquiry found that the general was indeed treated roughly and unfairly; it renders its verdict several years before Warren's death.

Often called the "Waterloo of the Confederacy," the defeat at Five Forks confirms to Lee that he is in imminent danger of losing his rail links running west from Richmond and Petersburg. Desperate as the situation is, however, all is not lost—unless the Federals exploit their success.

General Grant responds to the good news about the Union victory at Five Forks and issues special orders to General Meade. At 10 p.m., Federal artillery all along the Union lines opens fire upon the Confederate positions protecting Petersburg. Following the artillery bombardment, Union infantry move forward at 4 a.m. on April 2 and advance against the Confederate lines.

Men of Horatio Wright's VI Corps quickly rip through Lt. Gen. A. P. Hill's line of defense near Confederate Fort Fisher, and overrun the earthworks defended by brigades of Brig. Gen. James "Little Jim" Lane and Lt. Col. Eric Erson. In the confused fighting General Hill is killed by two Federal skirmishers. Wright's Federals pivot to the left, rolling up the Confederate line as far as Hatcher's Run. Maj. Gen. John Gibbon's XXIV Corps breaks the Rebel lines at Hatcher's Run and pushes northeast up the Boydton Plank Road across the front of Wright's attacking corps and storms Forts Gregg and Whitworth. Maj. Gen. Andrew Humphreys's corps takes the Crow Redoubt. On orders from Grant, Brig.

Gen. Nelson A. Miles's II Corps division advances north up Claiborne Road toward the South Side Railroad. By 3 p.m. they overwhelm hardcore troops from four of Maj. Gens. Henry Heth's and Cadmus Wilcox's divisions at Sutherland Station. Only Maj. Gen. John Grubb Parke's IX Corps finds it rough going against Maj. Gen. John B. Gordon's Confederate II Corps, which holds the stronghold that guards the Jerusalem Plank Road, known as "Fort Damnation." Sheridan pushes north from Five Forks and reaches the South Side Railroad shortly after Miles has taken Sutherland Station.

Hours after the Union offensive begins, President Jefferson Davis enters St. Paul's Church in Richmond for Sunday morning worship. As he sits down, an usher hands him a communication from Lee informing him that the Petersburg lines have been broken and that Richmond must be evacuated immediately. President Davis rises, leaves the church, and proceeds to the War Office, where he issues orders for the evacuation of Richmond to begin. Lee continues to struggle to hold the lines at Petersburg until nightfall permits the evacuation of Petersburg. Throughout the afternoon, the Confederate government in Richmond is busy packing and making preparations for leaving the capital of the Confederacy.

Under cover of darkness on the night of April 2, Lee's army—consisting of units from Lt. Gen. James Longstreet's I Corps, John Gordon's corps, which has stood tall resisting repeated assaults of IX Corps, and the remnants of A. P. Hill's corps, soon to be merged with Longstreet's corps, which has retreated eastward—evacuates Petersburg, destroying the bridges behind them. Lee then heads west with the remnants of the Army of Northern Virginia, following the River Road on the north side of the Appomattox River. Retreating on the south side of the Appomattox River are remnants from the Confederate brigades that had defended Sutherland Station and escaped from Five Forks and the White Oak Road defenses. The Confederate cavalry covers the retreat of the various units as they flee.

A ruined Richmond is visible across the James River in this 1865 photograph. On April 2, Lee was forced to order the evacuation of the capital after Union forces broke through his lines at Petersburg.

Commanding the forces that abandon the Confederate defensive positions north of the James River and in Richmond is Lt. Gen. Richard Stoddard Ewell. In the early morning hours of April 3, 1865, the last units to evacuate the Confederate capital burn the remaining bridge across the James River and begin the long westward retreat. The withdrawing Confederates set fire to military warehouses and depots, but the flames quickly spread to civilian property. Union troops enter the abandoned capital of the Confederacy and are set to work putting out the fires.

Lee has established Amelia Court House as the point of rendezvous for the Confederate columns retreating from Richmond and Petersburg. Orders have been sent to Danville directing the quartermaster to send three trains loaded with rations and supplies to Amelia Court House. The Confederates have left Richmond and Petersburg much more rapidly than they expected to, and many of the troops have not received rations. So, the troops are looking forward to arriving at Amelia Court House, where they expect to find at least 80,000 rations. Once they have received their rations, the Confederates will march along the Richmond & Danville railway to Burke's Station and then on to Danville. But there will be confusion created by the orders issued and the instructions received, which have a significant impact on future events.

Grant prefers that the Union army keep the pressure on Lee's retreating forces and issues orders to the commanders of his two armies, George Meade and Maj. Gen. Edward O. C. Ord, who has replaced Butler as commander of the Army of the James, to instruct their corps commanders to begin the pursuit of Lee's army. Grant orders Sheridan to pursue the retreating Confederates along the South Side Railroad. Sheridan and his cavalry will ride along a route parallel and south of the Confederates to cut them off at Burkeville Junction. IX Corps marches along the South Side Railroad in pursuit of Lee's forces with Ord's XXIV Corps under John Gibbon in advance. XXIV Corps has with it Brig. Gen. William Birney's division of blacks, and one of Birney's brigades will make the incredible march of 96 miles in three and a half days. The men are given the task of repairing the railroad and the telegraph lines as they march. On April 4, Custer's cavalry division, after besting a Rebel cavalry brigade at Namozine Church on the third, turns south before it wheels west heading toward Jetersville.

By the morning of April 4, the scattered elements of the Army of Northern Virginia have assembled at Amelia Court House. When Lee arrives, he is upset by what he finds. He expects several trains loaded with badly needed rations and supplies for his men and his horses to be there. A snafu at the quartermaster's office in Danville has resulted in the non-arrival of vital supply trains at Amelia Court House. There are, however, lots of cannon here and much powder, but unfortunately, an army cannot eat either of these.

Lee now makes a decision. He feels compelled to give up some of the time he has gained on Grant so that he can properly feed his men. He issues a desperate public appeal to the inhabitants and farmers around Amelia Court House to share what they can with his hungry soldiers. The army quartermasters and commissaries go out into the countryside with their wagons hoping to find rations. But the area has already felt the hard hand of war, and the foragers find that there are few in the vicinity of Amelia Court House who can answer Lee's desperate appeal. The army spends the day in the vicinity of Amelia Court House vainly foraging for food. The animals are in worse shape than the men, for they were in terrible condition when the march from Richmond and Petersburg began. Army wagons return to their camps with little to offer the hungry troops and animals.

Lee's army has lost a precious day at Amelia Court House. Lee must now make another crucial decision. Where does the Army of Northern Virginia go from here? Lee decides to move his army down the Richmond & Danville Railroad. From Amelia Court House the rail line runs southwest through Jetersville and then on to Burke's Station (today's Burkeville). At Burkeville Junction it crosses the South Side Railroad and then continues southwest to Danville. The South Side Railroad heads west to Lynchburg. Lee orders the Army of Northern Virginia to march from Amelia Court House on the morning of April 5. The cavalry takes the lead: they use the road paralleling the railroad.

Lee's men are now subsisting on what few rations they may have been able to bring with them in their haversacks when they left Richmond and Petersburg on the night of April 2. There have been few if any rations issued to the troops, and many of the soldiers will go without food for another day unless they stop alongside the road and raid nearby homes. There are lots of stragglers. Many of them simply wander off and don't come back. On April 1, before the Five Forks debacle and the evacuation of Richmond and Petersburg, the army numbered about 56,000 men.

Lee will surrender 28,000 men at Appomattox Court House. He is going to lose about half of his army by the time he reaches there.

Lee is aware that there is Union cavalry supported by part of the V Corps at Jetersville. When his army leaves Amelia Court House, he places Fitz Lee's cavalry division in the lead. Sheridan and his cavalry reach Jetersville late on the afternoon of April 4, and they tear up railroad tracks, cut the telegraph wires, and take position, throwing up fence rail barricades.

The important question is: Will Union infantry arrive there before Lee's army reaches Jetersville? Unfortunately for Lee, two Union infantry corps arrive at Jetersville on the morning of April 5. These are the men of Andrew Humphreys's II Corps and Horatio Wright's VI Corps; they take position on the right and left of the cavalry and throw up breastworks. As Lee closes on Jetersville, his cavalry reports that the Federals are there—infantry as well as cavalry in force.

Lee now faces another key decision. Should he try to fight his way through the Union force now blocking his path of retreat at Jetersville or should he go around them? He decides to avoid a fight at Jetersville and turn his army north through Amelia Springs. At Amelia Springs there is a road running east and west that passes through Deatonville and on to Farmville by way of a place that Lee is going to wish he had never heard of, Sailor's Creek. By turning his men into the road to Amelia Springs, they have to spend another night on the road. This is another day in which his men will face the hardship of having to locate food. Lee calls for a night march on April 5.

As soon as the Federals learn that Lee has turned north and is passing through Amelia Springs, they make plans to continue the hot pursuit. Their plan is as follows: Pursuing on a road that goes west out of Jetersville toward Farmville will be Sheridan with his three cavalry divisions commanded by Tom Devin and George Custer under the close supervision of Maj. Gen. Wesley Merritt, as well as the division led by Maj. Gen. George Crook. Following General Sheridan's Cavalry Corps will be Wright's VI Corps, which arrived in Jetersville on April 5. Griffin's V Corps and Humphreys's II

Corps will pursue Lee's army by heading north out of Jetersville toward Amelia Springs, before turning west. When they reach Rodophil, Griffin will veer to the north and march toward Painesville, where he will turn west again.

Ord's Army of the James will follow the South Side Railroad. His two infantry corps will comprise the Federal southernmost column. Ord will be accompanied by Brig. Gen. Ranald S. Mackenzie's cavalry division. John Parke's IX Corps is to follow Ord's column, realigning the railroad gauge as it marches. With all of these columns on the move, Grant casts a net hoping to ensnare Lee's Army of Northern Virginia somewhere between Jetersville and Farmville.

On April 5 both armies continue to move westward, with Lee becoming ever more desperate in his efforts to escape Grant's advance and make his way toward North Carolina. Absent that, perhaps he will seek refuge in the Blue Ridge Mountains.

Lee's army spends the night of April 5 passing through Amelia Springs and beyond. But there is little rest for Lee as his army trudges westward. Since leaving Richmond and Petersburg, the army has marched through the night on April 2. The men have marched all day and a good part of the night on April 3. They rest at Amelia Court House on April 4, but awaken on the morning of April 5 and marched west once again. They continue to trudge through the night on April 5. They are not marching continuously. There will be periodic halts, which give the men a chance to catch a few winks. Some of them sneak away when their officers are not looking and fade into the woods alongside the road.

Not all the Confederates are as lucky on April 5. Custis Lee escorts a wagon train, carrying with it Confederate military records, when he runs into a Union cavalry unit at Painesville, about six miles northwest of Amelia Springs.

This is the first time that any officially "mustered in" black Confederates will participate in the fighting. Of course, there will be black teamsters and black body servants, but they have not been officially mustered into the army. Lee had earlier authorized the creation of a black battalion. They are trained and drilled in the ways of combat and learn how to march. This battalion is accompanying Custis Lee's command, and become engaged in the defense of the wagon train at Painesville.

On April 6 both armies continue to press westward. Part of Grant's forces sweep south of the retreating Confederates; the other part presses hard upon Lee's rear. Portions of the two armies collide at Sailor's Creek, less than 10 miles east of Farmville and about 30 miles east of a place called Appomattox Court House.

Phil Sheridan is confident at this point because he has VI Corps with him. He and Horatio Wright, commander of VI Corps, get along well, having fought together in the Shenandoah Valley. Sheridan sends the cavalry commanded by Crook, Devin, and Custer down the road to Gill's Mill, a short distance from a Little Sailor's Creek crossing. Then the horse soldiers swing north in an effort to cut Lee's line of retreat at Marshall House.

Lee has already passed Marshall House, riding with Longstreet's I Corps. Following behind Longstreet's corps is the division commanded by Maj. Gen. William "Little Billy" Mahone. These units have reached Rice's Station, several miles beyond Marshall House. A wide gap has opened between the rear of Billy Mahone's division and Lt. Gen. Richard H. "Dick" Anderson's corps, consisting of Maj. Gens. Bushrod R. Johnson's and George Pickett's divisions.

When Anderson's vanguard approaches Marshall House, they find Union cavalry in front of them. Following Pickett's division, with no artillery, are units commanded by General Ewell. His force of nearly 6,000 men is composed of Confederate marines, sailors, heavy artillerists, and the men of Maj. Gen. Joseph Kershaw's infantry division. With Union cavalry blocking the road at Marshall House, Lee's army has been divided into two columns, with Union infantry bearing down on them.

The first Union cavalry to arrive at Marshall's Crossroads is George Crook's division. Johnson and Pickett must fight their way through Crook's people if they are to reach Lee and Longstreet at Rice's Station. Anderson's corps is unable to advance. Union cavalry has blocked the road in front of them. Worse, Anderson's infantry must also ward off attacks on their left flank by Custer's and Devin's cavalry.

After these commands pass through an intersection known as Holt's Corner, the Confederate wagon train arrives. There is difficulty ahead in crossing Little Sailor's Creek because the stream is two to four feet deep. If you are a short fellow, the water would be up to your belt. The banks are steep, and the crossing of Little Sailor's Creek is slow. Because of the difficulty in crossing the creek, the teamsters turn the wagons into the road heading northwest from Holt's Corner.

Gordon's corps is not supposed to follow the wagon train, but there is a breakdown in command and control. Gordon assumes that he is to trail the wagon train. So he turns his corps at this location and follows the wagon train, away from the remainder of Lee's army. You can imagine what is going to happen when they go down the steep grade into the area known as Double Bridges. Here the road crosses first Little and then Big Sailor's Creek.

Sheridan sees his opportunity. He orders Wright to take VI Corps, turn into the road that leads southwest from Holt's Corner, past the Hillsman House, across Sailor's Creek, and attack Ewell's rear. Humphreys's II Corps takes the road that leads to the Double Bridges and pursues Gordon's people. The Union cavalry continues to occupy their roadblock on the high ground between Little Sailor's Creek and Big Sailor's Creek at the Marshall Farm. The horse soldiers have brought to a halt the westward movement of Dick Anderson's two divisions and Ewell's column behind them.

Wright deploys two divisions of his corps adjacent to the Hillsman House northeast of Little Sailor's Creek. The Confederates are positioned on the opposite ridgeline on open ground. Dick Ewell's command is posted with Kershaw's division south of the road on the high ground. The Confederate naval battalion, sailors and marines from the James River fleet, is astride the road. On the Confederate left are the men of Brig. Gen. Seth Barton's brigade that had manned the Richmond defenses. Alongside these troops are the heavy artillerists, gunners from the Richmond defenses—without their artillery—commanded by Maj. Gen. George Washington Custis Lee.

When the Yankees advance, the Confederates show their spunk. Capt. John Randolph Tucker of the naval brigade orders his men to charge the enemy, yelling, "Board them, Board them," just like if they were fighting a ship-to-ship engagement. The men go forward with cutlasses and pistols, joined by the men of the heavy artillery. The Yankees, not expecting a charge, fall back across Little Sailor's Creek. All except the 37th Massachusetts, who are armed with Spencer repeating rifles. This regiment waits for the Confederates to cross to the other side of the stream and then opens fire upon their ranks as they get closer. The Confederate counterattack is thrown back.

The Federals then launch a counterattack, which sends the Confederates retreating to the safety of their lines, where they are quickly overwhelmed. The last men to surrender are the men in Commander Tucker's naval brigade. The Federals capture seven Confederate generals as Ewell's command disintegrates. One of the captured generals is Ewell himself. General Kershaw is taken prisoner, as are five other Confederate generals, including Robert E. Lee's son Custis.

Disaster also strikes to the north at the Double Bridges. Hundreds of wagons, trying to get down the steep grade and cross the bridges, block the movement of Gordon's corps. Gordon is forced to form a brigade east of the Double Bridges. Humphreys deploys an entire division and attacks. Panic grips the Confederate teamsters: 350 wagons are either captured or destroyed. The Federals capture another 1,700 Confederates, three cannon, and 13 stands of colors. The Confederates have had a very bad day here. Almost 6,000 Rebel prisoners will soon be en route to City Point. Lee has seen a quarter of his army disappear in one battle.

Custer and Devin do the unexpected. They mount a charge against Anderson's front. Tom Custer, George's brother, captures a Rebel flag, his second in the last 72 hours, and receives a second Medal of Honor. Crook's horse soldiers continue to hold their roadblock, and Anderson's corps breaks and flees.

Lee sits astride Traveller, up on the high ground on the far side of Big Sailor's Creek, when he sees a mob headed his way. He exclaims in anguish and disbelief, "My God! Has the Army been dissolved?" Billy Mahone then tells Lee that he will form his division and prepare to repel an attack. Lee soon sees "Old Man" Brig. Gen. Henry Wise among the steady stream of panic-stricken men. Wise is Meade's brother-in-law and was ex-governor of Virginia when John Brown raided Harpers Ferry. Wise comes up to Lee and tells him that he will make an attempt to create some kind of order out of the chaos that surrounds them.

Lee soon learns from some of the retreating soldiers that most of Ewell's command has been captured as well as large numbers in Johnson's and Pickett's divisions. Many of the wagons have been destroyed or captured, but most of Gordon's corps has managed to escape via the Jamestown Road. Lee is now left with Longstreet's corps and Billy Mahone's division as well as the cavalry divisions of Tom Rosser, Rooney Lee, and Fitz Lee. He orders what remains of the army to push on to Farmville.

Lee also sends instructions to army quartermasters in Lynchburg to assemble trains with rations and supplies for the soldiers and animals and rush them to Farmville. Finally, on the evening of April 6, Lee tells Richard Anderson, Bushrod Johnson, and George Pickett to go home because they no longer have commands. Unfortunately for Pickett, he makes the mistake of hanging around, leading to Lee snapping on seeing him, "Is that man still with the army?" So, there is going to be another night march for Lee's weary, hungry men as they trudge on toward Farmville.

On the morning of April 7 Lee and Longstreet arrive at Farmville.

The hungry, exhausted Confederates are excited by what they see. There are cheers in the ranks. There are five trains loaded with much needed rations and forage waiting for them. The officers immediately issue rations to the men and forage for the animals. While this is taking place Lee receives horrible news. Billy Mahone's division had been sent to the High Bridge, four miles downstream, where the South Side Railroad crosses the Appomattox River, with orders to destroy the bridges. His men managed to partially destroy the railroad bridge, but before they could torch the wagon bridge, it was captured by Yankees. The Federals will use it to cross the Appomattox River.

Upon learning the bad news, Lee orders the trains to leave Farmville and move to Pamplin's Depot, where they are captured the next day. Those sent from Lynchburg arrive at Appomattox Station and there await the arrival of the army. Soldiers of James Longstreet's corps and the Confederate cavalry gather up what few rations they have been issued and cross the Appomattox River at Farmville and burn both the railroad bridge and the highway bridge. The Federals soon close on the Confederates who regroup at Cumberland Church. But the Rebels stand tall and fend off the attacks of Humphreys's II Corps. Able to reassemble his army at Cumberland Church, Lee prepares to move out again on another night march to Appomattox Court House.

When the Union troops enter Farmville, their morale is sky high. There is a torchlight parade, and as the troops march by, Grant stands on the porch of the Prince Edward Hotel. The soldiers raise a cheer for their commander as they pass by with bands playing. Grant has recently run into one of General Ewell's relatives, who tells Grant that Confederate morale appears to have been broken by recent events. Perhaps Lee would now be willing to entertain suggestions for surrender. While he is in the hotel Grant drafts his first message to Lee—a formal request for a cease-fire between the two armies—and gives it to a courier. Under a flag of truce the staffer rides to Cumberland Church, Lee's command post, three miles north of Farmville.

Lee reads Grant's message to his assembled officers. Lee's right-hand man, as he has been since his October return to duty, is James Longstreet. Personally, Lee is closer to Longstreet than he was to Stonewall Jackson. Upon hearing Lee read the message from Grant, Longstreet says, "Not yet!" Lee agrees. He responds to Grant, saying that he doesn't think he needs to surrender, but inquires as to the proposed terms.

Lee orders his army to begin the march to Appomattox Court House on the night of April 7. They march throughout the night, and on the morning of April 8 Lee is feeling better. He's beginning to think that he might escape the trap that Grant is weaving to snare his army.

On April 8, Lee approaches Appomattox Court House late in the day. His lead elements pass through the village. This is an artillery unit commanded by Brig. Gen. Reuben Lindsey Walker of III Corps. They push ahead to secure the area around Appomattox Station. Lee establishes his headquarters several miles east of Appomattox Court House. His army is strung out over a distance of five miles, from Appomattox Station, through Appomattox Court House, and on to New Hope Church. Lee is feeling more confident as his men have made a good march and appear to be temporarily out of danger. There have been no attacks by the Federals against his rear guard or flanks since leaving Cumberland Church. He does not believe that there are any Federals in front of him. He knows that the supply trains ordered west from Lynchburg have reached their Appomattox Station destination.

Having some free time available, Lee sits down late in the afternoon of April 8 and replies to a new message from Grant at Clifton, near New Store. Grant tells Lee that he is willing to discuss surrender terms, either face-to-face or through intermediaries. Lee shakes his head. He's not willing to surrender; at best he will meet to chat about terms. When Grant receives Lee's reply, he develops a bad headache. Lee has regained some of his confidence and now seems to be of the opinion that he might be able to escape with his army. It seems to Grant that Lee is stalling for time. Grant tries to sleep off his headache. He has mustard plasters applied to the back of his neck and his wrists. But he is unable to get some much needed rest and relief from his headache because several young staff officers are downstairs at the parlor piano singing songs. Grant is tone deaf and says he knows only two tunes: One is "Yankee Doodle" and the other isn't. Grant is tolerant of the staff officers who are singing downstairs in the parlor.

If Grant had a headache, what happens that evening was sure to give the Confederates a more serious one.

We must turn our attention to General Lee's chief of artillery, Brig. Gen. William Nelson Pendleton. It would have been better for the fortunes of the Confederacy if he had remained a minister. He had been an Episcopal rector in Lexington prior to entering service as commander of the Rockbridge Artillery. Through much of the war he had served as Lee's chief of artillery. He is a kind, godly man but not very effective in high command. Pendleton rides from Lee's headquarters tent near New Hope Church east of Appomattox Court House via the Richmond-Lynchburg Stage Road and heads for Appomattox Station. As he approaches Appomattox Station about 8 p.m., he hears the reports of several cannon in the distance. George Armstrong Custer and his cavalry, leading the Union column approaching via the road paralleling the railroad, have reached Appomattox Station. When Custer arrives, he finds the Confederate supply trains with rations for Lee's army sitting on a spur near the station. He orders his horse soldiers to attack, and they scatter the small force defending the Confederate trains. After seizing the trains, Custer's cavalry bears down on the camp of Walker's artillery. Walker manages to get a few of his guns into position, and they fire several rounds before they are overrun. Custer's people then form up again and turn into the Lynchburg Stage Road and head for Appomattox Court House.

Upon seeing the approaching Yankee cavalry, Pendleton and his staff wheel their horses around and ride back to Lee's headquarters with bad news of Yankee cavalry in the Appomattox Station vicinity. This means that Walker's artillery has been captured as well as the supply trains. Even worse, the enemy is now astride the Lynchburg Stage Road, blocking Lee's escape route to the west.

Custer's cavalry closes on Appomattox Court House from the west. Confederates posted near the court house fire upon them, and one of the approaching Union cavalrymen bites the dust. Having been fired upon by Confederates, Custer's cavalry hesitates and falls back toward Appomattox Station. Meanwhile, Sheridan, Ord, and Griffin call upon their men to make a night march. Sheridan soon arrives at Appomattox Station with Crook's and Devin's cavalry divisions to join Custer's. Col. Charles F. Smith's cavalry brigade rides east along the Lynchburg Stage Road and takes post a half mile west of the court house. He also unlimbers a section of artillery. Soon the rest of Sheridan's cavalry arrives as well as the vanguard of Charles Griffin's V Corps. Ord reaches the station with Gibbon's XXIV Corps. Now there is a powerful Union force in control of Appomattox Station.

So night falls on April 8 with Lee not fully aware of the situation. He seems determined to press on. No wonder Grant had a migraine headache; it looked as if Lee meant to fight it out to the end.

When Lee awakens on Palm Sunday morning, April 9, 1865, he knows that the supply trains at Appomattox Station are in Yankee hands. He also knows that Lindsey Walker's artillery brigade has been captured.

Lee decides to gamble on a last attack. He knows that there is Federal cavalry along with two cannon astride a ridge west of the courthouse. He has John B. Gordon bring his men through the village. Once the Confederates have cleared the village, they deploy into line of battle. If he encounters only Union cavalry, Lee feels that Gordon will brush it aside without much difficulty and open a route toward Lynchburg.

On the Confederate right are the small cavalry divisions commanded by Gens. Tom Rosser and Rooney Lee and Col. Tom Munford. In the center are three small divisions of the once proud II Corps. Brig. Gen. Bryan Grimes's division of North Carolina troops is on the right. Col. James A. Walker's division of mostly Virginians is in the center. Brig. Gen. Clement A. Evans's Georgians are on the left.

Gordon's battle-hardened veterans advance, raising the old familiar Rebel Yell for the last time in the Army of Northern Virginia. They proudly move forward, their tattered, blood red battle flags billowing in the breeze, and they quickly overrun Charles H. Smith's cavalry brigade, brushing them aside and taking two cannon—among the last the Army of Northern Virginia will capture during the war. They reach a ridge perpendicular to and south of the stage road, and just as they begin to think that the way is open to the west, they see a long line of blue infantry filing into position on a distant ridgeline. They are the men of John Gibbon's XXIV Corps, and as they arrive on the field they block the Confederates' escape route to the west. Also present are soldiers of William Birney's black division.

Brig. Gen. William Cox's North Carolinians halt. Gordon rides to the front and looks across the field through his binoculars at the lines of infantry supported by artillery. He sends a message back to Lee stating that he has fought his corps to a frazzle and cannot advance any farther unless reinforced. Lee has no available reinforcements to send. Longstreet's corps is several miles to the east, protecting the rear of Lee's army, which is threatened by Humphreys's corps. Lee is faced with another critical decision. There is now Union infantry in his front, and Gordon has been checked. More important, the Yanks are astride the Lynchburg Stage Road.. Lee has Gibbon's infantry to his front, Griffin's infantry to his left front, and Custer's cavalry threatening his flank from the southeast. Lee turns to his officers, including Longstreet, and tells them there is nothing left for him to do other than go see General Grant—and that he would rather die a thousand deaths than do this.

Lee rides back to the rear of his army, where Longstreet has deployed his men on both sides of the Lynchburg Stage Road. He goes out in front of Longstreet's picket line. There he sees a Union skirmish line beginning its advance against Longstreet's front. He sends a Confederate messenger out in front of the lines under a flag of truce and with a request to meet with the commander of the Union skirmish line. Lee then rides out along the skirmish line. That officer soon arrives, and Lee tells him that he wants to see General Grant. The Union officer returns to his lines and refers the message up the chain of command to General Humphreys. Thank goodness there are no trigger-happy Federals on the skirmish line that day, who might have gunned down Robert E. Lee at this critical moment.

Soon a Union staffer rides back to Lee, still standing in front of the Confederate picket line and delivers a note from Grant, which he had written to Lee earlier in the morning, calling for his surrender. Lee quickly scribbles a reply and requests that it be immediately delivered to Grant. In it he asks to meet with Grant to discuss surrender.

Lee lies down under the shade of an apple tree beside the Lynchburg Stage Road near the Appomattox River. He's had enough of fighting. Before Lee rode away from Longstreet's lines on Traveller, he had been told by Longstreet that if the Federals did not offer favorable terms of surrender, then they should continue to fight. Artillery commander Brig. Gen. Porter Alexander has already come to Lee with a proposal to break up the army and retreat to the mountains and hollows of Virginia and continue the fight, employing guerrilla warfare tactics. Lee turns down Alexander's proposal. He tells Porter Alexander that if they scatter the army and continue the fight using guerrilla warfare as he proposes, then the enemy will pursue them to all parts of the South, and the entire countryside would be devastated. Alexander later writes in his memoirs that the general was thinking on a higher level than he was when he made the proposal to Lee.

That same morning, Grant mounts up and rides over to visit with Generals Ord and Sheridan. He wears a simple sack coat, similar to the uniform of a private, with twin three-star shoulder straps. He does not have his sword with him, only a pair of binoculars hung around his shoulder. He is hardly a well-dressed officer on this day. He still has a splitting headache, primarily due to the rowdiness of his staff officers in the Clifton headquarters parlor the previous evening. If I had been Grant, I would have put them on the front line the next day. But Grant is a much kinder man than I. He soon leaves the Lynchburg Stage Road and cuts cross-country toward Appomattox Station. About 11 a.m. a courier catches up with the general and his party. The courier hands Grant the dispatch from Lee—the one agreeing to meet with Grant to surrender his army. He reads it and passes it to his chief of staff, Brig. Gen. John A. Rawlins. Miraculously, his headache disappears.

While all this is going on, George Custer rides into General Gordon's command. As Longstreet later describes it, Custer's wearing the biggest stars, a handsome red neckerchief, and a gold stickpin. He tells Gordon that he demands "in the name of General Sheridan, the surrender of this army." Gordon is somewhat taken aback by Custer's brash, flamboyant behavior and display of arrogance. Longstreet happens to be standing nearby. Longstreet is a big, burly man, and he happens to know Grant. He had been one of Grant's groomsmen at his wedding in 1848. And Longstreet will respond in a rougher tone to George Armstrong Custer's demand, saying, "How dare you come into our ranks when you know that a flag of truce is out! You are insulting General Grant! And you are insulting General Lee! Get out of here!" Having been chastised in such a forceful manner by Longstreet, Custer turns his horse around and rides off without muttering another word.

The two unluckiest men in the Union Army are going to be killed about noon on Palm Sunday. One belongs to the 155th Pennsylvania, now wearing Zouave uniforms. Pvt. William Robert Montgomery, not yet 19 years old, will be struck by Confederate artillery fire and die. First Lt. Hiram Clark, of the 185th New York, will be killed near the courthouse. His regiment belonged to Joshua Chamberlain's brigade and was advancing toward the court house on the morning of April 9, 1865, when Clark was killed.

That afternoon Grant and Lee prepare to meet in the village near the courthouse.

Grant sends a staff officer, Col. Orville Babcock, an engineer, to meet Col. Charles Marshall of Lee's staff for the purpose of finding a suitable location to meet in the village of Appomattox Court House. The two men enter the village and are impressed by the house occupied by Wilmer McLean. When the war broke out in 1861, Wilmer McLean had owned a farm on Bull Run near Blackburn's and McLean's Fords. His farm had suffered some damage from Union artillery fire on July 18, 1861. Both armies had foraged liberally on his farm and had demolished many of his rail fences during the Battle of Manassas. The two armies returned again 13 months later, during the fourth week of August, and again his property was damaged during the engagement.

So, he decided to move his family and purchase property in a place that will be out of the way of the two warring armies. In 1863, he bought this house. As Marshall and Babcock ride through the village looking for a place for the generals to meet, they come to the conclusion that the Wilmer McLean House is the place. McLean does his best to discourage the two men. The two staffers ignore his request that the meeting be held elsewhere and insist that his house be used.

General Lee, Colonel Marshall, and Pvt. Joshua O. Johns arrive first, about 3 p.m. Lee is riding Traveller and is dressed immaculately in a new uniform and carries a dress sword. Lee and Marshall go into the parlor of the McLean House; Johns remains outside to hold the horses. Lee takes a seat at one of the two tables that have been placed in the room and awaits the arrival of General Grant. Grant soon comes up on horseback via the Lynchburg Stage Road from the west. When he arrives, he dismounts and enters the parlor where Lee is sitting, with Marshall standing nearby.

The two commanding generals stand and greet one another and reminisce about their service in Winfield Scott's army during the Mexican War. Grant remembers Lee from the war. Lee had been a member of Scott's staff and was one of his most important officers. Grant was a lieutenant in the Fourth U.S. Infantry Regiment. He was a brave soldier and the regimental quartermaster. But there's no way that Lee would have known every regimental quartermaster in an army of 13,000 soldiers. Grant seems reluctant to focus on the reason for this meeting between the two generals. After several minutes of courteous conversation have passed between the two, Lee takes the lead and brings the conversation back to the subject at hand. The two generals then take their respective seats in the parlor.

There soon assembled in the parlor a large group of Yankee officers. The room couldn't possibly hold all the officers who later claim they were in the parlor when the surrender takes place. Custer is out in the hallway and will occasionally peek in through the doorway to see what is happening.

Now, if you're a "good Confederate," you think that General Grant comes into the parlor dressed in a private's uniform and Lee will hand him his sword and be too kind to take it back, thinking that Grant was some kind of flunky. But that isn't how the meeting between the two men goes. The two sit down to negotiate the surrender terms for Lee's army. Grant thinks rather rapidly, but not as quickly as Sherman. Sherman can write almost as fast as he thinks. Hence, he has very bad punctuation, or none at all, in much of his writing.

Grant had left his Clifton headquarters early that day, and he had not expected Lee to offer the surrender of his army at this time. So he had dressed as he usually did in the field. Grant is not the type of person who believes in shiny brass buttons and braid, or fuss and feathers. He modeled himself in many ways after General Zachary Taylor in the Mexican War, who dressed plainly. But he will later regret it when he arrives here and sees how Lee is dressed for the meeting. It appears that he is patronizing Lee by showing up in a plain uniform with mud on his trousers and boots.

Grant drafts the terms of surrender on his manifold. The surrender document will contain much of what was previously referenced in correspondence. The Confederates are to prepare muster rolls and to be paroled and not fight again until exchanged. Public property is to be turned over to the United States government. Officers will be allowed to retain their private property. Grant will go far beyond anything Lincoln has authorized him to do. The Confederates, upon receiving their paroles not to fight again until exchanged, will be allowed to return home. And as long as they remain there and observe the terms of their parole and the laws of the land, they will remain "undisturbed" by the U.S. government. Grant has inserted himself between those in the government who want to exact revenge and retribution upon high-level officers in the Confederate Army.

Upon reviewing the surrender document, Lee adds smalls changes to the document where Grant has left out a word or two. He wants to add a clause allowing the men to keep their horses and mules for the planting season. Grant explains that the surrender document will remain as written, but he will issue orders that allow the men to keep their horses and mules. Lee says that this will foster better relations between the two sides. Lee then says that his men and the Union prisoners in their custody are in need of food. Grant then issues orders to have army rations distributed to the hungry Confederates and to the Union prisoners they have captured.

Having signed the surrender document, Lee rises and shakes hands with Grant. Lee and Colonel Marshall leave the parlor with their hats and gloves in hand. They step out onto the porch of the McLean House. Lee puts on his hat and slaps his gloves into his left hand before slowly putting them on. He and Marshall slowly descend the stairs of the front porch and walk toward Private Johns. Lee slowly takes Traveller's reins and gently pats his nose. And then he puts his left foot in the stirrup and swings slowly into the saddle, uttering an imperceptible groan or sigh.

Meanwhile, Grant and other Union officers have come out onto the porch. As Lee and his small party prepare to ride away, Grant and the Union officers remove their hats. Lee tips his hat in acknowledgment of their courteous gesture and slowly turns his horse away to begin the difficult journey back to his headquarters camp. Thus ends one of the great moments in American history.

One can argue that this is the high point in the lives of these two great Americans. Because as much as they are able to have any control over the course of future events, they have placed the nation on a path to peaceful reconciliation before any of the politicians can get involved.

As Lee returns to his headquarters and rides east along the Lynchburg Stage Road, large numbers of his men crowd around him. He has yet to issue his now famous Farewell Address. Many of the soldiers ask him if it is true about the rumor circulating through the ranks that the army has been surrendered to General Grant. He slowly rides on through his men and arrives at his headquarters in a rather foul mood. After slowly dismounting, he is seen by his staff pacing back and forth in camp, remembering the day's fateful events. He can hear cheers in the camps of the enemy as he continues to pace back and forth.

During the next several days both armies prepare for the formal surrender of the Army of Northern Virginia. Commissioners meet to iron out procedures;

The stately Wilmer McLean House in Appomattox, Virginia, where Robert E. Lee surrendered his Army of Northern Virginia to Ulysses S. Grant.

Union soldiers commandeer a local printing press and begin to churn out parole forms. While the remaining cavalry units surrender on April 10 and artillery units turn in their cannon on April 11, the climax of the surrender ceremony is on April 12, 1865—four years to the day after Confederate forces opened fire on Fort Sumter.

As the infantry of the Army of Northern Virginia prepares to march into Appomattox Court House to surrender their arms and colors, Union soldiers in two ranks line both sides of the old Lynchburg Stage Road. They are drawn from the first division of the Union V Corps. Brig. Gen. Joshua Lawrence Chamberlain has been given the task of overseeing the formal surrender of Confederate arms. The 20th Maine will be one of the regiments standing in double ranks next to the road. Also present is the 185th New York as well as the 198th Pennsylvania, new regiments that Chamberlain had led in the final campaign. Chamberlain takes position next to the road, sitting on his horse Charlemagne.

If we were here on April 12, 1865, we could look east and see a long line of butternut and gray winding its way along the road in the distance. Out in front of the long gray column is the famous Stonewall Division. And in the van of the division are the pitiful remnants of the once proud Stonewall Brigade, the 2nd, 4th, 5th, 27th, and 33rd Virginia. As the long column approaches the Appomattox River, the Rebels temporarily disappear from view and then slowly reappear as they ascend the hill leading to Appomattox Court House. The column appears to be moving slowly and listlessly as it ascends the hill, with blood red battle flags, crowded together in the depleted ranks, blowing in the breeze or hanging limp on their staffs as they approach the top of the hill.

General Gordon is at the head of the column, riding a magnificent black horse with his head tilted downward. And as Gordon approaches, Chamberlain sits astride Charlemagne. Chamberlain issues an order for his men to go to right shoulder shift, and the soldiers lining both sides of the road come to the marching salute. Gordon hears the sound of shifting of arms. He quickly turns and gives a similar order to his men, and they come from right shoulder shift to shoulder arms, a salute, as they continue to march forward. When he reaches the spot where Chamberlain and Charlemagne are positioned beside the road, Gordon wheels his beautiful black steed to the left to front them. He takes the reins in his left hand, forcing his mount's head downward; to Chamberlain, it looks like Gordon and his horse have become one. He then raises the sword hilt to his chin, with the blade turned sideways, and then he lowers the blade so that its tip touches his boot. Chamberlain smartly responds to Gordon—honor saluting honor. Gordon wheels his steed to the right and rides forward again, but this time sitting erect in the saddle, with his drawn sword held tight by his side.

The long column continues to pass for more than four hours as regiment after regiment passes in front of Chamberlain and his men lining the road. They march by the court house and past the McLean House, and there they form into ranks in the road. They then stack arms and place their accouterments on top of the stacked arms. They then lay their furled regimental colors on top of the stacked arms and turn to march off down the road to the west, many of them with tears in their eyes. Some soldiers rush forward to tear fragments from the flags they have followed for four long years.

After a brigade has passed through the village in this manner, Union troops gather up the arms and accoutrements and battle flags and load them into wagons and drive off. The process will be repeated for the next Confederate brigade until all of the Confederates have surrendered their arms, accoutrements, and battle flags. By the end of the day, approximately 28,250 Confederates will be paroled. And as soon as the men have been paroled and have received their passes, they head off for their homes, using the best means available. Many of them must walk home if they have no horses, or bum rides on wagons, or catch a train, if possible.

EPILOGUE

HARDLUCK IRONCLAD *CAIRO*

In late April 1861, Abraham Lincoln approved the construction of seven ironclad gunboats. Built of wood and covered by iron plating, they were named for cities and towns along the Mississippi and Ohio Rivers where they would navigate, and upon them rested the Union's hope to regain control of the Mississippi River and prevent the Confederacy from making use of the river systems of the West. After her sister vessels participated in the battles of Forts Henry and Donelson, the Cairo *was sunk in 1862 by "infernal machines"—floating mines then called torpedoes—on a bend in the Yazoo River near Vicksburg, Mississippi. Union plans to recover the gunboat stalled, and the* Cairo *remained undisturbed for more than 90 years, buried—and preserved—by the river's silt and mud. In the mid-1950s, National Park Service employee Edwin Bearss, stationed in Mississippi, along with two companions, studied the paper trail of the* Cairo *and using rudimentary equipment discovered her, unmoved from the position where she sank. The recovery of the vessel took nearly ten years, but produced a treasure trove of artifacts—a time capsule from the Civil War. Today, the* Cairo *and her treasures are on view at the Vicksburg National Military Park.*

THE HISTORY

The ironclad gunboats *Cairo* and her sisters were designed by Samuel M. Pook and built by James Buchanan Eads, a St. Louis millionaire and riverman. When

Eads learned of the bombardment and surrender of Fort Sumter and Abraham Lincoln's call for 75,000 militia to serve in the Union Army for 90 days to quell the rebellion, he wrote a letter to the President describing how to win the war quickly by building a fleet of gunboats to patrol the Mississippi and her tributaries, effectively splitting the Confederacy. It was a good idea. Eads is familiar with the Mississippi River system and he also has personal relations with two of the seven members of Lincoln's Cabinet: Postmaster General Montgomery Blair and Attorney General Edward Bates. They write letters of endorsement, and Eads comes to Washington in the last week of April 1861 to meet with the President and his senior advisors. Eads urges the government to let him convert his huge salvage vessel *Submarine No. 7* into a gunboat as the core of a fleet to operate on western waters downstream from a base to be established at Cairo, Illinois. The President likes what he hears. But Secretary of War Simon Cameron, a machine politician from Pennsylvania, and Secretary of the Navy Gideon Welles, a Connecticut newspaperman who had been a Navy Department clerk in the Polk Administration (1845–49), raise jurisdictional issues. Cameron, alert to "pork barrel" issues, argues that since the vessels will operate in inland waterways they should both be built and be under operational control of the Army. Welles disagrees, but Mr. Lincoln sides with Cameron. The Army has won this turf battle.

As soon as Congress convenes on July 4, 1861, and the necessary appropriation is secured, Army Quartermaster Gen. Montgomery Meigs calls for sealed bids for constructing seven ironclad gunboats. Eads, who is a salvager, brilliant engineer, and idea man, but not a boat-builder, gets the contract. He will be the Civil War's Henry J. Kaiser. He proposes to build and deliver the desired number of gunboats in 64 days at a price of $89,600 a vessel. If he fails to accomplish this, he will be subject to a penalty of $250 per day on each vessel. The contract is awarded on August 7; therefore Eads's drop-dead date is October 10.

Eads leases two boatyards, one at Mound City, Illinois, and the other at Carondelet, Missouri, then a St. Louis suburb. He encounters major problems: The government fails to pay for work done on dates due, there are more than 120 change orders, et cetera, and Eads doesn't meet the completion date. It is January 15, 1862, before the last of the seven "City Series" ironclads is accepted, 97 days after the date specified in the contract. The United States argues that Eads owes a penalty figure of $250 a day for 97 days times seven.

Cairo and her six sisters are the first ironclad vessels built from the keel up in the Western Hemisphere. They are 175 feet long and 51 feet 2 inches wide at the knuckle—a point just above the waterline. Forty feet wide on the keel. Forty feet wide on the spar deck. From the keel up to the hurricane deck, it is 16 feet. Chimneys add another 28 feet to the height. The average crew is 158 enlisted men and 17 officers. Each boat is armed with three guns firing forward, four starboard, an equal number to port, and two aft.

Federal gunboats—including three of *Cairo*'s sisters—enter into combat against Confederate Fort Henry on February 6, 1862. The government hasn't paid for them yet, so Eads owns or has a claim on the vessels. Under operational control of the United States Army, they are officered by United States Navy personnel, and the crews are a mixture of Army and Navy. Fortunately for the Federals and Eads, the gunboats prove themselves at Fort Henry and the fort is blasted into surrender while Brig. Gen. Ulysses S. Grant's columns are still approaching the scene. This is important for Eads. After the victory, U.S. Treasury auditors, on evaluating the claims of Eads and the government, rule in favor of Eads, and he is paid the more than $148,000 due on his contract. It is also fortunate for Eads that Fort Henry occurred before Fort Donelson or he might not have not gotten paid. The gunboats, including four of *Cairo*'s sisters, suffer a severe repulse at Fort Donelson on the Cumberland River on February 14.

Unlike her sisters, *Cairo* doesn't see serious action as part of the Brown Water Navy on the Mississippi River until the Battle of Plum Point Bend,

On December 12, 1862, the first armored warship to be sunk by an electronically detonated mine, the ironclad gunboat Cairo, *sank on the Yazoo River and quickly filled with mud and silt.*

near Fort Pillow, Tennessee, on May 10, and at Memphis on June 6. In mid-September she visited the Vicksburg area as an escort to steamboats loaded with thousands of Confederate prisoners being transported down the Mississippi to be exchanged in accordance with the Dix-Hill Cartel.

As the river war continues in the West on the Mississippi and her tributaries, *Cairo*'s date with destiny comes on December 12, 1862. In late November General Grant's army, in northern Mississippi, crosses the Tallahatchie River and compels the Confederates to retreat south of the Yalobusha River and take position at Grenada. To pressure the Rebels, Grant sends a request to Rear Adm. David D. Porter—the Navy had in mid-October 1862 secured operational control of the Brown Water Navy—that he send gunboats down the Mississippi to the mouth of the Yazoo. The gunboats would, Grant hoped, ascend the Yazoo as far as Greenwood and then go up the Yalobusha and threaten the Rebels' hold on Grenada.

The Yazoo is as muddy a river as you have in America. When the gunboats arrive, there is only five feet of water over the bar of the Yazoo, but to cross it the City Series ironclads need a six foot depth. The advance squadron is commanded by Cmdr. Henry Walke, a well-known senior officer, who has seen much combat afloat. His squadron includes three of Eads' ironclads—*Carondelet* (Walke's flagship), *Cairo,* and *Pittsburg*—several less heavily armored "tinclads," and a ram.

On December 11 two light-draft tinclads—*Marmora* and *Signal*—enter the Yazoo. Soundings taken as they cross the bar show that the Yazoo is rising and there is now six and a half feet of water. About 12 miles upstream, as the mariners continue to make soundings, a sailor sees a block of wood floating in the water. He takes his rifled musket, aims at it, and "Boom!" A geyser of water leaps up and douses the deck. He has fired into and detonated what is known as an "infernal machine." As *Marmora*'s captain, Lt. Robert Getty seeks to turn his tinclad about, there's another explosion, followed by a geyser of water, but again no damage. Whereupon *Marmora* and *Signal* return to the fleet anchorage at the mouth of the Yazoo. Getty goes aboard *Carondelet* and informs Commander Walke that the Confederates have infernal machines up the Yazoo and he knows how to safely remove them. But to do so he must be supported by ironclads. Walke is down with malaria, but he decides to follow up on Getty's recommendation and entrusts the next day's mission to Lt. Cmdr. Thomas O. Selfridge, an 1854 graduate of the U.S. Naval Academy. Walke's instructions to Selfridge, who has captained *Cairo* since September 12, are to take his vessel, the *Pittsburg,* the tinclads *Marmora* and *Signal,* and the ram *Queen of the West* up the Yazoo. When they go upriver Selfridge is to cover the light drafts as they remove the torpedoes. However, under no circumstances is he to take the ironclads into unreconnoitered waters.

It is a mizzly day on December 12 as the squadron enters the Yazoo. *Marmora,* followed by *Signal* and then *Queen of the West,* takes the lead. As ordered, the ironclads *Cairo,* trailed by *Pittsburg,* follow. About 11 a.m., well above the mouth of Thompson Lake and abreast of Benson Blake's levee, *Marmora* stops, and the crew lowers and mans her cutter. Hearing firing ahead where *Marmora* has stopped, Selfridge takes his vessel forward.

At the same time the gunners manning the big ironclad's starboard battery open fire into the woods on the south bank. Passing *Queen of the West* and *Signal, Cairo* draws abreast of *Marmora.* As *Cairo* closes on the tinclad, Selfridge puts a bullhorn to his mouth and calls out, "Getty, what is your problem?" Getty answers, "This is where the torpedoes are." Getty does not run a tight ship. His men have difficulty getting the cutter away. Their inaction angers Selfridge. The *Marmora's* bluejackets finally get the cutter underway, and they pull toward the south bank. They locate and recover a glass demijohn, which proves to be an infernal machine. Returning to the tinclad, they disarm and disassemble the demijohn. Meanwhile *Cairo's* stern begins to drift toward shore. Once again Selfridge calls to Getty to take the *Marmora* ahead. Getty doesn't react fast enough to satisfy Selfridge, so he orders Chief Pilot Charles Young to go ahead, and the *Cairo* shoots out into unreconnoitered waters.

There's a Boom, followed by a second Boom! Geysers of water leap up, and a report comes up from the fo'c'sle, "that the water is rushing in like the roar of Niagara." Selfridge issues orders for the *Cairo* to back up and be driven aground bow-on. Sailors leap ashore with lines and secure them to cottonwood trees, but within 12 minutes the hawsers have tautened, parted, and the *Cairo* slips off into 36 feet of water. Only the tops of her chimneys and jackstaffs extend above the foaming waters. Fortunately no one is killed and only half a dozen people are injured. The other vessels take the survivors aboard; the *Queen of the West* comes alongside and pulls down the *Cairo's* jackstaffs and chimneys to prevent the Rebels from locating the boat. Within an hour nothing else protrudes above the waters of the Yazoo. Selfridge returns to the mouth of the Yazoo and goes aboard the *Carondelet* to report to Commander Walke the loss of the *Cairo.* She has earned a place in history, for on this day has occurred a "first:" Electrically activated torpedoes (mines) sink an armored warship, inaugurating a new era in naval warfare. One of Selfridge's critics in the Western Squadron, Master George Brown, dryly reports that on December 12

"Commander Selfridge of the *Cairo* found two torpedoes and removed them by placing his vessel over them."

A word about what the Yankees called "infernal machines," what the Confederates called torpedoes, and what we today identify as mines would be appropriate at this point. The Confederates seek to nullify Union superiority afloat by ways small naval powers always try. "Unsinkable warships," such as the *Virginia, Arkansas,* and *Tennessee,* are employed, but they are nullified by Union numbers. Like the Germans in World War II with their V1s and V2s, the Confederates give priority to the development and deployment of explosive devices and enjoy considerable success with these weapons, sinking or damaging more than 25 Union warships.

The Recovery

The *Cairo* is at the bottom of the Yazoo River. Union plans to salvage her in the summer of 1863, following the fall of Vicksburg, are scrapped because Confederate guerrillas are too active. The Yazoo carries as much silt as any river in the world, and within a year the *Cairo* is buried in the bed of the Yazoo. This is good. If she's buried in the bed of the Yazoo, she's not a hazard to navigation and is soon forgotten. As first the years and then the decades pass, the *Cairo* will remain in her resting place, her location obscured in mystery and speculation. This changed forever on Veteran's Day 1956, which at that time was officially marked on the closest Monday, November 12. Two friends and I had the day off. My companions for the day's adventure were Warren Grabau, a geologist with the U.S. Corps of Engineers, and M. Don Jacks, a man of the river and a fellow National Park Service employee in Vicksburg. We had long researched and studied the paper trail of the *Cairo* to establish likely sites for the sinking. To conduct the physical search, we had hoped to secure a dip-needle, an extremely sensitive magnetic device that would react to the *Cairo*'s hidden metal cladding, but we were compelled to use instead a World War II military compass.

We boarded Jacks' runabout at the Vicksburg Landing and headed up the Yazoo. We began our search near the south bank of the river adjacent to the site of Benson Blake's 1860s lower plantation. Jacks conned a course some 15 yards offshore. After one earlier wiggle, the compass needle went wild at a point seven-eighths of a mile downstream from Blake's plantation. We probed the mud with a metal rod and struck the sloping sides of a large object sheeted with iron.

In 1960, reinforced by James "Skeeter" Hart, a Jackson, Mississippi, fireman, and S. Ken Parks, a local TV personality, we returned to the site. Beside being qualified scuba divers, the two were interested in further documenting the site, and if it was truly the *Cairo*, to see if she could be raised. We borrowed a World War II pumping unit from the Jackson Fire Department and a work barge from someone else, and proceeded up the river to the *Cairo* site. It took a lot longer to relocate the *Cairo* than it did to find it the first time. When we found it originally we had secured metal targets to trees that when sighted in on from shore zeroed in on the pilothouse. This was the only part of the vessel that extended above the mud cocoon. But the Yazoo's banks are unstable, and all a tree has to do is tilt a few degrees to throw your markings off target. The Yazoo here is controlled by the water level in the Mississippi. The level can be 5 feet above the *Cairo* or it can be 50 feet—depending on the stage of the Mississippi at Vicksburg. We had to spend much time reestablishing contact with the pilothouse. Then we had to remove the mud from outside and inside the pilothouse. Mud had impacted around the sloping sides of the pilothouse, so Parks and Hart had to jump up the engine to put a lot of power on the hose to jet the mud loose from the pilothouse. After two weeks they had exposed the four upper feet of the pilothouse above the mud cocoon. They also jetted mud loose from inside, and we were finally ready to try to raise the pilothouse.

I'm not going to tell you how to lift a pilothouse, or an ironclad gunboat. I'm going to review the problems of raising one and you'll agree why

I titled my book *Hardluck Ironclad: The Sinking and Salvage of the Cairo.* We are now ready to challenge the river. We were fortunate that my neighbor knew Mr. Bart Tully of Anderson Tully Lumber Co., who agreed to lend "Operation *Cairo,* Inc.," as we designated the project, the tug *Porterfield.*

On September 14 we were ready, and up the Yazoo came the tug *Porterfield.* Naive as we were, we thought that a line from the crane would separate the pilothouse from the sunken hulk. But such was not to be. Fortunately, the floating crane had an A-frame on its bow with a 50-ton lift capacity. Parks and Hart, working in black water, threaded two 1.5-inch wires through opposite ports in the octagonal pilothouse, and we began the lift. We wanted to bring the pilothouse to the surface in the presence of Johnny Holland, the personable mayor of Vicksburg, who happened to be chairman of the Mississippi War Between the States Centennial and wanted publicity for that effort. It was getting dark.

As we began to lift, the bow of the barge sank lower and lower. Instead of six foot of free board it now had about a foot and a half. We worried that the barge might sink when a line of bubbles shot to the surface and an object that no living human had seen surfaced—the eight-sided pilothouse of *Cairo.* By the next morning we had lifted an eight-inch naval gun. This was the *Cairo*'s number two starboard gun. We knew from the paper trail that the gun carriages were made of green white oak. The cannon was loaded with canister, and the cap on the nipple ready to be fired.

We cleared away the mound of mud that remained on the pilothouse site. The removal of the impacted mud disclosed a McClellan saddle that probably belonged to Commander Selfridge, as he wrote of going on horseback rides with Maj. Gen. William T. Sherman. We also found a Colt .44 caliber pistol, artillery short swords, and a folding chair, among other items.

In 1962 the Mississippi Agricultural & Industrial Board contracted to have a survey made of the vessel by the New England Naval and Maritime Museum. The investigation revealed that the *Cairo* was

After more than 100 years submerged beneath the Yazoo, Cairo's *casemate shield emerges from its muddy resting place as her namesake barge struggles to raise the rest of the boat.*

positioned at nearly a right angle to the Yazoo's south bank and her stern was well beyond mid-channel. Her back was not broken and the situation was favorable for raising her. On the dark side, the cost of such an undertaking was placed at $300,000, and while Operation *Cairo,* Inc. had lots of enthusiasm, money was a problem. Money can be hard to come by and would always plague us.

More than half the money to fund a volunteer effort to raise *Cairo* in 1963 came from two sources: J. W. Williams, of Corr-Williams Tobacco Co., contributed $20,000, and I won $10,000 on the *$64,000 Challenge.* The game show gave an amateur the opportunity to win $100,000. A professional could win a $1,000 bond, and $10,000 for a project of his interest. The Civil War, as we know, is always popular with the American people. It was also one of the subjects that doomed the *$64,000 Question* in the late 1950s, because that's when the sponsors fed answers to a very popular young man. The *$64,000 Challenge* was designed to guard against a repeat of this embarrassment. The Vicksburg Chamber of Commerce put me up for the show and the sponsors asked me to come to New York. I flew to New York, and on Saturday morning a private "dick" showed up. He informed me he would be with me until the program was over, because this show has to be purer than Caesar's wife. He stayed with me till I entered the "bubble." The format was: You formulated your questions for the other contestant. The first question was one-part, the second two-part, and the third three-part. The rules were that the questions had to appear in two of four standard references. I can remember two of the references: Ralph Newman's and Otto Eisenschiml's *The American Iliad* and the American Heritage book on the Civil War published in 1959. To ensure that the questions weren't too vague or had more than one answer, each contestant, with the private eye in attendance, had his questions reviewed and certified by a two-person panel, one a Civil War historian and the other a generalist. I then entered on a stage with the master of ceremonies in the middle, and they dropped a glass bubble over me. Since I was the challenger I had to answer first. Got through the first question, as did the amateur, then I got through the second question. On the first part of the second question I put him down. The question he went down on was this: Who was in charge of the pontoons that were drifted down the Tennessee River to open the Cracker Line into Chattanooga? My opponent answered "John Geary," but the answer was "William Hazen." Operation *Cairo* was $10,000 richer.

So that gave us $30,000 to begin the raising of the *Cairo*. Inexperienced as we were, we priced out what a cutter-head dredge would cost. It was $100 an hour, and even with $30,000 that was too much money. So we decided to go with a gravel dredge, the *Mary Ann*. We also built a sluiceway to screen out artifacts that came up in the mud.

Cairo-watching soon became popular as hundreds of people assembled on the banks of the Yazoo daily, with particularly large crowds on Sundays.

In the autumn of 1963 there were still 12 cannon aboard. So whenever possible we planned a good show for the Lord's day. Unfortunately we didn't take advantage of the popularity of *Cairo*-watching until too late. No fees for this activity were charged until late fall 1964.

The summer and autumn of 1963 were months that saw the civil rights spotlight shine on Mississippi with the assassination of Medgar Evers and the murder of the Philadelphia Three. Standing by waiting for something to break were CBS's Nelson Benton and NBC's Jay Barbree. And they were frequently there for cannon raisings.

Because of the huge number of explosive shells in one of the boat's magazines, the U.S. Coast Guard requested that personnel of the U.S. Navy's Explosive Ordnance Disposal Unit 2, based in Charleston, South Carolina, be sent to the site. On October 19, Nelson Benton with his CBS team was present as well as Chief Wesley Collins and other members of the EOD team. A 30-pounder rifled Parrott gun was raised from the stern. When examined by Chief Collins it was found to be loaded and fused. While the camera crew filmed and Benton described what was happening, the men of Unit 2 removed and disarmed the projectile, which could have been a hazardous undertaking. The next night Walter Cronkite featured the recovery and disarming of the Parrott gun and shell on his prime-time evening news program.

Through the assistance of U.S. Senator John Stennis of Mississippi, we secured the lease of two large fuel barges, 235 feet long, 40 feet wide, and divided into nine compartments. Mud and silt that had entombed *Cairo* were removed to a considerable distance both up- and downstream from the hulk by mid-February 1965, and the weather had turned cold.

If we were to use buoyancy to raise the Civil War ironclad, divers would have to go down and, by feel, position three-quarter-inch wires under the stern. One barge was anchored parallel to and upstream from the *Cairo* and the other downstream. A dragline positioned on the upstream barge was fastened to one end of the wire and the other end secured to a bollard on the downstream barge. First one wire and then six more were sawed into position under the *Cairo;* seven evenly spaced lifting points were established. The barges were then flooded so that less than 18 inches thrust above the river surface. The ends of the wires that provided the give for the sawing were secured to the upstream barge's bollards. We were now ready to pump out the barges. When this was done, strain would be placed on the lifting points and the *Cairo* hopefully would be raised from the grave in which she had rested for more than a century.

Unfortunately, heavy rains had fallen. Upstream someone was clearing an area of timber for construction of a pulpwood plant, so against the upper barge there were soon wedged seven acres of debris. This put more stress on the lines securing the barges to anchors ashore than they could resist: The anchors were uprooted; the barges were swept downstream, and the *Cairo* sank back into her grave. Daybreak on March 6 found the barges on the Vicksburg waterfront. All our work since September 6 had come unraveled. Worse, on January 12, Dr. Walter Johnston, one of Operation *Cairo,* Inc.'s hardest and most dedicated workers, fell overboard from a workboat and drowned.

All, however, had not been lost; we had recovered and curated a collection of artifacts documenting life aboard a Civil War ironclad. The largest of these were her 13 big guns, 12 of these had been entombed in the *Cairo* for 101 years, and the one salvaged earlier for 98 years. When the mud and crud were removed, marks left by machine tools used in their manufacture were clearly visible.

Officers always have it a little better. In the officers' quarters there was water for a shower and the head's commode. How did they get the water? As the paddle-wheel turns, runoff from the bucket drains into a storage tank. Thus the officers had water for their "head." The enlisted men made use of heads that extended over the fantail. We found castor oil and all sorts of bottled medicines in the sick bay. I played with an iodine bottle too much, let the vapors out, and the iodine soon crystallized. It turns out that the treatment for syphilis and gonorrhea was the same as they used in the 1930s:

Blue Mass. One rather interesting artifact was an ice chest. No beer in it. We found a barrel that had contained beer; we could still smell a musty odor of beer in it. The ship's brass bell came up and shone as brightly as it had more than a century earlier. When it was exposed to oxygen in the air, it tarnished before our eyes. Among the most numerous objects recovered were wrist and ankle shackles, like those used during the Revolutionary War. You had to go to the blacksmith to have them removed. The large number of pistols recovered consisted mostly of personal weapons.

We salvaged thousands of artifacts but the vessel still sat on the bottom. Soundings showed the *Cairo* had silted in again, and was once more entombed. Perhaps not as tightly packed as heretofore, but it was back to square one. The Vicksburg Chamber of Commerce and the Mississippi A & I Board took the lead in putting together a financial package, including $40,000 made available by the Warren County Board of Supervisors and $50,000 by the state. With more money available, hopes high, and a realization that this was a major undertaking, a contract was signed with Capt. William "Billy" Bisso, the most experienced salvage man on the lower Mississippi. His company would raise the *Cairo* and place her on a barge for $40,000, and better yet, the contract included a "no cure no pay" provision.

Bisso, his crew, and his equipment—the tug *Rip Tide* and the powerful floating steam derrick cranes *Boaz, Atlas,* and *Ajax*—reached the *Cairo* site on July 25.

A take-charge guy, Captain Billy began work on August 3, a Monday. A dragline excavated a trench where the riverbank had sloughed and covered the forward part of the ironclad's bow. This was necessary because Bisso needed to seesaw 2.5- and 3-inch wires under the hulk from fore to aft to establish six lifting points. The gravel dredge *Mary Ann* returned and, assisted by cutter-head dredge *Benalo,* removed thousands of cubic yards of buckshot mud and silt that enclosed the *Cairo*'s grave. Several lifting wires were positioned under the ironclad's bow with mighty *Boaz* and *Rip Tide* acting as seesaws. Heavy rains associated with Hurricane Hilda struck the Louisiana coast, enabling Bisso to call up from New Orleans his giant floating steam dredge *Cairo,* the largest on the Gulf Coast, with a lifting capacity of 320 tons. She arrived on site October 4.

Much cleanup and tidying kept Bisso's people busy during the next two weeks. On Sunday morning, the 18th, everyone was at his station. Upstream of the ironclad were moored the mighty floating derrick *Cairo,* nearest the bank, and the *Boaz.* The *Atlas* and the *Ajax* were on the downriver side, the latter opposite the *Cairo.* Wires were attached and the lift began at 11 a.m. It was interrupted at noon. Soon one of the engineers shouted that the strain on his derrick had lessened. Back to their stations Bisso and his hands raced, and within minutes the water boiled and churned. Moments later the tip of the ironclad's starboard casemate shield poked above the brown water. Employing winches and spring lines, the four floating derricks eased the submerged *Cairo,* cradled in her nest of six lifting wires, upstream more than a hundred feet and gently lowered her. This had been a banner day, but what the future held we fortunately did not know.

A hectic ten days followed. A gasoline barge similar to those used in the ill-fated 1963–64 raising was readied and sunk in *Cairo*'s late grave downstream and parallel to where she now rested. We knew that the barge and the *Cairo*'s bottom had identical widths, which in zero visibility water could be a problem. Also the river was low, which meant that several feet of the casemate must be above water in positioning her on the submerged barge.

The lift began on a warm October 29 afternoon. A huge crowd gathered; both CBS and NBC television crews are there. Bisso deployed his floating derricks as they were on October 18. Initially all seemingly was on schedule. The *Cairo*'s casemate shield was in view; we saw the three gunports; the iron, shut off from oxygen for more than a century, was blue-gray; out near mid-channel we saw the paddle-wheel spiders. Soundings showed that about two more feet of the casemate needed to be exposed before the keel could clear the barge. The ironclad's namesake increases the strain on her end of the lifting wires. There was a crack. A surge of water swept across the *Cairo's* deck forward of the casemate, the paddle-wheel spiders disappeared, and the casemate shield slanted at a rakish angle.

Bisso shut down operations while he assessed what had gone wrong. It was determined that two of the six lifting wires cut deeply into the vessel's bowels below the knuckle like a hot knife through butter. We had a disaster. To cut losses we determined to use these two wires to cut the ironclad into three parts: the bow aft of No. 1 gunports, the amidships containing the five boilers, and the stern aft of No. 3 gunports and forward of the paddle-wheel raceway.

This was done and the bow was positioned with little difficulty on the barge. We saw that, as with the cannon, the iron on exposure to air rusted before our eyes. When Bisso sought to position the heavy amidships section aboard the barge, it turned 90 degrees in its wire slings. The amidships was then "walked" ashore and dismantled. The stern was placed successfully on the barge, but the rains had come and the Yazoo was rising rapidly, some six feet in 30 hours, and the current accelerated. On Thanksgiving Day the pumps were started to expel more than 750,000 gallons of water from the barge and bring her to the surface. But before our dreams were realized, a powerful eddy caught the lifting barge, causing it to list and tilt at a rakish angle. The *Cairo's* stern slid off the barge. Fortunately it was still nestled in its lift wires and, although the raceway was crushed, two of the floating derricks beached the two sponsons, each containing an engine and a treasure trove of artifacts. On December 22 Captain Bisso complied with the "no cure no pay" condition in his contract. Taking in tow two barges on which rested the battered remains of the *Cairo,* the tug *Rip Tide* chugged down the Yazoo.

In late winter of 1965, still on the barges that took her to Vicksburg, the battered *Cairo* was towed to Pascagoula on the Mississippi Gulf Coast. The parts were off-loaded at the yard of Ingalls Shipbuilding Corp. There she was entrusted to the care of the firm's chief naval architect Clyde Leavitt. Under his careful supervision the vessel was laid out, the armor removed, the engines disassembled, and measures taken to preserve the historic fabric.

With the end of the Vietnam conflict, responsibility for restoration, preservation, and interpretation of the *Cairo* was turned over to the National Park Service. In 1977 the vessel was returned to Vicksburg. At the national military park, the ironclad has been restored. In exhibiting, the surviving historic fabric has been used where possible. To give size and support to the *Cairo,* a skeleton of laminated wood of a distinctive color is used. This replicates in shape and form a framework to support the historic fabric, the cannon and carriages, boilers, engines, et cetera.

Adjacent to the vessel is the *Cairo* museum and interpretation center. On display are thousands of representative objects that interpret the material culture illustrative of a moment in time in the lives of the officers and men of *Cairo.* You can see one of Commander Selfridge's gold oak leaves and a watch. Sailors have always like to whittle, and one of the *Cairo*'s bluejackets has carved a naval eagle and shield. Another, perhaps homesick for the open sea, has carved a ship. The large number of civilian shoes of various sizes and looks underscore what the paper trail told of the ironclad's interception of a boat smuggling shoes across the Mississippi from Memphis into Arkansas. We also found many different kinds and shapes of pipes. Archaeologists find pipes like these of value because they're datable. Coins were drilled for wear in the ears as good luck pieces. Artillery shells were stored in color-coded boxes—red fused to explode in 15 seconds, white 10 seconds, blue 5 seconds. We found toothbrushes. We tried the tobacco. It wasn't too bad except its muddy taste. The Navy until World War II wore flat hats, and one flat hat we found still has its blue silk ribbon embossed in gold with the name of the vessel, *Cairo.* Silk fabric held up very well in the Yazoo mud, and we found lots of it. Wool pea jackets were not as durable. We found a bluish coloration in the mud sporting four Goodyear-patented buttons.

I had a close association with *Cairo* from 1956 until the late 1970s, when the National Park Service assumed responsibility for her restoration and interpretation. Beginning in September 1960 with recovery of the pilothouse, *Cairo* became a part of the Bearss family, particularly because of my wife's interest in material cultures of the past. Thousands of artifacts were recovered from *Cairo*. My wife headed the volunteers who, like herself, spent hours washing mud from artifacts, inventorying them, and taking measures to preserve them. She then researched and cataloged these "bits and pieces from the past."

Since the mid-1980s the *Cairo* has been a feature at the Vicksburg National Military Park, which displays the restored *Cairo* and her artifacts. Today when I tour the Vicksburg park and the *Cairo* museum I hark back a half a century to that day when Grabau, Jacks, and I set out to see if we could find the all but forgotten ironclad. In the years since, much has happened, and as time marches on most of those who were associated with raising the *Cairo* have answered the last roll call and have joined Lt. Cmdr. Thomas O. Selfridge and his crew.

ACKNOWLEDGMENTS

This book would not have been possible without the dedicated service of the Blue and Gray Education Society and its tireless director Len Riedel. Since 1994 Len and I have worked together to build a definitive record that interprets the war as I have seen and understand it. Len has matched me with a supportive and impressive set of historians at more than 100 Civil War battlefields. It has made a great difference as we play off against each other. Over a typical three day tour we would generate dozens of hours of tape, which in turn produced over 2,000 typewritten pages of transcript.

The task of transcribing more than 300 hours of tapes for this book was cost prohibitive and so we sought volunteers from the membership of the BGES. Each tape was raw material with the imperfections of background noise, wind, distance from the speaker and countless other challenges. A single hour of tape took as much as 8 hours of review to produce the manuscript. Every volunteer started with 16 hours of raw tape and 3 months to complete the work. Rick Williams and Beth Cromwell supervised the effort. When some volunteers were unable to complete their work others stepped up to accept additional tapes. Four people, Will Smith, Kathleen Colburn, Cecil Jones and Jack Dawson led this effort. Each of them transcribed at least 32 hours of tape and some did in excess of 50 hours or nearly 250 volunteer hours of transcribing. The others who volunteered their time to make this work included Henry Trawick, Art Espinoza, John Coski (and his staff at the Museum of the Confederacy), Stewart O'Bannon III, Dennis and Nancy Buttacavoli, Rick and Ann Whaite, Craig Clark, Joe Pierro Jr., Melissa Krause, and Karen Needles. I cannot thank them enough they are true friends.

When your life revolves around battlefields you become involved in the issues that are important to the preservation of them. Some of the great visionaries for preservation are members of the public at large—no two people ever took a stronger stand than my late friends Annie

Snyder and Jerry Russell. They were preservationists before it was fashionable to do so and paved the way for many of the efforts that are ongoing today. Some of the people who walk in their footsteps include men like Joe Whitehorne, Dan Laney, Joe Smyth, Tom Clemens, Dwight Mottet and Dr. Mike Stevens. Jim Lighthizer and his staff at the Civil War Preservation Trust have given a national urgency to the effort and established a much needed presence in Washington D.C. Collectively the preservationists' passion inspires people and produces results.

Numerous "Friends" organizations advocate the preservation and interpretation of various sites. My friends Jim Cass and his wife, Maxine are leaders in the preservation of Camp Wildcat in Kentucky. Alan and Arleen Hoeweler have invested heavily in Perryville and sites around the country. The Mill Springs preservationists have done an equally magnificent job in preserving the story of that early but robust encounter in Kentucky. Dan and Peggy Beattie, Richard Guilder and Irvin and Nancy Hess are all preservationists of the first magnitude.

I am asked to read many manuscripts and want to thank gentlemen such as Rick Williams, Bob Eberly, Ed Urban, and Lester Horowitz for excellently representing the craft of Civil War scholarship. Specialty publishers such as my friends Mary and Bob Younger at Morningside Books and Dave Roth at Blue and Gray Magazine have made this proliferation possible. They maintain good inventories and offer unique services. All contribute to a growing body of literature that enhances our understanding of the war.

The countless artifacts of the war continue to find suitable and prestigious homes either in museums or private collections. Dr. Bob Pamplin has built the premiere private Civil War Park in the country under the supervision of A. Wilson Greene at Pamplin Historical Park; however, no site can top the wonderful White Oak Museum in Stafford, Virginia. D. P. Newton and his mother have harvested a camp full of Union artifacts and their documentation is a primer for anyone who does archeological work on a battlefield site. Van Hedges at Corinth has collected the best set of artifacts documenting the Civil War in Corinth. My good friend Tom Sweeney built a Trans-Mississippi artifacts museum that is simply superb—so much so that it is now a part of the National Park Service's exhibit at Wilson's Creek. Gordy Dammann set the standard for Public-Private partnerships with the National Museum of Civil War Medicine in Frederick and its satellite center at the Pry House on the Antietam Battlefield. Carl and Jeannette Christman in Kansas have selflessly accumulated an impressive set of artifacts that they are using to tell the story of the war and support preservation causes.

My professional and personal papers are now at the Marine Corps Archives at the library on the Marine Corps Base at Quantico, Virginia. Soon tapes and transcriptions of my tours will be handed over to the supervision of archivist Mike Miller. Mike has done an oral history with me and in cooperation with a fine young archivist, Laura Lacey, is bringing my work to the internet for researchers to use.

During my time in the National Park Service and in various special assignments I met some of the best academic scholars this country has to offer and a number of people that I enjoyed spending time with. I count men like Jim McPherson, Dick Sommers, Jack Waugh, Richard McMurry and Brian Steel Wills as some of my close friends. I find men such as Greg Mertz, Chris Calkins, Terry Winschel and Jim Ogden as representative of some of the dozens of great young historians the National Park Service has grown.

The tours that I have done for the BGES are noteworthy for their intellectual components. They are well organized and superbly supported with personal amenities—no one does them better. With the BGES' programs, I get to visit sites that are rarely seen. Indeed in this series, I have visited sites that I had never personally visited or taken groups to before such as the Swamp Angel; Castle Pinckney; Camp Wildcat and Fort Hood to name but a few. The company has been superb—I look forward to seeing The Texans—Bart Allen and Bill Rogers; Char and Becky; Reb and Yank and other regulars like Chuck Bristol, Lee McDowell and Mike Green.

I also enjoyed the chance to work on this program with historians Jim McPherson, Rick Hatcher, Steve Wise, Ethan Rafuse, Bill Shea, Bill Piston, Wiley Sword, Mike Andrus, Chris Bryce, Lynn Sims, Tom Clemens, Dennis Frye, Gerry Prokopowicz, Brian Wills, Neil Mangum, Brooks Simpson, Greg Mertz, Frank O'Reilly, Keith Alexander, Parker Hills, Jim Ogden, Mike Miller, Gary Joiner, Steve Davis, Chris Fonvielle, Mark Bradley, Kendall Gott, Art Bergeron, Chris Calkins, Jack Friend, Joe Whitehorne, Gary Echlebarger and Thomas Cartwright. Each contributed to a better experience for the group and I enjoyed the dialogue with each of them.

As this book came to fruition I am grateful to Len for organizing a "who's who" list of volunteer "fact checkers" for each chapter. Dennis Frye, Rick Hatcher, Becky Cumins, Jim Burgess, Parker Hills, Wiley Sword, Wayne Motts, Tim Smith, Donald Pfanz, Chris Calkins, Mark Bradley, Steve Wise, Gordon Rhea, Greg Mertz, Tom Clemens, Terry Winschel, and Elizabeth Joyner gave me a "last chance look" at items that might have been in error or overlooked. I appreciate them taking time from their full schedules to promptly check and challenge my facts. Any errors that remain are my responsibility alone.

I hope this book and the labor that went into it will enable many worthy preservation and educational organizations to work together to raise funds for their important causes. I also hope that the remaining text of these transcripts will find a publisher so that future generations may have them as a baseline for increasing our common understanding of the significance of the Civil War.

I am optimistic that outstanding organizations such as the Central Virginia Battlefield Trust, Cedar Creek Battlefield Foundation, the Brandy Station Foundation, Save Historic Antietam Foundation, Friends of Newtonia and the Friends of Raymond will receive support from the Civil War Preservation Trust and others to save all the battlefield land that can be saved. Sam

Hood is passionately advocating the preservation of the operations of the Confederate Museum in New Orleans, while Waite Rawls fights a tough battle against encroachment upon the Confederate White House and Museum of the Confederacy in Richmond. Efforts like theirs are important. I know the Friends of the Wilderness Battlefields will succeed in raising the funds needed to restore Ellwood, the Lacy House and that the Blue and Gray Education Society will continue to lead the way into the Sesquicentennial Commemoration by presenting the Civil War in a probative and interesting fashion while developing and installing the signs needed to tell the story for future generations. Finally, I hope the new American Civil War Center at Tredegar in Richmond will be a unifying symbol for all Americans—Blue, Gray and Black to tell this marvelous story for the next generation of Americans.

This book is a tribute to so many people and yet a few deserve specific thanks: Jim McPherson, Harris Andrews, Brooks Simpson, and Walton Rawls have brought this to life in a fashion that I hope will educate and please you. As for Len Riedel and the BGES I am never disappointed. He is a person you can turn any problem over to and it gets solved in a seemingly effortless way. Lisa Thomas at National Geographic Books saw the potential of this project and shepherded it to a successful conclusion. Jane Menyawi edited the photographs in this book, and Carl Mehler led the cartographic team that created the maps. The maps in this book are based on A Battlefield Atlas of the Civil War *by Craig L. Symonds and William J. Clipson. Cartography was originally produced by William J. Clipson and authorized for use by Irma B. Clipson. Map production for this volume was carried out by Matt Chwastyk, Steven D. Gardener, and The M Factory with my research consultation. Cameron Zotter executed the layout with aplomb. Judy Klein, Jane Sunderland, and Mary Beth Oelkers-Keegan copyedited the text. I also want to thank my friends who helped fund the BGES' leather-bound special edition especially Laurie and Corky Lowe, Sharon and Gene Dennis, Ann and Bart Allen, Candy and John Richards, Rick Williams, Dru and Bill Vodra, Jan and Herbert C. Miller, Jeanette and Carl Christmanm Jim Davis, Kathy and Don Shafer, Char and Bill Lambert, and Janet and Bill Riedel.*

I would like to especially recognize my dear friends in "The Joe Hooker Society." This group is headed by Wendy Swanson, George Evans, Van Vanderwahl, Nancy Wentworth and Kieran McAuliffe. They are assisted by many other friends who have channeled a personal loyalty into an "Official Annual Birthday" celebration that has raised tens of thousands of dollars for preservation causes such as rehabilitating Gettysburg's Coster Avenue mural, the preservation efforts of the Friends group at the Newtonia battlefield,, the BGES' interpretation of the North Anna battlefield, and the purchase of land at the White Oak Road battlefield.

Finally, I could not enjoy the pleasures I do without the loyal and selfless support of my wife Margie. She has endured much to permit me to engage in a seemingly endless parade of programs.

ABOUT THE BLUE AND GRAY EDUCATION SOCIETY

The **Blue and Gray Education Society** is one of America's leading Civil War education organizations. Based in Danville, Virginia, the BGES organizes and leads approximately 20 Civil War tours per year to sites both familiar and nearly forgotten. In addition to its ambitious tour program the BGES has engaged in a multi-pronged program to enhance the visitor's experience at selected battlefields by presenting detailed, quality educational signage. BGES has worked hard to assist other nonprofit preservation groups in funding and achieving their objectives. Members have donated valuable primary documents to public libraries. Some members have produced scholarly papers that document and inform people about heretofore unknown aspects of the war. Staff members analyze new publications to determine which books are the best from a long list of releases. BGES has also consulted with local communities and the National Park Service to complete battlefield preservation plans that are now being implemented.

Fields of Honor is the product of a fruitful collaboration between Ed Bearss, a man we consider to be the nation's foremost public historian, and the BGES. It is a work that in Bearss' mind has been nearly 60 years in the making and in the BGES' life has been developing over its entire 12 years of existence. The text is the edited product of more than 300 hours of videotaped Bearss BGES battlefield tours transcribed by BGES volunteers into nearly 3,000 pages of narrative text. The total effort makes a substantial contribution to Bearss' growing archives. A copy of the tapes and text transcriptions will be given to the curators of his archive at Marine Corps University in Quantico, Virginia.

Ed Bearss asked the BGES to take an active role in this project based upon their long and mutually supportive relationship. Since its inception, the BGES has worked to build an unparalleled video archive of America's Civil War battlefields. The project now spans 12 years and includes recorded tours of more than 220 battlefields. BGES tours take people to places that are rarely seen and often accessible only by van, boat or foot. Each hour of tape documents their comprehensive commitment to take heritage tourists to each of the nation's 385 primary Civil War battlefields. Many programs have left the hotel hours before dawn or returned late in the evening—whatever it takes to do it right. For information about BGES tours, please visit our website, listed below.

BGES depends upon the tax deductible support of donor members from the general public and the patronage of the public for these tours. If you would like to be a part of living history the "BGES Way" please consider joining their organization by calling toll free 1-888-741-2437 or visiting their web site at www.blue-and-gray-education.org.
Email blue-grayedsoc@mindspring.com.

Illustrations Credits

Front and Back Cover: © Jan W. Faul/ artfaul.com, 2006

All interior photographs from Library of Congress Prints and Photographs Division unless otherwise noted.

2-3, © Jan W. Faul/artfaul.com, 2006; 11, Ohio Historical Society; 16, Hulton Deutsch/Getty Images; 20-21, © Jan W. Faul/artfaul.com, 2006; 25, William J. Clipson; 27 (RT), Courtesy of the Medford Historical Society & Museum; 32, Corbis Historical/Getty Images; 41, Cook Collection, The Valentine; 43, William J. Clipson; 60-61, © Jan W. Faul/art faul.com, 2006; 65, Corbis Historical/ Getty Images; 67, William J. Clipson; 76, William J. Clipson; 84, Corbis Historical/ Getty Images; 86, Courtesy of the Medford Historical Society & Museum; 96, William J. Clipson; 107, Corbis Historical/Getty Images; 118-119, © Jan W. Faul/artfaul .com, 2006; 128, William J. Clipson; 145, William J. Clipson; 162, William J. Clipson; 176, William J. Clipson; 196, William J. Clipson; 206, William J. Clipson; 227, William J. Clipson; 248, Old Court House Museum Collection, Vicksburg, Mississippi; 252, Courtesy of the Medford Historical Society & Museum; 261, William J. Clipson; 266, Corbis Historical/Getty Images; 268, Richard F. Carlile Collection; 272-273, © Jan W. Faul/artfaul.com, 2006; 281, William J. Clipson; 326, William J. Clipson; 342, The U.S. National Archives; 347, The U.S. National Archives; 349, William J. Clipson; 352-353, © Jan W. Faul/art faul.com, 2006; 362, William J. Clipson; 367, Mathew Brady/Corbis Historical/ Getty Images; 372, William J. Clipson; 384-385, William J. Clipson; 417, Courtesy NPS/Vicksburg National Military Park; 423, Courtesy NPS/Vicksburg National Military Park.

Index

Boldface indicates illustrations.